ARCHITECTS
of the WEB

ARCHITECTS
of the WEB

1,000
Days that
Built the
Future of
Business

Robert H. Reid

John Wiley & Sons, Inc.
New York • Chichester • Weinheim • Brisbane • Singapore • Toronto

ISBN: 0-471-17187-5

Printed in the United States of America

10 9 8 7 6 5 4 3 2 1

For Mom and Dad

CONTENTS

ACKNOWLEDGMENTS

This book would not have turned out as it has without the help and involvement of literally hundreds of people. I would especially like to thank the eight people profiled in its chapters—Marc Andreessen, Rob Glaser, Kim Polese, Mark Pesce, Ariel Poler, Jerry Yang, Andrew Anker, and Halsey Minor—for taking the time (in some cases dozens of hours) to share their recollections, opinions, and predictions during what will no doubt prove to be the busiest period of their lives. I would also like to thank the hundreds of other people, many of them quoted in these pages, who also gave generously of their time in the form of interviews, extended E-mail dialogues, back-and-forth faxing, and even the exchange of good old-fashioned U.S. mail while I was researching this book.

None of these chapters would be as complete as they are were it not for the thoughts and critiques of those from the industry who read them while they were still works-in-process. I would like to thank all of these people for their time, their insights, and above all, their *courage* for wading through what was, in many cases, some highly unedited writing. They include: Linda Buckel, Rikk Carey, Elizabeth Collet, Teri Elniski, Julie Farris, Lisa Friendly, James Gosling, Jeff Huber, Steve Jurvetson, Tim Lindholm, Miko Matsumura, John McCrea, Jon Mittelhauser, Ho Nam, Greg Sands, John Taysom, and Mary Warner.

This book would also certainly not be as complete as it is if it were not for Neil Weintraut, who did a wonderful job of framing many of the issues it considers and reviewing the history of the Internet in its Introduction. Neil distinguished himself for years as one of Wall Street's leading technology analysts while at Hambrecht and Quist, and I was both honored and delighted when he agreed to kick things off for me here. Neil and I now work together at Twenty-First Century Internet Venture Partners—a development that followed Neil's writing of the Introduction, and one with which I am equally delighted.

Before writing this book, I worked at Silicon Graphics, Inc. It was there that I first encountered the World Wide Web. It was also there that I first became a Web full-timer, when I joined the team that was marketing and developing our WebForce line of Web authoring workstations and Web servers. I would like to thank my manager, John Mc-Crea, and his manager, Jim White, for bringing me over to the Web at an early and exciting moment in its history, and for recruiting me to (and I say this without hyperbole) the finest professional team I had ever been a part of. I would also like to thank everyone associated with WebForce for being so great to work with, and Brian Bennett of Netscape Communications for being a great partner to Silicon Graphics and also a very good friend.

This book was edited all over the place—on airplanes, in cafés, on StairMasters, and (primarily) in my own apartment. But for the most part, it was *written* in two wonderful homes that were far from my own home in both atmosphere and place. I would like to thank their owners for their hospitality, and for giving me much needed changes of scenery during some fairly demanding weeks. First, I would like to thank my parents, to whom this book is dedicated, for seeing to my care & feeding throughout Chapters 1, 2, and 3 out in way-rural Connecticut. Second, I would like to thank Jocelyn and young Sheba McArthur of San Francisco for giving me frequent run of their glorious city "sky pad" during Jocelyn's long international journeys. I would specifically like to thank Jocelyn for generously letting me stay in her room during said journeys, and would specifically like to thank young Sheba for sharing her home with me, for putting up with my bizarre hours, and for not shedding too much on my computer.

Finally, no drama would be complete without the heroic arrival of the cavalry toward the end or (in this case) the middle of the action to save the protagonist from near-certain disaster. The writing of this book was certainly a dramatic episode for its author, and the cavalry was Katie Burke. Katie arrived in the midst of an overwhelmingly busy summer and spent two months catching dropping balls, interviewing dozens of people, digging up hundreds of seemingly-unfindable facts, considering and commenting upon every syllable contained herein, fixing my computer, and generally enabling me to keep my act together. I don't know how this book would have turned out without the enormous bolts of energy, wisdom, and good spirits that she directed at it and its author during a very critical period—and I'm grateful that I'll never have to find out. Thank you, Katie—it looks like we're finally done with this one.

Robert H. Reid

December 1996
Mountain View, CA

INTRODUCTION

J. Neil Weintraut

Through a combination of foresight, intuition, and mostly luck, I was one of a then relatively small number of people who grabbed onto the tail of the commercial Internet tiger when it was a mere cub in mid-1994, launching my career from a technology industry analyst to an Internet industry insider and spokesman. Since late 1994 the Internet has been all-consuming for those—including myself—in its vortex.

"All-consuming" is not meant casually. Indeed, I have yet to hear of a description that encapsulates the surreal hyper-speed/happening/different virtual world of the virtual world. Its speed, scope, and scale—plus its uncanny and intrinsic nature to warp or obviate experienced-built knowledge, principles, and concepts—is unlike anything mankind has experienced at least in this century, if not in all time. And for us in the Internet vortex, we even get *paid* to do this. As Rick Adams, the founder of UUNET Technologies, described it in December 1994: "We haven't spent a cent on marketing, the phone never stops ringing, and every time we answer it, it's another new customer." This was a precursor, an understatement, of what was to come; in Rick's case, his company went on to be the largest Internet service provider, growing to a size in the subsequent two years like what it normally takes the fastest-growing non-Internet technology companies five to seven years to reach—that's Web time. Put another way, the transformations brought forth by the technology industry over the past 20 years, exemplified by the invention of the microprocessor, the advent of the personal computer, the rise of Microsoft and fall of IBM, are mere gusts of wind compared to the tornado, the hurricane, and the tsunami wave of the Internet.

Furthermore, the Internet is becoming *more* intense. Remember those nonstop customer calls Rick Adams was fielding in 1995? It has gotten even headier; many Internet companies cannot respond to all of the calls and opportunities—jammed switchboards may be the best symbol of the spiraling white-hot intensity of the Internet of 1997. It is appropriate to say that the Internet has gone nuclear.

WHAT IS THE INTERNET?

The Internet—and this is important—is a lot of things. Important because although the Internet is prima facie a technology, it is most significant as the stimulus and means to a new—and better—world, ultimately touching virtually every facet of our lives. Furthermore, for all of the attention and impact of the Internet to date, it's about to get more exciting (more on this later). The Internet is more important in what it enables than what it is; more phenomenon than fact. Yes, the Internet is networks, software, computers, and other technologies; but more so, it is a catalyst of change, a new mass medium, a culture, a mindwarp, new things never before imagined. In the same manner that the world we live in is attributable to a major meteorite collision with the earth (which transformed our world from its previous era of the dinosaur), the Internet is a modern-day meteorite noteworthy not only because of itself, but rather because of the new world resulting from its aftermath.

It's one thing to "online-ize" a business; it is another to unleash pent-up forces of change that existed long before and are bigger than the Internet, that shatter, upset, revolutionize, and reformulate entire industries and even change the products that they sell. The former is a boring half-step of progress, while the latter is profound, tremendously beneficial, and opportunity-rich—this is the Internet. Similarly, rather than being yet another technology that widens the chasm between affluent and poor schools and students, the Internet promises to equalize the opportunity to be technology-fluent, due to the intrinsic nature of the Internet to provide everyone and anyone—regardless of economic class or geographic circumstance—with access to resources far beyond anything most of us have ever experienced. Additionally, just when conventional media such as print, radio, television, and film have run their course, the Internet provides a profoundly different medium that is spawning a new era of creativity. Indeed, the Internet will even recover great things now lost; notably, writing as an art form, a communications medium, and a lubricant within our society—lost for the past 40 years—is rapidly resurging on Internet E-mails and chat forums.

Transforming the fundamental structure and nature of business, equalizing and empowering us as individuals and as a society, providing a new and better medium both for communicating and for enabling creativity, and challenging our conventional thoughts . . . these are aspects of the Internet. Thus, just as the word "Hollywood" is really a metaphor (films, stars, lifestyle, creativity, and mass-influencer) rather than a location, the Internet is really a metaphor and stimulus to a new world (i.e., its consequences are what's really important, not its substance) rather than just a thing. And yes, the Internet is also a profound collection of computer and network technologies that are revolutionizing computers and communications.

The Internet is also a cauldron of activity, notable both in its seeming omnipresence (e.g., affecting every industry, every function, every principle), but also in its mindwarping ability to encourage activities and trajectories that in more stable environments are mutually exclusive. The Internet is chaos—chaos on a scale beyond any of our experiences; that is why attempts to pigeonhole Internet topics or issues as black or white engender confusion rather than understanding. Indeed, the Internet's vibrancy is its diversity. Where else can one simultaneously agree that high-bandwidth connections such as cable are the future (see Chapter 8), while at the same time project that sales of low-bandwidth modems will accelerate in the future? Similarly, many newspapers dismiss the Internet as an insignificant threat to their business, while simultaneously scrambling to become content providers to major Web sites and to sell Internet-based classified advertisements as a complement or alternative to their print classifieds.

Recognizing then that the Internet is more about the phenomenon of a new world and less about a technology, some statistics help to substantiate its profound size, speed, and significance, as follows:

• Calculating the number of individuals using the Internet has become as common an event as assessing the weather—and just about as accurate. Nonetheless, many separate studies indicate that more than 30 million people use the Internet in the United States alone, and perhaps another 10 million internationally.

•Many Web sites already have *more* regular subscribers than the national magazines and newspapers—the ones that influence the very soul and beliefs of Americans. More people regularly visit Netscape, Yahoo!, and ESPNET SportsZone Web sites on the Internet than read *Newsweek*, *Forbes*, or *Sports Illustrated*. PointCast, for example, has attracted over 1.5 million subscribers in the first *six months* of its release, which equals the subscriber base of *The Wall Street Journal*, the most read newspaper in the United States.

•The Internet has enticed more people to jump from the security of their well-situated jobs and lifestyles into the uncertain but heady world of the Internet than any other phenomenon since the California gold rush of 1849. Previously unseatable midlevel managers and engineers are suddenly surrendering their peaceful $100,000-a-year jobs for Internet jobs at half the salary but with the opportunity for the ride of their life and of course stock options that may be worth millions. Even more significant is the trend of nontechnology people—including senior executives—deserting their cushy jobs in traditional banks, manufacturing, retailing, and media in pursuit of the Internet brass ring; many seek nothing more than to be able to tell their grandchildren that they were part of the phenomenon that created the future world.

•The number of host or so-called server computers on the Internet has grown exponentially from under one million two years ago to over five million today.

•Starting with NETCOM Online Communications in December 1994, the Internet has spawned more than 20 initial public offerings, more IPOs than the entire technology industry in 1994. Moreover, Internet IPOs forever changed technology finance, blowing away rules of thumb for going public that held true for 20 years, and increasing valuations of technology companies at large by up to 50 percent. Recent Internet IPOs included four Internet service providers, six Web software companies, three firewall software companies, four directory services, three transaction services, and a media company.

•Within one year, the Internet accelerated the demise of (non-Internet) online services, such as eWorld, Imajination Network, and Interchange—names that seem silly today to recall. Similarly, the Internet precipitated wholesale transformations of other online services, as evidenced by the dramatic transformation of the largest—namely, America Online—from a private into an Internet service.

The Internet spawned Netscape, which is the fastest growing soft-

ware company ever, and second only to the personal computer manufacturer Compaq as the fastest growing company of any kind.

•Where IBM in its heyday and the federal Department of Justice
failed, the Internet has succeeded in being the first threat to Microsoft,
the world's most powerful and treacherous software company, since it
was created.

INTERNET: THE TECHNOLOGY

Technologically, the Internet is a network of computers. Not just a few
special computers, but millions of all types of computers. Similarly, it
is not just a network, but a network of networks—internetworks—and
hence, its name.

This borderline technogobble, however, does not identify the key
values that lead to the Internet's profoundness. There are many other
networks, including the technology, online service, and private networks such as those used on Wall Street or within major companies.
Each of these, however, is expensive, constrained in its functionality,
and/or limited to private—and hence small—communities of subscribers or employees. In contrast, due to both its technology and
philosophical underpinnings, the Internet is trivially inexpensive, can
be used for seemingly any type of communication, and—most importantly—is open equally to *everyone*. These factors make the difference
between the Internet being just yet another computer network and being the platform for the most phenomenal event and (virtual) thing
during our lifetime.

A comparison to the telephone network will help here. With a telephone network, you connect to a single point (e.g., your grand-
mother), and you communicate with a simple device such a telephone
(or to a lesser extent a facsimile machine or computer, albeit in a cumbersome fashion). With the Internet, you or more specifically your
computer connects to the Internet of *millions* of computers (as opposed to a single end-point), and you communicate, well, with just
about anything in any way. Each computer is the technological agent
representing and maintaining interaction with a company, activity, or
individual. Simply put, you can do far more things on the Internet that
are either cumbersome or not possible to do with plain old telephones
(of course the Internet is cheaper too).

With no more than a point-and-click hyper-link, you can entertain
yourself at a Walt Disney site, send electronic mail to Grandma, check

employment opportunities at a French winery, get real-time stock quotes at Quote.com or have them effortlessly broadcasted to your home via PointCast, track a Federal Express package, or participate with many other individuals simultaneously in a chat forum in topics ranging from sex to multiple sclerosis.

Furthermore, recognizing that the Internet is designed for computer-to-computer communications and that—via the advances of microprocessor technology—computers can be used for seemingly anything and anything can be computerized, the Internet thus can be used for, well, anything. And so it is. The Internet is being used for telephone calls, video transmissions, and even "radio" broadcasts (via software from companies such as Progessive Networks, which is discussed in Chapter 2). Similarly, computer-in-disguise appliances such as cellular telephones are being applied to the Internet through companies such as Unwired Planet, thereby enriching otherwise vanilla consumer devices with the potential power of millions of Internet computers. Finally, a plethora of so-called network computers, with breakthrough significance ranging from being able to carry a device with powerful information access capabilities in your pocket, to slashing computer costs to the sub-$500 threshold, making computers and networks available to the masses of people, are forthcoming.

Moreover, beyond a small fixed monthly fee, the communications cost of all of this activity is, well, nothing; using a computer in Montana costs the same as using a computer in Australia: *nothing.* Telephone usage is priced according to the length of time and the distance between points for each time a connection is made. In contrast, the Internet is an invisible connection to all computers all the time; distance, time, and number or frequency of connections don't matter; these concepts don't exist on the Internet. Want to wantonly surf across the computer of every company whose name begins with the letter "Q"? No problem; no charge either. Want to broadcast New Year's wishes to two thousand of your closest friends? Its easier than licking the stamp for one envelope and even cheaper than the stamp!

Thus, while the ubiquitous telephone shares the same level of openness (i.e., usable by anyone anywhere) as the Internet, it lacks functionality; many of the activities or capabilities of the Internet are either too cumbersome or impossible to do with a telephone. Meanwhile, there are many computer networks that already exist that theoretically could provide power similar to the Internet; however—and this is key—they lack the openness of the Internet. Therein lies the unique and breakthrough capacity of the Internet: It provides both powerful and even new networking capabilities, and makes them available to everyone—that's exciting!

The limitations of contemporary non-Internet computer networks underscore the problems—perhaps even the absurdity—of their lack of openness, which is ultimately manifested in severely restricting the networks' impact relative to their potential (and hence, indicate some of the breakthrough that was to come via the Internet by eliminating these restrictions). Consider, for example, a Wall Street stock service such as Bloomberg. Powerful stuff, but it requires a dedicated and one-of-a-kind computer that is useful only for Bloomberg-based information—hardly the basis for attracting millions of subscribers; hence, its use is restricted to fewer than 100 thousand elite users. Similarly, prior to the Internet, consumer online services such as Prodigy and CompuServe were isolated online private "clubs." This balkanization was even worse, as the content was also segregated according to network (when is the last time you were told that to call Philadelphia you needed to use telephone network A versus telephone network B?). If you want *USA Today*, that's America Online, CompuServe is *Newsweek*, and Prodigy is *Home and Garden* (see Chapter 1). Pretty stupid. As if the closed nature of computer networks wasn't enough of an eviscerating barrier to profound utility, each non-Internet network required the use of different software that both worked only on that specific network and entailed learning yet another set of commands and syntax.

The Internet, in contrast, is accessible by everyone; and everything, be it *The New York Times*, *The Wall Street Journal*, or *Wired* magazine, is available on it. Moreover, by its very design, the Internet employs technology, especially software technology, that is both widely available and usable across a broad range of applications from transaction processing to animated games to personalized newspapers. Indeed, symbolic of the global and community nature of the Internet (whereas private networks use technology ironically as a barrier, an impediment to their usage), the Internet uses technology in order to be as useful to as many people for as many applications as possible.

(The ability of Internet software technology to be applied to essentially every application known to mankind—including even non-Internet uses such as so-called intranets used by companies for internal communications—engenders enormous market potential for its software. As discussed in Chapter 1, this potential is so profound that it came to launch the fastest-growing software company ever, namely Netscape, which is the market-share and spiritual leader of Internet software.)

NUCLEAR PACKETS

No discussion of the Internet would be complete without mentioning its roots in the age of nuclear defense. Indeed, despite its potential as the most significant phenomenon during our lifetime, the Internet shares some background with other technological innovations such as the integrated circuit (invented in 1956 and flourished in the late '70s), and the personal computer (prototyped in 1977 and flourished in the mid '80s); it is one of the longest overnight successes.

The Internet's roots trace back 27 years to a project of the Defense Agency Research Projects Administration (known as DARPA). The project, appropriately enough christened ARPAnet, was to prototype a communications infrastructure for the U.S. military that could withstand a nuclear attack. Indeed, some of the best attributes of the Internet—its architecture, technology, and gestalt—are all legacies of this unwitting nuclear parent.

The design goal of nuclear resilience inspired a network architecture and technology unlike any other, and certainly unlike the standard telephone network. Where the telephone network architecture requires connection through a central switch (which by virtue of its centralization makes thousands of connections vulnerable to a single nuclear strike), the ARPAnet, and hence Internet, allows any computer to tap in anywhere, analogous to tapping many holes down the length of a garden hose. Furthermore, whereas the telephone network architecture is predicated on transferring information along logically-fixed and defined pathways between two points, the Internet instead slices information into small "packets," and each one then bounces around from computer to computer across the nation until it lands on its destination computer, where the collection of packets is reassembled into the original message. This packet technology again complements nuclear resilience; if a nuclear attack compromises one path to a destination, each packet will just keep being rerouted between computers until it finds a path that still exists. Most importantly, the packet-based architecture of the Internet enables many of its fundamental capabilities: Packet communication is far better suited to computer communication—which is of course what the Internet is, namely a network of networks of computers—than the point-to-point technology of telephone networks, and the packet and distributed architecture engenders the openness that sets apart the Internet from all other networks and underlies much of its mass utility.

A handful of universities were invited to be the development partners of the project, and shortly thereafter many major universities connected to the ARPAnet as a means of exercising both the technology and the communication. This flourished into a sister network for the research community sponsored and funded by the National Science Foundation (NSF), called the NSFnet, which quickly infiltrated most universities not only in the United States but worldwide. This led, quite naturally, to the permeation of the NSFnet and technology into corporations, as engineering students who had used and established relationships on the NSFnet brought their university accounts and electronic mail (E-mail) addresses with them to their jobs subsequent to graduation. As a result, many corporate computers began being connected to the Internet through the informal efforts of former college students cum employees (although often without the knowledge or approval of senior management or the legal department).

Amongst other consequences of this evolution of the Internet from nonprofit to commercial usage is the now-familiar ".com" (pronounced "dot com," an abbreviation for "commercial") suffix that you hear promoted on the radio, and indeed that has become part of pop lingo. For example, the Internet addresses of Netscape, Book Stacks, and Federal Express, respectively, are "netscape.com," "books.com," and "fedex.com." (In comparison, government and educational entities are assigned the ".gov" and ".edu" suffixes, and countries outside the United States are assigned specific acronyms, such as ".uk" for the United Kingdom.)

In response to this proliferation of corporate users of the Internet—albeit substantially techwennies exchanging E-mail—the NSF established an acceptable use policy (AUP) for commercial use in 1990. This AUP cleared the Internet for applications beyond strict academic research and development, although no significant uses surfaced until late 1993. This policy, however, set the stage for a number of Internet engineers to start businesses to provide "turnkey" Internet access services to a local region, spawning over a thousand mostly mom-and-pop companies (called Internet service providers or ISPs). These ISPs took advantage of the fundamental capability to append additional connections and networks to the Internet "backbone" networks running across the country, essentially anywhere by anyone. Internet access service enabled businesses and individuals to easily and cheaply get access to the Internet over standard telephone lines that are already in existence; the ISPs own and maintain big network switches that on one side directly tap into one of the Internet backbones, and on the other side connect or bridge thousands of companies and individuals via standard phone lines. For example, one of the top-four ISPs today, PSInet, originated as a spin-off of the network community servicing the Greater New York area anchored around Cornell University.

Meanwhile, the NSF became increasingly and appropriately antsy as commercial users and applications began consuming significant amounts of capacity of the NSFnet; after all, the NSF was subsidizing the NSFnet for academic purposes. As a result, what were to become the major Internet service providers, namely, UUNET Technologies, PSInet, NETCOM On-line Communications, BBN Planet, and MCI, went beyond providing mere local access to the NSFnet, and rather, installed their own nationwide trunk lines that paralleled and carried traffic independent of the NSFnet. Exhibit I.1 shows how UUNET's trunk lines crisscross the nation; regional areas are serviced as spokes connected to major hubs.

As a result, what today we loosely call the Internet is predominately a collection of nationwide and international networks independently operated by UUNET, PSInet, NETCOM, BBN, and MCI. Each one is literally a separate network; but to us as users they appear as one amorphous network. (For those more technically inclined who are wondering how these different networks interoperate, the national ISPs set up

Exhibit I.1   UUNET High-Performance Network

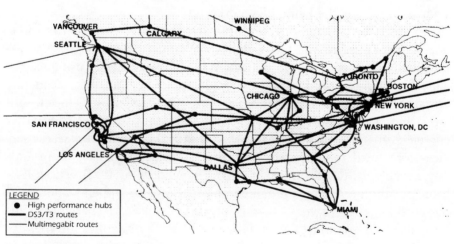

Source: UUNET Technologies.

massive interchange points at key locations—for example, near Washington, DC, Boston, and San Francisco—where traffic is crossed between the otherwise independent networks.) Ironically, the commercial Internet networks quickly overshadowed the research and educational activity and purpose of the NSFnet; consequently, funding for the NSFnet, and hence its operation, was terminated in April of 1995.

WEBBING THE INTERNET

For all of its technological wonder, the Internet was an obscure scientific endeavor. This would be changed and changed markedly by the innovation of an idea and technology called the World Wide Web—or the Web—in 1993.

Prior to the Web, the Internet was a world that only a technologist could love, much less use. It required adeptness at painfully cryptic computer programs, and even if one mastered these, other than E-mailing your buddies, where to go or what to do on the Internet was, well, a mystery. The Internet was a massive library of some of the most advanced information and discussion forums in the world from the leading research institutions, but locating and getting the information was obtrusively difficult. It was akin to walking down each aisle of a library, scanning each book just to figure out what is there, but doing all of this in the dark! Furthermore, once you found something relevant to your needs, you then had to read (i.e., download) the entire book, rather than skim or browse parts of it. Worse still, once found, one piece of information often referred to other valuable information but provided no means for locating it, thrusting you into a seemingly endless cycle of hunting in the dark to browse and gather information that was all but impossible to aggregate. Enter the World Wide Web.

Tired of the hunt-and-peck process for locating and obtaining information, a researcher named Tim Berners-Lee at the CERN atomic research center in Switzerland proposed software and networking protocols (protocols are sets of commands and sequences that computers use to communicate over a network) in 1989 that any computer could use to browse—rather than find information by brute force. This effort gained momentum by 1993, culminating in the development of the critical piece of software called a Web browser—and the rest, as they say, is history. (Quoting a report by Matthew Gray of MIT in 1994: Technically, "the World Wide Web was originally proposed in 1989 and the first implementation appeared in 1990. The Web, however, did not gain any widespread popular use until NCSA Mosaic [browser software] became available in early 1993.")

Berners-Lee's software and protocols created the ability to browse documents and navigate among not only different documents but among different computers—and in fact throughout the Internet—with simple point-and-click commands. Key to the technology was the concept of "hyper-links," which are highlighted words or symbols within documents that when clicked on, cause your computer to automatically and instantaneously jump (in a virtual sense) to, well, anywhere, ranging from the next page in the same document to a different report on a different computer, located, perhaps, halfway around the world. Clicking on a highlighted (i.e., hyper-link–enabled) name of a team in a sports article, would, for example, change the screen to details about the team, recent games, players and positions, and upcoming events. In turn, clicking on a player's name presents a detailed biography of the player, including education, statistics, and commentaries (these notions are all reviewed in Chapter 1).

This hyper-linking functionality spun the Internet from an information terra incognita into a web of information spanning the world; hence, the moniker World Wide Web.

The Web is the Rosetta stone of the Internet for the masses. The Web makes the Internet ubiquitous, easy, and useful—useful in particular by the masses versus only the technologically elite. Notably, Web software has become easier to use than even the Apple Macintosh computer, a computer long heralded for its ability to be used by almost anyone, yet the Web offers more power, more information, and more services to just about anyone for anything. Not even the most sophisticated computer networks on Wall Street or within major businesses like IBM, or American Airlines' SABRE reservation system, have the power of the Web—and the Web is accessible by anyone for $19.95 a month or less.

Within months of the release of an early version of a Web browser developed by Berners-Lee, Web software spread like wildfire throughout the research community; by June 1993 more than 130 server computers (i.e., the computers where information is stored and served to client computers such as yours and mine) were Web-enabled. As a tip-off of what is to come, the number of Web-enabled server computers grew a thousandfold—yes, 1000 times—to over 150 thousand server computers by July 1996! Exhibit I.2 highlights the exponential growth of the Web. The statistics of the Web also mirror the transformation of the Internet from academic to commercial, as only 1.5 percent of Web

Exhibit I.2   Proliferating Web Sites

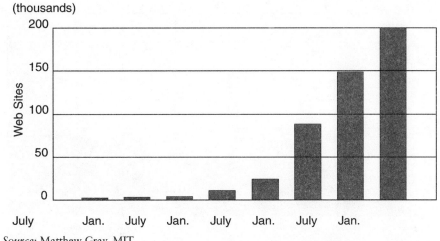

(thousands)

Source: Matthew Gray, MIT.

servers (i.e., 2 out of 130) were ".com" addresses in June 1993, whereas that fraction transformed into 90 percent of a markedly higher number, namely 200 thousand, by the end of 1996.

One of the places where the primordial Web software spread during 1993 was the University of Illinois, where it engaged a small group of students including one named Marc Andreessen. They took it upon themselves to rectify many of the shortcomings of the very primitive prototypes then floating around the Internet. Most significantly, their work transformed the appeal of the Web from niche uses in the technical area to mass-market appeal. In particular, these University of Illinois students made two key changes to the Web browser, which hyper-boosted its appeal: they added graphics to what was otherwise boring text-based software, and most importantly, they ported the software from so-called Unix computers that are popular only in technical and academic circles, to the Microsoft Windows operating system, which is used on more than 80 percent of the computers in the world, especially personal and commercial computers. Marc's team circulated a version of the NCSA Mosaic browser that ran on the Microsoft Windows operating system in October 1993; this fact is represented by the Web statistics collected by Matthew Gray in Exhibit I.3, wherein the number of Web servers jumps markedly shortly after the release of the NCSA Mosaic software for Windows.

Exhibit I.3   Web Site Growth—Pretakeoff

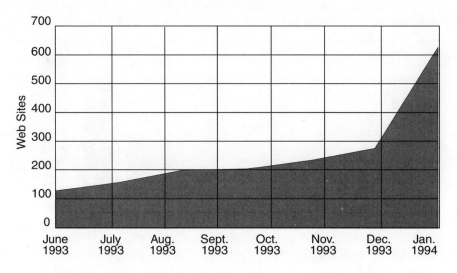

Source: Matthew Gray, MIT.

FROM TECHNOBABBLE TO SOCIETAL CHANGE

Via the Web, the Internet suddenly provided access to far more information than ever before possible, and that access was available to the masses at dramatically low cost and effort. This capability is profound; it is the makings of another exciting technology market, akin to the multibillion-dollar database or semiconductor industries. However, these facts by themselves do not explain the phenomenon of the Internet.

The Internet unwittingly struck a nerve in factors far bigger than the Internet itself. The Internet is the catalyst, the means, and the metaphor unleashing pent-up forces of change throughout both commerce and culture. In addition, the Internet itself has become a new—virtual—world that is as much a mass and cultural activity icon and mindset in the pre-twenty-first century as, for example, the Beatles were in the 1960s. That is to say, the Internet is the lightning rod drawing a lightning bolt of world-change.

The Internet is stimulating wholesale changes in essentially every industry and every business—changes that have long been ready to occur, but have been held back by a variety of factors including sheer inertia and physical limitations. To emphasize, if all the Internet amounted to was yet another communications channel (i.e., a computer version of a telephone), it would be interesting but inconsequential—and you wouldn't be reading this book right now. Instead, the Internet enables profoundly different, new, and better ways of doing things. Simply put, the phenomenon is not about doing things on the Internet, but rather it's about using the Internet to do things differently.

Broad but essentially inevitable evolution of business—markets, industry structures, practices, prices, and practices—is waiting for wholesale response and transformation. Consider these trends:

•Markets are switching from production-driven to customer-controlled. Fifty years ago when mass production was the breakthrough, it made sense to drive markets based on production issues (remember the tag line for Ford's mass-produced Model T: "You can have any color you want as long as it is black"). Today, production is no longer a significant issue—it is commonplace. Instead, markets are saturated, and customers are the scarce resource. Witness, for example, how the cereal and automobile industries each recently unilaterally reduced prices. The cost of producing these products did not change. Instead, what changed was the market environment; prices are no longer based primarily on the cost to produce goods, but rather on customer-perceived value.

•Similarly, basic offerings are being commoditized, while the service and knowledge associated with the basic offering is increasingly the primary value or differentiation as viewed by the customer. Customers have become so used to receiving well-made products at reasonable prices that this is considered a requirement rather than a distinctive aspect of a product or service. Accordingly, people increasingly base their choice of whom or what they do business with—be it a bank loan, automobile purchase, or trading partner—based on how a company does business (i.e. service and knowledge) rather than the actual product. Delivering service and knowledge is a defining capability of the Internet, making the Internet a natural catalyst to unleash this broad trend.

•Proliferating product options and complexity are changing the seller/buyer interaction from one of selling products to that of helping customers select products. There are now so many choices in virtually every product category—beds, magazines, stereos, loans—that finding and configuring the best option to individual requirements dominates a customer's need and, most importantly, decision process. This need again plays to—and has been waiting for—the abilities of the Internet,

which is a natural medium for identifying individual customer requirements and selecting and configuring the best option.

The Internet plays to each of these trends—and then some. The interactive, personalizable, and communications capabilities of the Internet enables businesses to drive their operations around customers—
including establishing priceless customer relationships—while providing more service and knowledge than was ever before possible.

As if that wasn't enough bang-for-the-buck, the Internet provides
these breakthrough benefits at lower cost and greater customer involvement and satisfaction. Notably, the Internet empowers "everyone to be
an operator." An anecdote from the phone industry applies here. Fifty
years ago, the telephone companies realized that the only way that they
could meet the coming surge in telephone usage was to rid themselves of
manual (i.e., clerk-based) switchboards, and instead have everyone dial
his or her own calls (i.e., make the customer the operator). That is of
course what we do today; we dial our own phone numbers—and we prefer it that way. Similarly, the coming surge in service and knowledge just
discussed can be met only if we let everyone service themselves (i.e., be an
operator) at least for the top 20 percent of our needs that account for 80
percent of our time; there are simply not enough clerks in the world to
support all of the coming demands for service and knowledge, and even
it there were, the system would collapse under its own cumbersomeness
and complexity. Furthermore, by making "everyone . . . an operator" we
all benefit: We get better and more personalized service (who knows better what our individual preferences are than ourselves?) and it cost less.
Thus, one of the single most important uses of the Internet is and will increasingly be companies empowering customers to service themselves.
Notable examples include banks letting customers check their account
balances, retail operations order books, and shipping companies such as
Federal Express enabling customers to check package status.

Furthermore, the Internet is the catalyst to change—make that
obliterate—outmoded business models, models that are vestiges of by-
gone eras dating back to the 1920s or even late-1800s, when most industries were formed. Indeed, the fact that car buying is ranked as the
single most painful consumer experience in the United States tells more
about the potential for the Internet than the most sophisticated network protocol devised by Netscape or the CERN. Accordingly, some
of the early successes on the Internet are car-buying services (which,
consistent with the fundamental trends discussed earlier, implicitly

shift power from the supplier to the customer) such as Auto-By-Tel. Similarly, most industries that are founded upon transaction-based business models—such as banking, stockbrokerage, and travel—are up for deconstruction and reformation; transactions are a commodity and the value-add lies in incremental and associated services. Accordingly, other early Internet successes include E*Trade, Lombard Securities, and Charles Schwab, all successful because they fundamentally altered the business model by marginalizing transactions to a trivial cost and nondifferentiable process, while empowering individual investors with investment information never before available.

Conventional media, namely television and radio broadcast; newspaper, magazine, and book print; and film, are stale and stagnant, leaving an opportunity, indeed perhaps begging the Internet to provide a refreshing antidote.

Conventional media are losing or have lost their zip; they are increasingly more (and the same) formula than creative. Indeed, the first print media to come along in some time that is refreshing in content and context is *Wired* magazine, which also happens to be an icon of the Internet world (see Chapter 7).

Plots in situation comedies and movies (consider, for example, *Mission Impossible*, *Terminator*, or *The Mirror Has Two Faces*) are the same ones that have been used 10 or even 30 times over since the 1950s. From one television station to the next, news broadcasts are mostly the same content organized in the same order (for example, could anyone tell the difference between stations or newspapers in the coverage of the O. J. Simpson trial?). In desperation, they have sunk to shock versus substance as a means to retain viewer interest. Hollywood has resorted primarily to packing more sex and violence into each minute of film rather than plot or intrigue, in a spiraling race to stimulate viewers' senses, which are already overloaded and callused.

The statistics bear out these trends: The fraction of the population watching prime-time newscasts, which were once the keystone of television, has halved over the past 10 years. Similarly, city after city around the country is witnessing the collapse of two or three local newspapers into one, as increasingly apathetic readers find little need for two or more papers.

Most significantly, conventional media is doomed to mediocrity. The business model of conventional media—including its broadcast orientation, which implicitly entails onerous economics of mass appeal, whereas the interactive world of the Internet leverages mass participation and access—relegates most of its endeavors to least-common-denominator subjects and presentations in order to appeal to as broad a base of viewers as possible.

The Internet changes—indeed obviates—the root sources of the problems of conventional media. Whereas the limitations of technology and business models condemn conventional media to generic and homogeneous content in order to appeal to a broad base, to fixed schedules, and to a lack of diversity by virtue of their small numbers, the Internet is personalized down to an individual, available anytime to anyone, and diverse even to a fault.

The other energy driving the Internet phenomenon is its adoption by our society at large as everything from a cultural icon and identity to a new world. In the same way that baseball is a unique activity, identity, way of life, pastime, means of inspiring young minds, business, and national treasure, so has the Internet become.

Of all the important messages he could have given, Bob Dole chose to end his closing comment at the final debate of the 1996 Presidential election with a reference about using the Internet, in a pitiful attempt to suggest that he and his entourage were in sync with cultural trends and the future. (His attempt was pitiful because his subtly incorrect enunciation of the address of the Dole campaign Web site signaled the he did not have a clue about the Internet. His failure to use the "dot com" suffix was akin to a visitor trying to act like a local by calling San Francisco "Frisco," which is a sure tip-off that he or she is a tourist.)

Indeed, much of the sudden interest in the Internet by the masses is attributable in large part to a non-Internet but cultural phenomenon called America Online. America Online is a private consumer online network that introduced and inspired millions of people to experience and use so-called online activities long before the masses had heard of the Internet or Web technology had been commercialized. Reflective of its role in making online a cultural phenomenon, as much as 50 percent of the activity on America Online is online chat forums, where the masses of people meet and interact in a virtual world with its own rules and environment. Until very recently, America Online had little to do with the literal Internet. Conversely, the term "Internet" has come to be a metaphor for the culture and concept of doing things online, be it literally on the Internet, on America Online, or on private corporate networks.

As a result of the Internet increasingly becoming an integral component of our lives, and certainly of the future, E-mail addresses are becoming as commonplace—and expected—as phone numbers. Indeed, it's not uncommon for the decreasing portion of the business population that do not yet have an E-mail address printed on their business cards to sheepishly make preemptive excuses or scribble their newly acquired address on the back of the card.

Meanwhile, more and more people are using the Internet for legions of pedestrian uses. Importantly, pedestrian does not imply unimportant, rather quite the contrary. While the press tends to be fascinated with sensationalized but relatively useless applications—so-called "pizza-over-the-Internet" stuff, the Internet is simplifying, chipping away, or obviating a myriad of the little things that add up to marked improvement of our lives every day. Take, for example, getting directions to a business, store, or friend's apartment. With about the same number of keystrokes as to dial a phone number, the Internet provides directions and a map faster and better than verbal explanations or facsimiles. Accordingly, as a routine part of life, executives are increasingly simply clicking on Yahoo!, BigBook, or Vicinity to get directions to literally every business or household in America—wow! Similarly, got an interview tomorrow? Smart job seekers pop over to the Web site of the prospective employer—or check out other Web sites with related information—to get insights that not only are otherwise unavailable, but may be the edge that lands the job during the interview.

The essential point of all these seemingly intangible activities is that the Internet is becoming . . . part of our life. That's important.

SCOPE, SPEED, AND SCALE

All of this Internet-borne activity—the unprecedented access to information, wholesale transformations of industry, and a new cultural entity—is exciting and bewildering enough. Yet there is more, as all of this is occurring at unprecedented scope, speed, and scale. That is, the Internet is affecting essentially everything and it is doing this faster and impacting things to a much greater degree than anything we have ever before encountered.

•**Scope.** The Internet is affecting almost everything imaginable—publishing, education, entertainment, banking, industrial arts, health care, government, travel, the Olympics, employment, retailing, cellular phones, and the First Amendment, to name a few.

The Internet has impacted medical studies, albeit so far adversely, as participants previously isolated by the physical barriers of conventional media found and communicated with each other en masse on chat forums, enabling them to surreptitiously determine who was being given placebos and who was not. Meanwhile, the publishing industry, long used to tying their content exclusively to their physical media (i.e., a magazine), is confronted with the reality that content will be sold à la carte over the Internet in many cases. Government is finding their sovereignty—the ability to censor information and tax—undermined by the Internet. Creative people, such as graphic artists or game-software programmers, are finding their stature and pay jump from back-office clerks with sub-$40,000 salaries to prime stars commanding $60,000 or even six-figure salaries. Laws that easily demarcated the difference between so-called real-time sports data sold to radio stations and public (i.e., free) information published in the newspapers the next morning are proving impotent to define Internet-based data (e.g., is the difference between real-time and public data 10 seconds, 2 minutes, or 20 hours, or is a distinction even appropriate in the Internet era?).

Thus, far from merely being the latest twist to fire up the technology world, the Internet is affecting essentially everything in our world. . . . Now, that's a phenomenon!

•**Speed.** Whereas most technological innovations take 5 or even 10 years to achieve a scale of significance, the Internet is impacting industries and our culture in time frames measured in months or at most a few years. That is to say that the Internet is impacting our world at a rate of 5 or even 10 times faster than most technological innovations.

Fundamentally, whereas most innovations—essentially by definition—necessitate a time-consuming stage of building a new infrastructure to support the innovation, the Internet, by its very design, uses the existing infrastructure and existing industries. Thus, during the same time that most technological innovations are laying groundwork for their ultimate takeoff, the Internet has already rushed ahead into mainstream ubiquity. For example, the widespread use of the personal computer was impeded by years not by computer hardware technology that makes a personal computer, but rather by the lack of availability of useful commercial-grade software to run the personal computers. In contrast, the Internet harnessed existing telephone lines, computers, and even software to be an "overnight success" subsequent to the advent of Web technology.

Hence, we have one of the many mind-numbing, reality-bending aspects of the Internet—instantaneous speed. Our time-honed practical experiences that left us comfortable knowing that if and when a new innovation comes along, we would have plenty of advance warning to study, understand, and respond to it is a sense of reality that no longer holds true in the Internet era. Indeed, the speed of the Internet confounded even the world's most powerful technology company, Microsoft. Microsoft literally resorted to midnight telephone calls over cellular phones during the first week of December 1995 in a mad scramble to amass a strategic response to a "thing" (i.e., the Internet) that had been a technical oddity only a year earlier (see Chapter 3). If the Internet's speed surprised the people that live and breath technology every day, imagine the bewilderment of some poor retailer, media executive, lawyer, or other nontechnologist, as it sweeps through their relatively measured-pace world.

• **Scale.** Finally, as if it weren't enough that the Internet affects essentially everything and affects it at mind-boggling speed, the Internet's impact is not one of mere modification, but profound and substantive transformation.

For example, whereas most software takes 5 to even 10 years to permeate markets (for example, relational database software became commercially available in the early 1980s, but it did not significantly impact businesses until the early 1990s) Web browser software has populated more than 40 million computers within two years. Forty million copies—that's more than the population in each of all but the 10 most populous countries in the world.

Most significantly, as described earlier, the Internet is important not because it is a means to do the same things online, but rather because it enables us to do things differently. Thus, the impact of the Internet on most industries, companies, and government is not merely limited to providing yet another communications channel, but rather it is a shockwave shaking—perhaps destroying—fundamental structure and philosophies. That's deep! For example, in the investment industry, the Internet not only augments operations with electronic order entry, but it shakes the foundation of the industry itself by empowering individuals with information and flexibility that greatly diminishes the role of stockbrokers while radically altering the underlying business model from transaction-based to service-based.

WHERE WERE YOU WHEN THE INTERNET HAPPENED?

Although the Internet has been the most profound and heated phenomenon during our lifetime since it broke onto the mainstream scene—thereby officially demarcating it as a happening—in early 1994, we ain't seen nothing yet. Indeed, much of what has transpired has been the build-out and permeation of the Internet groundwork; build-out and permeation in preparation for the phenomenal impacts about to be realized.

Indeed, during the past three years, many people involved with the Internet had a moment akin to a religious experience when they discovered the Internet with its potential and promise; they describe the experience as an epiphany. For example, the author of this Introduction remembers vividly his epiphany, which was caused by an article in a February 1994 issue of *The New York Times* describing how the Securities and Exchange Commission (SEC) had just begun publishing corporate financial filings on the World Wide Web. Suddenly, important information that had previously been difficult and costly to obtain in a timely fashion was available to everyone, instantaneously, for free; it hit me that the Internet was—finally—happening and was going to be big.

Despite all of its greatness, there is actually a relatively limited range or depth of things to use the Internet for today; it is, for all intents and purposes, still a novelty (see Exhibit I.4). Indeed, the Internet in 1996 is analogous to air travel during its propeller era—neat but not particularly relevant to most activities, and limited to special uses,

Exhibit I.4 The Four Stages of the Internet Evolution

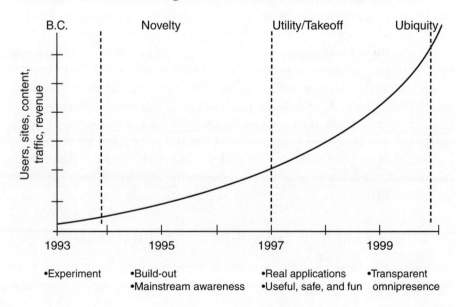

such as airmail. The Internet is in the throes of entering its jet age; it will become not only useful for a variety of functions and for most people, but we will actually come to depend on or require it.

As discussed earlier, prior to the advent and dissemination of Web technology in late 1993, the Internet was a wonderful global experiment in computer networks; this was the "before commercialization" or B.C. stage of the Internet. The operative word in the B.C. stage was "experiment"—an arcane experiment known to relatively few individuals and used for relatively few purposes. Nonetheless, this experiment, perhaps unwittingly, was priming the pump for the rocketshiplike takeoff of the Internet. Ignited by the advent of Web technology in late 1993, thousands of companies and millions of individuals began to harness this "overnight" wonder; and here we are today, in the second—build-out and novelty—stage of the Internet.

While the exact date when the Internet went mainstream is debatable within a seven-month time frame between, say, September 1993 and March 1994, this was the critical build-out stage when it captured the attention and imagination of everyone. In early 1997 the convergence of a variety of forces presently afoot has ratcheted the Internet to its next and profoundly more significant and exciting jet age . . . and a new world. Hence, this book's subtitle, *1,000 Days that Built the Future of Business*, refers to the mainstream making of the new world, the new era of the Internet that transpired over an approximately three-year or thousand-day period beginning in late 1993/early 1994 and ending in early 1997.

For the period between late 1993 and early 1997, the Internet has been captivating the awareness if not direct participation of literally everyone in the United States, transforming the technology industry, drawing the attention and involvement of almost every company ranging from Joe Boxer to Microsoft, stirring up legal quandaries and public issues such as fallacious reports about the downing of a TWA airliner, and accumulating a critical mass of more than 40 million users. All the while, the Internet has been superheated by the energy of thousands of vendors or all sorts ranging from Internet service providers to new startups of Java-based software (more on this later) that have been racing to build out and be part of what will be the biggest opportunity of their lifetime. In many regards, one could argue that these thousand days have been the preparation for the rest of our life.

And here comes the rest of our life. For all the attention that the

Internet has already deservedly received, things are about to get even more exciting. Until recently, a variety of factors, such as—amusingly enough—the lack of anything substantively useful to do, has restrained the Internet to being a novelty of mass interest but a novelty nonetheless. As these restrains are removed or rectified, the Internet is ratcheting from a neat curiosity to a profound and powerful medium, capability, even a world.

For example, the absence of proven security for financial transaction mechanisms (e.g., electronic cash or credit cards) has impeded commerce applications of the Internet, and conversely, commerce will dramatically take off as this issue is resolved. This is currently happening; companies such as CyberCash and VeriSign are in the midst of deploying electronic cash and authentication services, respectively. Similarly, rating, auditing, and syndicating systems necessary for large-scale advertising are being deployed and reformulated by companies such as I/PRO (see Chapter 5) and IMGIS. Many other impediments exist, and most are being addressed. For example, a facet often overlooked but very significant is the involvement of people and players outside the United States; country after country is coming to grips with removing anachronistic telecommunications, legal, and information regulations, whereupon the Internet will truly become global.

The most important impediment by far, is, very simply, lack of useful things to do! Here too, many recent developments, such as PointCast, Travelocity, Amazon.com, and pcOrder.com, have transformed the Internet from a neat place to observe to a powerful thing to use. For example, the first application of the Internet that is powerful enough to entice people to remain connected to the Internet 24 hours a day recently surfaced; the application, the PointCast Network, streams relevant information to the people 24 hours a day. Similarly, people recently gained direct access to the American Airlines SABRE airline reservation system, which is the most powerful system in the world, through a new Web site called Travelocity. Meanwhile, many other powerful and smartly-done cross-media activities have surfaced that cross-fertilize between the popular mass media and the Internet. Indeed, one of the most significant trends in 1997—and one that will markedly boost the mass prominence of the Internet—is the cross-linking of conventional media with Internet media. These include CNET (see Chapter 8), MSNBC, and ESPNET SportsZone. The essential point is that within the last half of 1996, the utility of the Internet has been turbocharged by no less than 15 powerful services spanning a multitude of real-world needs . . . and you ain't seen nothing yet.

BUCKS, BITS, AND BOXES

Although the persuasiveness of the Internet challenges the ability to precisely define markets, it is projected to produce $15-billion bits and boxes industries, each, by the turn of the century. *Bits* refers to the technological infrastructure of the Internet, plus other Internet-related technology markets (notably the application of Internet technologies within companies, which will actually account for more than half of the $15-billion bit industry). *Boxes* refers to the applications of the Internet, be it electronic commerce, such as selling hard goods; entertainment, such as games or media; or information services, such as a personalized electronic version of *The Wall Street Journal*, to name a few.

These numbers quantify three aspects of the Internet: (1) It will be *big*; (2) It will become big fast; and (3) Companies need and are going at the Internet will all their might and speed to stay on—rather than be overwhelmed by—the Internet tidal wave. Notably, the bits industry is expected to grow tenfold over the next five years from $1.5 billion in 1995 to $15 billion in the year 2000—that's fast. Nonetheless, the use of the Internet is expected to blossom even faster, as it is going from a cold start (it is estimated at $50 million in 1995) to $15 billion in only five years!

This growth profile has fostered a mind-warping mentality and behavior for Internet companies; tossing aside just about every experience-honed tenet of business to build businesses in a methodical fashion, Internet businesses have adopted a grow-at-any-cost, without-any-revenue, claim-as-much-market-real-estate-before-anyone-moves-in approach to business. This mentality has come to be known as "Get Big Fast." Behind it lie two key strategic points: The first is that Internet opportunities—whether in software or in banking—are new and unclaimed, and hence available for the taking. Secondly, these opportunities will ultimately deliver big rewards to whoever gets claim to them. Hence, Internet company after Internet company is wisely going for it, spending lots of bucks far, far in advance of revenues to both develop offerings and claim market real estate in order to claim stakes in the Internet gold rush that will—hopefully—reward them with unprecedented returns. This is the hyper-growth, hyper-speed, hyper-bucks business world of the Internet.

The $15-billion bits industry spans at least five major sectors (see Exhibit I.5). These include Internet service providers, equipment vendors, software vendors, enabling services, and professional services.

Exhibit I.5 Internet Technology Industry—Representative Vendors

ISPs	Equipment	Software	Enabling Services	Professional Services
UUNET	Cisco	Netscape	I/PRO	Organic Online
NETCOM	Ascend	Open Market	Yahoo!	
PSInet	Cascade	Check Point	CyberCash	
BBN	Silicon Graphics	Marimba	InfoSeek	
Digex	Sun Microsystems	DimensionX	Lycos	
@Home	US Robotics	InterVista	Excite	

Notable in the software category are Netscape, Marimba, and Inter-Vista, and in the enabling services sector Yahoo! and I/PRO—all of these companies are featured in this book.

The Internet software sector is particularly noteworthy because not only will it prove to be the largest of the technology sectors, but also it will be distinguished with headline-grabbing news as Internet software turns the existing software industry upside down. In particular, the switch in computing from desktop computers of the recent past to the networked world of the Internet inverts, undermines, and indeed obviates 30 years of computer science. In other words, it pulls the rug out from under essentially every software company and product that originated prior to late 1994. Other disruptive and sensational transformations, consolidations, and implosions of traditional software companies are expected.

In particular, there are two essential points to know about Internet software. The first is that Internet software introduces a whole new set of technologies that are both powerful—more powerful than we have yet to harness—and that undermine existing software technology and products. The second is that most of the so-called Internet software market will be for *corporate* usage, which may or may not have anything to do with the literal Internet.

The first point portends that Internet software—also known as Web software—will reinvent (and repopulate) the $100-billion software industry. This explains why and how Netscape is the hottest company in all of software history, as well as why the dominant force of the previous generation software industry, namely Microsoft, is scrambling to get in front of the Internet software wave. Similarly, the industry-shattering aspects of the Internet arise from the profound technologies begotten for it and underlying it. Notably, key Internet-borne software technologies include the Web metaphor, Java, VRML, and Channels; this is pretty arcane stuff, but it is also the makings of entirely new capabilities, companies, concepts, and industries. In particular, it is the making of hot companies such as Netscape, Marimba, and InterVista, and hence their showcasing in this book.

The $15-billion application opportunity of the Internet is most noteworthy in both its shear breadth or diversity as well as innovation and creativity (see Exhibit I.6). Applications of the Internet span the range of stockbrokerage, mortgage exchange, and travel services; wine, book, flower, and food retailing; affinity-group chat forums; multiplayer games and gambling entertainment; and a plethora of news and information services. These are here today; much more is to come tomorrow.

Although beginning with a cold start, the $15-billion boxes industry of the applications of the Internet appears to be a no-brainer in view of the enormous and existing industry opportunities to be tapped by the Internet. For example, if all the Internet did was to capture 10 percent of the existing $100-billion publishing industry, it would have $10 billion of the $15 billion target . . . and that is only one of many industries.

Consistent with earlier themes, the applications of the Internet are particularly worthy of our attention not because they are online versions of things that already exist in our physical world, but rather because these applications are innovative, unique, and valuable. For

Exhibit I.6   Representative Applications of the Internet

Internet Service	Application
PointCast	TV news—Internet style
CNET	Technology information on TV and the Internet
Quote.com	Real-time stock quotes
BigBook	Any business, anywhere
Healtheon	Health information
Amazon.com	Books
Travelocity	Travel
CDNow	Music CDs
ESPNET SportsZone	Sports news
WebTV	Television over the Web

example, the PointCast Network is both unlike anything we have seen before, and well, entrancing—as evidenced by the fact that within six months of the start of the service PointCast has attracted more regular viewers than all but the top five magazines in the world! Equally innovative is a company called CNET, which pioneered the previously heretical notion of fusing television with the Internet, creating a whole that is greater than the sum of its parts. The accuracy of this concept is borne out by the many imitators of CNET's idea (see Chapter 8).

BETTERING OUR WORLD

The transformation, technology, and prosperity brought about by the Internet will be on a scale unmatched during our lifetime, yet the ultimate value of the Internet lies in its potential for it to better our society, culture, and indeed our world, both for us to benefit from in the immediate future, and for our children tomorrow.

The Internet obviates physical impediments of geography and cost, and empowers the masses with automation and information greater than even the most powerful company or government. Amongst the many ramifications of these subtle but key capabilities will be to make the 21st century the century of equality, creativity, and time. Specifically, the Internet promises to equalize many opportunities across our society, unleash creativity on a scale never before imaginable, and enable us to optimize our ultimate asset, namely, our time.

Following are a few examples to underscore these grand hopes:

•**Equalization.** The Internet promises to equalize the opportunity for everyone to become technology-literate, particularly within our schools.

Historically, computers in schools have mostly both been a failure, except in the rare instances where they were successful in favored affluent schools. Why? Because the stand-alone nature of computers (i.e., versus networked computers) necessitated very high and costly efforts to keep them current, and even when they were kept up, they still offered only a spartan collection of useful things to do, all done by isolated users—hardly the makings of an educational tool.

In contrast, the Internet fundamentally obviates these structural problems, thereby both equalizing the ability for anyone or any school of almost any economic means to have use of computer technology, but moreover to gain access to more power and information than has ever been available to anyone, including even the most affluent of schools. Specifically, rather than requiring the latest and most costly computer and software, essentially any computer of recent means can gain access via the Internet to, well, anything, ranging from national magazines to E-mailing to the President of the United States. That's equal opportunity.

• **Creativity.** Except for the limits of human imagination and resources, the Internet has removed essentially all barriers to being creative—a profound capability that will likely take decades for us to exploit, but when we do, it will be tremendous.

What a refreshing change. Unrelenting broadcast media over the past half-century has inculcated our society into being passive observers rather than making any effort to develop and capture our own sense and opinions about life. Furthermore, even if one could retain sufficient motivation to create, how and to whom would such creativity be distributed beyond the confines of our home and family? Meanwhile, the advent of convenient and relatively low-cost telephone communication has caused the art of writing—including its thoughtful process and resulting insights, as well as command of the language as a skillful tool—to be all but lost in our society.

The Internet changes this predicament. The Internet provides essentially anyone with electronic canvas—be it audio, graphical, textual, animated, or video content—and a means to make available creative work to the masses. Similarly, E-mail and chat forums promise to restore the lost arts of writing and debate—talents that both better us as a culture and become increasingly important in smoothing the increasing factionalization of our society at the same time that the world is getting smaller. Most importantly, the creativity-enabling capabilities of the Internet promise to empower our children to be more creative, expressive, and intelligent than ever before.

• **Time.** The Internet at once is potentially the greatest means of preserving significant amounts of time to spend at our discretion, as well as the greatest threat to consuming even more of our time. Indeed, time more than anything else will be the resource of the next century.

The Internet obviates space as a consideration in our world, leaving only time, and hence amplifying its significance. For example, by eliminating geographic constraints that inherently and conveniently introduced minimum amounts of elapsed time—that could be used, for example, to think—the Internet is making our world instantaneous. This is not necessarily all good. On the positive side, however, in both the automation and the ability to better understand our world and do so more efficiently and conveniently (i.e., select the best product that matches individual needs), the Internet promises to recoup significant amounts of time wasted on geographic "overhead" (i.e., driving to and from stores).

Forecasting the future is difficult. Accordingly, it is amusing to think how naive the grand projections previously discussed will sound five years hence—naive not in the fundamental idea but in the interpretation of the consequences.

Similarly, in the face of such unquantifiable opportunity and tumultuous change one can't help but hope and wonder about what will become of today's star companies creating the Internet. Some will literally become the General Motors, General Electric, AT&T, Microsoft, and Intel—the major corporate icons—of the next century, and many are destined to be the De Lorean, People Express, and Kaypro—erstwhile hot innovative stories forgotten by time. To date, over 500 companies are estimated to have been capitalized with at least $1 million each to attach the Internet opportunity; history suggests that fewer than 100 will even exist five years from now, and that thousands more are yet to be formed.

The subsequent chapters of this book are written so that they can be read in a stand-alone manner, but can best be read in sequence. Each considers the career of an important Internet "entrepreneur" (literally in seven cases, more figuratively in the case of Mark Pesce, Chapter 4), the company he or she has founded, that company's technology, and its markets. These people were selected for profile because they have all played central roles in the Web's business evolution, and also because they are a diverse enough group that learning all of their stories will give the reader a broad understanding of the Web's history and business relevance. The profiled people and companies (in order of their appearance) are:

•**Marc Andreessen/Netscape.** While still an undergraduate, Marc wrote the "Mosaic" software discussed above that made the Web popularly relevant and touched off the revolution discussed in these pages. Netscape, the company he cofounded, is certainly the highest-profile, largest, and (for now) most successful company to build its business on the Internet and the intranet. Netscape's history is arguably that of the Web itself, and Chapter 1 is that history told in greater detail than it has been told elsewhere. The chapter also reviews some of the concepts discussed in this Introduction for the benefit of those who habitually skip over any page with a Roman numeral on it.

•**Rob Glaser/Progressive Networks.** Rob was a Microsoft vice president with 10 years of successes behind him when he established the company that taught the Web to talk and sing. Progressive Networks' RealAudio software enables the distribution of live and prerecorded audio over the Internet, and has over 10 million users as of this writing. It has already helped hundreds of radio stations broadcast their signals worldwide using the Internet as their transmission tower, and could soon enable thousands of artists to reach their audiences without the intercession of traditional radio stations, or even music stores. Chapter 2 considers the rise of RealAudio and its long-term significance for radio, broadcast, and audio content in general.

•**Kim Polese/Marimba (Java).** Sun Microsystems' Java language is one of the technology industry's great marketing success stories. And throughout its early history, Java's "marketing department" was Kim. After the language's success was assured, Kim and three of the Java team's lead engineers founded Marimba, in part to help further the language's development. Java has a long and fascinating past, and an even longer and more fascinating *future*, in that it is completely altering the economics and competitive dynamics of the technology industry. Chapter 3 considers both past and future, as well as Kim's and Marimba's contributions to them.

•**Mark Pesce/VRML.** Mark is not an entrepreneur in the strictest sense of the word. But as Chapter 4 indicates, he has helped build the community of companies and individuals furthering the development of the VRML language "with all of the zeal and focus of a founder-CEO." VRML enables the distribution of 3-D scenes over the Internet. It could one day foster the rise of vast, shared virtual reality "worlds" of the sort that so fired the popular press's imagination at the start of the decade. VRML's impact is only just being felt on the Web today. In this, the story of its relevance is more one of the future than of the past. But the story of VRML's future is intriguing—and perhaps terrifying.

•**Ariel Poler/I/PRO.** Ariel was still a business school student when he started investing the money he had saved up as a teenaged DJ in Caracas, Venezuela, in I/PRO. Two years later, I/PRO had over a hundred employees and had become the most widely-used auditor of Web "audiences"—much as Nielsen Media Research is the most widely-used auditor of television audiences. The Web has unbelievable promise as a marketing and advertising medium—in part because of its extraordinary auditability. This power—and Ariel's and I/PRO's story—are considered in Chapter 5.

•**Jerry Yang/Yahoo!** It has been a long time, perhaps since Apple Computer's establishment, since a couple of guys have burst out of a Silicon Valley garage (or, in this case, a trailer) to become celebrity entrepreneurs. Jerry Yang and his partner David Filo did just that when they created their company. Yahoo! is an Internet directory. As such, it is like the Web's yellow and white pages, or its table of contents. Millions of people (literally) now interact with Yahoo! directly every day. Within a few years, tens of millions probably will. Chapter 6 tells Yahoo!'s exciting story, and also explains why Yahoo! could soon become "the most powerful media property in the world."

•**Andrew Anker/HotWired.** No industry other than the technology industry itself has embraced the Web as thoroughly as the publishing industry. Perhaps that industry's most important Internet pioneer, and certainly the one that created the economic model now followed by most of the Web's commercial publishers, is HotWired—a creation of the people at *Wired* magazine. Andrew has been running HotWired since its launch in 1994. Its history, his involvement in it, and the relevance of the Web to publishing in general are explored in Chapter 7.

•**Halsey Minor/CNET.** CNET is publisher of technology news, reviews, and analysis, and sits at the intersection of the coolest and sexiest new medium—the World Wide Web—and the most popular and ubiquitous old medium—television. It is now competing with some of the most powerful and deep-pocketed periodicals publishers in the world for both advertising dollars and audience. Halsey, CNET's founder-CEO, has created a business that is leveraging both on-air and online content to maneuver against his gigantic in-print competitors. CNET's vast and growing audience, and its successful IPO in the summer of 1996, indicate that he is on the right track. Chapter 8 discusses all of this, as well as the relevance of the Web to broadband media (like video) in general.

It will be interesting to read this book in the year 2001 to look back at these companies and see what became of them and their industries and technologies, particularly relative to what we thought of them today. Certainly, the answers will be interesting!

ARCHITECTS
of the WEB

CHAPTER 1

MARC ANDREESSEN
Netscape
Portal to the Web

The tidy, tidy town of Mountain View, California, is bordered by the still tidier town of Sunnyvale in the south and by tony Palo Alto in the north. It has no Mountain, really, nor even much of a View of one, although clear days offer glimpses of some foothills to the west. Much of Mountain View is orderly to the point of Swissness. Lawns are clipped, roads are straight, and intersections are wide with left-turn, U-turn, and straight-only lanes that red, red lights cautiously activate only singly, or in pairs. The tonier residential areas are ones of pet-free apartment complexes with Shangri-la names like The Waters, The Shadows, and Village Lake. The downtown strip is one of understated mom-and-pop shops and mostly Asian restaurants. There isn't a national franchise among them, other than a teensy Domino's Pizza outpost on the eastern fringe. And things get awfully quiet after dark. There's a microbrewery, some coffee houses, maybe a pool hall or two, and that's about it. The real centers of Mountain View's nightlife are the highways leading *outtahere*, particularly to San Francisco, 40 miles to the north.

But shrink-wrapped, tidy, and (let's face it) kind of forgettable as much of the town may be on its surface, its still waters do run deep. Because beneath and above it, in its fiber, cable, and copper, a hidden matrix howls with all of the chaos that the choreographed street traffic lacks. This over-and-underpinning is Mountain View's corner of the

Internet, the busy data blanket that now swaddles the earth. Like the planet it overlays, the Net has its rutted lanes and its interstates, its backwaters, hot spots, and mega–magnet attractions. And of these, its Grand Central Terminal, its O'Hare Field, its Times, Red, and Tiananmen Squares is now found at 501 East Middlefield Road in tidy, tidy Mountain View.

This is the home of Netscape Communications Corporation, whose busy data furnaces scream around the clock. These were first hooked to the ether back in the ancient days of 1994. They immediately drew a curious trickle of traffic, which quickly grew into a daily Niagaran deluge—well over 100 million unique requests for information per day by 1996. These requests came from engineers, from businessfolk, from academics, government workers, and others in every nation with an Internet hookup. Each was answered with a packet of text, an image, or some other kind of media file; bits and parts of pages that assembled on their requesters' computer screens. And as its traffic grew from trickle to deluge, Netscape itself grew into arguably the hottest startup in history. In August of 1995, scarcely 16 swift months after its formation, it debuted on the capital markets, attaining a market value of over $2 billion during its first day of trading. Some months after that, it added its thousandth employee. And not long after that, it could claim that its flagship product, the Netscape Navigator, had become *the world's most popular PC application.*

Netscape owes its astonishing rise to its pioneering, dominant, and briefly hegemonic position among the companies making their living on and around the Internet's World Wide Web. Within weeks of its release in October of 1994, its Navigator became the preferred portal for peering into the Web's ether, the preferred joystick for steering its traffic. Other Netscape products soon became popular tools for serving Web data, for authoring Web content, and for building Web storefronts. Abetted in part by Netscape's technical and marketing acumen, the Web's user base quickly quadrupled and requadrupled, in scarily tight, months-long cycles. And as this happened, Netscape itself quickly quadrupled and requadrupled in head count, revenues, and value.

But important as the company has been in the Web's history, the Web itself is no Netscape product. Nor is it a Mountain View, nor Californian, nor even United States of American invention. The Web rather emerged from a Swiss physics institute, where a

British researcher one day reckoned that he could come up with a better way of organizing documents and other professional information than the usual haphazard methods. By 1991 that researcher, Tim Berners-Lee, had specified the Web's underlying protocols and had built its basic tools. Late the following year, a University of Illinois undergraduate named Marc Andreessen reckoned that he could come up with a better way of displaying the information that the Web had so brilliantly organized. And within a few months, he and a friend had added a critical piece to Berners-Lee's foundations—one that gave the Web visual allure it had lacked, while also making it far more understandable to the nontechnical masses. This facelift helped draw millions to the new medium in little more than a year. It also set the stage for the dramatic emergence of the company that Marc cofounded after his migration to the tidy town.

Marc first encountered the unfacelifted Web at the National Center for Supercomputing Applications (NCSA), a gleaming modern institute quartered on his university campus. Marc came to NCSA through its usual channels. He grew up in the University's hinterland (well, almost: in a small town in nearby Wisconsin). He honed his technical chops long before college (starting at age nine when he learned the BASIC computer language from a library book). His background was modest enough—his father was a seed salesman, his mother a Lands' End shipping clerk—that part-time work made a great deal of sense during college. And given his technical interests, hanging out in a building stuffed with supercomputers for $6.85 an hour seemed like a reasonable job.

And so Marc became one of the NCSA guys, one of the 10 or so core people you'd bump into at the soda machine at two in the morning if you happened to be on hand polishing up some code, or tending to some supercomputer's fires, or just pulling down another helpful $6.85. He blended in fairly seamlessly with the rest of the crew. Sure, he was a bit bigger than most—6'4", and with enough heft and brawn that you wanted him on your side when the Chair Football began (although that wasn't until later). He also had these odd fixations on classical music, certain literature, geopolitics; that kind of stuff. But like almost everybody, he was from the hinterland. He liked computers, he needed the money, and that was pretty much that. Certainly nobody expected him to become the first underage hacker to become rockstar famous since Apple's Steve Jobs. And surely no one was calling him *The New Bill Gates* (as he was later dramatically labeled). And absolutely nobody, least of all Marc himself, imagined that he would become *Time* magazine's first barefoot coverguy since Mahatma Gandhi (but after that, almost anything seemed possible).

By and large, Marc found NCSA to be a snooze. He worked in its software visualization group for a while, writing code that helped its big, sweating machines model and render objects in three-dimensional space. His own workstation was ironically made by Silicon Graphics, the company founded by (and at the time still employing) his future business partner, Jim Clark. The Silicon Graphics machine was awesome. But supercomputing itself "basically was dying then, and should be dead now," Marc says. Sure, supercomputers were better, faster, and stronger than anything else in their narrow fields of excellence. But their excellence came at a dizzying price. Fast microprocessors from Silicon Graphics, Digital Equipment Corporation (DEC), and others were meanwhile starting to make workstations like his far more useful to many researchers than shared time on NCSA's pricey behemoths.

During his NCSA yawning and thumb-twiddling, Marc became very familiar with the Internet, the vast network of networks that linked the University of Illinois and NCSA to thousands of other organizations throughout the world. Designed as a hedge against nuclear annihilation (see Introduction), this network had become a wide-reaching and useful tool whose popular relevance was limited only by its tremendous embedded arcaneness. The Internet derived much of both its usefulness and its arcaneness from the diversity of *protocols* that ran across it. Simply stated, a protocol is a set of commands that enables computers to implement specific operations across a network. On the Internet, protocols create unique functional spaces with their own rules and uses. For instance, the Simple Mail Transfer Protocol (SMTP) enables E-mail, or the posting and delivery of electronic messages between computers. FTP, or File Transfer Protocol, lets users download programs and other files from distant machines. IRC, or Internet Relay Chat, lets users swap messages with one another in real time. And NNTP, or Network News Transfer Protocol, enables users to access and post messages to electronic bulletin boards whose themes range from the technical to the trivial.

By the time Marc arrived at NCSA, these and dozens of other protocols had helped make the Internet a rich and lively environment. But they had not made it very accessible to noninitiates—or *user-friendly,* in the cozy post-Macintosh parlance of the computer industry. Indeed, if anything, the Internet was a little *user-hostile*. Most of its protocols required unique pieces of software to retrieve information, and other pieces to send it. Users had to know where to find that software—it was invariably tucked away somewhere out on the Internet—and then "FTP it" to their own machines (yes, FTP is a verb as well as a protocol), configure it, and run it.

In addition, much of the Internet's software worked only on systems running Unix. Unix is an operating system—like Windows, DOS, or the Macintosh operating system—favored by manufacturers of high-powered workstations like Marc's Silicon Graphics machine. Unix machines tended to be terrifically powerful tools, far more powerful than the PCs and Macintoshes of the mass market. But they also tended to be terrifically expensive and difficult to operate. These twin barriers of cost and complexity had kept almost all Unix machines in the hands of academics or professional engineers. And since these were precisely the communities in which Internet connections were most common, they inevitably came to form most of the Internet's user base.

From all of this, a paradox gradually arose. Academic, international, and apparently free (Internet connections came with the professional or academic territory for most users back then), the Internet developed into an almost militantly egalitarian and cooperative community. Nobody owned the network. Virtually nobody made money from it directly. And almost every piece of software that governed or accessed it was free (the people who wrote it generally did so from the goodness of their hearts, or to make names for themselves, or as parts of funded projects). But its egalitarianism aside, the Internet's tight de facto admission requirements of technical acumen, access, and pricey tools also made it a very elite realm. Marc even suspected that the Internet community deliberately kept its complexity barriers high as a way of keeping the unwashed masses *out*.

But then Tim Berners-Lee cooked up the World Wide Web, and it soon became a tiny outpost of elegance in the Internet's sea of arcana. Like E-mail and FTP, the Web was a functional space with its own rules of engagement. It required a special piece of software, called a Web browser, to retrieve information, and another piece, a Web server, to send, or publish it. It made it possible for users to navigate between files on distant computers not by rattling incantations into their keyboards, but by simply typing in numbered references, like footnotes.

"Footnoted" words were typically linked to other documents elsewhere on the Web. An article about Unix workstations that included a numbered reference to Silicon Graphics, for instance, might be tied to another document that discussed Silicon Graphics in more detail. A user could summon that document simply by typing in its reference number. The computer hosting the referenced document would then send it over the Internet. Documents that referenced one another could well be hosted on computers that were continents apart. But the distances between hosts were invisible and irrelevant to users, who navigated the entire Web as if it were a single global patchwork document (as indeed it was).

The Web's metaphor for organizing information is known as *hypertext*, and had been used for years in software help files, CD-ROMs, computerized kiosks, and other unnetworked settings. But bodies of unnetworked hypertext were inherently hobbled in that they could only leverage and reference the content with which they were bundled. They could not grow richer from the contributions of outside authors, nor could they be plugged into the context of other bodies of knowledge. In this, they were like office buildings outfitted with intercoms, when what they really needed were telephones to connect to the bigger and more important outside world. For this reason, visionaries like Ted Nelson (see Chapter 4) had long proposed the development of networked hypertext systems. But these people were often out "to solve these really deep research problems," Marc explains. For instance, Nelson intended for his system, which he called Xanadu, to know and track where each of its many documents' many hyper-links pointed. This would allow it to keep them all updated as documents were moved and removed. But as systems scale, or grow, the challenge of tracking their every node and change can grow more complex at exponential rates. For this and many other reasons, Xanadu forever remained only a nice idea.

But then the Web appeared, and it "sort of had the philosophy that if something doesn't work, oh well," Marc explains. This allowed it to scale, and deliver on much of the maximum promise of networked hypertext with the occasional *oh well*. But the Web's *oh well* robustness alone did not make it ready for the MTV mainstream. The earlymost Web was bland for one thing. Based wholly upon text, it had no imagery, sound, or color. It also lacked a windows-based graphical interface of the sort that was becoming de rigueur in desktop computing. And much of its earliest software ran only on NeXT computers, whose virtually nonexistent installed base was almost wholly confined to academia.

In late 1992, Marc, technically capable, Internet-savvy, and *bored off his ass*, decided it would be fun to take a crack at giving the Web the graphical, media-rich face that it lacked. This notion was starting to surface in Web circles around that time (and by some accounts the idea of building an NCSA Web browser of some sort had already emerged at the Center). For this reason it was perhaps inevitable that somebody would soon take a stab at making the Web visual. But in the end it was Marc who seized the initiative and drove the months-long and exhausting project that actually achieved this. A necessary first step was recruiting Eric Bina to the task. Bina had a few years on Marc—he was a full-fledged NCSA employee—and was known as a quiet, careful programmer. He knew plenty about the Internet, and was a pretty good friend of Marc's by then. But despite all this he wasn't an easy sell ("He was like, 'No, no, I'm doing other stuff that I'm happy with,' " recalls an early NCSA associate). So Marc campaigned hard. He even built a prototype to showcase what his proposed software would do. Bina had never before seen Marc so excited about something. But he initially "assumed it was just a reaction to previous boredom," he recalls (there was a lot of that going around). Faced with this skepticism, Marc stepped up the pressure, and eventually Bina caved in.

The subsequent months were a blur. The two of them would "work three to four days straight, then crash for about a day," Bina recalls. "Haunts were the local twenty-four-hour convenience store for Marc's cookies and milk, my Skittles and Mountain Dew." Early in the project, the two of them cohered terrifically as a team. In the words of one NCSA colleague, Bina became "the heart and soul of the code," while "Marc was really the one coming up with the ideas." This balance served their project well. It needed an incredible programmer to code and debug it into existence in the lightning time frame they took on. But it also urgently needed a *just do it* pragmatist driving its agenda. This latter role was, and still is, Marc's. Because while Marc is a capable engineer, it is his "surprisingly wide field of interest" that really sets him apart among engineers Bina notes, as programmers "tend to be rather narrowly focused in general." For this reason, Marc's most important and unique contributions at both NCSA and Netscape have not arisen solely from his engineering knowledge, but from its intersection with the broad matrix of nonengineering matters and media that he has always plugged into. As such, they have not been lines of code (he has indeed not written any shipping code at Netscape) but have rather been insights, strategies, and designs. The first of these contributions came as he catalogued, drove, and shaped the project that resulted in Mosaic, as he and Eric eventually named their software. But they were not the last.

By February of 1993, Mosaic was nearing completion. It was a Web browser, a far more polished, stable, and graphically capable one than any of its forerunners. Like the other early Web browsers, it was able to read and display pages written in the Hyper-Text Markup Language (HTML), the Web's own lingua franca. HTML documents include both text and some simple commands that describe their layout. Browsers are designed to interpret the commands and display the text as indicated by them. For instance, if a browser were to receive the following HTML code from a Web server:

```
<CENTER> Welcome to Netscape </CENTER>
```

it would know to display

```
                  Welcome to Netscape
```

because <CENTER> is a command (or "tag") that indicates that the text between it and the </CENTER> endpoint should be centered. Mosaic supported all of the standard HTML tags of its day (which did not, incidentally, include the center tag, as this was created later by Netscape). But it went beyond other browsers in the richness of its presentation. It supported a more visual form of hypertext than certain other browsers for one thing, in that words that linked to other documents were not numbered like footnotes, but were rather highlighted. This let users navigate from document to document by simply positioning their cursors over highlighted words and clicking on them, rather than typing in reference numbers (words that linked to other documents were commonly referred to as hyper-links, or hot-links). More importantly, it was also designed to interpret a new, special, extra tag—the <IMG>, or *image* tag. This let Web page designers populate their work with images for the first time. Mosaic's richer presentation was also wrapped up in a graphically intuitive interface that included niceties like buttons that let users "back up" and view Web pages they had previously seen, and controls that let users scroll pages up and down easily. All of this made the Web far more engaging and accessible than it had been before.

As Mosaic took form, a rare buzz of excitement began to build amongst the NCSA crew. All of its core members were fluent in the Internet, and most were even familiar with the tiny Web by then, so nobody needed much explaining about what Mosaic might mean. *It could be the next Gopher!*, people thought (Gopher, one of the Internet's few other intuitive quadrants, organized information into hierarchically nested "folders," much as computer file systems do). And although nobody foresaw what was actually coming, the possibility of beating Gopher, or just enabling something cool and new on the Internet, was plenty exciting in itself. Because basically it was high time that something happened at NCSA. And now that something was happening, people wanted *in*.

As it turned out, there was plenty of work for them to do. Marc and Eric were writing Mosaic on their Unix machines. This meant that if it wasn't to become yet another exclusive toy for the technical elite, somebody had to port, or translate it into code that the more democratic Macintosh and PC platforms could run. Jon Mittelhauser, an upbeat, easygoing graduate student, ended up working on the PC port. Joining him on this project was Chris Wilson, one of his best friends since childhood. A Yugoslav with an opaque accent known as Aleks "Mac Daddy" Totic took on (surprise) the Macintosh port. In this he was later helped by a younger student named Mike McCool, whose last name absolved him of having a nickname. Mike's identical twin brother Rob, likewise absolved, wrote the Web serving (or publishing) software that the team eventually released along with Mosaic (before that release the only available Web serving software had come from CERN or *Conseil Européen pour la Recherche Nucléaire*, where Tim Berners-Lee did his work).

Marc and Eric first posted the Unix version of Mosaic on NCSA's servers in the winter of 1993 "and it spread like a virus after that," Marc recalls. Within a few weeks, tens of thousands of people had downloaded copies of it, and within a few months, it was estimated that hundreds of thousands had (the team lacked a precise system for tracking downloads, so nobody was ever exactly sure about the numbers). As Web servers proliferated along with the client software, almost any computer with a full-time Internet connection and CERN's or NCSA's free server software could double as a Web server. So for those already on the network, becoming a Web publisher involved no real economic hurdles. Despite this, there was only a tiny handful of Web servers in the world when Mosaic first released. But soon, there were thousands.

Mosaic attained its early popularity because it turned the Web into a publishing medium that was both expressive and uniquely democratic. "It was the sort of thing where people realized all of a sudden, here's the most convenient possible way to share information, publish information," Marc recalls. "In some cases very useful information they had to show other people anyway, and in some cases it was just for the pure hell of it, which is something that still continues." The newly visual Web did not of course offer all the graphical richness of traditional print publishing. But it did offer immediacy (no delays for printings, mailings, and waitings) and unmatched affordability (the marginal cost of distributing any document of any size to anyone in the world was effectively zero).

And perhaps most powerfully, it offered tremendous efficiency in that its content was distributed by information consumers *pulling*, or summoning it, rather than by publishers pushing it out. In this, the Web differs from traditional publishing channels, which generally distribute information by pushing it to its audience. The push model has its advantages and is indeed becoming popular on the Web (see Chapters 3 and 8). But efficiency is not traditionally among its advantages. This is because all pushed information inevitably reaches many people who just aren't interested in it. Consider the Sunday newspaper. As a pushed document, it delivers the same sections and articles to all of its readers. So although a page 11 article in the Automotive section may be read by only one out of every 300 people who receive it, it will still be pushed to the other 299, incurring newsprint, distribution, and disposal costs on behalf of all of them.

The many misses of pushed communication mean that every spot-on *hit* is expensive to reach, and this expense prices a tremendous amount of would-be content out of the distribution channel. A narrowly focused technical tract, a detailed paean to an obscure musician, and an English-language guide to the nightlife of a provincial Italian town might each be enormously relevant to a tiny audience. But when audiences are small, dispersed, and anonymous (i.e., when publishers do not know precisely who will want to receive their content, and therefore have to make it generally available) they can rarely be reached economically. In such cases, content is all too often denied an audience, and information consumers are denied access to content. Even information that clears the costs of the pushed channel cannot possibly reach its full natural audience, because no pushed information can be ubiquitous. For instance, train schedules that are handed out by the thousands are often not in pockets or desk drawers when they are needed. Hometown papers that are easy to find at home are often inaccessible to residents who are traveling. And back issues of magazines that reach millions when they are published can be impossible to find when researchers or reminiscers want to see them decades later.

The inefficiency of pushed channel *misses*, priced-out content, and available-but-not-ubiquitous pushed information can be reduced by placing content on a shelf from which anybody can *pull* it. That shelf needs to be big, so that every provincial train schedule and obscure lab report can find room next to the *Time* magazine cover stories and the Pamela Anderson photo galleries. It also needs to be widely accessible (if not necessarily omnipresent) so that content can reach as many of its constituents as possible. The Web is precisely that shelf. It is a shelf that extends to any computer with a modem and a Web browser. And it is one that content can board easily, because its shelf space is infinite, and therefore (unlike the shelf space in an urban boutique) practically free. Once content arrives on the shelf, its audience's interest in it becomes its distributor, and the frictionless ether its channel.

For all of these reasons, the newly visual Web quickly became an ideal distribution vehicle for all kinds of information in the professional and academic circles in which it was known. And as Marc notes, many people also started publishing things "just for the pure hell of it." Personal "home pages" (as the entry points to Web sites, or discrete collections of Web pages, are known) proliferated as thousands posted scrapbook photos, ruminations, and collections of links to their favorite Web sites. Countless sites meanwhile arose around cultural, technological, athletic, and other themes. Like almost everything connected to the Internet—its software, its news groups, its E-mail lists—these were built and maintained mainly as labors of love by their architects. Many were also amateurish, even narcissistic creations. But the Internet was always about the exchange of ideas—of all ideas without constraints imposed by popularity or production value thresholds. And since the shelf was infinite, there was no harm in piling it high with the outpourings of anybody who felt like they had something to outpour. If only two or three people found enough value in a particular site to pluck its pages from the shelf, they at least would be enriched for it, its author would get an audience, and some idea or creation that would not otherwise have had one would gain a voice.

As the spring and summer of 1993 progressed, it seemed that almost everybody who experimented with Mosaic was delighted with it. Almost. But some people were concerned about what the Web's new look would do to the network that suddenly had to play Sherpa to its profusion of wedding snapshots, *Star Trek* photo albums, and unclad models. The trouble was that digital media dramatically ups the ante in the old adage about pictures being worth a thousand words. Images can in fact take up more digital space than many thousands of paragraphs; and so some people worried about what would happen as the *what the hell* clickings of the Web's growing audience threw the frivolous girth of countless idle snapshots into the Sherpa'd slipstream of the crowded Internet. It seemed that this could easily make the system buckle or gag, could make it *run out of Internet*. If this happened, the responsibly formatted treatises and lab reports would be snuffed along with all the new trivial clutter.

Tim Berners-Lee himself was among the concerned ("Tim bawled me out in the summer of '93 for adding images to the thing," Marc recalls). The frivolity that the visual Web invited worried him because "this was supposed to be a *serious* medium; this is serious information," Marc remembers. "Absolutely, dead serious. This was all very serious stuff." And now suddenly there were Klingon portraits tripping through the wires. NCSA earlytimer Jon Mittelhauser characterizes the differences between Berners-Lee's group at CERN and the NCSA crew as a matter of orientation. "The one thing that probably separates all of us who were on the original team is that we're all very pragmatic," he points out. "Academics in computer science are so often off to solve these obscure research problems. The universities may force it upon them, but they aren't always motivated to just do something that people want to use. And that's definitely the sense that we always had of CERN. And I don't want to mischaracterize them, but whenever we dealt with them, they were much more interested in the Web from a research point of view, rather than a practical point of view. And so it was no big deal to them to do a NeXT browser, even though nobody would ever use it." To someone with this perspective, "the concept of adding in an image just for the sake of adding an image didn't make sense, whereas to us, it made sense because face it, they made pages *look cool*."

Once it was out of the bottle, there was no recorking the NCSA team's hell-bent pragmatic energy. And so by the time X Mosaic (named for the "X" windows operating environment common on Unix systems) debuted in the winter of 1993, the Macintosh and PC versions of Mosaic were already deep in development. The teams assigned to them ended up working every bit as hard as Marc and Eric. They were driven by an unreasoning urge to *catch up with X* and, since this was impossible, an almost maniacal urge to beat one another to the finish line. "We're all pretty independent, and pretty cocky programmers, and think we can do whatever we want," Mittelhauser explains. So once the Windows and Mac ports started in tandem, "it was like, which of us could get something transferring across the network first? And which of us could do this thing that X Mosaic did?" And once the head-to-head competition started feeling bland, the teams started adding "trivial little things" to their software, Mittelhauser recalls—little featurelets that the X version lacked: a cursor that changed shape when it was positioned over hot-links, making it clearer where hot-links were located, for instance. Subtle and small features that made Mosaic more functional, and just as importantly, kept the X guys in their place.

The PC and Macintosh versions of Mosaic were first posted to the Internet late in the spring of 1993. And with their debut, the stage was finally set for everything that followed. Tim Berners-Lee had given the Internet an interface that the masses could manipulate. Mosaic had given it a look that could draw and hold their attention. Now the ports put it all on the consumer-class computers that they had in their homes and offices. In this, the Internet itself was primed to become popularly alluring and accessible for the first time.

It didn't take long for Mosaic to gather some early momentum (see Introduction). And once it did, it was almost unstoppable. Because as more and more people started using the Web, the information that was posted there was able to reach bigger and bigger audiences. This of course attracted more information providers, who piled the Web's shelf higher and higher with more information and content, which in turn attracted even more people, which in turn attracted even more information. A similar self-feeding cycle is behind almost all network growth, as networks get their value largely from the people and organizations that they connect. More people make for more attractive networks, which draw still more people, which make for still more attractive networks. This dynamic made telephones increasingly attractive as the phone network expanded and more people could actually be reached with telephones. It made fax machines more interesting as the number of businesses that could receive and reciprocate faxes increased.

The Web's growth was therefore driven by the same forces that fueled the growth of many other communications channels. But the Web was able grow with unprecedented speed. Because unlike the telephone network, whose architects had to lay lines, hire operators, manufacture telephones, and invent all manner of complex switchery, the Web rode upon an infrastructure that was largely in place before it took root. By the time Mosaic was released, desktop computers had been commonplace in offices and homes for years. Modem penetration was also surging, as communications hardware had become standard in most new PC configurations. Internet connections were already installed in thousands of companies and institutions. And computers in offices everywhere were by then networked in LANs (local area networks). The LAN boom of the 1980s and early '90s had generally been driven by very local economics; the need to share printers, files in small work groups, and other such resources. This had made LANs very inward-looking. But then "all of a sudden in '93 and '94 people just started realizing that these networks could do very interesting things," Marc explains. Specifically, they could look outward, bringing the content and resources of the broader world into the enterprise. Or they could look sideways at the rest of the company, and spread all of its information broadly, rather than just in small local compartments.

Given how ripe the infrastructure for connectivity had grown, it is in a sense odd that the pieces took so long to connect. But proprietary barricades of all kinds had been keeping the world's growing networks isolated, sequestering outward-looking and inward-looking networks alike. For instance, by the time Mosaic debuted, commercial online services like CompuServe, Prodigy, and America Online were flourishing, their combined subscriber bases having grown over 50 percent in the previous two years to over 3.5 million. This growth indicated an increasing interest in connecting and communicating among computer owners. But while the commercial services helped satisfy that urge, none ever attained the kind of content and user growth momentum that the Web generated. A big reason for this was that each commercial service's subscribers and content were sequestered from the others'. Subscriber growth at CompuServe therefore did nothing to help Prodigy's content reach more of its natural audience, and growth in America Online's content did nothing to enrich the CompuServe or Prodigy experiences. Segregated and barricaded, the aggregate online population could never achieve the full benefits of mutual affiliation that open networks offer. Also, the commercial services' content channels were never open like the Web's. Content didn't flow in continually from countless unaudited sources, but was rather created, or at least approved, centrally. This meant that while the content on the commercial services' shelves may have been better designed and produced on average than the Web's, it was nowhere near as diverse, deep, rich, or (ultimately) interesting.

As for the LANs, they had not initially been designed to be robust collaborative systems. A number of "groupware" packages therefore eventually emerged that enabled people to interact and communicate over them. Some, like Microsoft's Windows for Workgroups and Novell's Groupwise, were little more than word processors and spreadsheets integrated with rudimentary document sharing and E-mail capabilities. Others, like Collabra Share and especially Lotus Notes (which pioneered and defined the groupware category), were more fully-featured. But these packages were not designed with one another in mind. They didn't interoperate; indeed, they could barely pass E-mail messages back and forth unless some arduous infrastructural work was done to enable this. This meant that they often became quite entrenched with the customers who adopted them, blossoming into annuities for their makers. As their installed bases grew, it therefore became all too tempting for their makers to maintain them as closed systems.

The early groupware products were therefore the architectural opposites of the cooperative, interoperable, egalitarian Internet. But in this, it was the Internet that was the oddball, that was marching to a different drummer, because the groupware packages were following a well-established pattern in the software industry: one of proprietary competition. In locking customers into a solution and keeping competitors out, this model could be very profitable. And in allowing for the possibility of winning and taking all (customers tend to flock to proprietary standards that become truly dominant, because they don't want to get stuck using a standard that the rest of the world shuns), it even offered a shot at de facto monopolyhood. For this reason, the proprietary competition game that the network suites played was both a popular and well-established one. Early word processors that couldn't read one another's files were among the many others who had played it. So, certainly, were the major operating systems.

To one accustomed to the proprietary game, the Internet looked rather like the void of space. There was no money out there. There were no corporate *players*. There were just the weird quarks and leptons of its profitless open protocols. And so the early groupware companies didn't think much about the weird, open Internet as they built their profitable proprietary bastions. Their bastion walls and airlocks were primarily meant to defend against encroachment from one another, not the Internet's profitless void. The commercial online services' barricades likewise defended each from its rivals. And the operating systems' barricades—towering things, fortified with *sunken investments* and *switching costs*—likewise sequestered operating systems from rival operating systems, as each player sought to expand and harvest from its installed base.

But there is always information worth grabbing out in the big broad world, or in the parts of the company that aren't connected to this or that little LAN. For this reason, the economic logic of connection eventually started asserting itself. As it did, the pressure on the airlocks of the enterprise networks started to build. Networks started peering outward, and sideways. This meant they had to peer into other networks. As this happened, it was the harmless Web, which in many cases needed only some free software and a small administrative flourish to slip through the proprietary barricades, that proved to be the ideal peer-enabling medium. Mosaic (and later its many descendants) then proved to be the ideal portal to peer through. And suddenly the weird quarks and leptons of the Internet's profitless void were hissing through the airlocks of the enterprise network. And they didn't stop there.

Early signs of Mosaic's march started showing up in the monthly traffic tallies of the North American high-speed Internet backbone almost immediately. This backbone by no means transported all of the Internet's traffic. But it did transport a greater proportion of it than any other link, and as such presumably offered the most representative view of its aggregate composition (until the federal government decided that the Internet was commercial enough to stand on its own, and shut down the publicly-funded backbone in April of 1995). In January of 1993, just before Mosaic was first released, the Web accounted for all of one five-hundredth of 1 percent of the backbone's packet traffic, making it the 127th-largest source of traffic among the Internet's many protocols. By June, some months after Mosaic's first Unix release, it had risen to 21st place, now with a quarter of 1 percent of all traffic. By September, it had reached 16th place. Gopher was still ahead at that point, running in 10th place, and FTP reigned supreme. But neither of their leads would last for long.

The summer of 1993 brought the first Web developers' conference in Cambridge, Massachusetts, and with it, the first opportunity for many of the Web's early architects to meet face to face. Tim Berners-Lee and several of his colleagues from Europe attended. So did Lou Montulli, a University of Kansas undergraduate who had written a popular text-only Web browser called Lynx. Montulli's first impression of the NCSA team was that they were "your typical computer science kind of people," although Marc really stood out in the crowd. "You could definitely see that everyone was kind of just falling around him, and when he would talk, people would listen," Montulli remembers. Perhaps picking up on this, Marc conspicuously filled out a conference badge not with his full name and home institute like the other attendees, but with only his first name—just *Marc*—as if no further introductions were necessary.

By then, everybody on the Mosaic team was getting a big kick out of their software's early popularity and the growing notoriety that it was bringing them. But success had its drawbacks. The biggest of these was the heightening attention of NCSA's administrators. Before Mosaic became popular, none of them seemed to "have any clue who we were, and we liked it that way," Jon Mittelhauser recalls, but "as soon as Mosaic took off, we suddenly found ourselves in meetings with forty people planning our next features, as opposed to the five of us making plans at 2:00 A.M. over pizzas and Cokes. Aleks, who had basically done the Mac version, suddenly found out that there were three or four other people working on it with him, according to NCSA. And they were like his bosses, telling him what to do and stuff. And how can I put this politely? We didn't think that any of them had Aleks's ability or foresight."

The *who's in charge* tension heightened in December of 1993, when Mosaic and the Web made it as far as the front page of *The New York Times* business section. There, a lengthy article about the software prophetically noted that it was perhaps "an application program so different and so obviously useful that it can create a new industry from scratch." The article ran with a big picture of NCSA's director Larry Smarr, who declared that Mosaic was "the first window into cyberspace." Also quoted were Tim Berners-Lee and a number of giddy Mosaic users. But no Binas, nor Mac Daddies, nor McCools, nor Mittelhausers were mentioned. Mosaic's lumbering co-author and catalyst was likewise unnoted, as was the dramatic Skittle-and-cookie-fueled hackathon that produced it. From this, it seemed to the outside, Mosaic was no Marc-and-Eric-Bina thing—it was rather an NCSA thing.

Marc attributes NCSA's ballooning enthusaism for Mosaic to supercomputing's doldrums. "They were raking in millions of dollars per year in federal money for supercomputing," he remembers, "and no one really wanted to use supercomputers anymore, so they sort of had two alternatives. One was to give up the federal funding, and one was to find something else to do. If you're an academic, you're certainly not going to give up your grant. So you look for something else to do. So they figured out that this was it fairly quickly." And Marc figured out fairly quickly that *they* weren't going to let him remain the de facto head of the Mosaic project if he stayed at NCSA after he was done with his studies. "It was just weird," he now shrugs. "The motivations were weird, the effects were weird, the fallout was weird, the debates were weird, the politics were weird, so I said, 'OK, I'm graduating.' So I graduated in December and I just basically took off." Marc headed West, far away from Mosaic's suddenly annoying birthplace. His *outtahere* trajectory inevitably took him straight to Silicon Valley, where he tarried briefly in tony Palo Alto before coming to rest in Mountain View.

At about that time, one of the tidy town's most notable notables was fortuitously getting ready to move on to something new himself. This was Jim Clark, the brilliant, self-starting, and famously outspoken founder of Silicon Graphics, Inc. (SGI), one of the many high-flying technology companies quartered on Mountain View's eastern landfill fringe. Clark had been with his company for about a dozen years by then. He had come to SGI and Valley entrepreneurship by way of Stanford University (the Valley's own alma mater, as some like to think), where he served on the engineering faculty. But though a professor by training, Clark had not exactly lived a sheltered scholarly life. His academic career had indeed been much more of a scrappy entrepreneurial episode than a coddled saunter up the ivory tower steps. His first stop after high school had been the Navy. Through its good offices and under a great deal of his own steam, he eventually made his way through college, and then onward through the scholarly ranks until he earned a Ph.D. in computer science in 1974. He taught for several years after that, first at the University of California and later at Stanford. His specialties were 3-D visualization and computer graphics (see Chapter 4). Feeling that the time was ripe to commercialize some of the notions that he had pioneered, he recruited a handful of his best graduate students in 1981 and established his company. A dozen years later, it had grown into a multibillion-dollar giant whose workstations were being used to design some of Hollywood's most spectacular special effects and some of the industrial world's most sophisticated products.

SGI became a tremendous success by dominating the high end of its markets. But over the years, Clark grew convinced that it also needed to start building "very, very powerful, small, low-priced machines" to counter the rising low-end threat posed by Microsoft and the rest of the PC industry. He lobbied hard to effect the strategic changes that he wanted to see. But in the end he did not prevail (he had not been running the company directly since early in its history). Frustrated, he eventually decided to leave and start something new. His plan was to create a networked, online gaming sort of business. Or perhaps some interactive television software. Or maybe interactive television services? Basically, he didn't know what he was going to do, and left SGI in January of 1994 with "this kind of feeling of stepping into empty space in a free fall," he recalls.

One of Clark's closer associates before his dive into the void was a plain-speaking jack-of-all-digital-trades named Bill Foss. Foss helped manage the flashy "briefing center" where SGI customers were wowed, and had occasionally doubled as Clark's roadie during his flashy, customer-wowing, speaking-and-deal-cutting tours. Foss and Clark got to know each other well through these tours, and Foss came to view his boss-of-bosses as "a great guy, although somewhat irascible at times," he says. "Temperamental, and definitely always spoke his mind at the expense of pissing people off occasionally. Which is great. That's something I really enjoy in somebody. It's nice to know where you stand." Another thing that Foss came to value in Clark was that "he doesn't discount you based on who you are or what you are. He listens to everybody," even a "midlevel marketing grunt." And this turned out to be a good thing. Because if Clark hadn't gotten into the habit of listening to Foss, *midlevel marketing grunt* though he was, Netscape as we know it would not now exist.

Many of Clark's speeches and efforts during the time leading up to his departure from SGI touched upon the information superhighway notion that was so heavily touted by President Clinton and others early in his first administration (Clinton himself even addressed the SGI cafeteria once). Within this broad theme, "interactive TV had been my push," Clark remembers, and to that end he had gotten SGI involved in Time Warner's ambitious interactive TV experiment in Orlando (see Chapter 3). As his occasional roadie, Foss grew very familiar with Clark's ITV pitch. And when he first encountered Mosaic, it struck him that "as it relates to what Clark was doing, this *is* an information superhighway," he recalls.

This notion was in the back of Foss's mind when Clark called him into his office during his last day at SGI to see if he knew any good engineers. Clark was looking for a few of these, because he knew that his *free-fall* startup was going to need some, whatever it did, and "most of the good engineers I'd ever known I had recruited into SGI, and I wasn't going to recruit from there," Clark explains. Foss knew from one of the Web-related news groups that Marc Andreessen had moved to Silicon Valley. He had never met Marc, but given the ITV/Web link that he saw, this struck him as "a great coincidence. . . . So I located Marc's phone number and basically put it in front of [Clark] and said, 'Give him a call, if you want—he's reportedly a bright engineer,' " Foss recalls.

Figuring he'd show Clark some proof, Foss loaded Mosaic onto his system and watched him "go up to it and do this thing where he kind of sits up, and kind of squints a little at the screen. . . . He said, '*Uhhhh.*' I just remember leaving him, clicking his way through the interface on that thing." It was Clark's first glimpse of the Web. Before he was done, he E-mailed Marc. You may not know me, but I'm the founder of Silicon Graphics, his message began. He asked Marc if he would like to meet the following day. Marc, who certainly did know who Clark was, agreed immediately.

At the time, Marc had just started working for Enterprise Integration Technologies (EIT), a small Palo Alto–based company that was developing some interesting Web security products, among other things. He had joined EIT because it was in California, it was doing Web-related work, and it was small (a semester spent working at IBM had cured him of big companies). The only trouble was that "EIT turned out to be a research environment" just like NCSA, Marc recalls. Other than that, things were already off to a fine start in California. It was exciting to be in the Valley, the weather was great, and he had already met his soon-to-be girlfriend (and later-to-be fiancee) Liz Horn. And now he had *Jim Clark* on the wire. *Hmmmmm.*

Marc and Clark met up at a Palo Alto hangout called Café Verona for breakfast and discussed Clark's various startup notions at length. "He was big on the idea of software," Marc explains. "He wasn't sure what the platform would be, so he was talking to the Nintendo people, he was thinking about PC software, he was thinking about ITV software. You know, the idea of working on some of the [interactive TV] trials came up, the idea of building sort of an online network for the Nintendo, the next-generation game box." The trouble with all of these ideas was that it "would be two years or more before you would be actually making any money—if at all—and even then you would be taking a bet." The notion of starting a Mosaic-related company didn't really come up (still fresh from the debacle with NCSA's administrators, Marc "had kind of a bad feeling about it, and he didn't want to be involved with it," Clark remembers). And so, with no idea really breaking out of the pack, Clark and Marc adjourned and agreed to stay in touch.

Marc then became a core member of an informal group that met periodically over the next few weeks to discuss Clark's startup plans. It was at one of this group's meetings that Bill Foss met him for the first time. Foss remembers Marc as "this kind of ungainly twenty-two- or twenty-three-year-old kid [who] doesn't quite know what to make of this corporate culture, so he's put a *tie* on" (ties were passenger-pigeon rarities in the corridors of the company Clark had founded). "He's sitting over there and he's super-quiet, doesn't know what to say." But while the *Just Marc!* confidence of the Cambridge Web conference might have been dormant that day, Marc "kind of built up his comfort level with Jim" over the subsequent weeks, Foss recalls. Soon he was lobbying hard for the idea of—bad NCSA memories be damned—starting an Internet company. This idea had been in the back of his mind all along. He had in fact first considered the possibility of building a business around Mosaic back in Illinois. But he hadn't known the first thing about starting businesses. And "there's no infrastructure at all in Illinois for a startup company," Marc explains. "It's not there. No one does it. They just don't know how to react to it. No one really knows if it's a good or bad thing."

But Jim Clark's background, bank account, and Rolodex by themselves were plenty of infrastructure for a startup. And the more Marc thought about it, the clearer the Web's business potential seemed to be. Even before he left NCSA, "We started to get a lot of licensing requests from companies for different reasons," he remembers. "Internal use, distribution rights, commercialization rights, things like that. So I sort of knew just based on that that there was a business opportunity, although it was not fully articulated, because it was a brand-new thing." This sense was corroborated by the Web's awesome march down the Internet backbone, which had continued to gather steam throughout the summer, fall, and winter.

All of this indicated a pretty serious market opportunity to Marc. And the market seemed wide open, because there was a blanket expression people used, where "nobody makes money on the Net," Marc recalls. To him, this was like saying, " 'Who is going to sell the first phone? Who's going to buy it? Who do you call?' 'Cars? There are no roads!' It's that same type of thing." After all, every network had to start *some*where. And the Web's growth already seemed to have achieved self-sustaining momentum.

Clark—*he doesn't discount you based on who you are*—took all good ideas very seriously, however inexperienced and tie-wearing their progenitors might be. So he listened carefully to Marc's arguments about Mosaic, and eventually "said, 'Well, I'll put money behind that,' " Clark recalls. "Personally, we don't know how in the hell we're going to make money, but I'll put money behind it, and we'll figure out a way to make money. A market growing as quickly as that is going to have money to be made in it." But first they needed an engineering team, so Marc E-mailed the NCSA crowd. His message told them to pack their bags, because he and Jim Clark were coming to town. And that was about it.

Marc's mysterious E-mail touched off a wave of sorely missed hysteria back in Illinois. The politburo that was managing the Mosaic project was proving to be about as unfun to work with as everyone had feared. And so life was generally "sad, and much quieter," since Marc had left, Eric Bina remembers. Now suddenly Marc was coming to town with *Jim Clark* in tow to talk about . . . something. It was a business-something. But beyond that, Mystery Marc was tight-lipped. Excited, perplexed, and deeply annoyed by this, Jon Mittelhauser eventually got him on the phone and demanded to know what the hell was the going on. Marc mysteriously told him to—*heh heh*—read *Game Over*, a book about Nintendo. As Mittelhauser obediently chased that wild goose, harumphing about how he didn't know a blessed thing about programming game machines, Marc and Clark made their travel arrangements.

Everything was running behind schedule the night they flew out— bad weather in Denver or something—and the team waited up late for them in their hotel. Most of the core Mosaic group was on hand, although Chris Wilson, who had helped Mittelhauser with the PC browser, had moved to Seattle (where he eventually ended up working for Microsoft). The team had filled out its numbers with another Chris from NCSA—Chris Houck—and also with Lou Montulli, the University of Kansas undergraduate who had written the text-only Lynx browser. Once Marc and Clark finally arrived, the group went to the hotel bar so that everybody could meet Clark. By then the business idea—*Mosaic Killer!*—had been revealed to everyone. The following morning each of the guys had a half-hour chitchat with Clark that ended with a job offer. Everyone got the same package, a generous mix of salary and stock options.

Once the interviews were over, the NCSA group retired to a local bar called Gully's while Clark typed up an offer letter on his laptop computer and faxed it to the hotel lobby seven times. He and Marc then powwowed briefly, and Marc carried the seven faxed offer letters over to Gully's, where everyone celebrated like mad. Someone had made a set of commemorative sweatshirts and everyone signed everybody else's. A few days earlier the new company had been officially incorporated as Mosaic Communications Corporation. The day after its incorporation, top executives of the world's most powerful software company, Microsoft, had coincidentally convened in their first Internet-related off-site retreat with their chief executive officer. There they had considered a 300-page briefing on the growing network, and discussed what it might mean for their company.

Mosaic Communications set up shop in a tiny office on Castro Street, Mountain View's eerily franchise-free main drag. The company's business model was still under discussion. But its mandate—*Beat Mosaic!*—was clear. The engineers were chartered to remake both the Web browser and the server, and to make them faster, more stable, and more fully-featured than their predecessors. They were also chartered to do this from scratch—completely. At Clark's wise insistence, they had already burned, deleted, and otherwise eradicated everything that they had ever owned pertaining to the original Mosaic code. This was important because Mosaic had been developed on university time and equipment. As such it belonged to the university—not, sadly, to the people who had written and named it. By then a number of companies had already started licensing and bundling Mosaic into Internet connectivity kits that were becoming hot items in software stores. But Mosaic Communications had no intention of signing a licensing agreement, and as a result its products had to be wholly original implementations.

This did not worry the engineers. They had already been through this drill once, after all. And they didn't view their own first-draft work as being very serious competition. For one thing, the earliest versions of Mosaic were notoriously crash-prone, because at NCSA "we were students; we were just having fun," Mittelhauser explains. "We had no thoughts about quality, really. I mean, we didn't want it crashing so much that nobody could use it and see how cool it was. But the idea was if you did some weird thing and it crashed, then you shouldn't do that weird thing again." This time around, however, stability would be a priority, not an afterthought. The team would also focus on performance, something they had ignored when it seemed that their core audience would be other people using fast workstations tied directly to the Internet backbone.

And perhaps most importantly, they would now be directed by seasoned engineering managers, as Marc was moving on to other things. This had been the plan from the beginning, as Marc was now more interested in focusing on the company's strategic issues. And the engineers didn't want to report to him anyway, because he had "no experience managing people," Mittelhauser explains. "He's incredibly bright at coming up with ideas; he's very good at knowing what's important; he's incredibly good at taking forty different pieces of information and putting them together. But these are all very different skills from managing engineers on a day-to-day basis." Marc did end up serving briefly in "sort of a management role" before experienced managers were hired, a position he personally felt he was "terrible at," Marc says. Soon enough he was relieved of being an engineering manager, and became more like the *Vice President of Thinking Stuff Up*, in the words of one company old-timer.

Marc's first replacements at the head of the engineering team came from SGI. Clark could not recruit directly from his old company, but people were allowed to call him, and most knew where to find him. So Tom Paquin came over early in the summer and started managing the engineers. Bill Foss turned up pretty quickly too (his first job was managing the company's Web presence), as did Rosanne Siino. Siino came from SGI's public relations department, which badly confused Marc at first. "I was like, 'We're a startup company and we don't need to hire a full-time PR person,' " he recalls. Mosaic Communications had yet to make its two-dozenth hire, after all. "But Jim was like, 'Trust me on this one.' "

So Marc trusted him, and hooo boy, was Jim right. Because within weeks of Siino's arrival, a gale force of press attention hit the tiny company, bringing it more profile-heightening coverage than any multimillion-dollar marketing campaign could have. Siino acknowledges that the Mosaic story "wasn't a hard sell" to the press because it had so many intriguing elements. "We had this twenty-two-year-old kid who was pretty damn interesting and I thought, 'There's a story right there,' " she recalls. "And we had this crew of kids who had come out from Illinois and I thought, 'There's a story there too.' " And then there was the founder-of-billion-dollar-company-tries-to-make-lightning-strike-twice story, the mounting-

Internet-craze story, and of course, the good-Lord-something's-happen-ing-in-Mountain-View story. All of this gave Siino something interesting to offer to almost every publication that came through the door.

Marc's transition from minor Internet folk hero to media property was sudden, and it wasn't always entirely smooth or enjoyable. Marc was in fact already squirming a bit when Siino first happened across him in the Castro Street building's lobby. She had not yet started work-ing for Mosaic, and was passing through for a quick meeting just as Marc was being photographed for a local newspaper article (which was eventually titled "He's Young, He's Hot, and He's Here"). "He was obviously not having a good time," Siino recalls. "He hates hav-ing his picture taken, and he's been difficult about it ever since." But the parade of cameras, microphones, and notepad-toting journalists had only just begun. Certain aspects of the ensuing frenzy never sat well with Marc. Photo shoots remained unhappy events for him, and personal profile pieces could irk him terribly. But he enjoyed giving in-terviews on professional topics that he cared about, particularly tech-nical ones. And through these, he quickly blossomed into one of the industry's most sought-after voices. Marc variously embraced, toler-ated, and endured the many aspects of his exposure, because he under-stood their business value from the outset. "If you get more visibility," he figured, "it would count as advertising, and it doesn't cost any-thing." And so, *Young, Hot, and Here,* Marc got visible.

One of the most important pieces of coverage that he and his com-pany received early on came in *Fortune*'s annual "25 Cool Compa-nies" survey in July of 1994. This led off with a profile of Mosaic Communications, and ran with a big picture of most of the NCSA crew and Jim Clark. The splashy article did much to lift spirits down on Castro Street, and also helped put the company on the map with a number of people that it was trying to talk to. The most important of these people was Jim Barksdale. Barksdale, who *Time* describes as "one of a handful of corporate managers who make up the varsity squad of American CEO's," was then the president and chief operating officer of McCaw Cellular. He had been at Federal Express prior to that, where he had served as chief information officer and later as chief operating officer. McCaw was in the process of merging into AT&T, and Clark thought that Barksdale might make a good CEO for his company once the merger was completed (he had never intended to run the company himself for very long). Clark wasn't alone in courting Barksdale; he understood that Microsoft was also trying to recruit him to be its president. But Barksdale happened to see the *Fortune* article right before Mosaic's recruiter called, so he was intrigued and willing to talk.

Clark flew up to Seattle (where McCaw was headquartered) with John Doerr of venture fund Kleiner Perkins Caufield & Byers (or KP, as it is usually known). He had accepted Doerr's offer to help fund his new company just a few weeks before. Doerr, whose influence has been compared to that of Microsoft CEO Bill Gates, was arguably the Valley's premiere venture capitalist. The companies in his portfolio included the workstation industry's largest player, Sun Microsystems; the personal finance software market's by far largest player, Intuit; and the fastest-growing company in the history of the world (in that it got to the $1 billion revenue mark quicker than any other company), Compaq Computer.

Doerr and Clark had known each other well since Clark's Stanford days. Doerr was living in a garage apartment near the campus at that time, dreaming of starting a technology company of his own. To this end he did a fair amount of networking in the university's engineering department, where he got to know Clark, as well as future Sun Microsystems founders Vinod Khosla and Andy Bechtolsheim. Doerr was an associate at KP throughout this period, helping around the shop while looking for a venture to start or join. One thing led to another and he eventually found himself starting *not companies, but industries* (to paraphrase technology investor Roger McNamee).

Sun was one of Doerr's first investments, and since Silicon Graphics and Sun became competitors, it was not appropriate for him to back Jim Clark. But "when finally it came time for him to do a new company, we both wanted to work together," Doerr recalls. Clark, who had done well by his success with Silicon Graphics, didn't really need help with its financing. But Doerr offered much more than cash, as his fund had built a tremendous network of hundreds of successful companies that its capital had seeded (its *Keiretsu*, as it calls it, is said to include over 200 companies with over 120,000 employees among them, and over $44 billion in combined revenues). Affiliating with this network could open countless doors for any young company. Doerr and his associates were also known for assembling crack management teams, and Clark was definitely going to need one of those. To this end, "job number one" became recruiting a world-class CEO straightaway, Doerr explains, and one of the most attractive candidates was Jim Barksdale, with whom he had once spoken about running Intuit. The meeting in Seattle went well. But Barksdale was unwilling to make any new commitments until McCaw's deal with AT&T closed. And so Doerr and Clark persuaded him to join the company's board of directors, with an eye toward eventually bringing him on to run the show.

By then things were going full throttle down in Mountain View, where the engineering team had long since shifted into overdrive. "It was really intense," Lou Montulli remembers. "You [would] wake up, go to work, sit at your cube, type a lot, and go to a lot of impromptu meetings. It was basically continuous work until you hit a major road-block. And a major roadblock would be something you couldn't solve by yourself. . . . Then you'd quickly form a quick meeting at twelve midnight and figure it out in ten minutes, and then go back to work." *Back to work* could mean staying at it through the night, or into the next morning, or through the next afternoon, or into the following night. Bill Foss remembers that "a lot of times, people were there straight forty-eight hours, just coding. I've never seen anything like it, in terms of honest-to-God, no BS, human endurance, to sit in front of a monitor and program. But they were driven by this vision. Part of it was Marc being this fanatic cheerleader, saying how everyone was going to prosper in the end, that we were fighting some war and that we could win."

Despite the hours, nobody was miserable. The team drew energy from its own camaraderie, from Marc's exhortations, and from the almost unlimited opportunities for competition that came from having the Mac, PC, and Unix browsers all enter development at once. The new versions squared off continually. The teams benchmarked them by summoning Web pages across the network and clocking their download times with stopwatches. They raced one another, and also the NCSA Mosaic software, which they started clobbering early on. When the time trials starting feeling a little too collegial, the engineers sometimes released their competitive energies in games of Chair Football. This was a brutal two-on-two sport in which people rolled around on office chairs, threw savage blocks, and generally tried to muscle past one another (and yes, a football was somehow involved too). "We probably took out about ten chairs in that game," Bill Foss recalls. "Took a big chunk out of Mittelhauser's ankle. It was pretty physical." Once the injury toll hit a certain threshold the pastime was quietly dropped. The next mania began when Rob McCool showed up at work with a radio-controlled car. Soon everyone was one-upping him and one another in a model-car arms race of flashiness, complexity, and speed. The cars took hours to assemble and cost small fortunes, and mostly ended as rubble in the hallways or in the brush outside.

When not trashing cars, chairs, or bodies, the engineers labored under the banner of Mozilla, a floor-to-ceiling paper lizard that hung from their wall. *Mozilla* the word originated as the code name for the new browser (it was a play on "Godzilla," as it was supposed to anni-hilate Mosaic—the software, not the company). Mozilla the Lizard (who came later) quickly became an engineering mascot, and it wasn't long before the marketing folks decided it would be fun to integrate him into the company Web site. But of course Marketing needed to give the company a kind, gentle, *user-friendly* sort of face, and Engi-neering's Mozilla was anything but that. So they had an artist draw up a Marketing Mozilla, a goofy, friendly, salamander kind of thing that the engineers found revolting. Eventually a balance was reached, and Mozilla started capering about the company's Web site, where he be-came immensely popular (Siino remembers "just this outraged cry from the public" when the company made the disastrous—and very temporary—mistake of deleting him).

Marc remained engaged with the engineers throughout their chaotic summer and fall, first as their quasi-manager, then through some ongo-ing involvement in product design. But he increasingly focused on his bigger-picture duties as *Vice President of Thinking Stuff Up* (or offi-cially, vice president of technology). This included working very closely with Clark, figuring out the company's strategy, visiting with customers, and recruiting senior management. Also, the "the flow of [press atten-tion] coming in was just overwhelming," by then, Marc remembers. This made for a full agenda. But Marc kept up with everything tirelessly, obsessively. Bill Foss remembers that he "put in more hours than any in-dividual in this company," because "he was just consumed by this. He enjoyed this more than anything else. No hobbies, nothing. This is all he would do. When no one else was around the building—if everyone had fallen asleep, or no one was there—he would just sit and read through newsgroups or magazines. A stack of old newspapers and magazines just fill[ed] the back of his car. His office was a pigsty, just full of every book in the world that he wanted. He had books on Gates, on every-body. He wanted to know what was a great entrepreneur. So he spent far more hours that I would consider healthy just living and breathing and thinking this. Far more than Clark, far more than anyone."

Marc's commitment was contagious, as was the confidence he was always trying to instill in the rest of the team that this thing was going to be *huuuge*. He did this through countless impromptu pep rally harangues with the engineers, and also at the weekly "all-hands" meetings that Clark convened on Fridays. One early employee remembers these for the "professorial, almost fatherly" approach Clark sometimes took. "It was like he really wanted to show the business world to these young programmers, explain who the companies we were working with were, and why they were significant."

Through the Friday meetings, some early successes with corporate partners, the engineers' benchmark results, and the relentless growth of the Web itself, the company's optimism built throughout the summer and fall. Greg Sands, the company's first marketing hire, coauthored its first business plan and recalls that even that sober document was giddily bullish. "We estimated '95 revenues of fifty million dollars," he says, "which is totally audacious for a software company's first full year of operation. But we were convinced that this thing was going to be vast. There was just no question about it. If not the company, then certainly the market" (Netscape's revenues ultimately exceeded $80 million in 1995).

Another early duty that Sands and the teensy marketing staff took on was making up names, as the company needed several of these for its products and (it turned out) for itself. Sands made the mistake of inviting the engineers for one of the first naming sessions. In it, Mac Daddy Totic went bonkers over "InfoCar" for the browser. Lou Montulli remembers lobbying hard for InfoSuck for the browser and InfoNipple for the server ("I think we could have gone a long way with that," he insists). InfoJockStrap and InfoCondom were meanwhile batted around for security software. Sands politely wrote down all of the engineers' suggestions and left them to their engineering after that. Naming sessions then continued fitfully for months. Almost all of the good names that fell out of them had at least a few loyal partisans. But one that was almost universally disdained at first was one of Sands's own. It was *Netscape*.

Late in the summer, the grown-ups started arriving in force. The first to show up was Jim Sha, a former engineering vice president from database giant Oracle. Sha came on to manage the company's big-ticket software business. "The idea was to sell large, integrated systems that would help 'pull through' the client software," he recalls (i.e., that would help drive the browser's proliferation). The first deal Clark handed him was one that he had initiated at MCI. MCI was interested in developing an online mall that could host storefronts for several merchants, and execute credit card transactions securely. "I started on a Monday, and Jim told me to close it by the end of the week," Sha laughs. The deal didn't close quite that quickly, but Sha did have a letter of intent by September. The contract that was ultimately signed allowed his team to productize the technology that they developed for MCI's mall, and to resell it to other companies. The MCI software later became the heart of a product family called the Integrated Applications (also confusingly known as the Internet Applications, then later as Commercial Applications). The I-Apps were the first integrated products designed to both market and sell goods and services over the Web.

The Kleiner Perkins recruiting machine kicked in shortly after Sha's arrival. In the span of 150 days, John Doerr, his partners, and the headhunters that they worked with brought the company a world-class team of seven vice presidents and a CEO (Sha was the only early VP to arrive without Doerr's intercession with the exception of Marc himself, and three earlier VPs who departed quickly—two of them when asked by Clark to step down for performance reasons). One of the new VPs whom Doerr had known personally was Mike Homer, who became vice president of marketing after a brief trial period as a consultant. Homer had previously spent nine years as a marketer at Apple before serving as vice president of marketing at GO Corporation, a high-profile pen-based computing company that ultimately imploded with the rest of its industry. Doerr had backed GO, and hand-picked Homer for his new job.

Homer spent much of the early fall working on the company's pricing model. When he started, plans were in place to charge $5000 and $25,000 for its two server products and $99 for browsers. He felt the server prices were particularly unrealistic, given how cheap (i.e., *free*) CERN's and NCSA's software was. After surveying pricing models in some other markets, Homer determined that the company should charge $1500 for its baseline server (the Communications Server, as it was called), and $5000 for its premium server (or Commerce Server). The Commerce Server differed from the entry model in that it could encrypt its communications using the company's Secure Sockets Layer (SSL) technology. This meant that traffic between it and a browser could be scrambled so that outside parties could not snoop on it. The Commerce Server was so named because its technology was meant to encourage Web commerce by enabling consumers to transmit credit card numbers and other sensitive data securely.

Browser pricing was a more complex matter. By then, Marc and others were determined that any browser price should be a bit of a *nudge-nudge, wink-wink* affair, because "we knew that the key to success for the whole thing was getting ubiquity on the Navigator [i.e., browser] side," Marc recalls. "That was the way to get the company jump-started, because that just gives you . . . essentially a broad platform to build off of. It's basically a Microsoft lesson, right? If you get ubiquity, you have a lot of options, a lot of ways to benefit from that. You can get paid by the product that you are ubiquitous on, but you can also get paid on products that benefit as a result. One of the fundamental lessons is that market share now equals revenue later, and if you don't have market share now, you are not going to have revenue later. Another fundamental lesson is that whoever gets the volume does win in the end. Just plain wins."

The *Microsoft lesson* that so impressed Marc was the triumph of that company's PC operating systems (first DOS, later the many versions of Windows). A computer's operating system (OS) is its most important piece of software because it determines the look, feel, and functionality of its interface, and also attends to countless vital housekeeping tasks below its surface. Also, applications written for one OS will generally not run under another OS unless they are arduously translated, which can take almost as much time as writing them in the first place (although the Java language is starting to change this; see Chapter 3). This traditionally made the proprietary airlocks tighter in the OS market than anywhere else. It also helped Microsoft parlay a big early lead in the PC OS market into a position of all but unusurpable dominance, as application vendors were naturally drawn by the larger markets that its OS's serviced, and wrote their software to run under them. Starved of applications, many rival OS's disappeared, and the Macintosh gradually foundered (although other factors contributed to this as well). Numerous hardware manufacturers prospered by building the machines that ran Microsoft's OS's. But none ever approached Microsoft's influence in the industry because the OS was the real computer, was the *platform* that software was written to.

As Microsoft's share of the OS market marched toward 80 percent and beyond, its distribution channels and its unrivaled intimacy with the platform that everyone else was writing to positioned it immaculately to compete in the application software market too. Throughout the 1980s and early '90s, Microsoft steadily rolled to dominance in category after application category. Some it won through traditional sales and distribution channels. Others (like screen savers and file compression tools) it simply subsumed into its operating systems. The company's extraordinary success drew many cries of foul play, as well as governmental inquests (one of which resulted in a negotiated consent decree that set restrictions on the company's conduct in the OS market). But no amount of finger-pointing or bureaucratic saber-rattling could change the fact that Microsoft had *just plain won* the PC software market.

By the fall of 1994, Marc was growing convinced that the Web was a computing platform just like the PC. In light of this and Microsoft's example, he concluded that "There has to be just one single big winner in a market like this." Winning therefore meant being as ubiquitous in the browser market as Microsoft was in the OS market. And it was clear that ubiquity would not come from charging money while the competition was free. By the time Mike Homer came on to run marketing, the notion of offering a free, or somewhat-free, or free-to-some browser had become gospel in the company. Homer recalls that there was "a lot of oscillation" about what all of this meant, but in the end "Marc came up with this notion of 'free but not free,' " which was eventually implemented. The meaning of *free but not free* oscillated quite a bit itself. The hope was to make the Navigator free for noncommercial use and not free for commercial use. But it turned out that there were a lot of gray areas in this. For instance, if someone wanted to use a browser at work, that copy should of course be *not free*. But if it was only going to be used to check movie listings and horoscopes, then perhaps it should be *free* . . . ?

In the end, the policy stabilized around making browsers free to students and educators, and in theory not free to all others. *Not free* meant $39 (then $49, about a year later). But even the unfree masses were granted access to "beta software," or new versions of the browser that were released to the Internet while they were still works-in-progress. The browser remained in constant development from the day it first released, so free beta software was ultimately available as often as not. Even when there wasn't an in-process version of the Navigator in beta testing, all users were always permitted to download and "test" its current version for a 90-day trial period without paying for it. And since the trial period was never really enforced, the *free but not free* policy as it evolved meant that the browser could be de facto free to almost anybody, except for businesses with MIS (management information systems) staffs, software budgets, and consciences.

By early October, the company's revenue model was all but finalized, and the first beta release of the browser was all but ready to be posted to the Web (its final not-beta version was not released until December). Everything seemed to be falling into place. The one unsettling exception to this was that the University of Illinois, as universities do, had decided to come tin-cupping to its newly-minted alums. But unfortunately, it wasn't coming at them with the usual dinnertime phone calls, fund-raising tailgate parties, or commemorative ashtrays; but rather with *lawyers*. The university "essentially tried to extort a fifty cents per copy royalty" on the browser, Clark recalls, with the idea that it somehow infringed on its intellectual property rights. This infuriated Clark, who reckoned that his company hadn't "taken anything from the university except what was in these guys' heads, and after all, the purpose of the university is to put stuff in their heads." There was also no way that his software was going to be *free but not free* if it was saddled with a per-copy royalty payment. So Clark retained a forensic software expert who determined that there was "no similarity in form, only in function" between the company's code and the NCSA code, he recalls, and on October 13th the software was posted to the Net.

Exhausted but jubilant, the engineers held vigil the night it went up. Beer was *brung*, pizza was summoned, and somebody set up a big display screen to track the downloads as they happened. The engineers huddled around this breathlessly after the software went up. A few minutes that seemed like an eternity went by, then the first connection was made. It was somebody in *Japan*! Everybody cheered. They swore they'd send the guy a T-shirt. (They didn't.) Then another download was logged, then a series in rapid succession. And within an hour, the poor Silicon Graphics machine that they had conscripted as their server fell under a siege from which it never emerged. Thousands of people from throughout the world were sticking their digital reeds through the ether and sucking down copies of Mosaic Netscape, as the browser was named. For a little while the Drinking & Downloading passed in a haze of convivial unity. Then somebody snapped out of it and realized that the screen was of course indicating the *versions* of the browsers that were being downloaded and that—*WIN!!!*—somebody should be keeping score. In a heartbeat the system was rigged up to sound-code the downloads—a cow mooing for PC browsers, a bell for Macintoshes, an explosion for Unix—and the Drinking & Downloading moved onto more familiar competitive terrain. For a while it was shaping up to be a close race. But then the PC version took off, and at least one of the Unix guys stomped out of the room, reportedly somewhat pissed off.

Of course, the only race that really mattered in the end was the one between Mosaic Netscape and its rivals out on the Internet. And in this race, all of the engineers *kicked ass*. Because in the course of just a few weeks, Mosaic Netscape was being used by a plurality, then a majority, then a crushing majority of the Web's population. Performance had a lot to do with this, as when it came to downloading, the software screamed, it jammed, it *went to eleven*—company benchmarks clocked it as running 10 times faster than the competition. Mosaic Netscape also offered the promise of displaying more interesting pages, as it supported several new extensions to the HTML language. These included a "center tag," which centers text in the middle of a page, and a "blink tag," which makes it flash (like the "12:00" on most of our VCRs).

The extensions dismayed some HTML purists, who saw them as the first step down the path of turning the Web's Esperanto into a balkanized Babel of warring browser dialects. But the Mosaic Netscape team had already extended HTML once before (remember images?). And they were convinced that the language still needed to be far, far livelier. They had in fact come close to dropping HTML entirely and introducing a new language (MDL, or Mosaic Description Language). But while this would have brought the Web a far more vibrant content language all at once, it would have required the company to support two languages (MDL and HTML) in its browser instead of just one (it also would have enraged much of the Web community). So in the end the company decided to leverage the fact that HTML already existed and to gradually evolve it, unilaterally, in the ways it saw fit.

But unilateral as they were, the new extensions to HTML were never proprietary. They were instead publicly documented, and the company urged all of its competitors to adopt them. Its competitors did ultimately adopt them, as well as the sets that followed them. But thousands of Web page designers, whose expressiveness was hobbled daily by HTML's limitations, beat them to the punch. Soon armies of Webmasters (as the builders and tenders of corporate Web sites came to be known) and Web developers (as the for-hire builders of sites for multiple companies came to be known) were tagging their pages with notices indicating that they were best viewed with Mosaic Netscape (and later, the Netscape Navigator). Millions of Web users eventually heeded these notices, and followed their accompanying hot-links to the company's weary FTP servers to download new browsers. In this manner, the Web's creative community became Mosaic Netscape's distribution network, helping to spread its proliferation even further.

Another unique feature that Mosaic Netscape offered was security, as it was embedded with the company's Secure Sockets Layer (SSL) technology. SSL enables browsers and servers to conduct secure dialogues with one another in which all communication is encrypted. The exportable version of SSL uses 40-bit digital "keys" to encrypt traffic, while the far more secure United States–only version uses 128-bit keys. SSL's underlying algorithms (which the company licenses from RSA Security) are very powerful. Shattering even a humble 40-bit key would on average require the full attention of a Pentium-powered PC for roughly nine months, according to Jeff Treuhaft, who spearheaded much of the SSL effort. Anybody that anxious to get a credit card number could far more easily take a job at a department store cash register, and have dozens within a few hours. Even harder to break than this, 128-bit keys are deemed to be unshatterable even by intelligence agencies. This is not to say that security breaches are inconceivable. Glory-seeking hackers have in fact been prodding at SSL for security leaks since its maiden release, and have found holes (the company in fact encourages this rigorous stress-testing by offering prize money to those who spot weaknesses). But these holes are plugged as they are found. And of the hundreds of millions of dollars' worth of secure Internet commerce that had occurred as of this writing, Treuhoft knew of no case of a credit card number being stolen, or a transaction being otherwise hijacked by a malevolent party. Few if any traditional retail businesses with comparable sales volumes can make a similar claim.

SSL represented a significant point of differentiation for Mosaic Netscape and the Commerce Server, which also supported it. But it also led to a small PR debacle for the young company. Because not long before it released, EIT (Marc's brief one-time employer) released a rival security technology called S-HTTP (Secure Hypertext Transfer Protocol). EIT then did a very effective job of positioning S-HTTP as an open industry standard, one that would be thoroughly documented and available to any company that wanted to implement it. Mosaic Communications later declared that it meant for SSL to be an open standard too, but the technology released without any documentation. Many in the industry, their suspicions fanned by EIT's superior PR efforts, then came to view SSL as a proprietary solution, which was of course badly contrary to the open, egalitarian precepts of the Internet ("it took us a good six months to a year to overcome that 'anti-standards' label," an early employee recalls). In the end SSL became far more of a standard than S-HTTP ever did (documentation and a reference implementation were eventually released, and all of the major browser companies came to support it). But the experience was a hard one, and taught the company a great deal about how to promote and propagate technology on the open Internet—although the uncomfortable politics surrounding SSL did nothing to slow Mosaic Netscape's wildfire adoption by Web users.

The competition it was soon routing consisted mainly of unimposing descendants of the original NCSA Mosaic code. Spyglass, the university's master licensee, was already distributing a Mosaic browser itself. Other companies that had or were expected to release NCSA-based browsers included Spry (which CompuServe later bought), Quadralay, DEC, and IBM (all of these other licensees acquired sublicenses from Spyglass). But while there were already some big names in this group, the biggest looming competitor, Microsoft, had yet to make a move. And so, with a mind toward perhaps keeping the software giant out of Spyglass's camp entirely, Clark and others had talks with Microsoft in which the possibility of Microsoft licensing their code was discussed. But Microsoft was willing to pay only a paltry onetime licensing fee for rights to the code, and Clark refused. He later joked that he might have sold if the fee was, say, a billion and a half dollars. And in retrospect, that might have been quite a bargain.

But Clark didn't sell. And he didn't end up devoting as much time to the Microsoft issue as he would have liked. Because by the late fall, the *gimme gimme* gadfly chorus from the University of Illinois and its henchpersons at Spyglass had come to take up "one hundred fifty percent" of his time, he recalls. The spat also became very public as it escalated. By December, Spyglass President Douglas Colbeth was complaining to *The Wall Street Journal* that his rival's "development wasn't done in a 'clean room,' " implying that Clark's engineers were inadequately insulated from their knowledge of the NCSA code when they wrote their new browser. Colbeth also accused the tiny startup of being "monopolistic."

Clark speculates that the hostilities escalated because the university "began to see themselves disenfranchised" when Mosaic Netscape's popularity took off. Whatever the motivations, Clark soon received a letter demanding that he "change the name of the company and stop allowing the program to be downloaded over the Net," he remembers. He decided "fine, I'll change the name. But I said, 'I paid for the writing of this code. I choose what I'm going to do with it, and you don't tell me what to do with it.' " The company then became Netscape Communications Corporation, which was expedient, as the Netscape name had already been trademarked for the browser.

But this reflagging alone did not bring a cease-fire, and eventually, Clark recalls, "Spyglass salesmen were telling people that we were stealing from the university," and both Spyglass and the university were flatly refusing to examine his code to verify that it was independently authored. All of this took his attention away from running his company, which suddenly had 120 employees, and only $1 million left from the $13 million that he and KP had funded it with. So in the midst of all this, "we burned $12 million in six months," Clark recalls, "and it was my foot on the floor. But I began to get hesitant." He implemented a reorganization, asked some temps to leave, and the company held its collective breath.

Luckily it soon cleared a major hurdle when shipping versions of its maiden software released on December 15th. This allowed some revenue to be collected before the end of the year. Six days later an agreement with the University of Illinois was finally announced, in which the university asserted no wrongdoing on Netscape's part, and made no further claims on its revenues. The agreement's specific terms were never publicly disclosed. But Clark says that he simply estimated the costs of fighting a lawsuit, and offered that amount to the university's lawyers to go away (industry rumor pegged the settlement at around $2 million). He also offered an allotment of Netscape stock as an alternative, but the university took the money. Ten months later, the value of the spurned stock peaked at over $17 million. And so the University of Illinois not only burned every bridge that it ever had (or might have built) with Netscape, not only squandered its chances of one day boasting an Andreessen Library, a Mac Daddy Computer Center, and a Mittelhauser (Chair) Football Stadium, but it also opted out of one of the hottest initial public offerings in history.

Over the Christmas holidays, Clark contacted Jim Barksdale and told him that he was really needed at Netscape. Things were wrapping up between AT&T and McCaw by then, so in January Barksdale finally came aboard and "put his foot on the floor again," Clark says. Temps were called back and the hiring started afresh. The company's head count doubled in a matter of months, then doubled again. Growth was fueled both by its products' early successes and by Barksdale's bullishness about its prospects. This was itself partly driven by his bullishness about the Web, because in early 1995, Netscape's exposure to the Web's growth and popularity was almost total. The Navigator handily maintained the overwhelming market dominance that it achieved in its first weeks, and this helped fuel thousands of server sales (although Netscape's servers never matched the Navigator's market share, as several capable competitors were on the scene by the spring of 1995, and most of the market retained its affinity for freeware).

Barksdale's faith in the Web was not misplaced, and the Web quickly carried Netscape into thousands of businesses and millions of households. The roughly one million Mosaic users at the time of the company's establishment in April of 1994 had already doubled by the time of Mosaic Netscape's debut in October, according to Rosanne Siino (who kept track of these numbers for PR purposes). Those two million Mosaic users translated into almost two million Netscape users in fairly short order. And this group grew to more than ten million users by the next summer. Driven by the surge in its user base, the Web went from being the 11th-largest source of traffic on the North American Internet backbone when Marc and Clark first met, to number five by the time the first beta copy of their browser was ready in October of 1994. It then rose to second place by December, when the final, shipping version of the Navigator was released, and then finally to number one before the federally funded Internet backbone was shut down in April of 1995. By then, the Web had a 21.4 percent share of the backbone's traffic—a several-hundredfold increase in its share since Mosaic debuted in the winter of 1993. In two short years, then, the Web's traffic had come to dominate the network whose creation had preceded its rise by over two decades.

Much of this early growth was driven by the Web's rapid acceptance among businesses. The first corporate sites, which started appearing as early as 1993, were typically mere shelves; they were little corporate patches on the Web's infinite shelf from which information like product literature, annual reports, press releases, listings of regional offices and phone numbers, and technical specifications could be pulled. Simple as they were, these shelves quickly proved to be very useful tools. Because while successful organizations had long maintained robust channels for pulled communication, traditional pulled channels (e.g., investor relations departments, customer service staffs) are very expensive. Activating one can require phone calls to operators, trips to stores, visits from sales representatives, use of the public mail, and the creation and distribution of printed matter. These are expensive "media" for a company to maintain, and are likewise expensive for its constituents to activate, as doing so requires time and interpersonal involvement. Many companies therefore realized early on that putting pulled information on the Web's shelf could have a measurable benefit every time it obviated the use of a traditional channel. An obviated request to an investor relations department, for instance, could save dozens of dollars' worth of staff time, postage, printing costs, and 800-number charges. An obviated request for a company price list could save a similar set of expenses.

Corporate shelves on the Web also brought the less measurable (but potentially far greater) benefit of inviting and fielding inquiries that would not otherwise be made. For instance, a customer curious about pricing or product specifications might not have the time to visit a store or call a sales representative. But that customer might—*ah what the hell*—be willing to spend a few minutes pulling information from the Web, which could well result in a sale that would not otherwise be made. In this and many other like circumstances, the alluring accessibility, anonymity, and (increasingly) media-richness of information shelved on the Web can invite a degree of impulsive exploration that salespeople and phone calls cannot.

Some companies quickly went beyond mere shelves and built their sites into full-blown *user interfaces* to their organizations. These sites were not merely stocked with pulled-channel documentation, but also sought to emulate some of the more sophisticated functions of sales representatives, customer service people, and others. For instance, a mere-shelf Web site might save a shipping company several toll-free calls by publishing its pricing schedules, office locations, and hours of operation. But a user interface site might save it hundreds of thousands of calls by tracking its customers' packages for them. Federal Express set up a celebrated site that did just this back when such feats were still novel. Visitors to this site type in their "Air Bill" (or package ID) numbers, and instantly receive detailed logs of their packages' progress and locations. For someone with continuous Web access (generally, someone working at a computer connected to a corporate network) this is a much quicker way to check up on a package than calling the company's 800 number, which makes Federal Express an easier company to do business with. Federal Express meanwhile saves a few dollars for every query that it satisfies over the Web instead of through its operators.

User interface sites like Federal Express's are powerful in part because they create a new and efficient means for customers (or partners, or other outside stakeholders) to query corporate databases. And this is significant, as outsiders query corporate databases all the time. Whenever somebody asks an airline about schedules and prices, a bank about balances, or (of course) a shipping company about a package, a database query is being made. Queries like these are the currency of many companies' customer relations. But the traditional broker for them—an operator who parrots customer requests to a database, and then parrots the database's replies back to the customers—is very expensive. The Web can obviate this expense by "making everyone an operator" (as Neil Weintraut points out in the Introduction of this book). This is a highly precedented strategy that has often worked brilliantly. Telephone companies made everyone an operator—literally—by bringing technology to the home that let people dial their own calls, rather than request connections from operators. Banks made everyone an operator by bringing technology to the street corner that let people withdraw cash and settle other transactions without a teller's intercession.

Making everyone an operator has traditionally been a very expensive proposition, because it involves distributing the operator's infrastructure to the public. But the investment can have an enormous return, because it lets companies "outsource" much of their labor-intensive work to their own customers. More importantly, it often leads to far more satisfied customers because people are inevitably more familiar with their own needs than a distant operator can be. Once they are empowered to act as their own operators, they are therefore often able to get what they want more speedily and efficiently. The Web can make the decision to invest in making everyone an operator a far easier one, because it lets companies leverage infrastructure that already exists when they distribute the operator's infrastructure. And when the operator's infrastructure consists largely of access to a database (as it often does), the Web can easily and affordably give it more access points than every automatic teller machine network in the world.

The distributive power of the Web drew cost- and customer-conscious companies by the thousands throughout 1995. A similar logic meanwhile started drawing content providers of all types. These included hundreds, then thousands of bricks-and-mortar periodicals, as well as countless Web-only publishers, distracters, and entertainers. Their professionally-authored content entered the Web's shelf alongside that of thousands of evening-and-weekend Web designers, alongside an explosion of school, government, and philanthropic sites, and alongside a jumble of online boutiques and malls whose ranks began to swell after Netscape released its secure servers and browsers (see below).

And as the Web's shelf grew increasingly crowded and rich, its charms drew new users to the medium at a rate of thousands, then millions per month. This mushrooming audience drew still more content as the network's self-feeding growth surged. Realizing that they could never replicate the torrent of content that the open network was drawing, the commercial online services soon joined the network themselves by integrating Web access with their proprietary services, allowing the open Internet to come hissing, then cannonballing through their airlocks. This delivered millions of new users to the Web in the span of a few months. It also eventually delivered the online networks themselves, as by the end of 1996 all but one of them (America Online) had partly or wholly abandoned their expensive proprietary networks to deploy on the Web.

The wild momentum that the Web attained in early 1995 was astonishing to some in light of the medium's look and feel. This was almost wholly static; its content neither morphed nor zapped, but just kind of *sat* there against an off-white background. Certain Web sites had offered richer media like audio and video since the Web's earliest days. But since traditional audio and video files take up vast amounts of digital space, they took ages to download over the consumer modems of the day. As such they remained novelties, not core elements of the Web's media environment. This started to change dramatically in the spring and summer of 1995, when a number of independent developments began to make the Web a more inherently alluring environment. In April, Silicon Graphics released Web Space, the first Web browser designed to interpret and display three-dimensional scenes written in the Virtual Reality Modeling Language (VRML). VRML brought the Web navigable, manipulable content with depth (see Chapter 4). Also in April, Progressive Networks released its RealAudio technology (see Chapter 2). This brought the Web audio content that could be played within moments of being summoned, rather than after minutes of downloading, and soon enabled live Internet broadcasts. And in May, Sun Microsystems unveiled Java, a secure programming language that could in theory make it possible for any type of application or interactive content to run in a Web page (see Chapter 3).

Java's rise was particularly momentous, because the language not only made it easy for applications to be distributed over the network, but it treated all operating systems identically. This meant that a Java applet that ran in the popular Windows environment could also run on a Macintosh, or on a Unix workstation. This had tremendous ramifications for the operating system market, which Microsoft had long dominated in part because of the unrivalably large selection of applications that its operating systems ran. This advantage would clearly erode if new applications started treating all operating systems identically. In this, Java threatened to bring the Internet's open, interoperable rules hissing through the airlocks of even the most powerful bastion of all—that of the PC operating system.

It also, along with the other Internet technologies that emerged in mid-1995, promised to heighten the Web's popular relevance dramatically. Because the Web's shelf, whose humble product pitches, package trackers, and digital newspapers were already drawing millions, would soon be dishing up radio signals, vast archives of computer programs, internetworked *virtual 3-D worlds*, and who knew what else. All of this would make the Internet a veritable hard drive, crammed full of enough digital content and computer applications to fill a boxcar of CD-ROM disks, to fill a train full of them. The Web browser, then, would be the interface that summoned that hard drive's countless programs and performances. In this, it would be rather like an operating system, like a *computing platform* in its own right.

The Navigator-as-platform notion took root at Netscape throughout the spring and summer of 1995. Marketing VP Mike Homer recalls that "there were two key things that we decided to do that kind of got us there." The first was licensing the Java language. Marc, who describes Java as being "as revolutionary as the Web itself," took the lead on this decision, and announced the licensing agreement personally at the language's official unveiling in May. Java support was subsequently built directly into the Navigator, starting with its 2.0 release (which was posted to the Internet in beta form in September of 1995).

The other key enabling step was the development of the Navigator's "plug-in API (application programming interface)," which also debuted with Navigator 2.0. This is an infrastructure that lets independent developers extend the Navigator's media capabilities with pieces of software called "plug-ins." For instance, the very first plug-in enabled the Navigator to display VRML content. This made it possible for rotatable 3-D models and navigable 3-D scenes to be viewed with it. Previously, VRML content had to be viewed with a separate browser, which meant that it could not be integrated with the text, images, and other media displayed in the Navigator's window. The plug-in API eventually extended the Web's capabilities in countless ways that Netscape could not have planned or effected on its own. In the months following its final release, scores of plug-ins were developed that let the Navigator display text and graphics in new ways, play video, play MIDI (Musical Instrument Digital Interface) music files, and more (see Chapter 2).

By the time Navigator 2.0 entered late development in the summer of 1995, Netscape itself had grown and matured almost as fast as its flagship product. It now had hundreds of employees, almost 10 million users, and a rapidly expanding product line. This already included a newsgroup server and a "proxy" server (proxy servers speed Web access by pooling large amounts of content from throughout the Web on fast local networks, like corporate networks; see Chapter 5). A number of other new products, like site development tools and the commerce-enabling Integrated Applications (I-Apps), were in or nearing their first releases. The company had meanwhile rung up two astonishingly successful quarters, and was starting to generate revenue at an unbelievable $80 million annual run-rate. Revenues were coming mainly from *not free* copies of the Navigator that were selling briskly both in the corporate market and in retail channels. But server sales had also ramped up quickly. With December's worries fading fast, and an apparently profitable quarter under way, it was time for what the company's venture backer John Doerr calls a "puck on the ice IPO." These are warranted when "the board management has the confidence that we can exceed investor expectations for the next eight quarters," Doerr explains, and "the team is in place." By late June Netscape seemed to have met these criteria. Also, Spyglass had already filed for a public offering. In light of this, Clark and Barksdale both felt that a Netscape offering could bring a tremendous marketing advantage, and the company filed to go public.

Bracing for a frenzy, the PR group immediately set up an IPO hotline staffed by three full-time contractors who were soon fielding up to 400 phone calls per day. People were calling to see if using the Navigator entitled them to stock, to propose marriage, to get *in*, get *in*, get *in* on the IPO. Some were charmingly finance-naive Internet denizens, many were Internet-naive Wall Street denizens, and some were just damn savvy investors. The tension finally broke on August 9th. Netscape's shares priced at $28 the evening before, implying a total value for the company of over a billion dollars. This was a tidy sum for a startup that had been shipping product for less than eight months, whose since-inception revenues totaled around $17 million, and whose since-inception losses were close to $13 million.

A number of employees came to work early to watch the ticker and cheer it on. At 6:30 A.M. the opening bell rang back in New York and . . . nothing happened. Ten minutes went by. Then a half hour, an hour, an hour and a half. The market was humming, millions of shares were trading hands, but not a single share of Netscape. Nobody understood what was happening. Then finally, around 8:00, *Kaboom!* The first trade finally cleared—at $71. The price then marched up to $74.75 before an inevitable round of profit-taking drove it downward. But even at its $58.25 close, the stock had gained over 100 percent on its (official) opening price.

Netscape's dramatic IPO put the Internet indelibly on the map with millions of people who hadn't yet been there. Callers to Charles Schwab that day encountered recordings that directed them to *press one* if they were calling about Netscape. *The Wall Street Journal*'s front page marveled that while "It took General Dynamics Corp. 43 years to become a corporation worth today's $2.7 billion. . . . It took Netscape Communications Corp. about a minute." Thousands of other periodicals also helped to spread word of the bonanza throughout the world. Its unhappy coincidence with the day of musician Jerry Garcia's death meanwhile immortalized it with folkloric jokes ("Netscape opened at *what*?" were of course the famous dying words). All of this eradicated whatever remained of the Internet's lab coat obscurity. The Net was now a front-page land that raced infant companies to the public market; one where people *got rich!* in months flat. To some this made it a realm of inspiring promise; to many others, one of unconscionable hype. But whatever it was, the Internet would never again be a *huh?* to the business mainstream.

The IPO was of course a giddy and roundly celebrated event at 501 East Middlefield Road (where Netscape had moved in January). And in filling the company's coffers, heightening its profile, and giving it the credible mantle of public ownership, it was one of the best-imaginable things that could have happened to it. But it also brought with it a certain loss of innocence. Because while Netscape was still that *Cool Company!* started by the bright-eyed undergrads grinning and yee-hawing in *Fortune*'s pages, it now also had a lot to prove to clucking minions of Internet skeptics who all but viewed its market value as a moral affront. Rosanne Siino's PR role particularly exposed her to the new *they're all a bunch of teenage gazillionaires* cynicism. She recalls that "after the IPO, people wanted to focus so much on the stock price that they forgot that there were real humans [at Netscape] trying to do some real things, and that they were working, and they weren't sitting and counting their money in the back room." Hoping to in fact keep back-room money-counting to a minimum, CEO Jim Barksdale quickly banned discussions of Netscape's stock price during work hours (an edict that inevitably was about as adhered to as those forbidding alcohol to minors on most college campuses).

Among the people who were most impacted by the IPO were the original NCSA boys, who were of course happy with the change in their material circumstances. But they had been told to expect it so many times, by Marc, by Jim Clark, by others, that for some it almost didn't seem like a change. "Jim Clark's such an optimist," Lou Montulli remembers. "He told us like right from the beginning, you know, 'I'm going to make you X amount of dollars.' . . . And at first I only kind of believed him. . . . And then within a couple of months, I had totally bought into it. It's like, 'Oh yeah. It's there. It's like money in the bank, almost.' " As a result, it was "kind of anticlimactic" when the IPO finally hit, he recalls. "It's like, 'Oh well, there it is. Now it's there.' " Despite this, Montulli still seemed lingeringly flabbergasted by it all many months afterward. "Take, say, a Chinese worker," he reflected. "I'm probably worth a million times the average Chinese worker, or something like that. It's difficult to rationalize the value there. I worked hard, but did I really work that hard? I mean, can anyone work that hard? Is it possible? Is anyone worth that much?"

For his part, Marc was almost militantly nonchalant about the wealth issue. He even slept through the IPO, having worked late the night before. When he finally did wake up, he checked the stock price and went straight back to sleep. His personal fortune quickly became one of his least favorite topics of discussion. When asked about it, he would typically point out that "there are a lot of both legal and practical restrictions" on what he could do with his Netscape holdings, which meant that it was "still all funny money." And then he would change the subject. Because as far as he was concerned, there were far more important things to discuss and (certainly) for Netscape to focus on than its IPO's aftermath. Looming large on his and many other radar screens by then was Microsoft, as just a few weeks after the IPO, Microsoft finally released its long-anticipated Web browser, Internet

Explorer, along with its much-longer anticipated new operating system, Windows 95.

Like most of the rest of the market, Internet Explorer (or IE, as it came to be known) was based upon NCSA code licensed from Spyglass. At first it was not much more impressive than any of the other NCSA derivatives. Alex Edelstein, who had just started working at Netscape as the Navigator's product manager (having previously spent a good number of years at Microsoft), found IE to be "very underfeatured," and accordingly lumped it in with "a whole range of roughly equal players" that Netscape was then competing with. These included Spyglass itself and CompuServe's newly acquired Spry unit (where busy young Edelstein had also worked). Unlike Navigator 2.0, which Netscape unveiled a few weeks after IE's debut, IE didn't support Java, and offered nothing like the plug-in API. It also didn't support Netscape's extensions to HTML, which had become quite rich and were being used at thousands of sites. This meant that IE users visiting those sites would miss out on much of the media experience that they offered—much as black-and-white TV owners miss out on much of the richness in a modern television signal. But most significantly, Internet Explorer ran under only one operating system: Windows 95. In this, Microsoft temporarily ceded the small-but-significant Macintosh and Unix markets to Netscape, as well as the unsmall and very significant Windows Not-95 market. This market included the vast base of computers running Windows 3.1, Windows 3.0, and their ancestors, which at the time accounted for the overwhelming majority of the world's PCs.

But IE did have one feature that Edelstein found "threatening" from the outset, and that was its price. Because just like the screen savers, the file compression tools, the calculators, and the other little doodads that were integrated into Windows 95, IE was *part of the operating system*. It came with the computer; it was just there. This meant that to win over Windows 95 users, Netscape would have to persuade them to evict an apparently-free piece of software, and replace it with a functionally-similar piece of rival software which was in most cases (at least theoretically) *not free*. This is a fairly unnatural act for most computer users. The evicting-and-replacing-by-FTP-download part would also be creepy territory for less technically-savvy users. And as the Web's constituency continued to expand beyond its elite early bastions and into the general population, the techno-savvy of its average user would inevitably decline.

All of this could mean serious trouble for Netscape over the long haul. Because like its forebears, Windows 95 was expected to take over the vast majority of the world's desktop computers in short order. This meant that for the Navigator to remain all-but-ubiquitous among Web users, it would eventually have to be all-but-ubiquitous among Windows 95–based Web users. And this meant that its features and performance would have to be compelling enough to inspire millions of diminishingly technical computer users to perform that unnatural act of replacing IE. In short, Navigator would not only have to be better than IE, it would have to overwhelmingly better, and it would have to be *always* better. It could perhaps achieve this by regularly adding tremendous new features that IE lacked. Or maybe it could provide access to vast shelves of compelling Web content that IE somehow couldn't reach. Or perhaps there was some other way. But whatever the strategy, beating IE over the long haul would mean continually staying far out ahead of the most entrenched, powerful, and (many felt) unfair competitor in the software world. And there was no question about whether Microsoft was coming. Some three months before Internet Explorer's release, CEO Bill Gates had in fact circulated an internal memorandum entitled "The Internet Tidal Wave," in which he asserted that the Internet's rise was "the most important single development" since the release of the IBM personal computer over a decade before. So far, wimpy little Internet Explorer 1.0 was the most tangible embodiment of that call to arms. But more was certainly on its way.

All of this was of course concerning. But it didn't dampen spirits too much at Netscape during what became a spectacular autumn for the company. With the debut of Navigator 2.0 (which progressed from its first beta release to its final version between September of 1995 and January of 1996), Netscape took precisely the kind of overwhelming functional lead that it needed in order to dominate IE. Java content alone looked like it would provide Windows 95 users with plenty of reasons to do the unnatural deed. And the plug-in infrastructure looked just as promising, at least in the short term. Netscape's sales meanwhile skyrocketed. The company racked up over $20 million in revenues in the fiscal quarter ending in September while also logging its first profit. Sales jumped to over $40 million the following quarter, making Netscape the fastest-growing startup in the history of the software industry (with *not free* Navigators still accounting for the lion's share of revenues).

This beyond-expectations performance helped boost the company's share price over 100 points in slightly more than 100 days. Also fueling this advance was the press's growing infatuation with both Netscape and the great leveling power of its medium. In August, *Forbes*'s George Gilder anointed Marc as the New Bill Gates, and thundered that the "desktop imperium" of the PC industry's landed gentry would "pale and wither before the telecosmic amplitudes of the Internet." In December, a *Business Week* issue whose cover proclaimed that "The Web Changes Everything" (a quote borrowed from Neil Weintraut, the author of this book's Introduction), raised the same possibility, observing somewhat more soberly that "In the face of the Web. . . . the huge profits that Microsoft and Intel get by setting the standards don't look so safe." A few weeks later, *Time*'s covergeek was none other than New Bill Gates himself, barefoot and snarling, and hunkering down on a regal red velvet throne.

As the flashbulbs popped and the ticker surged, Netscape continued to fill out both its operations and its product line. Offices opened throughout Europe, licensees and distributors signed up in droves, and corporate head count swelled to almost a thousand people by January of 1996. The company also began making acquisitions, starting with Collabra (a creator of networked collaborative tools) in September. This and several subsequent transactions brought a number of new products into the company's portfolio. Several in-house development teams meanwhile continued to ship more and more homegrown products. The biggest of these (in code base if nothing else) were the commerce-enabling Integrated Applications, or I-Apps (later renamed the Commercial Applications). Four of these shipped during the spring, summer, and fall of 1995.

The I-Apps were first-draft attempts to create Internet businesses-in-a-box. Each was designed to market and sell goods or services, and also to provide an infrastructure for clearing online credit card transactions. Two of the first four I-Apps, the I-Store and the Merchant System, were designed to create cataloglike environments on the Web. These drew considerable promise from the Web's native strengths as a pulled information channel. Traditional mail-order marketing is of course pushed, and must bear the pushed channel's tremendous costs (which can get very steep when every miss involves dozens of full-color pages). These costs are not only onerous, but they limit the depth of marketing attention that products can receive. For instance, depicting a chair from 10 different angles and in 7 different dramatic settings might double its sales, but could also devour several catalog pages, and might therefore be an uneconomical method of promotion. The Web, however, constrains neither product lines nor marketing messages. An unlimited array of products can be stacked upon its shelf, and acres of marketing collateral can stand behind each of them. The Web can also (at least in theory) let merchants enlist rich elements like video and 3-D models in marketing their wares.

But despite its promise, cataloglike merchandising met with mixed results in the year following the I-Apps' release. One problem was that consumer Internet connections were not yet quick enough to allow for products to be perused as breezily as in traditional catalogs. Many of the Web's richest media elements (particularly high-resolution video) likewise could not be browsed impulsively, and therefore could not really be enlisted by online merchandisers. The catalog-oriented I-Apps therefore met with mixed results. The I-Store (which was designed to run stand-alone online stores) vanished without a trace a few months after its release. The Merchant System (which was more fully-featured than the I-Store, and also enabled the creation of multiple-vendor "malls") performed far better, winning such customers as the Discovery Channel and Travelocity (which is affiliated with American Airlines).

But the Web's most successful early merchants were ones who enlisted the medium's native advantages to create not mimicries of traditional catalogs, but unique businesses that could not exist elsewhere. A Seattle-based bookseller called Amazon.com, for instance, adopted the Web's infinite shelf space as a competitive weapon. The company deliberately set out to offer the world's largest selection of retail books, and was listing over 1.1 million titles by the fall of 1996. A catalog this extensive "would be the size of seven New York City phone books," its founder, Jeff Bezos, estimates, and a store with such a selection would be unimaginable, as the largest bookstore in the United States has only 170,000 titles under its roof. The power of Amazon.com's digital shelf also doesn't stop with its breadth, as it can paradoxically lie almost bare even as it offers customers an unrivaled array of choices since the company has no physical store to stock. This allows it to hold only a few hundred titles in stock at any one time, which lets it turn its inventory 150 times a year, 50 times faster than the average bookstore, Bezos says. The savings this brings enables the company to offer discounts on over 300,000 titles—hundreds (if not thousands) of times more titles than most bookstores discount—and helped the company become profitable a mere six months after opening for business in July of 1995. Aggressive prices also helped fuel its revenues to a rumored $17 million annual run-rate scarcely a year after its first sale.

Another powerful advantage that the Web has over catalogs is its ability to connect customers to one another. Bezos enlists this power by inviting his site's visitors to post reviews of books that they've read. Another company, Onsale Inc., enlists it by pitting its visitors against one another in bidding wars. Founded by former GO Corporation CEO Jerry Kaplan (Netscape marketing VP Mike Homer's onetime boss), Onsale conducts lively online auctions for computer equipment. Less than a year after the company's establishment in 1996, its Web site was drawing over 750,000 visitors and over 36,000 active bidders every week. Auctions were by then bringing in close to a half million dollars apiece, putting the company's revenues on a $45 million annual run-rate.

Merchants selling tangible, shippable goods like Onsale and Amazon.com were expected to ring up over a half billion dollars in sales in 1996, growing to over $6 billion annually by the end of the decade, according to Forrester Research. This should support a reasonable market for commerce-enabling tools, in which Netscape established an early toehold with the Merchant System. But Netscape will not dominate this market as it dominated the browser market. The Web's native commerce models are still quite unknown, and practices are evolving too rapidly for the market's needs to be wholly met with off-the-shelf products. The most successful online merchants have therefore tended to roll their own tools thus far, and will probably continue to do so for some time.

A somewhat more "standardized" tools market (in that there are already thousands of companies playing in it) and a very profitable one for Netscape from the beginning is online publishing. Netscape's Publishing System (another I-App) first shipped in the fall of 1995, and within a year was in the hands of over one hundred customers, according to Jim Sha, the vice president who oversaw the I-Apps' development. These included *The New York Times*, the *Los Angeles Times*, and the Chicago Board of Trade. The Publishing System is designed to archive and serve traditional published content, as well as to manage sales and subscription services. The market it serves is vast and growing rapidly, and few question its significance to the broader publishing community. Many have, however, questioned publishing's viability as an online *commerce* category. While hundreds of online publications partly support themselves with advertising (starting with HotWired—

see Chapters 5 and 7), relatively few have successfully charged for access to their content. An obvious problem with the paid-access model is that it is hard to charge for something that others give away (*Subscription fee? Guess I'll check the sports scores at one of the other 1864 newspapers. . . .*) This problem could prove to be endemic to retail publishers whose content has many ready substitutes.

But publishers of highly-differentiated, professionally-oriented content like research and financial analysis have long sustained subscription-based businesses on closed proprietary networks like Reuters and Bloomberg. And there is no reason why such content cannot also thrive on the open network, with its broader shelf and far wider reach. Boston-based Internet Securities is one company that decided to distribute its subscription-based information services exclusively over the Web. Its products consist mainly of financial information and business news from developing countries, and its client base includes traders, bankers, consultants, and other professionals throughout the world.

CEO Gary Mueller says that his company "never could have gotten started on a closed network like Bloomberg or Reuters, because we have always targeted a diverse clientele, and no closed network goes everywhere that we need to be. The entry hurdles that building our own network would have entailed were also insurmountable for a startup, because creating and maintaining a global network infrastructure is dizzyingly expensive." But with no real entry barriers, and with increasing penetration in the diverse professional markets that his company targets, the Web provided Mueller with an ideal business environment. His company logged roughly $1 million in billings in 1996, its second full year of operation, and counted over 200 clients, including Merrill Lynch, Morgan Stanley, and Fidelity Investments. Revenues were expected to grow to more than $5 million in 1997.

The power of online publishing lies partly in the fact that published products can be distributed as well as sold and marketed over the Web. Many other such product categories exist, and all stand to thrive in the digital channel because they can benefit so fully from its frictionless efficiency. When a product is wholly digital, not only can its specifications be pulled from the Web's shelf, but it can be too. And not only can it be marketed and sold at the customer's desktop, but it can be sampled and experienced there as well. Web-portable products include digital entertainment (online video gaming companies like Mpath are especially notable), financial services (including simple banking services and complex brokerage services, both of which are widespread on the

Web), information of all kinds, and computer software (see Chapter 8). They could soon also include audio entertainment (see Chapter 2), and perhaps even video entertainment (see Chapter 8).

As much promise as Web commerce appeared to hold, a far, far larger market was already emerging by the time the first I-Apps shipped. This was the internal Web, or *intranet* market. This market first became a major focus of Netscape's shortly after the company's inception, even though internal Webs were all but unheard of at the time. Marc first identified collaborative software giant Lotus as a potential competitor as early as mid-1994. The first pieces of Netscape product literature that appeared later that year were full of references to internal uses for Netscape software. And by the time of the IPO it was clear that however much of an *Internet company* Netscape in fact was, the lion's share of its revenue was already coming from intranets.

Like the Web itself, intranets caught on quickly because they enable the exchange of information in a uniquely open, intuitive, and cost-effective manner. This can be even more valuable within enterprises than on the open network, because coworkers on average have much more to tell one another than strangers on the Web. They also work within an economic context that can capture the full benefits of their collaboration, which creates strong incentives to invest in it. By the time the Web arose, the benefits of networked computing had already entered many white-collar offices through the spread of LANs and other networks (see above). But the earliest enterprise networks enabled only the most rudimentary sharing and swapping of information. Seeking to build on their unmined potential, a category of software called "groupware" emerged in the early 1990s. The runaway leader (and most important pioneer) of the groupware market was Lotus Notes. Notes enables its users to swap E-mail, synchronize calendars, share documents, access remote databases, and much more. By the summer of 1995 it was running on millions of corporate desktops, and had so enamored the market that IBM was moved to pay over $3.5 billion in cash to acquire its maker just a few weeks before Netscape's IPO.

But popular and powerful as they were, Notes and its lesser rivals (like Collabra Share, whose maker Netscape eventually acquired, and Microsoft's late market entry Exchange) had their drawbacks. They were expensive, for one thing (for a long time, Notes user licenses cost up to $300 each). They were also complicated, with big installations often requiring large, dedicated staffs to run them. And they were closed systems, which meant that buying into one consigned a company to having a single supplier for much of its information infrastructure (although this changed after the Web's rise, as all of the leading groupware packages started supporting open Internet-related standards).

For these reasons, Web technology started capturing the attention of innovative network administrators early on. It was certainly priced to sell, as even Netscape's *not free* Navigators were fire sale cheap compared to the per-seat licensing fees of groupware packages. The openness of the Web's standards and protocols meanwhile almost guaranteed that a competitive market of suppliers would exist. Web technology was also easy to administer, and astonishingly accessible to end users (who often found it easier to retrieve information from distant nations over the Web than from resources on their own corporate networks or even their own hard drives using traditional tools). Early intranets did not come close to supporting all of the sophisticated features that the more powerful groupware products offered. But only a small fraction of corporate PCs were groupware-enabled by the time Netscape started marketing the intranet (even market leader Notes had less than three million users by late 1995). And for those still experimenting with collaborative computing, an intranet could be implemented far more quickly and cheaply than any robust groupware solution.

The early intranets typically started out as the simplest of publishing tools. But even as mere shelves, many of them offered their makers tremendous value. Intranets made it possible for all manner of directories, manuals, and product specifications to be made universally and instantly available without incurring distribution or production costs. This could inevitably bring far more information into an enterprise's channel than would otherwise enter it. The Web's simplicity and openness also meant that communicating within a company no longer needed to require the intercession of editors or printers, as almost anybody could author and post a Web page. This allowed published information to reside much closer to its source, which inevitably made it far more accurate and also timely (as pushing out changes and updates no longer involved physical production and distribution channels).

The intranet's openness and decentralization also meant that decisions to invest in and to expand its content and infrastructure could be made at a very local level, where either formal or intuitive return on investment calculations could be made by those with the greatest amount of relevant information. Does it make sense, for example, to publish the details of a company's benefits program online? An intranet's open and decentralized architecture can allow the human resources department, which is on the firing line of requests for this information, decide for itself whether this makes sense, and do the publishing itself. Better choices are inevitably made when the same people make, fund, implement, and live with decisions.

The fact that intranet content creation and maintenance can happen largely on the periphery helped the companies that adopted intranets get tremendous leverage from the central resources that administered them. Silicon Graphics, for instance, integrates content from over a thousand servers scattered throughout dozens of countries into its intranet *Silicon Junction*. Thousands of author/publishers contribute to *Junction*, as well as perhaps a hundred people who could reasonably describe themselves as "Webmasters," according to Brett Monello, who manages the site. But despite the tremendous scope of the system he oversees, Monello needs only a team of five full-timers to coordinate all of its participants' efforts.

Powerful as intranet publishing is, early intranet administrators learned that some of their networks' greatest leverage could come from distributing databases rather than documents. Almost all corporate databases at the time, even ones with wide natural audiences, existed in isolation. This was typically because they needed to be accessed with expensive and highly specialized client software, which was only distributed to the people who were trained to use it and who needed it most. But intranets were able to free databases from their architectural isolation by acting as their brokers to the enterprise, much as Federal Express's Web site acts as the broker between its database and the rest of the world. For instance, one of the hundreds of database applications on *Silicon Junction* is Pole Vault, which allows Silicon Graphics' worldwide sales force to track the progress of their orders from the factory to their customers' doorsteps (among other things). To access the information that Pole Vault now distributes, sales representatives used to make time-consuming and (from the company's perspective) costly calls to an overworked order administration staff, which was forced to spend much of its productive time parroting requests and responses between databases and people in the field. But by distributing its databases to all of its employees instead of just small centralized staffs, Silicon Graphics was able to make everyone an operator, saving thousands of its employees a great deal of hassle and itself a great deal of expense. The company now has hundreds of database applications on its intranet that automate tasks ranging from the simple (e.g., signing up for company events or ordering marketing collateral) to the deeply involved (e.g., an electronic requisition system whose development budget yielded a tidy 1400 percent return on investment).

The rise of the early intranet helped power Netscape's astonishing performance throughout the second half of 1995. Many were soon forecasting that 1996 would be the year of the intranet, and that Netscape, which had so mastered the Internet, would ride this new wave deep into the lucrative heartland of the corporate market. The company's putative archrival Microsoft meanwhile had little more than its underfeatured me-too browser in its Web quiver. Many took this as evidence that the industry's most feared titan was lost in a hopeless net.muddle even as a new platform swept the industry that it supposedly dominated. Talk of *withering desktop imperiums* and comparisons to Kitty Hawk–era railroads abounded. In November, an influential analyst at Goldman Sachs went so far as to remove Microsoft's stock from the firm's Recommended List due largely to his concern about its lack of a compelling Internet strategy. Microsoft's market value plunged 7 percent, or over $2.5 billion, in the rout that followed.

By early December, the software giant was ready to put a stop to this. In a daylong session that dramatically coincided with Pearl Harbor Day (perhaps someone forgot that the *bad* guys had attacked then, in most American minds), the company outlined its Internet strategy for over 200 journalists and analysts. Chairman Gates proclaimed to the assembled that Microsoft was "hard-core about the Internet," and proved it by detailing his company's plans for attacking the market on every front. Internet Explorer would be better, faster, and *free*. It would soon run on Apple, Windows 3.1, and Windows NT machines. It would also include support for the potent Java language that had so captured the industry's imagination. The new Internet Information Server would meanwhile be *free* itself with the server version of Microsoft's increasingly popular Windows NT operating system. In this, the deep-pocketed giant would generously offer *free but free* products in precisely those markets in which Netscape made almost all of its money. Microsoft also announced a few other coming attractions (including a proxy server and a Merchant System competitor—neither of them free just yet) and some major strategic moves, including the deployment of its commercial online service, the Microsoft Network, toward the Web.

Marc's confident reaction to all of this was that "In a fight between a bear and alligator, what determines the victor is the terrain," and that Microsoft had just moved "onto our terrain." CEO Jim Barksdale's still more confident reaction was that—*Allah-u-akbar!*—"God is on our side." But not even this formidable backing was enough to re-assure all of Netscape's investors, and the company's stock plunged a sobering $28.75 immediately after Microsoft's Pearl Harbor Day *Banzai!* This still left Netscape trading at more than twice the value it had settled to at the end of its IPO day. But it was clear to all that Netscape's spectacular autumn in the sun—that heady time of 100-point/100-day stock surges, of do-no-wrong press coverage, and of nigh Web hegemony—had ended.

Still, none of this meant that it was time for the Netscape eulogies. Most of Microsoft's announcements were after all just announcements. Many of the promised products were still far from release, and Internet Explorer remained far behind the Navigator. Netscape was meanwhile anything but a sleeping *Arizona*. Anticipating price pressure from Microsoft in the server market (although not quite as much as it got), Netscape had already cut its prices dramatically in October (from $5000 and $1500 for the Commerce and Communications servers to $1495 and $495, respectively). And now that Microsoft had revealed its plans, Netscape had time to react before its dive-bombing *zeros* started blotting the skies.

One early step that Netscape took was to aggressively expand its partnerships and cooperative efforts. The company soon announced that it would collaborate with Apple Computer and publishing software giant Adobe Systems to improve Internet font technology; with credit card processing giant FDC (First Data Corporation) to improve Internet payment processing services; with design software giant Autodesk to "extend the Internet as a virtual engineering environment." Through these and many other cooperative moves, Netscape seemed to be indicating that while a small company alone might not be enough to beat Microsoft, an industry just might be.

Netscape entered into one of its most important partnerships in the spring of 1996, when it formed a joint venture called Actra Business Systems with General Electric Information Systems (GEIS). Actra grew out of the group responsible for creating Netscape's commerce-enabling I-Apps, and was formed to play in the business-to-business electronic commerce market. Several billion dollars' worth of this commerce was already flowing over electronic data interchange (EDI) networks every year by the time Actra was established. Jim Sha, who ran the I-Apps group, saw a huge opportunity in directing some of that commerce to the Web. He points out that "the Web's openness represents a great advantage over traditional EDI," because the value-added networks (or VANs) that traditionally provide EDI services all use different data protocols. This presents major interoperability issues. But the Web is a universal standard, and unlike a VAN, it doesn't impose high closed-network usage fees. Sha believes that using the Web for interbusiness commerce can also "tighten supply chains, enhancing intercompany productivity greatly," because procurement decisions made anywhere in a company with an intranet can be centralized, approved, and forwarded to Web-connected suppliers instantly and seamlessly. Sha largely drove Actra's development with GEIS (which is the leading provider of traditional EDI services) and became its founding CEO when it was formed in April of 1996.

As Netscape expanded its partnerships, it meanwhile redoubled, requintupled its own internal development efforts. Most of the company's new products targeted the burgeoning intranet market, from which it was generating well in excess of 70 percent of its revenues by the summer of 1996. The blue-chip list of Netscape intranet customers soon included Time Warner, Bank of America, *The New York Times*, Mobil, Johnson & Johnson, MasterCard, Lockheed Martin, and AT&T. The company's many intranet successes helped drive revenues to $130 million for the first half of the year, up over 700 percent from 1995, and then to $100 million in the third quarter of 1996 alone. The most ambitious intranet-related solution to ship during this time was a family of products called SuiteSpot. Announced in March of 1996, SuiteSpot gave customers access to roughly a half dozen different servers and some tools. Each SuiteSpot license entitled a buyer to activate five servers from a roster including Netscape's proxy, E-mail, and newsgroup servers, some directory and access-related servers, and the Enterprise Server, which had succeeded the old Commerce Server on the high end of Netscape's Web server line (this renaming itself being indicative of the company's new market priorities).

Around the time of SuiteSpot's debut, Netscape took an important step toward advancing its (and indeed everybody's) intranet story by announcing support for a new standard called LDAP (Lightweight Directory Access Protocol). LDAP is designed to help intranet administrators manage lists of network users and their access privileges centrally. Access control is important on intranets because all corporate networks contain information that not all employees should see. For instance, an HR person might be allowed to query certain compensation-related databases that are off-limits to finance people, who might themselves have access to general ledger files that are off-limits to everyone else. Without LDAP, every server and database on an intranet had to maintain its own list of network users and their access privileges. This was not only an administrative hassle, but it posed data security risks, as it is all but impossible to modify every relevant directory in a complex system whenever an employee switches jobs or departments. LDAP resolved these problems by decoupling directory services from the servers that access them. In other words, it made it possible for all of an employee's access rights to be stored in a central LDAP directory server that any other server in the enterprise could refer to. This makes it far easier for corporations to populate their intranets with secure as well as open information.

LDAP filled a key hole in the intranet story, as directory services are critical to almost any robust enterprise network, and are integral to groupware packages like Notes and Exchange. It also filled the hole in a way that further differentiated intranet technology from its proprietary rivals. Because while proprietary directories serve to lock corporations tightly to their vendors (replacing an installed directory is an agony that no MIS director would take on gladly), as an open standard, LDAP locks its users to no one. Companies that choose LDAP can later switch directory vendors without changing their network architecture. They can also buy the components that reference and tie to their LDAP directories from a variety of companies, instead of just one (e.g., they can buy their LDAP directory server from one vendor, their Web browsers from a second, their Web servers from a third, and their news group and E-mail servers from a fourth). This keeps the power in the buyer-vendor relationship on the buyer's side, which buyers of course find attractive.

Netscape rallied more than 40 other software vendors to join it in announcing support for LDAP in April of 1996. These included Novell, IBM/Lotus, and Banyan—the incumbents in the directory business. When Netscape's directory server entered beta testing a few months later, it became the first LDAP product to enter the market. But it was not to be the last, as by recruiting so many other software companies to the LDAP standard, Netscape ensured that its own products would face plenty of competition. This did not mean that recruiting those companies was a strategic mistake, however, as only the rise of a competitive supplier market could make LDAP a standard in more than name. And the intranet market to which Netscape had acquired such exposure urgently needed LDAP to be widely accepted.

In promoting LDAP in this manner, Netscape brought to the intranet a pattern that it had already established and refined on the Internet. It consists roughly of:

- Developing or identifying a standard that, if widely adopted, will advance the state of the medium.
- Recruiting partners to support that standard.
- Announcing the standard and publishing its specification, so that other companies can enter the market.
- Implementing products and solutions based on the standard within the resulting competitive market.

Netscape first followed a derivative of this pattern as early as October of 1994, when it released its first extensions to HTML. While these extensions (and the other sets that followed them) did briefly distinguish the company's products in the marketplace, they soon ceased to constitute a competitive advantage, as other vendors quickly adopted them. Netscape's hard experiences in promoting its Secure Sockets Layer technology eventually followed this pattern too, and in fact heavily influenced Netscape's refinement of it. In pursuing this model, Netscape has not suffered from a *not invented here* syndrome. The company did not, for instance, create the Java or VRML languages. But its support helped turn them into de facto industry standards that advanced the medium dramatically, and that other companies profited from as much as or more than Netscape (see Chapters 3 and 4). Netscape likewise did not create LDAP, which emerged from the University of Michigan.

In following this pattern, Netscape has pursued a strategy of standards-based competition that flies in the face of the industry's traditional rules of proprietary technology-based competition. The standards-based model welcomes rather than abhors the innovation of a competitive marketplace. Netscape has embraced this model in part because it views itself as having exposure to a medium, not a product. Anything that builds the medium, that extends its usefulness and popular relevance, is therefore good for the company. And nothing can build a medium faster than robust competition. Netscape is not the first company to follow this model. Silicon Graphics, for instance, followed something similar to it when it successfully promoted its OpenGL graphics library to the rest of the computer industry (see Chapter 4). But no other company has pursued it quite so singularly and as successfully as Netscape. This is partly because standards-based competition turned out to be a very natural model for the Internet, which has always run (albeit profitlessly) on open standards. In adopting and promoting LDAP as it did, Netscape therefore helped open the enterprise network to the Internet's rules of competition—rules that marshal the innovation of industries to challenge the proprietary bastions of powerful companies.

And by the time its first LDAP directory server released, Netscape had come to know quite a bit about squaring off against entrenched giants, because Microsoft, a company of some 20,000 people, had already made good on its months-old vow to reposition itself around the Internet ("There is not one product we have where it's not at the center," Chairman Gates told *BusinessWeek*). Its net.muddle now history, the company was pouring far more resources into its Internet efforts than Netscape could hope to match. Created just in February of 1996, its Internet Platform & Tools division already had more than 2500 employees by the end of the summer—more than all of the companies profiled in this book combined. One inevitable beneficiary of all this deep-pocketed zeal was Internet Explorer, which by spring looked ready to give the Navigator a serious run for its money. Both browsers were slated to complete the beta testing of their 3.0 versions in the summer.

Netscape entered the battle of the 3.0s in a strong position. In June it announced that the Navigator had reached an installed base of over 38 million users, making it "the world's most popular PC application." This gave the Navigator tremendous market share—over 85 percent according to some surveys. But by then the Windows 95 juggernaut was steamrollering across the world's desktops, swallowing them at a rate of millions per month, and IE was riding shotgun. Over 45 million copies of Windows 95 were expected to ship that year alone, bringing the operating system's installed base to over 65 million users by the year's end—far more than the Navigator's.

Microsoft had meanwhile closed a stunning series of distribution deals with online services and Internet access providers, beginning with America Online in March. Although a proprietary dial-up service, AOL had become an important Internet player in that many of its then five million subscribers used its online service as a gateway to the Web. As a result of its deal with Microsoft, AOL designated IE as the browser that subscribers would now use by default when they accessed the Web via its network. This was a major victory for Microsoft. It was also an astonishing victory, as AOL had just one day before designated the *Navigator* as its browser of choice. The goodie that apparently snatched the deal for Microsoft was its willingness to build easy AOL access into its all-conquering operating system, as well as to put an AOL icon next to the Microsoft Network icon on the Windows 95 desktop. Two days later, CompuServe, the number two online service, signed up with Internet Explorer as well, also gaining a berth on the Windows 95 express. AT&T's Internet access service was similarly favored several weeks later when it agreed to distribute IE to its more than 300,000 Internet access customers. The leading independent Internet service provider, NETCOM (with over 500,000 subscribers), soon followed AT&T's lead.

By the middle of the summer, Microsoft had reportedly signed up more than 2000 ISPs to distribute Internet Explorer. This meant that in addition to coaxing the swelling base of Windows 95 users through the unnatural act of evicting IE, Netscape now to worry about millions of online access customers as well. The overwhelming feature advantage that it had enjoyed over IE just a few months before had meanwhile largely vanished, as unlike its predecessor, Navigator 3.0 was not a paradigm-shattering piece of code. It did offer several worthy new features, include better Java support, better security, VRML access, and PC-to-PC telephony. But all of this had been around in one form or another for ages—several *months*, in some cases. IE had meanwhile matched almost every one of Navigator's features, and even now offered some unique goodies of its own, like ActiveX support (see Chapter 3).

By the time the battling 3.0s reached feature-complete beta releases, it was clear that the race was going to be a close one for Netscape—at best. CNET (see Chapter 8), one of the Web's most respected chroniclers and reviewers, in fact declared in July that IE was *juuust* a bit better than the Navigator in its then-current form. And while Netscape later marshaled a lengthy list of reasons why the Navigator actually ran circles around IE (*Navigator is faster. Navigator is smaller. Navigator provides greater security. Navigator is more than just a browser. Navigator is available for 16 platforms.*), none were especially unnatural act–inducing. For instance, Netscape clocked its own speed advantage over IE at 42 percent—significant, but meager compared to the 1000 percent advantage it claimed over Mosaic back in 1994. The fact that Navigator was almost two megabytes smaller than IE also mattered little in an age of gigabyte hard drives. And the fact that Navigator included E-mail capabilities was a serious *who cares* to Windows 95 users, who now got E-mail software along with all of the other little doodads in their operating system.

And besides, IE still offered that one killer feature that Netscape just couldn't match: its non-price. And that bargain price wasn't just being dangled before Windows 95 users; it would also be offered to Macintosh and Unix system users, once the Mac and Unix versions actually shipped. New computers loaded with the Windows NT operating system—over 24 million systems in 1997, by some estimates—would also of course get free copies of IE. And buyers of the server version of NT (which cost a few hundred dollars more than the baseline version) would get that free Web server as well. All of this meant that however much speedier, smaller, and securer the Navigator might be, the "One thing to remember about Microsoft," as Chairman Gates pointed out to the press, was that "We don't need to make any revenue from Internet software."

But unfortunately, Netscape did. This made squaring off against Microsoft—with its $8+ billion in 1996 revenues to Netscape's $300+ million, with its 20,000-ish employees to Netscape's 1000-ish, with its non-need to make money to Netscape's need—an uncomfortable proposition. And to many observers, it didn't look like an especially fair fight. In fact, it looked an awful lot like Microsoft was using its muscle as a large, established company with roughly $2 billion in *after-tax* profits to develop products at great expense (2500 talented people don't come cheap) that it was then giving away to snuff out a young competitor.

To this, Microsoft could counter that in the market that mattered most—Windows 95—IE was *just part of the operating system.* And there was ample precedent for little doodads like Web browsers slipping into the OS, as well as for companies occasionally getting stomped in the process. After all, Stac Electronics wasn't especially delighted when Windows picked up disk compression capabilities in 1993, clobbering the market for its Double Space product. Nor was WinFax developer Delrina bawling for joy when Windows figured out how to send and receive faxes on its own. Nor was cc:mail maker Lotus exactly passing around the cigars when E-mail software was integrated into Windows 95. But these and many other feather-ruffling capabilities had nevertheless been added to Windows over the years, and Windows users were better off for it.

The only problem with this line of reasoning was that IE was not just part of the operating system on Macintosh or Unix machines; yet

Microsoft was planning to firehose free copies of IE into those markets as well. And so while adding a memory management gizmo to Windows might be a bit like GM throwing in a radio with the purchase of a car, Microsoft's browser strategy was more like GM standing on street corners and handing out radios to every passing Hyundai, Lexus, and Pinto.

To this, Microsoft could counter that in the Mac, Unix, and Windows Not-95 markets, it was merely following the same strategy that Netscape had so dramatically demonstrated—that of giving away Web browsers to win market share. And this was a strong argument. Because whatever its de jure pricing policy was, Netscape had de facto given away millions of browsers to nonstudent, noneducator types since October of 1994. It in fact regularly pounded its chest about user bases that, if you believed them and did the math (*38 million times $49 . . .*), and compared the results to Netscape's since-inception revenues of just over $210 million, didn't quite square with the notion of a company pushing predominantly *not free* products.

But to this, Netscape could counter, *tell that to the judge.* And that's what it did. In August of 1996 the company's outside counsel revealed that he had sent a letter to the Department of Justice complaining of anticompetitive behavior on Microsoft's part. This allegedly included offering hardware vendors $3 discounts on Windows 95 in exchange for bundling Internet Explorer with their systems and effectively paying off Internet service providers to shun the Navigator. Microsoft's Web site was soon fuming indignantly about these "wild and irresponsible allegations that have no basis in law or fact," about this "transparent attempt to divert attention from our progress." But in late September, the Department of Justice launched an antitrust investigation of Microsoft's practices. This was of course a big preliminary victory for Netscape. But government inquests can take a long time. After all, the famous consent decree that Microsoft negotiated with the Department of Justice in July of 1994 started out as a Federal Trade Commission investigation in 1990. So however this investigation went, it was clear that Netscape would be left to its own devices for quite some time.

The IE juggernaut continued to roll forward throughout the latter half of 1996. In August, Microsoft effectively introduced a new, lower price for its browser—*freer than free!*—by paying a number of leading Web content providers (including ESPNET SportsZone and *The Wall Street Journal*) to give IE users free access to otherwise-*not free* content zones. Netscape then quickly secured for its users free subscriptions to media-rich mailings from CNET, HotWired, and others. But while the company effectively saw Microsoft's raise in doing this, it clearly had no interest in entering an all-out content bidding war with its deep-pocketed rival. By fall, IE's share of active browsers had crept up from practically nothing to over 20 percent by some estimates (although these varied, as most were based on traffic observed at single Web sites). From this it was clear that whatever came of the Department of Justice investigation, the days of the Navigator sitting securely on 85 percent of the world's Web-surfing desktops were probably over for good. Because even if Microsoft was eventually compelled to start charging for its browser, even if it was in fact forced to strip it from Windows 95 and its heirs, IE had already essentially caught up, and in scarily short order. And the engine of its catching up—those 2500 people in Microsoft's Internet Platform & Tools division—were here to stay, and no doubt to multiply.

But despite all of this, it was no more time to eulogize Netscape than it was on the day after Microsoft's Pearl Harbor Day *Banzai!* Because even if Microsoft could wrest most of Netscape's Internet market share away, and even if it could also drive every mil of revenue from the Internet market, the vast majority of Netscape's income was now coming from another market: that of the intranet. This market is expanding as fast as the Web itself did during its earliest breakneck days. Almost unheard of in the spring of 1995, intranets had reached 64 percent of Fortune 1000 companies by the fall of 1996, according to a survey by Forrester Research—and 32 percent more of those companies planned to build them. Credible forecasts anticipate a $10 billion intranet market at the end of the decade, and Marc says that he has his sights set on owning half of it.

The market, at least, will almost surely deliver on all bullish forecasts, because the economic logic of turning to a crowded pool of competitors for something as strategic as a corporate information infrastructure instead of a lone supplier is overwhelmingly powerful. So is the economic logic of handing responsibility for the publication and maintenance of information directly to the people who generate it. So is the economic logic of decentralizing the funding and development of the information and tools that reside on a corporate network.

The logic of openness is already driving as profound a shift in office automation as we have seen—one at least as profound as the shift from the mainframe to the client-server model which so roiled corporate computing in the late 1980s and early 1990s. It grows ever stronger as businesses couple their operations and information infrastructures more closely to one another's. This will happen more and more, as the benefits of making everyone an operator can grow truly vast when the empowered and empowering parties are businesses that deal with one another thousands of times a year. So-called extranets— intranet/Web site hybrids that give outside parties selective access to an enterprise's internal information—can enable this in an unmatchably robust manner. One hint of the power of extranets can be found at Cisco Systems, the $6 billion internetworking market leader. Through its Web site, Cisco gives its customers secure access to extraordinarily detailed information about their accounts and the products that they have on order. Customers can monitor the progress of their orders from the factory to the shipping bay, if they like. They can also make pricing inquiries (the site fields more than 15,000 of these per month), place orders, and buy and download software, among other things. Cisco chief information officer Pete Solvik estimates that his company's site was obviating 300,000 customer phone calls *per month* by the fall of 1996, calls that would otherwise have to be fielded by an expensive staff of operators and customer-support professionals. The site was also already generating over $30 million in monthly sales—a volume that Solvik expected to grow almost sixfold to a $2 billion annual run-rate by late 1997. Online ordering can be far more convenient for customers and if done right is far less expensive to process for vendors. All told, Solvik estimates that Cisco's Web presence was saving the company at least $250 million per year by late 1996.

Examples like Cisco's make clear the benefits of tighter coupling between the information systems of customers, suppliers, and partners. As these benefits become more widely known, demand for the open standards tools that enable this coupling of intranets over the Internet will boom. Netscape, with its broad intranet product line, is tremendously well-equipped to contest this market. Microsoft certainly is as well. But Microsoft has less strategic leeway here than it does in the stand-alone browser market. Pricing shell games only work if you already own a huge slice of the infrastructure to bundle *free but free* goodies onto. And Microsoft is nowhere near as dominant in enterprise network server software as it is in desktop software. So by meeting it here, Netscape removes much of its rival's home field advantage.

Microsoft will also have another matter competing for its attention as it meets Netscape on this far leveler ground—the hissing at the airlocks of the software industry's most powerful bastion franchise, its own operating system business. Extraordinary as it was, the company's lightning recentering alone did not eliminate the threat that the Internet's open standards pose to this bastion. With every passing month the Java language is becoming more widely used and robust. As this trend continues, increasingly powerful and diverse applications will come to treat all operating systems identically, inevitably eroding the advantages that Windows gains from the unparalleled diversity of applications that it now supports. Meanwhile, playback technology (e.g., that enabled by the plug-in architecture) and network access speeds are also improving, making Web content—which also treats all operating systems identically—increasingly lively, engaging, and useful. These trends together will encourage users to spend less and less of their computing time in proprietary operating system environments, and more and more of it in the context of the Web browser, or some other cross-platform Internet environment (e.g., those of the PointCast network or Marimba—see Chapter 3). As this happens, the OS's relevance to the end-user experience will inevitably diminish.

Microsoft took a bold step that could well hasten this process with the release of Internet Explorer 4.0, which it unveiled to the industry in late 1996. IE 4.0 was designed to be a portal not only to the Internet, but to the PC and its resources. It could browse through the hard drive's files and folders as easily as it could browse through a Web site, making it a desktop finder as well as a Web browser. In this, Microsoft strengthened the proposition that IE was an integral part of the OS, rather than just a land-grabbing adjunct to it. IE meanwhile became far better equipped to integrate the Internet's content and other resources with the Microsoft desktop. It did this through an infrastructure called "Active Themes."

Active Themes are thematic content channels, almost like cable channels. They draw their content from the Internet, storing some of it on the hard drive. This allows users to access their themes whether they are connected to the Internet or not. If a user is off-line, content can be summoned from the hard drive speedily. If a user is online, the hard drive's content can be augmented or updated with new information. For instance, a news theme might pump the day's stories into a user's hard drive when the user is online early in the morning. The user could then disconnect from the Internet and summon those stories at any time during the day. If the user remained online, the content in the hard drive might be augmented with a live news feed, which could display continuously like a ticker on the bottom of the computer screen.

Through Active Themes and its finderlike capabilities, IE 4.0 brought the "Web browser as platform" notion closer to reality than it had been before. It also heightened the power and value of the Windows operating environment by drawing the Internet closer to it. But in doing this, it opened the proprietary desktop's airlocks wider, and raised Microsoft's stakes in the browser war. Because if a rival browser could figure out how to mimic IE 4.0's functionality, losing a user to it would also mean losing much of the computer's user interface to a rival software company. And if that rival browser treated all operating systems equally, the Microsoft desktop could start looking and feeling remarkably similar to that of any other computing device. This meant that for users who happened to run mainly Java applications, and who also happened to turn to the Internet for entertainment and reference resources, the operating system could quickly become a *who cares* adjunct to their computing experiences, much as PC hardware had long ago become a *who cares* adjunct to Microsoft operating systems.

Another threat to the Windows franchise lay not in the leveling of the OS playing field, but in the wholesale obviation of the traditional PC by an increasingly functional and ubiquitous open network. It was partly with this in mind that Netscape established Navio Communications in August of 1996. Navio seeks to build operating systems for a new imagined class of simple, small, network-oriented computing devices that will turn to the Internet for connectivity and content. These could include TV set-top gaming systems, handheld communicator/schedulers, and E-mail–enabled telephones, among other things. Cheap and mass-market oriented, such devices could come to outnumber PCs if they catch on. In this they could give Navio's operating system an even bigger installed base than Windows. But Microsoft of course knows a thing or two about operating systems too, and is also eyeing this glittering *maybe* of a market—which, after all, could turn out to be a complete mirage. In this, Navio is perhaps little more than a long-shot bet. But it is a bet that might just have a remarkable payoff.

Netscape took a more here-and-now step toward bolstering its position with Microsoft with the announcement of its Communicator in October of 1996. Scheduled to ship in early 1997, this would be a full-blown piece of groupware in which the Navigator would be but one of many features. In addition to accessing the Web, the Communicator would let users send E-mail (as the Navigator already did), synchronize their calendars, and collaborate on word processing and spreadsheet documents. Tuned for the intranet—where most of the Navigator's revenues come from—the Communicator would effectively bundle features with the Navigator going far beyond the functions of a browser. In this, it appeared to have the potential to move the Navigator's revenue base to higher ground in the face of a rising tide of *Freer than Free!* Microsoft browsers.

However the battle between Netscape and Microsoft ultimately unfolds (and the market opportunities are vast enough that both parties are likely to do remarkably well), the battle between the old and new order is over. That battle ended when Microsoft, the old order's grand master, cast its lot with the new. It did this by reinventing itself with dazzling rapidity, and by turning its own hand to the airlock's crank at the walls of its PC operating system bastion. Now that those airlocks are open, there's no shutting them again—just as there will be no rehoisting of the barricades separating the old commercial online services, nor resequestering of the teensy inward-looking LANs. The hissing infiltration of the Internet's open protocols and rules of engagement has already shifted the competitive landscape of the technology industry beyond recognition. It has also given rise to one of the most dramatic successes in business history, and is building a network that will soon extend into every major organization in the world, fundamentally changing the way businesses, individuals, perhaps even nations, mind their affairs and deal with one another.

Looking back on all of this, Eric Bina recalls being "surprised, proud, and frightened in about that order" when he started realizing how *huuuuge* this was turning out to be. These days, he notes, "It is the fear that sticks with me. It is quite scary to think that just a couple people could influence so many without really intending to." Perhaps. Although it would be much scarier for the rest of us if he and Marc had actually set this all off on purpose. But perhaps the most sobering thought is this: The revolution—the boom in connectivity and capital formation that Tim Berners-Lee, Mosaic, and then Netscape touched off—is quite unstoppable, and is only just now gathering its very earliest momentum.

CHAPTER 2

ROB GLASER
Progressive Networks

Uniting Sound with Sites

In April of 1995, Progressive Networks of Seattle started drawing a great deal of interested traffic to its Web site. The company had just launched the beta program (or prerelease test) of its RealAudio System, which promised to bring *audio on demand* to the Internet. Delivering on this promise would mean giving a voice to a "media rich" medium that was, for most of its users, effectively mute. This was a lot for a tiny new company to take on. It also seemed that there was more to Progressive than this towering mandate. There was the company's name for one thing. *Progressive* Networks. What were they saying? There was its Web site for another, which featured all kinds of urgent copy about the company's, well . . . *progressive* principles (something-or-other about "social responsibility"; something-or-other else about "giving back to the community").

And then there was Progressive's neighborhood. This was Pioneer Square, a bustling and bohemian district not far from Seattle's financial district. Pioneer Square is said to be the original Skid Row. It was first named for the skid *road* that mill operator Henry Yesler built to funnel Washington's forests into lumberyards and furniture factories during America's industrialization. Long after the neighborhood reached its nadir (giving rise to the connotations its onetime name now has), local boosters rechristened it during a face-lift initiative. Some two decades later, the area's smartly restored buildings hum with life and commerce. Eclectic shops catering to map aficionados and book lovers flank the inevitable Starbuck's outlet (this is Seattle, after all). At night, high-ceilinged bars throb with bass lines and bluesy croons. But the square also has its share of rasping panhandlers, and can at times have an almost menacing edge.

Along with its offbeat name and feel-good Web site, Progressive's decision to locate here instead of in some suburban officeplex seemed to hint at a company staffed by low-key, bohemian Internet idealists. But Progressive's office in fact turned out to be an energy-charged place that felt more like a frantic trading floor than a Unix hippie hangout. Quarters were close, desks teetered with stacks of expensive technology, and the staffers seemed to be universally young, driven, and frenetically focused on their computer screens. The man in the middle of it all, with his almost military short black hair and his broad, black-bordered glasses, was furthermore anything but a hippie. This was Rob Glaser, Progressive's blur of a CEO. Almost everything about Rob in the office (particularly in those early days) said *hurry*. Almost everything that didn't said *business*. Put differently, a lot about Rob said *Microsoft*, where he had spent the first 10 years of his career. One of Rob's more distinctive fast-forward mannerisms (and there are a few) is this knack that he has for squeezing the contents of one-hour conversations into 10-minute chitchats; of 10-minute chitchats into elevator rides. This useful trick is said to be very Microsoft. It's certainly very Rob Glaser. But more than anything, it is *audio compression*. And this is appropriate, as audio compression is what Progressive Networks is all about.

Stated simply, digital compression involves the careful removal of data from a file so that it takes up less space. Fax machines compress and decompress data. So do many computer hard drives. If audio is to run over the Internet in a meaningful way, it too needs to be compressed. This is because CD-quality sound is built on 44,100 16-bit digital audio samples taken every second. All of those high-fidelity samples make CDs positively bloat with data; a standard one holds roughly 660 megabytes (close to the total hard drive capacity of most new PCs in the mid-90s, and far beyond that of most older systems). Pumping this much information through a consumer modem at top speed without interruptions (a nigh unimaginable feat over the Internet) could literally take days. For Web-based audio to be accessible to humble civilians on home PCs, it must therefore be made compact. And this is what Progressive's engineers have done.

Rob has likewise learned how to compress his own audio channel. At times he talks fast—real fast. His *compression algorithm* meanwhile removes extraneous detail from his content stream. This does not mean that Rob talks too much. Quick as the words tumble out and the ideas spring forth, he is also not a "fast talker" in the traditional sense. His words are well considered and their idea density is high. It's just that time is tight, life is short, and the less time Rob spends talking, the more he gets to read, to think, to build his business, and to watch the Mariners (a team he owns a small stake in) play ball.

By the time of RealAudio's debut, none of Rob's lieutenants had picked up his compression trick, but they were still a fast-moving crew. His vice president of marketing was Maria Cantwell. Before joining Progressive, she had been in Congress representing a district whose corporate constituents included Nintendo, Microsoft, and McCaw Cellular. There she endeared herself to many technologists by leading the charge against the hated "clipper chip" (a proposed technology that would have made it easier for the government to snoop on electronic communication). Rob got to know Maria through social and political circles before the Republican tide of 1994 took her out. He also knew that she had previously earned her private sector spurs in marketing and PR, and he needed some help in those areas. So he took her on as a consultant, and after a brief stint decided to make Congress's loss his gain and hired her on full-time.

Rob's vice president of software development was Phil Barrett. A bespectacled and mellow engineer, Phil will modestly tell visitors that he ran "a couple of product development teams" over at Microsoft before joining up with Rob. It turns out that two of these teams created Windows 3.0 and Windows 3.1, the releases that turned a me-too novelty into a famed and feared hegemon that wildfired across the world's desktops to claim tens of millions of users in the blink of a cursor and help bring Apple Computer to its knees. Phil is one of those engineers that you hate to spot on the far side of the field when you're staring down the other team. Back when RealAudio first released, his new team was still smallish by his standards—it included a little more than half of the company's 30-odd employees. But in their own domain, the products they were creating had the potential to be every bit as market-roiling as the ones that he had spearheaded at Microsoft.

Although it has been around since long before even Mosaic, digital audio over the Internet presented a questionable proposition to most listeners before Progressive came along. Traditional audio clips had to be wholly downloaded before they could be heard, and download times could exceed playback times by ratios of five to one or more. This meant that hearing a five-minute song or news clip could require at least 25 minutes of up-front thumb twiddling. Sound therefore couldn't be explored impulsively, like text or images. So although some technically savvy groups had been using the Internet to distribute audio for years, most people avoided browsing audio on the Web, finding it rather like getting radio by carrier pigeon.

Progressive Networks broke the Web's sound barrier by bringing it "streaming" audio. Its RealAudio files are impatient; they don't wait to be downloaded fully before they start playing. Instead they play as they stream in from the Internet. When a RealAudio clip is requested, there is only a brief delay as a small "buffer" of data representing a few seconds of sound is pooled on the user's computer. The selection starts playing immediately thereafter and (ideally) runs without interruption until it's over (and when it's over it's gone, leaving not a trace on the hard drive). This is possible because RealAudio files are very small. In its original lowest-bandwidth version, RealAudio needs only eight kilobits of data (one kilobyte) to represent a second of audio. This means that even somebody with an older 14.4 kilobits per second (kbps) modem and a good connection to a RealAudio server can draw in more than enough data to keep a sound file playing constantly once it starts.

The only problem with this is that 8 kbps sound files are by definition heavily compressed. CD-quality sound needs to be shrunk by a 176:1 ratio to squeeze into those dimensions, and as digital media files are squeezed, their fidelity inevitably suffers. As a result of this, RealAudio 1.0 has an echoey, squalling quality. But RealAudio 2.0, released only six months after RealAudio 1.0, can transmit entirely listenable music. And RealAudio 3.0, which released in the fall of 1996, can sound as good as or even better than broadcast FM radio. All of this has the potential to bring "radio into the next century," as Rob said on the day when RealAudio was first released. And this alone is enough to make Progressive Networks entirely *progressive*.

But there is more to Progressive's progressiveness—and certainly to Rob's—than RealAudio. For one thing, the company largely sustains a Web site called WebActive that serves as a clearinghouse for politically progressive interests on the Internet. Progressive's early-days home page rhetoric (which is now largely gone) was also a direct descendant of its earlier-days roots as a maybe-for-profit/kinda-for-profit vessel for Rob's technical and political interests. However, none of this has made today's

Progressive anything other than a dead-run startup intently focused on products, performance, and profitability, because its founder/CEO is at least as much of a businessman as a social idealist. Sincere as Rob's (and many of his employees') social idealism is, he has also decided to keep most of its outlets *out*side the office. These outlets are many. Among them are five not-for-profit boards that Rob sits on, including those of the Electronic Frontier Foundation (the online world's answer to the American Civil Liberties Union) and the publisher of *Mother Jones* magazine (the left-leaning chronicle of politics and exposé).

A busy balance of social involvement and technology has distinguished Rob's life at least since college, where he maintained a weekly newspaper column called "What's Left" (pun intended) while partly paying his bills by writing video games. But Rob traces the roots of these interests back further than that, to the town of Yonkers, New York, where he grew up with his parents and older sister just two blocks north of the Bronx. Significantly, Rob is the son of an entrepreneur; his father owned a small printing business. Also significantly, he is the son of a social worker; his mother worked for both nonprofit organizations and the city of New York for years. Hearing of her daily dramas attuned Rob to issues of poverty and social disadvantage at a young age. Her practice focused on helping inner-city children who were at risk. Rob still remembers "feeling, and her saying . . . that for every kid that they were able to help, they'd see twenty they couldn't reach." He admired his mother's work. But the thought of all those unreached kids often made him wonder if there might be a way "to have an impact that was more structural and more leveraged" than one-to-one involvement.

Rob got an early hint that skilled communication could pack a great deal of social leverage (although he might not have been thinking precisely those words) when he was in third grade. The revelation came not long after a field trip to nearby Inwood Park, which he and his classmates were dismayed to find littered and covered with graffiti. They were moved (perhaps with some adult encouragement) to write letters to the park commissioner. And "For whatever reason, the park commissioner wrote back," Rob recalls, "and it was the biggest thrill for me that among the letters that [he] quoted was mine." *Mine!* Impressed with this, Rob has kept up the letter-writing, the column-writing, and (eventually) the broadcasting ever since.

Rob's other standout area in grade school was math. He was always a few textbooks ahead of his classmates, and this eventually got him exiled for a few hours a week to a nearby high school, which had a computer. There the set-up was "the kind of thing where if you plugged the coffee pot into the same outlet the computer would crash," Rob recalls. So he was careful with the coffee pots, and his interest in technology blossomed. It blossomed further after he gained access to a far stabler system upon entering high school himself. This was the Fieldston School in the Bronx, which offered an Ethical Culture program ("Unitarianism with even less God," Rob says of this orientation). At Fieldston, Rob was "surrounded by people who were oriented toward ethical and philosophical issues, but didn't wrap them around a particular religious tenet." This environment inevitably pushed his own philosophical thinking in political directions. Fieldston also gave Rob his first chance to experiment with something that felt (at least faintly) like mass media: a "radio station" that he and some friends set up using the school's intercom system. In this, Rob cut his *realtime audio multicasting* teeth by piping Pink Floyd and Barry Manilow to the kids in the halls.

College was Yale, where Rob's media interests migrated to writing. His outlet was the *Yale Daily News* where he served as the editorial editor ("a very exhibitionist way to learn how to write fast") and maintained his "What's Left" column. He also pursued his political interests off the page by organizing The Campaign Against Militarism & the Draft in response to "the massive Reagan-era military buildup at the expense of social programs." Rob balanced this creative and social extracurricular life with a very quantitative course load. At the start of his freshman year he enrolled in an "early concentration math program" that had only a dozen nervous enlistees on its first day. In less than a week, this group was winnowed down to "five guys who knew each other from math camp" and Rob. Rob toughed it out for a semester and got the lowest grade in the class (which was fortunately an A). But by the holiday break he had determined that he wasn't so good at pure math that he "would be hurting society by not doing it," and decided to let his *early concentration* widen. He went on to study economics and computer science, and put any lingering questions about whether he was still an overachiever to rest by completing three degrees (a B.A., a B.S., and an M.A.) in the time that most people take to finish one.

As graduation approached in the spring of 1983, Rob did his share of agonizing about what to do next. A summer at IBM had already cured him of wanting to work for a large company. An intriguing experience in entrepreneurship had meanwhile piqued his interest in working for a startup, or at least a smaller company. This began about midway through college, when he and a half dozen friends appropriated one of the first PCs to enter the state of Connecticut. In no time they were writing commercial-grade games on it. The young scholars self-consciously called themselves Ivy Research, and went on to release Slynx and Viper, two racing snake games that gained national distribution through Computerland. The games sold well and got some nice reviews. But they didn't put anybody in a position to retire. And by graduation, everyone was ready to move on.

One day during Rob's senior year, Microsoft's cofounder Paul Allen came to town. His company was still relatively unknown. But Rob was very familiar with it, since his summer at IBM had coincided with the release of the first IBM PC, which ran on a Microsoft operating system. He signed up to interview and was soon offered a job, which he accepted largely because of the high caliber of Microsoft's people. "At a lot of places you interviewed," he remembers, "you'd meet one or two impressive people, and three or four kind of mediocre ones." But at Microsoft, everyone struck him as "incredibly smart and dedicated." So Rob signed up, figuring, "I'll do this a couple of years, and when it gets boring I'll do something else."

Microsoft had roughly 250 people and annual sales of around $50 million when Rob joined. After that it grew explosively—50–100 percent per year—throughout most of his career. This created an endless flow of challenge and opportunity for those who could keep up, and Rob kept up just fine. He started out by managing the company's relationships with some outside engineering teams that were helping it develop products. After about a year of that he was staffed to relaunch Microsoft Word, whose market share subsequently surged from "fifth or sixth place" to second. By 1987, Rob's responsibilities were touching on product planning for all of the company's application software.

Around that time his interest in "the nexus of computing and communications" was rising. So when he was invited to join Microsoft's networking group he accepted, despite some concerns about its deeply technical orientation. He spent two years there. Then in the summer of 1989 CEO Bill Gates put him onto a project in the then-new area of multimedia computing. At the time, IBM was moving to "legitimize the category" of multimedia-enabled personal computers (MPCs), much as it had done with standard PCs when it released its first product in 1981, Rob recalls. Rob's task was to help IBM develop the specification of an MPC that would include a CD-ROM drive, built-in audio, photo-realistic graphics, and other niceties.

This turned into a bad bureaucratic flashback of his summer with IBM eight years before. Rob recalls that what began as a $1500 product scheduled to ship in June of 1990 slipped and slipped until finally "shipping in the spring of '92 as a $6000 product that was totally irrelevant." Rob saw the writing on the wall long before this, and shifted his group's focus to creating a "virtual hardware spec." He later rallied 8 of the world's 10 leading PC manufacturers to support and build to this specification. The MPC project was a success. By the time it was over, Rob was Microsoft's vice president of multimedia and consumer systems, and a de facto direct report to Gates himself.

Exciting as all of this was, Rob grew restless as his 10th anniversary with Microsoft approached. He gradually realized that his "job satisfaction had gone down from 90 percent to 70 percent." And while this meant he was still pretty pleased with Microsoft, he had "kind of gotten spoiled" by his early years at the company, and he expected more from his job. Part of the problem was structural. His short-lived Ivy Research days had only whetted an entrepreneurial interest that he had had for years. And while Microsoft gave him many opportunities to act as an "intrapreneur," this just didn't compare to the real thing.

Things were also just more exciting back "when Microsoft was the David to the IBM Goliath." David had by now grown fiftyfold since Rob left Yale, and had traded in the old sling for a neutron bomb or 12. But however clear it may have been that Goliath was now signing the checks in Redmond, Rob didn't think his company had really acknowledged that. His boss certainly seemed to take the David fantasy rather seriously ("In [Gates's] mind's eye," Rob says, "Microsoft is still eight guys in a garage").

Another issue was that Rob was feeling the tug of his more public-sector interests. He had at least contributed money to some of his favorite causes and organizations while at Microsoft. But it had been years since he had thundered, pleaded, and cajoled in the college press. Since he had Campaigned Against Militarism & The Draft. For these reasons it seemed that maybe it was time to revisit some of his older beliefs. To read through some of his old columns. To maybe write to a park commissioner or two. So with mixed objectives and (perhaps) emotions, Rob left Microsoft in March of 1993. Gates wasn't happy about this. But he eventually understood that Rob needed to "up periscope" for reasons that had less to do with Microsoft than with himself (if it

weren't for the fact that Rob was barely past 30, they could have politely called it a midlife crisis). Rob spent a couple of months traveling,
first in Germany, then in Greece, finally in Egypt. Upon returning he
dove headlong into the not-for-profit world. But although he was soon
on the boards of several organizations that he believed in, a certain element of excitement and chance seemed to be missing from his days.

By summer he was trying to think of a way to bring his technical
and political interests together. He figured that there had to be some
leverage in such a combination, as it had long frustrated him that people who were "progressive in terms of world outlook" were "often
downright Luddite when it came time to use new technology, particularly communication technology." That backwardness contrasted dismayingly with the facility that televangelists and their ilk had developed
with new-ish mediums like cable TV. In response, Rob began toying
with the idea of "using interactive multimedia technology to create a—
think of it as a cable channel focused on politics and culture."

The notion of interactive television (ITV) was by then all the rage.
Many smug pundits were even viewing the PC as downright dowdy.
For his part, Rob was at first agnostic about whether to use ITV or the
PC as the medium for his half-formed vision. Then he encountered
Mosaic—a "total epiphany," he remembers. He almost immediately
concluded that "interactive TV was going to be stillborn," and that
"the whole mechanism that Mosaic had used to bootstrap itself, *A*,
was a big deal in its own right, and *B*, once established, itself could be
used as a bootstrapping mechanism for other stuff." That *other stuff*,
or rather some of it, turned out to be RealAudio.

Once he had settled upon the Web as his distribution vehicle, a
simple calculus of bandwidths and data rates drove Rob to focus on
audio. The then-standard 14.4 kbps modem was a claustrophobic tube
for any kind of media. Given that video can be well over a hundred
times the size of audio, Rob decided that dancing pixels would just
have to wait. The notion of creating his own *progressive* content was
soon lost in the excitement about creating the tools, the *media type*,
that would give the Web voice. Rob called a compression expert that
he knew from Microsoft days. Together they reckoned they could get
an intelligible audio signal through a 14.4 modem, resolve the latency
issues with buffering, and use the PC's horsepower to decompress the
signal in real time while managing the incoming data stream. The core
notions behind RealAudio were fixed in no time.

Rob started ramping up his company in the summer of 1994,

shortly after Netscape's incorporation. In June he hired Andy Sharpless to help manage its nuts-and-bolts operations. A Harvard-trained lawyer and McKinsey-bred consultant, Sharpless was the vice president of the Museum of Television and Radio in New York City when Rob met him through consumer-interest crusader Ralph Nader. Sharpless was truly a fish-in-water in Manhattan, and forsaking it for the distant and mellow Northwest was a real leap of faith for him. But luckily, he recalls, the "Watson, come here" moment (when the company's "working prototype" first truly worked) came just a few weeks after his own arrival, validating the plunge.

Before things really accelerated, Rob settled firmly on the notion that Progressive (which had been named and incorporated back when much was still undecided) would be a for-profit company. He did this because he knew that to keep up with the mandate he had settled on, employees were going to have to move fast and work hard. And at Microsoft, which had by then already minted thousands of millionaires, it was hard not to be "very impressed by the leverage you have by using the economic system in an effective way," Rob recalls. This meant that Progressive would be out to make a buck like any other company—but it did not mean that it would lack a conscience. Instead it would look to successes like The Body Shop, Working Assets, and Ben & Jerry's for examples of how profit motives and social agendas could be aligned.

Rob settled on Progressive's revenue model around the time of Sharpless's arrival. He decided that the company would give away its client, or end-user software (the RealAudio Player, as it is called), and the compression software that creates RealAudio files (the RealAudio Studio, later named the Encoder). But it would sell the software that served RealAudio files over the Internet (the RealAudio Server). Server prices would vary with the number of simultaneous users they could support. A server licensed to serve 100 simultaneous RealAudio signals, or *streams* (whose price eventually settled just north of $10,000, including upgrades and support) would of course cost substantially more than one licensed to support 20 (around $3000).

The genesis of Rob's decision to give away his client software lay in his decade on the (now) far side of Microsoft. There he learned that "if you make your business beholden to making money from initial-use client software," the result could easily be that "Microsoft would just sort of suck away your core business, either by putting a feature in Windows, or by aggregating a set of things like with Office," he recalls (Office bundled a word processor, a spreadsheet, and other tools into a single package). "And I'd say that happened with WordPerfect, and with Borland and with Lotus. And I was really struck by the fact that if you look at the long-term survivors against Microsoft—Novell, Oracle, even Intuit . . . they didn't try to make all their money on initial-use client software. They made their money on a mix of things."

So however similar Rob's business model might seem to be to Netscape's, it was in no way inspired by it. Rob indeed settled on it months before the Navigator even shipped. His model also represents an intriguing departure from Netscape's in that he built his company not around the Web as a whole, but around an extension to its look and feel, a useful and interesting *media type* that rides atop the Internet's protocols and operates seamlessly in the Web environment. His approach—evangelizing the client software to read his media type and selling tools to reach those people who acquire it—is now known loosely as the "plug-in business model."

The logic behind this model now amounts to conventional industry wisdom. But there was nothing conventional about it when Rob first arrived at it. Other companies, such as Macromedia (with Shockwave), Adobe (with Acrobat), and Silicon Graphics (with the first VRML browser), did start pursuing similar models at roughly the same time. But these were mature enterprises whose plug-ins (or "helper-apps," as they were known before Netscape specified its plug-in architecture; see Chapter 1) were extensions of their core technologies. In its pure-play focus on Internet media extension, Progressive was therefore unique. The mini "plug-in industry" that has since arisen now includes dozens of companies, and has helped the diversity of Web content expand with astonishing speed. While all of this could well have evolved without Progressive's early example, the company without question blazed a trail that has since become a thoroughfare.

RealAudio debuted on the Web on April 10, 1995, along with content from ABC News, National Public Radio (NPR), and others. Tiny Progressive was soon covered by such publications as *The New York Times*, *The Wall Street Journal*, and *The Economist*. *USA Today* characterized RealAudio as "The technology of the '20s [meeting] the technology of the '90s," while *Time* meanwhile assured the image-conscious that "Glaser's system is not just for geeks."

With its products now out, Progressive's imperative became to push its software's distribution. In this task the company had a classic chicken-and-egg hurdle to overcome, because while any Webmaster

could appreciate RealAudio's potential, most wanted to see a significant listener base before they would invest in it. Meanwhile, nothing
would inspire Web users to go through the trouble of downloading the
Player more than a big and alluring RealAudio content base. Making
the RealAudio Player free and easily available through download was
an essential first step to its proliferation. But for the Player to become
truly widespread through this channel, millions of people would first
have to become aware of it and then get excited enough about it to actively seek it out and acquire it. Engendering such high intent and involvement in a population as dispersed and diverse as the Web's would
not be easy, particularly before a big content base developed.

So long before the Player's debut, Rob identified the popular Web
browsers as potential vehicles for jump-starting its distribution. Most
of the Web's users were by then well into the habit of periodically
downloading new and more capable browsers as they became available. This meant that if the Player could be integrated into the next
crop of browsers (which was never more than a few months away), it
could become ubiquitous almost by default. Rob moved fast to clinch
deals. Within two days of RealAudio's launch, Progressive announced
that Microsoft, Spyglass, and Spry had agreed to distribute the Real-
Audio Player with their browser software. These were big wins for the
young company, as Spry and Spyglass were both still clinging to significant market share, and it didn't take a clairvoyant to know that Microsoft's browser would matter once it shipped (it was then still months
from release).

But potentially more helpful than all of these companies combined
at the time was Netscape, whose share of active browsers comfortably
exceeded 70 percent and was climbing. Progressive courted Netscape,
and in the end managed to cut a distribution deal with it too. But this
never got the Player much more than a berth in Netscape's Power Pack
(a collection of value-added software that relatively few Navigator
users purchased). A comprehensive Netscape distribution arrangement
could have made the Player all but ubiquitous. But in retrospect, Rob
says that not having one did not really hurt Progressive. For one thing,
it turns out that there are real benefits to distributing software directly,
as Progressive learns the names and E-mail addresses of every user
who downloads software from its site, making it easier for it to communicate with its user base and understand its composition.

People also proved to be surprisingly, almost shockingly, open to using the electronic distribution channel. Before the Player's initial beta test

period ended in July of 1995 more than two hundred thousand Players were already downloaded—a number that tripled over the next three months. The million-Player threshold was then crossed around the start of 1996, the 10 million mark astonishingly less than a year after that (in October of 1996). Progressive refined the RealAudio system continuously throughout this time. A live broadcast product suite was first demonstrated in September of 1995, when a Seattle Mariners–New York Yankees game was served up on ESPN's Web site, ESPNET SportsZone. ABC used the same technology a few days later to serve up the Web's first live news broadcasts (a historic event that was further dignified by the network's decision to devote them exclusively to the O. J. Simpson trial). RealAudio 2.0 was announced the following month. At 18 kbps, it ran at more than twice the data rate of its predecessor. This advance gave it far greater fidelity and brought a whole new stratum of content to RealAudio's realm. Vocal content (e.g., talk shows and newscasts) in RealAudio 1.0 was intelligible but hard on the ears. Echoey and flanged, it could grate after just a few minutes. Music in 1.0 was just not something that anyone would listen to for pleasure. But RealAudio 2.0 made immaculate use of its expanded data space. Progressive compared its fidelity to "mono FM quality." While this might have been a bit bullish, music in 2.0 can work in a pinch for anyone who grew up with a transistor radio or a vinyl Kiss album. Of course 18 kbps signals are beyond the reach of anybody using a 14.4 kbps modem, but RealAudio 2.0 was written for the expanding base of 28.8+ modems. And by the spring of 1996, a plurality of Internet connections (39 percent) were being made at that speed (versus 25.5 percent at 14.4 kbps, according to a survey endorsed by the World Wide Web consortium and others).

But it was RealAudio 3.0, which debuted in the fall of 1996, that started making the quality of Web-delivered music tolerable to all but the snootiest of audiophiles. RealAudio 3.0 runs at a variable data rate, but most connections are made at 20 kbps. At higher-bandwidth connections (which typically run over ISDN lines) its quality is literally indistinguishable from broadcast-grade sound. Progressive tested this proposition with a local classical music station called KING-FM shortly after 3.0's release. One afternoon during its heaviest "drive time" listening hours, KING-FM bravely shifted its broadcast source from its own studios to a RealAudio stream burrowing through the Internet from Progressive's headquarters on the far side of town. Apparently none of its thousands of listeners noticed the change, as no inquiring or complaining phone calls were logged.

As RealAudio's sound quality increased and its user population soared from six-, to seven-, to eight-digit tallies, the Web's base of RealAudio sites exploded into the thousands. Many sites simply used RealAudio to add narrations to their visual content. Unadventuresome as this may sound, vocal tracks can add real texture and personality to a site, helping it better connect with visitors. Many newscasters, led by ABC and NPR, also adopted RealAudio. Several news organizations that lacked traditional radio outlets, particularly technology-oriented ones (e.g., CNET and *PC Magazine*) meanwhile started creating their own daily feeds.

Putting content of the sort that already clutters the airwaves onto the Web may seem gratuitous. But the Web offers both broadcasters and listeners certain native advantages that terrestrial signals lack, certain of which can greatly broaden both the reach and usefulness of newscasts and other like content. Consider National Public Radio's Web site. NPR has been using RealAudio to post its popular "All Things Considered" program since the technology's debut. "ATC" is a long-format news program that examines the day's top stories in depth. It reaches legions of loyal listeners. But like all radio programs, ATC traditionally requires attendance of its audience at the time of broadcast. Miss the show when it airs, and she's gone, Jack. But RealAudio removes this constraint. Because once a show is "broadcast" (or posted) to the Web, listeners can access it at their leisure. They can tap into it as it is posted, or they can listen to it hours, days, even years later. This handy feat is sometimes referred to as "time-shifting."

Time-shifted content is not just a niche indulgence for technophiles. Stunning evidence of its popularity can be found in the multibillion-dollar VCR and video rental markets. VCR-enabled time-shifting now synchronizes millions of busy modern people with their favorite TV shows and movies every day. Master that mystifying digital timer and "Seinfeld" will always be waiting for you, no matter what time you come puffing home from the StairMaster. Miss Whoopi's latest in the cinemas and you'll find her at Blockbuster soon enough. Miss "All Things Considered" during the odd commute without a traffic snarl, and now that is accessible too.

Comparing the advantages of time-shifted and traditional broadcast is like comparing those of roadways and railways. Traditional broadcast can be reasonably compared to a train. It runs according to

posted schedules that its users consult. Someone interested in a particular itinerary has to get on at an appointed time. Like a train, broadcast derives efficiency by serving many users at once. Like a train,
broadcast is economically viable only to the extent that it can attract
large groups of people to its itineraries. And like a train, broadcast's
offerings are limited by its finite "shelf space." Broadcast's shelf is delimited by the number of channels in the spectrum. The train system's
shelf is delimited by its inventories of track and locomotives. Both
shelves are further delimited by the number of hours in the week.

Time-shifted media is more like a car. Its users can roam at will
without scheduling constraints or a programmer's arbitration. The selection of departure times is unlimited. The "shelf space" for destinations is virtually unlimited as well (any shop or home instead of a few
dozen train stations; an unlimited number of RealAudio sites instead
of a few dozen radio stations). But like a car, time-shifted media is not
wholly efficient. Infrastructural resources are used (be they roads or
bandwidth) whenever somebody goes out for a spin. This is not in itself a problem, provided that network resources are priced efficiently.
But if large groups of people start replicating precisely the same itineraries in their solitary cars, it can become a concern. This concern is
particularly relevant to the subject of real-time broadcasting over the
Web, as will be discussed.

By definition, live Web broadcasts forego the benefits of time-shifting. But they do a tremendous job of *place*-shifting. As mentioned,
Progressive sponsored the first live broadcast event in September of
1995. Countless content providers have since followed suit. Among
them have been many radio stations—more than 100 of them within a
year of the release of Progressive's live broadcast tools—that now
pump their broadcast signals through the Internet 24 hours a day.
Their number far exceeds the amount of "good [radio] signals you can
get in any major market" today, Rob points out. Some cynics have dismissed this small marvel by arguing that since the dial of any major
city is already packed with near-replicas of most of the stations now
crowding onto the Internet, RealAudio radio doesn't really offer anything novel or new. One response to this is that Internet broadcasts can
reach people where their radios are absent, such as in office buildings,
where PCs far outnumber radios. Another is that not all thinking people live in America's 10 largest radio markets. The Dakota steppes, the
Floridian swamps, and the hamlets of New England are now served by a
radio menu that rivals that of New York City. And while this broadcast

menu might not mean much in New York itself, it can sure be a big deal if you happen to live in Norfolk, Connecticut.

And interestingly, stations like WRRK, Pittsburgh; WBAL, Baltimore; and KNRK, Portland, Oregon, are now broadcasting live in Cairo, Warsaw, and Sydney as well. Staffers at Netcasting radio stations like these continually marvel at their signals' extravagant new reach. Peter Newman, program director at Seattle's KING-FM, has received mail from loyal listeners in Indonesia and Europe. Disc jockey Jeff K of Dallas alternative station KDGE has heard from a Jerusalem-based Texan who turns to his station to fight homesickness. KDGE now promotes itself (at home) with slogans like "Japan, are you ready to *rock*?"

Brent Alberts, the music director at KDGE sister station KZPS, compares all of this to a habit known as "DX-ing," which was popular in the heyday of AM radio. Late at night when the local stations dimmed their signals, Alberts recalls, "you could pick up the big guns like WLS in Chicago, and WABC in New York, and WOWO in Fort Wayne, and WBT in Charlotte anywhere in the country." There was a certain magic in "transporting yourself to a different place, in hearing what [was] going on" in distant and unknown towns, Alberts remembers. He now views Net broadcasts as "the DX-ing of the nineties." He believes that people will "put up with a lack of [sound] quality right now just for the thrill" of aurally connecting with faraway lands. And of course the geographies that today's DX-ers can access are far more diverse than Chicago, Fort Wayne, and Charlotte. Less than a year after the first live Internet broadcast, stations as varied as Commercial Radio Hong Kong; Radio X in Caligari, Italy; Radioactiva in Bogotá, Colombia; KISS-FM in Melbourne, Australia; and good ol' Rock 106 in Peoria, Illinois, were accessible to anyone with a PC, a good modem, and an Internet connection.

One ardent believer in the power of place-shifting is Mark Cuban, an entrepreneur with licenses to support over 10 thousand simultaneous RealAudio streams. He describes the mandate of his company, AudioNet, as "making the world a much smaller place" and providing "a cure for homesickness." Just a few months after its debut, AudioNet was already hosting dozens of radio stations. It was meanwhile sponsoring countless other live events, including sports broadcasts and talk shows. Cuban estimates that "on a Wednesday night during basketball season, we could have sixty events going on at one time" (this number would include his live radio feeds). Some of these events draw huge crowds. More than 32 thousand distinct listeners tuned in at least

briefly to AudioNet's broadcast of the 1996 Superbowl, Cuban estimates. His ambition is for AudioNet to support over a million simultaneous users by 1998.

Almost all of the early stations broadcasting on AudioNet and elsewhere on the Internet were simply redirecting the analog signals that
they already broadcast to their local communities. But the first Internet-
only stations also started cropping up as early as 1995. In November of
that year, two self-described "old radio guys" began broadcasting out
of Minneapolis as "NetRadio." Within six months of its debut, tens of
thousands of listeners from more than 70 countries had registered with
their service (and their total audience was probably a high multiple of
this, as listeners were not required to register). NetRadio was already
maintaining three discrete broadcast signals by then; a vintage rock format, a classical format, and an "emerging artists" format. Alternative
and country were soon added, and by the fall of 1996, NetRadio was
broadcasting over a dozen signals—a full radio dial in its own right—in
formats as diverse as Christian, Earth Beat, and Sports.

NetRadio cofounder Scott Borne points out that the Web offers
broadcasters a tremendous advantage by not requiring them to obtain
an FCC license. To him, this means "I don't have to fill out lots of pa-
perwork, it means I don't have to deal with government lawyers, it
means I don't have to worry about restrictions, and most importantly,
it means I don't have to pay $25 million for a piece of paper." This last
matter is of course not trivial. Metropolitan radio licenses have extravagant de facto prices because the shelf space for radio signals is local
spectrum, and that shelf is incredibly constrained. Borne notes that the
last Minneapolis station to sell before NetRadio's establishment went
for $22.5 million, less than 10 percent of which he estimates was for
its physical assets (the balance covered the scarcity value of its license).
This price was by no means a record, nor even atypical in the American market (radio auditor Arbitron ranks Minneapolis only 16th
among the country's largest radio markets). In industry jargon, "stick
value" is the value of a station's antenna or license. A "stick station" is
one whose total value barely exceeds that of its broadcasting rights. Industry analyst Richard Rosenstein of Goldman Sachs reports that a
New York–area stick station sold for $83.5 million in the fall of 1995,
another for $90 million in early 1996. The $250 thousand that Borne
and his partner spent on equipment during their startup phase was
pocket change by comparison.

Despite its advantages, Internet radio does have its detractors, and many of their complaints have concerned fidelity. But while it is true that early Internet broadcasts universally lacked the fidelity of clear radio signals, the same can be said of early *radio* broadcasts. Rob is fond of quoting the words of a journalist who wrote about the first live radio broadcast of an orchestra in November of 1921. "All that [came] out," he reported, "was grunts and groans and a strange crackling noise that the engineers kept referring to as *static*." From these humble beginnings we now have our thousands of high fidelity hit stations, rap stations, alternative stations, and even $90-million stick stations. The sound quality of RealAudio's broadcasts is likewise improving—far more quickly than that of terrestrial broadcasts ever improved. It is only a matter of time (and not very much of it; see below) before Internet broadcasts will sound at least as good as any traditional radio station.

So perhaps a more damning critique of today's Web broadcasts is that they are fundamentally "creatively challenged." Frank Catalano, an industry consultant and observer whose writing appears in such forums as *Windows World*, is among those who have leveled this charge. He maintains that "Internet vanity broadcasts may be nice for station owner egos or 'WKRP' wannabes without a real transmission tower. . . . But this is essentially audio shovelware, no better than dumping videos or books without interactive elements onto a CD-ROM or the Net." *Suck*, the Web's inimitable chronicler and critic (see Chapter 7), echoes this characterization, calling such broadcasts "shovelware with rabbit ears."

Shovelware is a marvelous term. It describes the brute grafting of one medium's native content onto another medium to which it is not native at all. And while the word obviously postdates the rise of digital media, shovelware has been with us for decades. Andy Sharpless, the New Yorker who has been with Rob since before his *Watson, come here* moment, gained an interesting historical perspective on this during his years at the Museum of Television and Radio. Today he is fond of the phrase "shooting the proscenium arch." The proscenium is the arch above a theatrical stage, and is as much a fixture in many early films as it is in physical theaters. This is because pioneering film directors often did little more than point a lone camera at actors on stage, then "shoot the play, but even show the proscenium arch, and show that [it was being performed] on a stage," Sharpless notes. If a Shakespearean text on a CD-ROM is shovelware, if KDGE on the Web is shovelware, then a single-camera shot of *Antigone*, proscenium arch and all, was certainly shovelware too.

The proscenium arch has many forms, and it lurks at the birth of all media. Early radio broadcasters whose announcers read directly from newspapers were shooting the proscenium arch. TV broadcasters who pointed their cameras at chitchatting radio announcers were shooting it as well. But the proscenium arch's day always passes quickly, as familiarity with a new medium grows, and content evolves in directions that its earliest pioneers could not have foreseen. This does not of course mean that those who shoot the proscenium arch are bumbling novices. They are rather pioneers, ones whose experiments are essential to whatever comes next. And even their most uninventive proscenium shots can create content with revolutionary power in its day. Consider what even the most shovelsome early *filmware* (to be very '90s) accomplished. Its forerunner was the play, a medium that required simultaneity of both time and place from its talent and audience. But the first movies of plays enabled place-shifting, a once-unimaginable feat. Millions, not hundreds, of people could now see an actress's finest moment in more venues than she could ever perform in personally. Film also enabled time-shifting. It may not have been Blockbuster, but even the earliest movies could fit with more people's schedules by offering more performances than even the most energetic repertory company.

In light of all this, it is unsurprising that the first directors were satisfied with just shooting the proscenium arch. After all, in the face of their new medium's raw power, a few close-ups would only have amounted to so much *who cares* icing on the cake. But however seduced they are by a new medium, audiences and producers alike quickly tire of raw demonstrations of its power (in the case of live RealAudio, *Suck* was yawning after seven months). Content then inevitably moves to the fore while the medium itself shuffles into the background. This can be a time of great excitement and creativity, which is what Sharpless, for one, finds so appealing about our moment. Speaking (figuratively) of RealAudio, he enthuses that "Nobody's figured out that you can do close-ups, nobody's figured out you can do out-of-sequence storytelling, nobody's figured that out you can do three-camera shots. . . . And that is the greatest and coolest thing about this medium."

So *cool* as digital DX-ing might be, the future of streaming audio on the Web inevitably lies somewhere beyond this, its proscenium. At this early stage, it is hard to know exactly what the medium's *three-camera shots* will turn out to be. But for now, the expanded shelf that the Web offers broadcasters alone should fuel enough unique output to sustain the newness of Internet broadcasting for years. There certainly is demand for something new, as the fact that radio dials are sold out in most of our cities does not indicate that local broadcast needs are being wholly met. It rather indicates the opposite: that the shelf is full, and if it could somehow expand, new content would rapidly fill the breach and connect with unserved listeners. Tight shelves tend to fill as they expand, because their expansion inevitably causes the cost of scarce shelf space to decline. In media, declining costs make smaller and smaller audiences economically interesting. Smaller audience sizes mean more audiences, and more audiences mean more diverse content.

The rise of the cable television industry demonstrated this phenomenon clearly. In the days before cable, TV's shelf could only hold a handful of stations, making shelf space costly—costly enough that a TV station catering exclusively to history buffs would have been a laughable notion. But in the 30-to-60-odd–channel cable environment, this format has proven to be surprisingly viable. Cable enabled the rise of niche content like the History Channel by expanding the shelf space available to it. It further enabled it by aggregating audiences from disparate areas. No single broadcast geography alone could sustain its own History Channel. But several hundred apparently can.

In radio, eight-digit stick values price out content that, like the History Channel, might be able to make it on a broader shelf. They also drive the content that does make it onto the shelf toward low common denominators. As NetRadio's Scott Borne notes, this is because "If you're a corporate radio station, you've got to spend twenty-five million dollars just to play. What are you going to do when it comes to recouping that money? You're gonna have to shoot for the broadest audience possible, which means you're not going to be able to service niche formats . . . [and] that's why all radio stations now sound the same." But this is not the case on the Web, where "if we want to do an all-Slovenian dance format, we can do that. We don't have to worry about making the twenty million dollars back on it. And if we want to do all Elvis all the time, we can do it, and if we've got a guy [who] sells straw hats and he wants us to build the barbershop-quartet radio network, we can do that too."

Uncommercial as it may sound, the future of broadcast audio on the Web lies more with the Slovenian dance format than with the me-too vintage rock-cast. Web broadcasters who offer choices that radio economics banish from the airwaves can (like the History Channel) create destinations, rather than shovelware novelties. And these destinations can pool audiences that have nowhere else to gather, either because they are too small to support a local station or because they are spread too thinly across the globe. If 30 thousand potential listeners is the minimum audience needed to sustain a broadcast presence (many rural radio stations make do with less), then any affinity or interest group with 30 thousand members worldwide could imaginably constitute a viable audience for an Internet radio station (particularly when wireless Web access becomes more widespread, making RealAudio signals accessible in cars, where most people do most of their radio listening). For this reason, Rob imagines that "basically any industry that has a trade publication will have its own Internet radio station" eventually.

For groups that don't find 24-hour signals to be economically sustainable, the Web grants broadcasters infinite flexibility to scale their programming hours downward. Groups can post an hour or so of fresh content per day (like "All Things Considered") or even just a few minutes per week. In this manner, even the smallest affinity group should be able to develop a nichecasted, time-shifted voice with which to reach its constituents and deepen their sense of connectedness. Smaller communities with strong ties of affiliation could be particularly drawn to this aspect of the medium. Places of worship might launch an explosion of nichecasting sites. So might kooks and zealots of all stripes. The typewriter gave us the Unabomber Manifesto. The Web might bring us Unabomber Radio.

Even groups that can afford 24-hour signals might ultimately find more concise programming to be a more efficient way of getting their messages across. CNET (see Chapter 8) is among the many computer industry chroniclers now offering daily audio briefings over the Web. Billed as "CNET Radio," these minutes-long newscasts are accessed by thousands worldwide. Posting them lets CNET make its headline stories available to listeners 24 hours a day. The company could also achieve this by going the CNN route, creating a 24-hour live news station that featured half-hourly news updates. But 24-hour formats are problematic when less than 24 hours of truly fresh content is created every day. They require that enormous amounts of creative energy be poured into maintaining the shelf lives of stories that have to be told and retold 18 times instead of just once. In this, perhaps the traditional 24-hour newscast is in an odd way shovelware itself. It seeks to offer benefits similar to those of time-shifted content (e.g., "the news you want is always available"). But its medium causes it to do this in an inefficient and imperfect way (e.g., a great deal of editorial attention is squandered on "fluffing" stories, and viewers can tune into the top stories only once every half hour or so, as opposed to at any moment they choose).

The Internet's ability to link disparate groups through highly targeted broadcasts could spark a rash of entrepreneurial activity. Desktop publishing made a flurry of highly-specialized publications viable by revolutionizing print production economics. Desktop broadcasting could spawn a similar outcome by revolutionizing broadcast distribution economics. Netcasting can also rid radio of free-rider economics, making ever more targeted specialized content economically viable. Traditional radio's ability to serve niche audiences is limited by its inability to collect subscription fees. A signal that needs 100 thousand listeners to draw a sustaining stream of ad revenues might get by on just 10 thousand listeners if all of them paid for access. The Web makes paid access possible, something that terrestrial broadcast has never done.

At the logical extreme of the nichecast is the pointcast, or the content stream crafted for and broadcast to an audience of one. A forerunner of this format can be found in Timecast, a free service that Progressive started offering on its Web site in the spring of 1996. Timecast users specify the RealAudio programs that they like to hear regularly (perhaps some mix of technology, sports, and world news). The system can then "drive" them through their personal mix whenever they like, launching from one program on the playlist to the next automatically. It is RealAudio's equivalent of a VCR that can play its owner's favorite programs in any order at any time without having been previously programmed to tape them (make that a *free* VCR that can do those things).

Music is particularly suitable for pointcasting. In this area, intelligent agenting technology coupled with point-to-point audio delivery could soon make the "personal DJ" an affordable mass-market item. No broker for starlets, Agents Inc. of Cambridge, Massachusetts, was a technology company started by several researchers at MIT's Media Lab and a Harvard Business School student in 1995. Now known as Firefly, the company develops a technology that purports to forecast a person's fondness for a musical artist (or a movie, or even a Web site) based on previously stated preferences and those of the general population.

For example, if you were to confide to the Firefly system that you were mad about Green Day, and if 98 percent of the other Green Day fans who used it before you also confessed to a weakness for Oasis, the system might suggest that you give Oasis a listen. The more preferences you log, the better the system can in theory predict your tastes. And the more people who use it, the better it can relate interest in one artist to interest in another. The company's CEO, Nick Grouf (the Harvard guy), has speculated that this technology could one day help pipe personalized mixes to firefly's users. These mixes could be advertiser-supported (now *that's* targeted marketing) or perhaps be funded with monthly fees. Whatever the revenue model, the days of *Me Radio* could be nigh.

But interestingly, there is no reason why the DJ in an Internet pointcast needs to be a computer, as sometimes we like to drive ourselves. We certainly do this when we *deejay* our own CDs at home. One of RealAudio's intriguing potentials is that of allowing us to do this over the network—without CDs. This practice could have tremendous economic ramifications for the music industry, because physical media like CDs are expensive to manufacture, truck, and stock on shelves. Physical shelf owners also need margin to cover their rent, heat, and (hopefully) profit. The result is a $15.99 price tag that draws as much for distribution and middlefolk as it does for talent and production. So what will happen when content can stream directly from artist to audience without the intercession of brokers and trucks? When it can be priced accordingly? When it can be purchased on a whim and accessed instantly, without a hasslesome, *ah-forget-it*-inducing drive downtown? It is easy to imagine that a fast Internet connection could one day become a fine substitute for a CD collection.

A number of things will have to happen first. Most obviously, fidelity and network bandwidth have to improve dramatically. But while this could take years, it won't take decades. Progressive's software development vice president Phil Barrett estimates that state-of-the-art compression technology can now "deliver content that is basically indistinguishable from CD [sound] by 95 percent of the population" at a data rate of roughly 128 kbps. He expects this figure to drop to 64 kbps by mid-1998. A rate of 64 kbps is not much faster than today's fastest analog modems. And digital ISDN service, which is widely available throughout much of the United States, can (at least notionally) support this speed. Cable modem and XDSL interests are meanwhile racing to provide consumers with much higher-capacity alternatives than this (see Chapter 8).

But faster Internet connections alone will not turn the Web into an infinite CD jukebox. An accessible end-user environment must also arise. People will want music delivered to their stereos, not to their computers. They will also need ways to manage lists of the music they have paid to access, and to summon it quickly. Certain system design questions will also need to be addressed. For instance, will purchased music download permanently to a customer's home and be stored there? Or will it rather stream in from the Net and play on request, like RealAudio? Either model could arise. Although if Web-based music is made as reliably available as, say, tap water, most listeners will probably no more clutter their hard drives with it than they would keep water towers on their porches.

A digital music distribution system would also raise many nontechnical issues. Rob, for one, believes that "getting the rights holders to get comfortable would probably be the bottleneck" to creating one. Ownership models will clearly be part of that discussion. Would listeners buy permanent rights to hear songs, as they do today with CDs? Would they instead be charged every time they accessed one? Or would they rather pay periodically to "subscribe" to an artist's output? These issues could prove to be even trickier than the technical ones. But despite that, it is easy to imagine a day when we will be able to select and draw high-fidelity sound from the Internet as quickly as we can pull a CD from the rack and insert it into a player. And when that day arrives, the need for physical media will fall into question. Rob believes that this will inevitably happen, although he thinks it could take "anywhere between two and twenty years," depending on ownership issues, payment models, and regulations concerning home Internet access.

The ramifications of all this could be devastating—or invigorating—for the corporate "Big Six" that dominate the music industry, as they are *distributors* as much as they are scouters and developers of talent. Tight shelves are of course good news for successful distributors, as they keep the competition *out*. And music shelves are tight all around. Radio, the shelf where customers sample product, is constricted by spectrum, homogenized formats, and the licensing economics described above. Shelf space in music stores is meanwhile as tight as it is in any retail environment. Through their muscle, relationships, and capital, the Big Six have created powerful (and expensive) distribution channels, and have conquered much of their industry's shelf. So what will happen when both channel and shelf are circumvented?

There will certainly be no shortage of content to fill the breach, as the musical world's creative capacity far exceeds its shelf space. For now this imbalance obliges artists to cross a high threshold before gaining a published voice. The height of this threshold is not driven by the public's tastes, nor even by production costs, but rather by the costs and constraints of distribution. In this environment, niche artists face the same problems as niche radio formats, in that drawing an interested audience is not enough; they need to draw an audience big enough to win them real estate on a hotly-contested shelf. An expansion of that shelf would therefore logically allow more artists to place themselves before their audiences. An infinite expansion of that shelf would almost certainly spark a renaissance of new voices flowering up from garages and street corners to connect with audiences so disparate as to have once been invisible. Musicians would clearly benefit from this. So would listeners, who would be spoiled by a once-unthinkable range of choice.

A big question, of course, is where will all of this leave the Big Six (and other middlefolk)? One answer is that they could well thrive, and end up in a similar, albeit probably diminished position to the one they occupy today, because even a digital distribution channel would need producers, promoters of talent, and arbiters of taste. Major labels that embrace the new channel (whatever its final form) could well leverage their capital and brand equity into roles like these within it. But those that particularly enjoy having the deck as stacked in their favor as it is now might reject the new channel, and fight to maintain the physical one. Such companies will invite the fate of the railroads. The railroads once had enough capital and managerial muscle to conquer any transportation market. But overly-enamored with the favorable status quo in their traditional markets, they stayed in them. These days, we buy most of our long-distance personal transportation from companies with names like "United" and "Delta."

For his part, Rob does not expect the major labels to suffer a fate as grim or as unanimous as the railroads'. He instead thinks that "ten years from now, one or two of [the majors] will have gotten ahead of this curve" to "grow their share, one or two of them will probably be treading water, one or two of them will have substantially shrunken share, and there may be one or two new record companies built around the new model that [have become] majors in a deeper way than is possible today." If Rob is correct, his one or two "ahead of the curve" majors may soon break away from the pack. But the most visible steps toward digital music distribution are for now being taken at the grassroots level. AudioNet, for instance, posts the work of scores of independent artists along with its live radio broadcasts, as well as the content of some "mini-major" labels like 4AD. This practice lets visitors sample an artist's work, often in its entirety. In some cases, pages are linked to artist home pages where the sampled CDs can be purchased directly.

"Try & Buy" marketing like this has proven to be very powerful in music stores that have equipped themselves with listening stations. It would seem logical that many customers would Buy more if they could Try in their homes or offices, rather than just at Tower—something that the Big Six could clearly profit enormously from. But as of this writing, none of them had really opened their catalogs to the Web. Some, like Warner Brothers, were posting selected new singles to their Web pages. Many others were permitting online music sellers to post brief excerpts of their songs. But in Rob's mind, such toe-in-the-water experiments amount to using the medium with "training wheels." And this is unfortunate, because "if you limit the customer experience too precipitously," he believes, "it's hard to really understand the true economics" of the system, and make an informed judgment of whether to embrace it.

It is hard to know where all of these new voices, digital distributions, personal DJs, and Try & Buyers will lead, although one pessimistic forecast might be to the *crash of the Internet*. The specter of such a collapse has been raised many times by industry observers including Bob Metcalfe. Metcalfe's credentials give pause to those who might prefer to dismiss his warnings with an eye roll, a chuckle, and a twirling finger to the temple. Metcalfe invented Ethernet, which underpins countless office networks today. He later founded 3Com, a company whose name is synonymous with "networking" in many circles (and is quite literally synonymous with "Candlestick Park" in many more, as to the lasting dismay of countless San Franciscans, the venerable ballpark recently sold its name to the highest bidder, and that bidder was 3Com. By then departed from the company, Metcalfe is blameless in the transaction, although he threatens that he is now "thinking of starting a new company named Candlestick Networks"). In his *Infoworld* column, Metcalfe has warned that "the Internet . . . will soon go spectacularly supernova," and, within a year, "catastrophically collapse." He identifies a number of bogeyitems behind his pessimism, including "the Internet's naive flat-rate business model" and a surge in high-bandwidth media traffic.

Patrick Naughton of Web content developer StarWave is one RealAudio user who shares Metcalfe's concerns. StarWave develops and manages popular sites like ESPNET SportsZone (which posts events like National Basketball Association games in RealAudio) and Mr. Showbiz, and Naughton is its chief technology officer. He came to StarWave from Sun Microsystems, where he was an originator of the revolutionary Java language (see Chapter 3). Naughton predicts that the Internet will crash not once, but several times, and "we will remember the dates just like we remember October [19th, the day of 1987's stock market crash]." He worries that "We're just gonna plain run out of bandwidth on the backbone, and the biggest culprit" in this is an imbalance between "the cost of a bit, the value of a bit, and the price of a bit." By Naughton's nomenclature, "the value is what do you get viscerally out of a bit, the price is how much are you paying to get that bit delivered to you, and the cost is how much did that OC-48 link from one city to another cost MCI to put [it] there."

Value can vary dramatically from one bit to the next. A packet with 64 bytes in it, Naughton points out, "can represent the stock prices of eight companies . . . or it could be somebody from NPR clearing their throat in RealAudio." However mellifluous NPR coughs may be, most of us would find far more to ponder in the stock quotes. But this fact is not reflected in the packets' pricing, as most people either do not pay directly for their Internet connections (i.e., their schools or employers pay), or they pay fixed monthly prices. This means that every incremental packet costs the average end user the same amount—which is to say, nothing.

As a result, end users lack incentives to restrict their packet consumption or (certainly) to steer it toward higher-value packets. But the costs of their innumerable Internet transmissions have to be borne by a very expensive network. A query to a stock quote server costs this network almost nothing, and can keep us amused or anguished for at least a few moments. But accessing a lengthy sound clip from a RealAudio server can involve thousands or millions of times as much data, and will inevitably deliver far less-than-proportionately valuable information. Despite this value gulf, there is no market force driving us toward the first type of exchange, creating a disequilibrium that could imperil the network.

Rob is aware of concerns like Metcalfe's and Naughton's, and is making big investments to allay them. One of these is a national "splitter" network that Progressive is developing to lighten the burden that live RealAudio broadcasts place on the Internet. This network should make it possible for a single RealAudio stream to reach not one, but several end users through a process of replication near the point of consumption. For instance, if 10 people in New York are listening to NetRadio's vintage rock station, a single stream should in theory be able to travel from Minneapolis to someplace near New York, hit a splitter, clone itself into 10, and then travel the last miles to its various destinations. Techniques like this are sometimes referred to as *multicasting*, and have become a hot topic in industry circles.

A multicasted RealAudio signal would clearly be easier on the network than 10 individual streams traveling the full Minneapolis–New York haul. The car/train analogy of media traffic is relevant here. Traditional broadcast media is like a train, in that it services many people taking the same itinerary at once. The Web gives its users carlike freedoms that no train can offer. But when many individual cars start following identical itineraries, finite public resources are squandered. Smog can result. Internets can crash. In building his splitter network, Rob is trying to enable a sort of digital carpooling for live broadcasts, which should help conservation efforts on the Net.

It should meanwhile heighten his product's value to broadcasters, because without multicasting, large live broadcast audiences are almost impossibly expensive to serve and maintain. Just 75 simultaneous RealAudio 2.0 signals can fill a T-1 line—a fairly fat and pricey pipe (depending on the market, T-1s can cost well upwards of $1000 per month, as well as thousands for installation). Servicing just a few thousand listeners without a splitter network could therefore require a broadcaster to maintain scores, or even hundreds of T-1s, which is far more bandwidth than most startups can afford. Multicasting will therefore become central to both cost- and bandwidth-efficiency as Netcasting leaves its proscenium days and becomes a mainstream medium. This is why Progressive is investing in it and is not alone in doing this. A competitor called Xing has been touting its own multicasting network since late 1995, and a little-known multicasting quadrant of the Internet called the MBone dates back long before Progressive's establishment. The MBone transports and multicasts audio and video signals, and is commonly used to host such gatherings as workshops, classroom courses, and meetings of the Internet Engineering Task Force (IETF). Its user base is still limited to a small and technically literate crowd. But the MBone could mature into an active and popular domain.

As Progressive develops its splitter network and otherwise builds for its medium's future, it will have to face down several direct competitive threats that have emerged in its category. RealAudio's more formidable rivals include Xing Technologies' StreamWorks system and the DSP Group's TrueSpeech technology. These companies each have their partisans and maintain well-regarded products. But Progressive got an enormous head start on both of them, and its tremendous marketing machine has helped widen its early lead. By the summer of 1996, RealAudio accounted for an extraordinary 85 percent share of the Web's audio content, according to industry chronicler *Web Week*. This indicates that Progressive will probably do just fine against its head-on competitors. But over the long haul, the company will probably face its most significant threats from far less predictable *side-on* competitors. Side-on competition is endemic to the Internet. It occurs when a (generally) larger company, fighting its own battles, expands its products' features in a way that encroaches on the functional space of an apparent noncompetitor.

Many early examples of side-on competition can be found in the Internet directory space (see Chapter 6). In competing with one another, search and directory services like Yahoo! and Lycos have added ancillary features to their sites like news feeds, stock quotes, and white- and yellow-pages services, thereby becoming significant competitors to sites that provide these information services exclusively. This does not mean that they are deliberately lunging for those smaller sites' revenues, or even that they count them among their "real" competition. It rather means that many markets and services lie in the strategic path of their competition with one another, and so do many companies that now have to learn to survive with some giants fishing in their waters.

Progressive encountered its first side-on competitor in July of 1996 when multimedia software giant Macromedia announced its own Web-based audio technology. Macromedia is the maker of a popular plug-in called "Shockwave" that plays multimedia titles. Like RealAudio, Shockwave arrived on the plug-in scene early. Also like RealAudio, it had drawn more than six million downloads by the time Macromedia announced that audio capabilities would be integrated with it. Macromedia tied no explicit revenue model to its audio software. Its files ran seamlessly within the Shockwave plug-in, which itself remained free. Shockwave's audio-serving software was likewise free, and was designed to run atop any ordinary Web-serving software. According to Ben Dillon, the company's sound products manager, Macromedia released its audio software in order to heighten Shockwave's popularity and to sell more licenses of the authoring tools associated with it.

Although the Macromedia system offered outstanding sound quality (it was superior to RealAudio 2.0, which at the time was Progressive's most advanced release) and a very competitive server price (*free*), Rob didn't regard it as a serious threat. For one thing, it was incapable of supporting both live events and multicasting, as these require a dedicated streaming server. RealAudio also more than caught up in sound quality just a few weeks later with the release of RealAudio 3.0.

But while its long-term competitive significance to RealAudio might be limited, Macromedia's entry to Progressive's market clearly demonstrated RealAudio's exposure to side-on competition. And over the long haul, Progressive's (and indeed, many companies') most serious side-on threats will not come from Macromedia, but from Internet software giants Netscape and Microsoft. The functionality of their browsers is expanding continuously, and it is inevitable that streaming audio interpreters will one day be as integral to them as VRML parsers, Java virtual machines, and their many other added-in features (Netscape in fact now integrates Macromedia's Shockwave with the Navigator, which means that it already has rival software on board). But while this could undermine the Player's position among Web users, it was not by accident that Rob chose not to base his revenue model on initial use client software. So even if the RealAudio Player is somehow usurped on both browser platforms, he will not have lost a nickel in sales.

A bigger worry is that Netscape or Microsoft might make a serious run on the server market, where Rob makes plenty of nickels. There have already been rumblings of this possibility (Netscape's SuiteSpot 3.0 is to offer an audio-capable "Media Server," and Microsoft has talked about building audio capabilities into Windows NT). But while Netscape and Microsoft are both huge compared to Progressive, they're busy enough with one another that neither is likely to put more resources into this market than Progressive's now 200-strong team. Rob also works hard to position himself as a partner, not competitor, to those two important companies. Microsoft is in fact one of Progressive's biggest customers. This, plus its crosstown location and the fact that Rob has 10 years of relationships to draw on there (including one with the Boss), makes it easy for him to keep the lines of communication and diplomacy open.

Rob also works closely with Netscape. In October of 1996, Progressive and Netscape announced the Real Time Streaming Protocol (RTSP) together, along with 36 other companies. Netscape and Progressive collaborated closely in RTSP's development and then presented it to other partners, including some standards bodies. RTSP will enable baseline interoperability between streaming media of all types, including audio, video, animations, and text (e.g., ticker tapes). It will make it easier to synchronize these media into coherent presentations or performances, and will allow for at least baseline interoperability between client and server software from different companies (e.g., if Xing released an RTSP-compliant server, the RealAudio Player would be able to decode its signal, although it probably wouldn't be able to interact with it as robustly as with a RealAudio server). Standards like RTSP make markets grow by making it less risky for new companies to enter them, or to create products that build upon them. RTSP will also make it easier for a RealAudio stream to act as the backbone and choreographer of elaborate multimedia creations. RealAudio was already being used in this manner before RTSP's announcement with a Netscape plug-in called Web Show (see below).

Despite the dramatic changes that its markets have gone through since the RealAudio system's debut, Progressive itself, or at least its ambiance, seems to have remained fairly constant. The company even hung onto its cheerful old brick and broad-windowed home on Pioneer Square well into the spring of 1996, when year-on-year quintupling finally forced a move to far more corporate digs. Rob, Phil Barrett, and Maria Cantwell still stand at the company's helm. They have been joined by several newer senior managers, including Bruce Jacobsen, who became Progressive's president and chief operating officer in February of 1996 (Rob remains CEO and chairman). Jacobsen spent many years at Microsoft, and had worked for Rob for two of them. Right before coming to Progressive he had served as chief operating officer at DreamWorks Interactive in Los Angeles. DreamWorks certainly has its share of sizzle, and Jacobsen was obviously playing an important role there. But Progressive's market promise and the opportunity to work for Rob again were enough to draw him back to Seattle—as was Seattle itself. Never crazy about the notion of raising his family in LA, Jacobsen claims that one of his tiny daughters adopted the phrase "do lunch," making it clear to all that the time had come to leave (although he points out that she still "lacks a lot of verbs," so this could have been a coincidence).

For his part, Rob seems as grounded in Seattle as a onetime New York lifer can be. He's married now. His parents have retired to his mother's native Northern California (his sister now lives there too).

His life also seems to have acquired a certain balance, one that perhaps eluded him at Microsoft. As noted, he keeps up with all five of his not-for-profit boards. He also keeps up with his Mariners, and there doesn't seem to be much of a chance of Rob leaving them. Despite his frantic schedule he makes it to most of the hometown games. These are played just a short stroll away from his office, and Rob strolls it five steps at a time. In the owner's box everyone knows him (surprise) and is clearly happy to see him. There, he can track the events on the field as closely as the boys in the press box, while maintaining a wide-ranging discussion on almost any topic.

Shift that topic to Progressive's future and Rob grows animated. Today, he absolutely sees its core focus remaining in the audio market. Streaming video could be an interesting follow-on product. But for now, Rob sees a real "impedance mismatch" between today's network and video services. Audio piped through a 28.8 modem is intelligible and useful, and can indeed be superior to the signals we tolerate in our cars. But real-time video over the Internet is often little more than a jerky, murky blob of pixels, and always falls far short of the standards we hold our TVs to. But this does not mean that Rob will ignore the video market. An idle reading of the tea leaves at his Web site (which has been known to host the odd help-wanted notice for video engineers) indicates as much.

More interesting to Rob and Progressive these days is the intranet market. Corporations with high-bandwidth networks can deploy denser media internally without inviting Metcalfe's *spectacular supernovas* or *catastrophic collapses*. This ability has helped Progressive do a great business inside the firewall. Rob estimates that 15–20 percent of his sales are intranet-related, and that this proportion will grow. He counted Boeing, Lucent, and NASA among his earlier intranet customers. Popular applications for RealAudio at those organizations have included training, internal communications, and presentations. This last category could itself become a growth area for Progressive. Rob has always viewed RealAudio as a potential backbone for synchronized multimedia environments. This vision is now a reality. At least one other plug-in (Web Show) can already use RealAudio to drive visuals on a computer screen. Others will likely follow.

New markets aside, Progressive of course has much to gain from tending to its core business. The Web continues to inhale the RealAudio product family, and the press continues to laud it. Progressive picked up several awards during RealAudio's first year, including the prestigious Outstanding Software Product of the Year Award at the 1996 Internet World show.

With such a successful core business, it is natural to wonder if the company might soon go public. Rob treats this subject delicately when it is raised, carefully detailing the pros and cons of such a move. One of his concerns is that an IPO could make it harder to attract top talent. It is one thing to get somebody's attention when you're offering pre-IPO stock options priced in pennies, but another thing entirely when you're offering options priced at the market rate, where they are already trading at a hundred times revenues. Rob himself once worked for a company that held off its IPO for years after it first became feasible. Microsoft's example must surely influence his own sensibilities today. Still, Progressive's market opportunity might demand the kind of capital that only an IPO could bring. After all, the transformation of industries as big as Radio does not come on the cheap.

This suggests the interesting question of what Progressive's rise might mean for the public valuation of other companies. Put differently, will Webcasting ultimately mean the demise of radio? Rob doesn't think so. He points out that the economics of one-to-many communication are "dramatically more favorable" over the radio waves than they are via the Net. Most radio listening is also not done at computers, but in cars and other settings where Web browsers are still rare (although they won't be forever; wireless Web service is already very popular in the San Francisco area and some other parts of the United States). But Rob does anticipate a "transformative event" when the signal clarity of Net-based audio exceeds that of FM radio. It is then that audiophiles will stop shuddering about sound quality and start adopting technology like Progressive's en masse. Rob believes this breakthrough will happen before or shortly after the end of the decade. Sometime afterward it could well become incumbent upon radio to reinvent itself. But Rob points out that if we can discern anything from radio's history, it is the medium's own profound "durability." He therefore has no fears for its future.

Rob falls into a brief silence that a Mariner kindly fills with the crack of a bat on a home-run ball. The crowd roars, the owner's box roars with it. For now, it's good to be here in the moment with all these un-time- and place-shifted thousands. Because powerful and enriching as the Web's shifting can be, the ideal of simultaneity still lies at the heart of all community.

CHAPTER 3

KIM POLESE
Java

Vitalizing the Web

For months the Marimbans were coming in so far below the radar that they had more to worry about from mine shafts than from radio towers. Nobody knew what their company was designing. Nobody knew where it was quartered. For a while, lots of people thought they knew its name ("it's *YAJSU*," insiders declared smugly, "for *Yet Another Java Start-Up*"). But then the name turned out to be a hoax, and nobody even knew that. The one thing everyone was clear on was *who they were*. Marimba was famous for being founded by four of the dozen-ish people who had shepherded the Java language from the red-ink obscurity of a Sun Microsystems skunk works into the limelight of the Internet's pantheon. By the time they left Sun to start their company in January of 1996, everybody in the industry certainly knew about Java. In just a few months on the public scene, the language had already been loaded onto over seven million computers (this tally would verge on 50 million by the year's end). It had meanwhile been licensed by over a dozen major companies that were building it into their products (these included IBM, AT&T, and Netscape). It had also been credited with much of a $4.5 billion surge in Sun's stock price, and was being heralded by many as the soul of the *next paradigm* in computing.

Java achieved all of this partly because the early Web had such a static feel. Few pre-Java Web sites did much more than spray pages onto the screen. Database links had turned some of them into powerful business applications (see Chapter 1). But they weren't exactly Hollywood. By early 1995, this had made the Web's early users hungry for something more. It made them ready for a Web that looked less like a televised pamphlet and more like *Terminator 2*. It made them ready for a Web that could *do* something—as the Web of their day could barely go *bleep*. It was into this sizzle-starved environment that Java exploded in the spring of 1995. It then became an instant sensation because it could do plenty. In fact, as a full-blown programming language Java can (in theory) do almost anything. It can play games. It can process words. It can balance checkbooks, run animations, analyze mutual funds, and even go *bleep*. Java applications (or "applets," as they were universally called early in the language's history) can also be embedded into Web pages as easily as images or lines of text. This means they can enliven, enlogic, or en*bleep*en Web sites in almost any imaginable way. And so as Java proliferated (along with several other technologies that appeared at roughly the same time; see Chapter 1), the once-static Web awakened. Countless sites started dancing with animations. Others became full-blown video games, while still others took on sober chores like tracking their visitors' stock portfolios. The early Java-powered Web may not have been as visceral as *Terminator 2*. But it was a lot more functional.

Significantly, it was also secure, because it is all but impossible for even the most malicious and brilliant of hackers to lace a Java program with viruses. It was also accessible, as Java can run on almost any computing platform. This means that Java applets that run on computers running the Windows 95 operating system can run just as well on Macintoshes, Unix workstations, or machines running Windows 3.1. They may also soon run on electronic datebooks, cellular telephones, and perhaps even toasters.

Java's security, cross-platform flexibility, and network friendliness led many industry sages to predict that it would roil the software industry's prevailing order much as the PC had roiled (and ultimately decimated) much of the mainframe's domain. If applications could really run equally well under all operating systems, the thinking went, the all-important operating system might become un-all-important. And if applications could really be summoned like Web pages, commercial software might stop shipping in a physical form altogether, and instead just breeze in from the Internet as needed to process words, balance checks, go *bleep*, and skedaddle. In such a model, software might be rented and discarded rather than owned and stored.

And if software wasn't stored, *who would need a hard drive?* Imaginations bored by years of evolutionary change (albeit fast evolutionary change) fired with speculations like these as Java fever gripped the technology industry.

Marimba's founders were in the midst of all this excitement from the outset. They were Kim Polese (ironically rhymes with *lazy*), the original Java product manager; Arthur Van Hoff, who wrote the second Java compiler; Sami Shaio, who along with Arthur prepared the language for its ubiquity-seizing integration with the Netscape Navigator; and Jonathan Payne, who wrote the first truly working version of the HotJava Web browser that demonstrated the language's Internet readiness. Together, Arthur, Sami, and Jonathan comprised roughly a quarter of Java's development team during its migration from the doomed foundries of interactive television to the Internet's booming frontier. And alone, Kim was Java's marketing department during its triumphant early limelit days in the spring, summer, and fall of 1995.

Kim's job required her to be one of Java's most polished explainers and promoters, and quickly turned her into one of its most public faces. She brought to her role a flair for making the complex and the obscure accessible, as well as a remarkable adeptness at broadcasting excitement along with some (face it) fairly dry information. Kim's Java was not just an *interpreted, object-oriented, multithreaded, garbage-collected, safe, and robust alternative to* C++ (although it was all of those things, and she could explain each of them in whatever detail her audience could bear). It was also *invisible technology.* It was *magic!* It was LIKE SCIENCE FICTION!!! It was an edge-of-your-seat combination of *Disneyland! memory management! string handling! and MTV!* Explaining all of this, she was liable to light up like a missionary remembering a particularly tough convert. Eyes would sparkle, words would tumble quickly, hands would weave and endanger tall glasses.

The public exposure that she and her cofounders received during the early Java boom helped make Marimba a high-profile startup from the outset. Its formation was noted in publications like *USA Today* and *The Wall Street Journal.* The *Journal* even speculated that the company's establishment triggered a $600-million slide in Sun's market value (see below). But dramatic as it was, the Marimbans had little time to revel in the attention that their company drew, as they had a full agenda. They needed to establish their company's product direction. They also had to refine its technical philosophy and ordain its strategic imperatives. In short, they had to figure out *what the hell they were going to do*, now that they had a (still nameless) company, a teensy office, and some business cards (Kim's own card said little but *Java Entrepreneur* for months). So after a final smile and wave on their way out the door at Sun, they vanished.

Rumors were rife for weeks. Some said the company was writing networked video games (it wasn't). Others speculated that its phone number was *something-something-something*-JAVA (it was). Marimba's founders meanwhile set up shop in a tiny Palo Alto office that a stationery store had been using as a warehouse (or *warecloset*, more accurately). Their new building was ironically situated across the street from a bustling café called Java Centrale. It was no less ironically situated next door to a Mexican eatery called Taqueria Ole ("OLE" was the predecessor of Microsoft's ActiveX technology, which many view as a Java competitor). Inside, the ex-warecloset was spare to the point of hilarity. There was almost no furniture, and, for a while, no phones. Once the company finally got dial tones, its incoming faxes fluttered leafily to the floor for months for want of a shelf.

For a while the Marimbans watched the fax machine's tiny autumn, thought, and planned. It took some time for their company to cohere. But eventually (after a briefly harrowing course adjustment) they had a product strategy, one aimed at fundamentally heightening Java's relevance and power. Not long after that they had a name. And not long after that they had a CEO, in Kim. This job fell to her for several reasons. Although technically trained, she had been working in marketing for several years. This balanced out her background with business experiences that her more wholly-technical cofounders didn't have. The CEO role is also a very public one, and her work on the Java team had given her a great deal of exposure to customers, analysts, and the press. Her networks within these groups, combined with her now-polished facility at *evangelizing* technology, seemed to make her an ideal emissary to investors and the rest of the outside world. For these and other reasons, Kim stopped being a *Java Entrepreneur* in the summer of 1996, and became a *President and CEO*.

Kim traces the passion for technology that started her on the path to all of this back to her hometown of Berkeley, California. The Berkeley of her early childhood is now remembered as a breeding ground for young radicals, not as a hotbed of budding *Java Entrepreneurs*. But it was a diverse community with diverse resources, and among them was a center called the Lawrence Hall of Science. Kim first visited that airy institute as an overly-energized sixth grader with an insatiable interest in roughly everything. She found it to be "a beautiful place with an amazing view," she remembers, hands weaving and words starting to tumble. "I started going up there, and they had computers, and a lab, and I started playing on the computers, and I had a lot of *fun*, and I was fascinated." Kim quickly became a Lawrence Hall regular. But she had other haunts, and many other hobbies. These included clarinet, tennis, swimming, cross-country running, and piano. When she was 14 she added dancing lessons to all of this. Years later, when the demands of school and then work inevitably pared her roster of passions and activities down, it was dance that, with technology, remained in her life.

Kim's home was as multinational as her famously diverse hometown was multicultural. Her father is from Italy, her mother is from Denmark, and she and her older brother were always wholly Californian in outlook. Kim is close to her brother, who, she laughs, "was supposed to be the engineer." But *he* became the artist, a pianist. And as early as high school, Kim began to suspect that not only might she become an engineer, but that she might become an entrepreneur as well. This notion first came to her shortly after her father opened his own machine shop (before that he had worked for General Electric). Kim recalls that he loved the independence this brought him. Perhaps coincidentally (she's not really sure) she soon found herself thinking about someday starting her own company too. Exactly what that company would do "was secondary to me," she remembers, but just "the idea of having my own company was so appealing, because of the creative aspect of it."

College was the internationally respected yet conveniently local University of California at Berkeley. Kim at first lived at home, then eventually found her own place all of five miles away ("call it the gypsy in me," she laughs about the big move). She continued to dance in college. She even thought seriously about turning professional. But then a troublesome Achilles tendon teamed up with a growing interest in technology to turn her focus "to this computer stuff." Much of her involvement in computing at the time was still through the Lawrence Hall of Science. She began to teach programming there early in college, and found that she loved "explaining and deciphering technology, and communicating my passion for technology." This propensity inspired her to start a tutoring program that taught local fifth, sixth, and seventh graders about computers and how to use them. She recruited several other students to help her, and eventually had every middle school in town covered.

Despite her interest in technology, Kim's undergraduate curriculum focused on natural rather than computer sciences. She even came close to applying to medical schools as graduation neared. But in the end she decided that this "looked like this huge long haul of ridiculous hours of years and years and years, and it just didn't look that fun." So instead of taking the Medical College Admission Test (MCAT), she signed up for a year of study in the University of Washington's computer science department (she had spent too much time in the biochem labs to learn her fill about programming). It was a fun year and she liked Seattle. But by the end of it she had had enough of this living abroad thing; she missed the Bay Area. So when the summer came she went home, and soon found a job with a company called Intellicorp in Mountain View.

Intellicorp specialized in artificial intelligence technology, and at the time (1985), AI was in its heyday. The companies pioneering it were awash with money from government contracts and deep-pocketed corporations that weren't sure what AI was, but knew they wanted *in*. This made for some workplaces that were as lush as they were stimulating. Intellicorp was one of those, and Kim remembers her stint there as "just an amazing first job." The high-flying company had "hot tubs, and cappuccino machines, and parties every Friday. It was just wonderful. It was like being in college, because everyone was really focused on the technology and how *cool* it was. Technology for technology's sake. That was cool, and for a lot of us the focus was not so much on products as it was on building the best rule system in the world, with every possible theoretical feature you could possibly put into it, because [it was] this beautiful work of art and research." Clearly, this couldn't last.

And it didn't. After a few years "it started not feeling like it was going to go so well," Kim recalls, and she began to look around. One of the first places she checked out was Sun Microsystems, which at the time was "the last hurrah of AI," she remembers, "the final frontier." Sun was the leading maker of high-powered Unix workstations and servers (see Chapter 1), and a lot of AI companies were then moving their software onto Sun systems to shed their own staggeringly expensive proprietary hardware. Sun was quite involved in this process, and this gave Kim an entrée to the company. She soon found that it met several of her criteria for a workplace in that "it was a lot of fun," and had "lots of smart people [and] lots of good energy." So in 1989 she took a post in its technical support group (she had worked in a similar position at Intellicorp). She was immediately delighted with her new employer. But eventually she found the job itself to be "depressing," she recalls. It didn't stretch her, and it felt like it fell far from Sun's mainstream. So when she heard about a job opening in marketing she decided to investigate. Kim had not thought seriously about marketing before that. But "product managers seemed to have a lot of fun," she remembers, "and they had a lot of responsibility for the destiny of the product. You got to decide a lot. It was very creative, and it just looked like a really interesting job."

And it was. Kim became the product manager for Sun's C++ programming tools at a time when C++ was an incredibly hot programming language. She found this to be at least as exciting as Intellicorp during the AI boom. Product management also rekindled her enthusiasm for entrepreneurship, because it was "like running your own company," she remembers. "You get to decide every aspect of the product. You get to stay technical, especially with a product like C++. The programming language is highly technical, so you get to keep your chops working. But the other parts are equally fascinating, like branding, the packaging. What should the product be called? What should the box be . . . ? What should the logo be, if there's a logo?" Kim remained a product manager for almost three years, and the job was always a challenge. But after a while it started to seem that she had learned most of what it had to teach her. She also became interested in applying her new skills in a small-company setting. Around the same time she started getting her first headhunter calls, and she took at least one of them seriously.

But then she saw *Oak*.

Kim encountered Oak through Patrick Naughton, one of its progenitors. She met him at a Sun VP-director conference in Monterey. Fairly clubby closed-door affairs, these were generally off-limits to mortals like her. But she got through the gate as a *demo jockey*, or displayer and explainer of technology. She was there showing off Helix, her new development environment. Naughton, who was demo-jockeying himself, was showing off . . . well, it was unclear. Naughton was from First Person, an intensely secretive Sun spin-off headquartered in Palo Alto's posh University Avenue area. First Person was so hush-hush, was so disdainfully aloof from its corporate parent, that mere Sun employees had to sign nondisclosure agreements just to hear about its products—and few were even handed the pen. Kim and Naughton were assigned to demo-jockey in the same room. They met, hung out, talked some Helix. Eventually Naughton spilled the beans, and told Kim all about Oak, the language that would one day be called Java. The Lawrence Hall nerd in Kim was immediately blown away. "It was like, 'You're *kid*ding!' " she remembers. "*No* language could have all those things, and be *so* small, be *so* compact, be *so* elegant, be *so* simple, be multi-threaded *and* garbage-collected, robust *and* secure, and platform independent! It's *not possible*!" Oh, but it was. And Naughton showed her *7 (or *star-seven*, as it was pronounced) to prove it.

*7 and Oak traced their roots back far before the VP-director conference, far before First Person even, to a rather blistering E-mail that Naughton once sent to Scott McNealy, Sun's no-nonsense CEO. Naughton knew McNealy reasonably well because they played hockey on the same team. One day in 1990, he informed his teammate (and boss's boss's boss's boss's boss) that he was leaving Sun. Naughton was just a few years out of college at that point, a youthful speck in a company with over 10 thousand employees. But McNealy thought well of him and hated to see him go. So he asked Naughton to send him an E-mail detailing his reasons for leaving, his complaints about Sun, and his suggestions for redressing them. Naughton was not one to demurely withhold his opinion. So he rattled out a few thousand candid words and sent them off (it was "the usual sort of thing when someone is terminally pissed off," recalls a senior engineer who read it shortly thereafter). Naughton wasn't just fuming—he made some astute points—and McNealy took them seriously enough to forward them on to his management team. A frenetic series of group E-mailings and brainstorming sessions soon followed. Several electrifying ideas about what Sun could or should be doing differently fell out of them. In the end, senior management decided to give Naughton and some other well-regarded malcontents enough funding to stomp off and pursue some of their wilder blue-sky notions more or less as they saw fit.

The group that formed around this attractive mandate came to be known as the Green team. Its most prominent member was a gentle genius named James Gosling, who had been one of Sun's best-regarded engineers for years. Gosling's most recent major project had been the ill-fated NeWS system, a powerful window-based interface for the Unix operating system. By most accounts, NeWS was technically superior to a standard called "X" that Sun's Unix rivals had united to promote against it. This and the fact that Sun held a dominant position in the Unix market had given NeWS some real weight.

But even dominant players with superior technology can have a hard time pushing a standard against an entire industry. NeWS's position was also severely undermined by Sun's famously hapless efforts to arrive at its business model. Jonathan Payne, a NeWS engineer, Green team member, and Marimba founder, recalls that Sun "insisted on [NeWS] being this proprietary thing that they sell for large quantities of money, and they only halfheartedly supported it, and all sorts of bad things happened. It was just a dismal failure. And even at the end, they said, 'OK, look. The only thing that we can do to make NeWS work is to give it away for free. . . .' [And] what they did was, they gave it away for 'free' for $999 or whatever, so they never actually did that." In the end, Sun essentially "killed NeWS by a thousand cuts," summarizes Tim Lindholm, a longtime Java engineer and associate of Gosling's. The project's undignified end left many of the engineers who contributed to it feeling very badly burned. Several of those engineers ended up on the Green team. Their lasting antipathy toward business-side bungling later figured prominently in Java's development.

As the Green team coalesced, its future members and their supporters held several discussions about its philosophy and mandate. One of the most important of these occurred at a VP-director off-site at Lake Tahoe in early 1991. There, "there was this series of epiphanies about all of this that we all had sitting in a hot tub," Gosling recalls. "That one hour or so really crystallized a lot of the stuff that we would then go off and do." The Greenies decided that they would focus their efforts on digital systems in everyday devices and their user interfaces. This seemed like a wide-open area, because microprocessors were by then turning up everywhere: in toasters, vacuum cleaners, VCRs, blenders. The digital innards of humble homes were starting to rival those of many not-so-long-ago computer labs. But despite this, it seemed that homes were only marginally better-functioning than they had been a decade before. If that.

Part of the reason for this disappointment was that the interfaces of the new *uber*-blenders and VCRs made no effort to shield their users from the complexity they governed. Instead they shoved it their users' faces and demanded that they *deal*. Many useful higher *uber*-functions therefore went unused. The 12:00 flashing on the VCR of anyone unwilling to spend an evening or three with an owner's manual was but one symptom of this problem. Another problem was that digital appliances didn't communicate with each other, even though they were often used together. Their intermediator, their *object broker*, was a human being who relied on a puzzling array of buttons to coordinate them. This task was aided only faintly by stacks of remote controls that each managed only one device, and in practice only two or three functions (*eighty-five buttons and all I ever do is hit pause . . .*).

In this environment, "what does it take to watch a video tape?" Gosling marvels. "You go *plunk, plunk, plunk* on all of these things in certain magical sequences before you can actually watch your videotape! Why is it so hard? . . . Wouldn't it be nice if you could just slide the tape into the VCR, [and] the system sort of figures out, 'Oh gee, I guess he wants to watch it, so I ought to power up the television set.' " And wouldn't it be nice if the tape would then pause automatically if the phone rang? And if the microwave could also pause the tape, and display a message on the screen saying that the popcorn was ready? And if people could travel with remote devices that would let them monitor their smart homes, and tell them to *boot up* whenever they were leaving the office? For all of this to happen, microwaves and VCRs would have to acquire a common language. And the Green team decided to give them that language. And that language, much later, became Java.

The Greenies built themselves a little Green Siberia out on Sand Hill Road, the Wall Street of the venture capital community that would later funnel millions of dollars into companies furthering their work. It was a good 20-minute drive from there to Sun's headquarters, and the distance was seen as a necessary buffer. "What we were doing was so different from what Sun does, we didn't want to be even in the same hallways as other people," Gosling recalls. The team even broke its link to Sun's corporate computer network for several months. Sun management indulged the Green team's appetite for independence and Dove Bar budgets because of its members' credentials. "James Gosling was an asset to Sun before 1990," explains Sun chief technology officer (CTO) Eric Schmidt. "When someone who is as smart as James wants to pursue an area, we'll do our best to provide an environment."

The Green team spent hundreds of hours studying seductive user interfaces in consumer products. They found few of these on blenders, but plenty on video games. "We spent a lot of time playing things like Super Mario," Gosling beams. "It's a job, right?" But life wasn't all joysticks and bonus rounds. Green's members were hard on themselves, and could be hard on each other. "Everybody [had] very strong personalities," recalls Jonathan Payne, the sixth person to join Green. "We were very vulgar, opinionated, obnoxious. We worked all hours of the day and night. Patrick Naughton and I used to go to Safeway at four in the morning. . . . I would come in on a Saturday morning and Patrick [would be] asleep under the table suffering from a migraine headache. It was just incredibly intense."

Gosling started working on the language early on. At first he just intended to work with C++, which had become the ascendant language for commercial-grade, speed-hungry applications. C++ is a *compiled* language, which means that it is comprised of high-level commands that are approachable for humans, but incomprehensible to microprocessors. For this reason, C++ programs have to be distilled by specialized tools (called compilers) into the low-level commands that microprocessors can understand. Gosling initially set out to build a customized C++ compiler ("compilers are something that I do on a relatively regular basis," he explains, the way some guys say "I often fish"). Through it, he hoped to work around the fact that compiled C++ code is very processor-specific. This means that code compiled for the Pentium chips that underlie so many Windows machines will not work on the Motorola chips that Macintoshes run on. And code compiled for Macintoshes will not run on the chips embedded in Black & Decker toaster ovens. Processor-specific code was troublesome for the Greenies, who wanted to create highly portable software that would run on a diversity of devices (electric razors! light switches! vacuum cleaners!). So Gosling went to work.

Unfortunately, his plans for making C++ more portable didn't pan out. He was also unable to work around the fact that it is very difficult to upgrade the capabilities of C++ programs without recompiling much of their code. This was a big issue for the Green team, as they envisioned a world in which appliances would continually learn to cooperate with new devices and do new tricks through software updates. They imagined that these updates would be distributed through tiny modular patches to the appliances' software that would be loaded automatically through a wireless network (nobody expected consumers to feed floppy disks to their toasters every week). But this system wouldn't work if every little update patch had to be compiled along with vast amounts of the target appliance's original code (unless blenders and light switches were to ship with compilers on board, which seemed like a bad idea).

Gosling eventually decided to toss everything and create a new language. He resolved the portability issue by placing his language in a "virtual machine." Virtual machines (or VMs) can buffer programs from the computers they run on by acting as their interpreters. A program running in a VM feeds it all of its instructions, which the VM translates into messages that the rest of the computer can understand. This can make a language very portable, because if its VM runs on 10 different operating systems (e.g., Macintosh, Unix, Windows 95), so can any program written in it. A program running in a VM just sits in its tidy wrapper, like a diplomat surrounded by translators, and issues the same instructions, regardless of the computer that is hosting it.

Gosling's new language addressed a number of issues in addition to portability, including the version management problem (Java programs are far easier to update incrementally than C++ programs). It was also quite robust, meaning (roughly) that it would oblige programmers to identify and eliminate bugs early. Its robustness came partly from its "garbage collection" services, which make it easier for programmers to manage memory allocation (this can both speed the writing of code and reduce errors). No one of these features was by itself revolutionary, or even new (Gosling, who borrowed liberally from several other languages, including LISP, Smalltalk, Cedar/Mesa, and of course C++, says that "In some sense, I would like to think that there was nothing invented in Java"). But the new language's many features cohered immaculately. And together, they added up to something that was truly unique.

The Green team knew that Gosling's language (which he christened "Oak," after the first thing he saw growing outside his window when it came time to name it) was hot. But they also realized that garbage collection and virtual machines alone weren't going to keep them in regal isolation forever. They also needed to come up with a physical manifestation of their progress. A tangible justification for their budgetary independence. Basically, they needed a *demo*, and a good one. So fairly early in their history, they started building *7. *7 was a prototype of the device that would control the smart homes of Green's imaginings (it was named after the push-button code that allowed any telephone to answer any other telephone in the Sand Hill office). It was the mobile remote unit that tomorrow's wired workers would use to program their VCRs during late meetings at work, or to get their microwaves cranking as they turned at the off-ramp heading home. *7 was digital particleboard, assembled from an almost shocking array of bits and parts. It was a teensy Sharp television, a set of Nintendo Game Boy speakers, some Sony Walkman connectors, a Sun workstation's innards, a couple of *batteries from hell*, and a military spectrum radio, all held together by solder and prayers, and emceed by a perky cartoon fella named Duke, who leaped about its screen pointing things out. *7 had no keyboard. Users navigated and managed it by poking and twiddling their fingers across its face.

McNealy and some other senior executives first saw *7 in September of 1992, and were immediately smitten by it. Soon the Green team was renamed, incorporated as First Person, and spirited off to far fancier digs at 100 Hamilton Avenue in downtown Palo Alto. Its longtime manager, Mike Sheridan, was meanwhile replaced by his more fancily-titled boss, Wayne Rosing. This change upset a lot of Green old-timers who thought well of Sheridan (and in some cases, not especially well of Rosing). But the new digs were great, the technology was exciting, and key players like Gosling and Naughton stayed with the project. In light of all this, much (not all) of the team stayed on, even after the popular Sheridan left Sun entirely.

After First Person became Wayne's world, its staff quadrupled and its mandate shifted dramatically. The Green vision was shelved because the products it encompassed wouldn't sustain its costs. A chip that could run Oak in those days would cost many dozens of dollars, even if mass-produced. But manufacturers in the price-sensitive consumer electronics markets got cold sweats over even single-dollar cost hikes. This didn't matter back when the team's mandate was to prove concepts and do *what if* research and development. But First Person was meant to be a business with real revenues. As such, it needed a here-and-now market. And before very long, it found one that seemed to be tailor-made for it on the seemingly booming frontier of interactive television.

ITV was the Web that never happened, and the excitement surrounding it in the early 1990s knew few precedents. The media, technology, and telecommunications industries were by then sold on the wholly accurate notion that their worlds were converging. But most of their big players weren't yet thinking of a grassroots-and-garage convergence like the Web's. They were instead imagining one of titans clashing, collaborating, even exchanging nuptials at Wall Street's altar (this notion was of course promoted furiously by investment bankers eager for the pornographically high advisory fees this would generate). Interactive television was the ultimate Big Convergence play. It would bring full-screen video *on demand* to millions. Vast archives of movies, a veritable Blockbuster in the living room, would be just a few pushed buttons (and a credit card validation) away. The ITV infrastructure would also be integrated with a marketing and transaction system that could seize the mega–billion-dollar catalog industry's jugular. This was big telecom, big technology, and of course the biggest of media (*teevee!*). Cable companies and telephone companies were alternately snarling and batting their eyelashes at one another as they eyed this vast potential market. Almost every major player seemed to be on the verge of setting up a well-funded ITV trial.

ITV seemed like a perfect market for First Person to pursue, as Oak's native properties were ideally suited to the ITV infrastructure as it was then conceived. ITV's set-top boxes were to be full-fledged computers. As such, they could easily host and run Oak programs. Content that responded to more than just play or pause commands could then be deployed into the network (interactive commercials! video games! online boutiques!). A few-dozen-dollar Oak chip could also fit much more easily into the cost structure of a $300+ set-top box than that of a $39.95 blender, so it seemed that the new market might just bear Oak's costs. And perhaps most appealingly (certainly from an internal political standpoint), big wins in the ITV market would mean big wins for Big Sun, because these ITV trials were going to require servers the size of *meat* lockers. Forget about cheap consumer devices; this was more like a few cubic feet of RAM. First Person needed to staff up to contest this vast new market. It needed more engineers, especially experts in operating systems. It needed more Dove Bars, more Super Mario. And (*what the hell*) it could probably use a marketing person too. It got that when Patrick Naughton met Kim.

*7 starry-eyed, Kim signed up with First Person as soon as they offered her a job. She arrived in the summer of 1993, about a year after the company's establishment. She found its atmosphere to be electrifying. It was full of brilliant people who were passionate about their technology. It was building products that might just change the world. It was posh as a night at the Ritz, with margarita parties on Fridays and hallways littered with every toy known to man. It was . . . *Intellicorp.*

There were several early hints of this. Soon after joining the company, Kim found herself in "lots of discussions of things that no one's really quite sure the people want, but we're all just sort of assuming they do. Like eight hundred channels on their TV. Stuff that sounds slightly odd, and really kind of off, but no one seems to be questioning it." And Kim didn't question it either, not at first, because in a lot of ways, First Person seemed so on-target. There was another elegant and powerful demo, this one showcasing the potential of ITV (it was called *Moviewood*). There were lots of Sun legends on hand, like Naughton and Gosling, whose mere presence validated the enterprise. But as 1993 drew to a close, that *Intellicorp feeling* started getting stronger for her and for everybody.

First Person's most obvious problem was that it just couldn't close an ITV deal. The biggest of those at the time (and, it may turn out, forever) was connected to a Time Warner trial in Orlando, Florida. The First Person team put in Green-like hours primping their technology and assembling their bid for that one. They also kept a steady and watchful eye on the competition, and felt certain that they were far ahead of it. Between this and a series of whispered *attaboy*'s from Time Warner executives, they grew convinced that they would win. But then an invisibly dark horse carried the day. This was Silicon Graphics, a crosstown rival that First Person hadn't even realized was competing. "As near as we can tell it, it was basically Jim Clark alone with nobody else involved," Gosling says, that won SGI its out-of-nowhere victory (see Chapter 1).

The Time Warner disappointment preceded Kim's arrival by just a few weeks, and other near misses followed it. The company came very close to signing a contract with video game startup 3-DO, which was also dabbling in ITV at the time. This fell through when 3-DO CEO Trip Hawkins offered to buy First Person's technology outright, and Sun CEO Scott McNealy refused. Then all eyes were fixed on a Sprint deal. After a while, it seemed like the tiny company was involved in negotiations and product demos all over the world. Things went well in that people seemed to like First Person's wares. But they went poorly in that there turned out to be little action behind ITV's brave talk.

As First Person's first (and ultimately only) marketing person, Kim didn't come into a job with much structure. A tiny business development group was already working the would-be deals by the time she showed up, so she spent her first few months learning the company's technology and its business model (such as it was). She also spent a good deal of time with the many looky-loo's that passed through, or *customers*, as they were called. A few months into her job, Kim received an unexpected request: First Person had a famous problem with its business plan at that point—it didn't have one—and Kim and a few others were asked to help address it. "I was kind of surprised," she remembers. "I thought, 'I'm a product manager. I normally wouldn't be writing a business plan for the company . . . but what the hell. I could learn something.'"

A number of people collaborated on the plan, but in the end she and Patrick Naughton wrote most of it. In it, they revisited some of First Person's basic premises. Oak had been targeted at ITV set-top boxes because it was assumed that developers (of content, applications, electronic storefronts, and so forth) would support that platform in huge numbers. But the set-top box was nowhere. Developers were instead more loyal than ever to the mainstream desktop platforms (i.e., Windows-based PCs and Macintoshes), and were starting to flock to the commercial online services (e.g., America Online, Prodigy). Aware of this, Kim and Naughton wrote a plan recommending that Oak be deployed to the PC and Macintosh—the platforms where consumers already were, rather than where the RBOCs (regional Bell operating companies) and cable companies decreed that they should be. They reasoned that Oak could be an excellent language for multimedia CD-ROM titles, and also for hybrid CD-ROM/online applications, which they expected to grow into a major software category. Only by building a broad user base in these markets today, they argued, would Oak be extant and relevant when broadband networks like ITV systems actually emerged toward the end of the century.

This logic proved to be wildly unpopular with many people. In the Tomorrowland world of First Person, PCs and Macs were the past, set-top boxes the future. Porting Oak to the desktop would be like pushing the Wright brothers into the railroad business just because there was no market for air travel in their day. The business plan must not have been very popular upstairs either. Because not long after it was presented to Sun's executive management group, First Person's long, agonizing dismantlement began.

This process got underway in the spring of 1994. By then, morale in the once aloof and whispered-about company had long since plummeted. One engineer remembers "a long stretch there where everything was in free fall. People were scrambling, a lot of people were quitting. A lot of people just went home for like three months." A number of other people were meanwhile scurrying about, trying to figure out if anything useful could be done with Oak. Both Gosling and Sun CTO Eric Schmidt cite another Lake Tahoe off-site as being critical to this process, and to everything that came next. There, a group that included them, Patrick Naughton, Sun cofounder Bill Joy, and the director of Sun's Science Office, John Gage, grappled for hours with the *now what* issue. Gosling recalls that it was at this meeting that the notion of Oak-on-the-Internet really took hold.

Sometime afterward, Patrick Naughton found himself in the First Person *penalty box*. By almost all accounts, Naughton is brilliant ("He's about the smartest person I have ever met," Kim declares solemnly) and knows it (he's "kind of an *enfant terrible*," another First Person alum explains). Some combination of his brilliance and knowing it involved Naughton in a row with management in mid-1994, and for a while after that, it was "like, 'Time out, Patrick,' " one First Person engineer recalls. Now with some empty hours to kill, Naughton was inspired to take a whack at writing a Web browser in Oak. He dove into the project in July of 1994, and after a couple of days had created a sorta-working prototype that could lay out some HTML text. It was "very minimal," in the words of one teammate. It lacked most of Mosaic's functionality and almost all of its polish, and it didn't execute code sent over the network, which is what today's Java is all about. But at least some First Person alums remember it as an important first tangible sign of the Internetward drift that Oak took on at April's Lake Tahoe meeting.

In retrospect, Oak's migration to the Net was an almost inevitable step in its evolution. The language was always about highly-distributed, heterogeneous computing networks that could extend to consumers. Put more simply, it was about useful networks for people, for civilians. It gradually came to be about several other things: openness (anybody could build upon the infrastructure, not just the company that designed it); extensibility (the infrastructure could be extended in ways not anticipated by its architects); and seamlessness, from a user's standpoint (*invisible technology!*, as Kim likes to say). The Internet turned out to be the optimal showcase for Oak's philosophy and virtues, as they eventually evolved. But the *consumer Internet* didn't exist in Green's earliest days. And networks had no place in the home—networks were for companies—nor did computers, in many minds. So the Green team dreamed of handheld devices without keyboards; *non*-computers for the computer-ambivalent home. And they dreamed of chitchatting appliances; *non*-networks for the unwired home. Green's non-networks would hide from their network-ambivalent masters by being embedded networks; networks as unobtrusive and essential as the plumbing, the wiring. *7 was just the first vessel of the team's early, still-forming philosophy. And it was a vessel so slick as to almost mask its contents. Everyone knew *7 was *cool*, but what seemed to be *cool* was its portability, its poke-me interface. But cool as all of that was, *7 was just the surface of something far cooler.

The evolving Green philosophy turned out to be portable—portable like a Java applet—in that it could run on many platforms and in many infrastructures. Its next platform was the First Person home. This was still a home of networks for civilians. But by then, the wildfire rise of the commercial online services and the public's apparent *sounds good to us* reaction to the ITV dream had made explicit, *here-I-am* networks commercially interesting. This allowed the dreamed-of networks to be not embedded within the home, but outward-looking—at Hollywood, at Madison Avenue, at Domino's Pizza. So Oak's architects replaced the lumens and pause commands traveling on their networks with content—*executable* content. It would be content in that it would be produced information or entertainment, but executable in that it would run, or *execute*, like any other computer program (e.g., the imagined interactive commercial or networked video game of the imagined ITV home).

Of course, not all of the network traffic would be Oak programs. Much it would be content of the sit-still-and-watch-for-three-hours variety. And First Person was still about *non*-computers, was indeed still about handheld devices, in that its consumer unit was a box with no keyboard that was controlled by a button-coated plastic pistol. But however much it might have behaved like a glorified VCR, the First Person network was very much of a distributed computing network. It was also a very open network, in that it was designed to host migrant content and logic from the community, from the local pharmacist as well from as from Time Warner, that could *live on the network* and enlodge in the networked home. Oak's move to the First Person vision was a step toward reality, and all 20/20 ex post facto snickering about ITV aside, it was a big one. It was a step driven by outside-world economics, and also by the economics and interests of Sun, its provider (*servers the size of* MEAT *lockers!*).

Oak's next leap was its best and (for now) final alignment with economic reality, with Sun's interests, and with consumer appetites. By then it was 1994. *Non-*'s be damned; Mosaic and its descendants were about to become bigger than the Beatles at their height. It was now fine for Oak to run on *non-non*-computers—big clunky things, with keyboards and disk drives. And it was fine for it to run on a *non-non*-network—the Internet; the granddaddy of 'em all. But the language retained the discipline of accessibility that its earlier *non-* platforms had imposed upon it. And today's Java derives much of its power from the elegant legacy of its ancestors. It is still as portable as the imagined *pause* command leaping from the microwave to the VCR. As understandable as Duke's mimed *Like* THIS, *idiot!* directions. And as entertaining as *Moviewood*'s studio-produced slickness. So much about Oak is unchanged, except now it has come to a new and wildly popular home—perhaps not its final home (the original Green vision is still very much alive), but the home that has given it relevance.

Unfortunately, Oak started moving toward this new home in the midst of First Person's vivisection. This culminated in the summer of 1994, when most (not all) First Person employees were given a choice between two new homes of their own. One of these was the Interactive Services Group, which was mandated to chase the *it's-gonna-be-huuu-uge* video server market. The other group would be the custodian of Liveoak, which would be Oak online, Oak on the PC, Oak on the Mac; wherever. Kim was at first given no choice, and was exiled to ISG for months ("Hated every minute of it," she still mopes). But org chart, shmorg chart; within days of this assignment she was spending almost all of her time with the Liveoak engineers.

One engineer recalls that at first she was just "sort of tolerated" when she showed up, because few saw the need for a marketing person on the team. After all, Liveoak was no product yet. It had no customers, no market. And so sort-of-toleration was the best that Kim could hope to win. An engineering-centric snicker was even embedded in the team's internal nomenclature. There was the A team—a core group of inner-circle engineers—and the B team, which was—not always, but for the most part—Kim. But of course, the A/B designation intended no varsity/JV condescension. "A" simply stood for *architecture*, "B" for *business* (yeah, right). Sometime during all of the vivisection, sort-of-toleration, and A/B apartheid of that unhappy summer, an unexpected cyclone started twisting anticlockwise in the Colorado hills. It gathered force, grabbed a few books, then *whooosh*ed off to 100 Hamilton Avenue in Palo Alto. That cyclone was Bill Joy.

Joy is a Sun founder, a true genius by many accounts, and an important patriarch in the history of the Unix operating system. These and other bragging rights lead one key Java architect, Tim Lindholm (who "*is* the virtual machine" in the words of an admiring colleague) to describe Joy as "a real scare for a nerd [i.e., an engineer]. Because in addition to having a thousand times the money you will ever have, and having incredible power, he's also really good technically, and he will work like a dog. I mean, he's a company *founder*, but will still stay up all night reading your code. And in the morning, he will have sent you five pages of E-mail telling you that your code is wrong. And he's right. Not that he's right by fiat, but he's right because he's correct. And so in terms of somebody who wants to be left alone to dork around, he's like the worst nightmare, because he's so capable and has so [many] resources." One could argue (fairly safely) that the Oak team had been *left alone to dork around* for quite a while by then. And many on the team were looking forward to dorking around quite a bit more. Now suddenly they had Joy to deal with.

Joy's *whooosh* began in Colorado because that's where he lived. He had been hunkered down in Aspen and fairly disengaged from Sun since the earlymost nineties. Despite his remoteness, he always had claim to a finger in Oak's pot (if not always an actual finger). He had been a key attendee at many of Green's and First Person's formative meetings, including the critical April meeting at Lake Tahoe that nudged Oak onto its collision course with the Internet. He had also had an office in First Person's building from the get-go. But First Person employees remember his office as being perpetually empty; no books, no mussy stacks of mail, no yellow sticky reminder notes—no sign of Joy, not even from the distant past. Now suddenly—after *years*, mind you (well, one and a half)—here he *was*. Joy had *whooosh*ed in with three linear feet of texts from Stacey's, a technical bookstore. These were a prop; he was making a point. Nobody seems to remember precisely what the point was. But it had something to do with the vast amount of technical muddle that one had to master in order to program in C . . . or C++ . . . or to write to Windows . . . Whatever. It was vivid at the time. But the main point that everyone really carried away was simply this: Joy wanted *in*.

Joy wanted in because he was excited about Liveoak, enraptured. As Kim remembers it, Oak seemed to be very "similar to this other vision he had which was called C++−−" (*C-plus-plus-minus-minus*). Joy had high, high standards when it came to making visions real, and this brought him to argue that "Oak wasn't perfect enough, and it needed to be more perfect, and it needed all these changes," Kim recalls. In this he had some strong theoretical points. But Oak's architects had been working in obscurity for ages, and they were ready to get this thing *out*. They didn't want to spend five more years in a skunk works building the perfect machine. Sun CTO Eric Schmidt recalls that a meeting was soon held in Aspen at which Bill Joy, Patrick Naughton, James Gosling, and the director of Sun's Science Office, John Gage, "screamed at each other for two days" (Schmidt deftly managed to absent himself from that particular bloodbath). "The screaming was that Bill believed that James was being too conservative with respect to the language. And Bill wanted a whole bunch of changes made to the language, and James was trying to get the product out," Schmidt recalls. Schmidt, for one, weighed in with Gosling, because after three years without products or (certainly) revenues, he "just wanted a customer."

And then Schmidt, Joy, and the other senior executives did the best thing they could do at that moment. They backed off. It was clear that the Liveoak people knew where they were going, and were in a hell of a hurry to get there. And there was no question about their technical brilliance. So the executives backed off, and let them continue to *dork around* and fumble their way to products, a business model, and a strategy. Schmidt later became the senior Sun executive most closely associated with Java in the public eye. But he insists that he "would not take the credit" for its famously successful strategy. "My contribution was making sure they didn't get squashed," he says frankly, "and creating an environment where they could succeed." But in this, his contribution was crucial. Because in lavishing Java with tremendously patient capital, and giving the brilliant *enfants* behind it years of leeway to be *terrible*, he, Joy, and Sun's other senior executives did as much to enable the language's rise as almost anybody on the team. And much as some in the trenches liked to rail about debacles like NeWS (and they did), it is hard to imagine many companies as young and impatient as Sun nurturing a wild-blue-sky project through quite as many hiccups as Java endured.

But while the executives backed off, they never took their hands entirely from the wheel. Schmidt insisted that the team commit to production and release dates. He also placed it into a managerial infrastructure that he knew would keep at least some tabs on it. Burt Sutherland, who ran Sun Labs, took official responsibility for the team (although for some baroque reason another manager picked up its bills). The team was also assigned two frontline managers. But Sutherland himself was fairly hands-off by most accounts ("He was kind of a godhead, but not an active participant in all this stuff," an engineer recalls). And even the frontline managers were eventually deposed in a mutiny, according to team members.

In September, Jonathan Payne picked up where Naughton had left off with the Oak browser and started building a far more robust from-scratch version of it. Naughton got excited and dove in to help before he was done. After a furious two-week hackathon they succeeded in making Naughton's "very minimal" prototype real. Jonathan then created the first Java applet, which was a box that colored itself red. It wasn't Doom, but it was a start. Gosling was impressed, so he dug through the old *7 archives and soon had Duke waving in the browser's window. Then Jonathan loaded up an old Oak demo that displayed a group of bouncing, spinning Coke cans, and the results were "just breathtaking," he remembers. "It wasn't just playing an animation. . . . It was *physics calculations* going on inside a Web page." In the static-Web days of 1994, this was big, big stuff. Bouncing Coke cans were soon swapped for bouncing heads (Jonathan Payne heads, to be precise), and excitement started to build both inside and outside the team. Patrick Naughton, now out of the *penalty box*, was briefly in the thick of everything. But shortly after the first working browser was completed, he left Sun for a Seattle-based startup called StarWave. StarWave subsequently produced a number of high-profile Web sites, including ESPNET SportsZone.

Naughton's departure wasn't the last from the Liveoak group, but the team became increasingly cohesive as it slimmed down. The browser (which was named "WebRunner" after *Blade Runner*, a favorite of moviegoers in First Person's boondoggle video lounge) shed light at the end of its long tunnel, helping to tighten its cohesion further. From this cohesion, a very strong consensus soon emerged about how Oak should be released and distributed. The group's adamant, militant *ideology* was that almost everything related to the language should be open and free. There should be no royalty charge for using the language to create content or applications. There should be no charge for downloading the browser. The browser's source code (i.e., the actual written lines of code from which it was built) should be freely available. And the entire system's specification, which could effectively allow anybody to recreate it from the ground up, should be freely available as well.

Freeness was essential because it was the way of the Net (the Java team included many Internet longtimers like Gosling) and also because Netscape had proven the model. The Navigator had shown clearly that relevance on the Web came from ubiquity, and that you didn't become ubiquitous by charging all comers for your wares. The team started dreading that some well-meaning blunderer from *Corporate* (this was a generic concept, not a specific group) would decide to price browsers at, say, five hundred dollars and Oak development tools at ten thousand dollars. A policy like this would be the language's death knell. And to those scarred by the NeWS debacle (as several on the team had been), it seemed all too plausible that *Corporate* would impose one.

Openness was important for several reasons (and with its source code and specification release, the Java team went far beyond even Netscape in this). For one thing, the team did not have enough resources to port (i.e., translate) Oak's virtual machine over to every operating system that it wanted to support (at the time the VM ran only on Solaris, Sun's version of Unix). It seemed that making the source code available might inspire "Tom Sawyer ports"; that is, it might lure affable outsiders into doing the porting work themselves (*not just* ANY *kid can port a VM—you've got to be a gooood arrow catcher . . .*). Openness would also let developers examine the innards of Java's security provisions for themselves, and thereby not have to take Sun's word for it that the language was secure. Finally, openness meant that if the team ever *got shot* by Corporate, Oak would be there for them in the afterlife. Because once the specification was out there on the Internet, any non- (or ex-) Sun employee would be free to work with it. This line of thought stemmed not from a cynical plan to make off with the company's jewels, but rather from a legitimate fear that after years of strained patience, management might finally pull Oak's plug.

Kim describes the team's philosophy about openness and freeness "as an organic group notion." It was not the work of one mind; it was not the result of one brainstorming. It rather arose inexorably from the logic of the language and the Internet. "It was this, leads to this, leads to this, leads to this," she recalls, and it was plain to everybody. Everybody on the team, that is. But there were other interests to align and other audiences to sell. There was that rather large part of Sun that was *not* on the team, for instance. And as the group's interface to much of the outside world, the B team—Kim—had some lobbying to do. To validate the team's viewpoint, she pored over every relevant pricing model that she could find in the industry. She identified a few earlier languages that had experimented with royalty-based schemes in which developers were charged "run-time" fees (i.e., small per-copy surcharges for software that they sold that was written in the language). Kim surveyed their histories and many others. She soon had plenty of hard evidence to support what the team knew viscerally: that charging royalties was "a good way to sink a programming language," and would be a great way to sink Oak. She presented this message up and down the line of command, and initially encountered "a lot of resistance," she remembers. "Not from the engineers, but from management. And I had to prove why, and I presented a case."

Between her efforts, the engineers' own lobbying, Gosling's influence in the company's upper echelons, and the team's vocal unanimity, this case was eventually heard, accepted, and approved. Nobody in Sun's topmost ranks made a serious move to veto Oak's unusual non-revenue model. But there were some anxious moments. Things got particularly tense as the language's first limited-distribution release approached in December. The team saw this as the litmus test of Sun's commitment to its philosophy, and eventually everybody was nursing a little Dilbert doomsday scenario based on their own traumas with prior managers. CTO Eric Schmidt had to deal with all of this anxiety from the other side. "The team was absolutely convinced that some unknown, unseen executive would somehow block the right thing," he shrugs. But in the end, no such ogre ever really appeared.

Oak was first put over Sun's firewall in December of 1994. Kim describes this distribution as "a pretty rudimentary alpha version" of the language and the browser. It was placed on a secret Web site and only a tiny group accessed it. Patrick Naughton at StarWave picked it up. So did some old associates of Gosling's at Brown University, an utterly unknown *somebody* in Australia, and Karl Jacob, then of On Ramp. Jacob was a particularly interesting test market because his company (which he had cofounded with former MTV video jockey Adam Curry) developed Web sites, and already had an impressive client list. He had also worked as a college intern on the NeWS team, and was well regarded by a number of Oak's developers. At the time, Jacob was anxious to find something new for On Ramp's tool chest. He had been marketing the company's services in Hollywood for several months, and remembers that "What I heard pretty constantly was that the Web sucked." Static images and text "just didn't do it" for the studios, which made Oak a revelation to him. "I took one look and thought, this is going to be the next thing," he recalls. "This is going to be the catalyst." He became such a believer that he soon left On Ramp and started Dimension X to focus more fully on advancing and commercializing the new technology.

Jacob's reaction certainly boded well for Oak's prospects with the development community. But while the team found it and its other universally positive reviews exciting, nobody really foresaw what was coming. Arthur Van Hoff remembers thinking that "if we would have a hundred applets written, and we would have ten thousand users, that would be success in a year's time." Tim Lindholm's "totally insane, farthest-out projection" was 100 thousand users after a year, a million after two. And Jonathan Payne's expectations were so modest that he left Sun in February to follow Naughton to StarWave ("*Doh!*" he now says of his timing).

Before Oak could disprove anybody's timid forecasts, the team had to come up with some new names, as it turned out that both "Oak" and "WebRunner" were already trademarked. There was a brief, tongue-in-cheek movement to save Oak by reverse-engineering what it "stood for" (O-A-K—*Object Application Kernel*. Yeah—that's what it always meant!). But it failed. Many of the engineers were disappointed to lose Oak, as they had always like its simplicity, its natural roots, its *Gosling-ness*. But Kim, who had always found the name to be somewhat snoozesome, was quietly relieved.

She soon recruited a charismatic and creative outside consultant to moderate a renaming session. She kicked the meeting off herself by writing words like DYNAMIC!, LIFE!, and ENERGY! on the board, and then let her emcee take over. Gosling remembers what came next as "sort of like a food fight." Everybody was "yelling names, and he's up there saying, 'How does it make you *feel*?' . . . 'How does *this* compare to *that*? What does *this* do to the *pit* of your *stom*ach?' " *Silk* was a favorite name with several people (although not with Gosling, who found it "really creepy"). *Lyric* also had some supporters. Nobody remembers who first suggested *Java*. But in the end, it cleared the trademark lawyers, and Kim was ecstatic. She thought the name was lively, accessible, *vowel*some. It was marketing name, it was *B team*. Sami Shaio, for one, believes that Kim "definitely deserves credit for steering the choices into the more nongeek variety. I think my personal suggestion for a name was *WRL*," he points out opaquely, eyebrows arching. "*That's* the kind of language I could get into. Java? I just hated the name." But Kim loved it. She presented it upstairs as *the* name (although she grudgingly offered some alternatives), and Schmidt roundly credits her with driving it through ("I don't *do names*," he explains).

By then, Sun was scheduled to announce its Internet strategy at the annual SunWorld conference in May. This would be a logical venue for Java's official release, and the engineers went into overdrive preparing for it. The work they were now doing was very different from the Green and even First Person teams' efforts, because for the first time, Java had to stop being a *demo* and start being a product. This meant it had to be thoroughly stress-tested, debugged, and (eventually) documented, which required a wholly different kind of engineering rigor (and perhaps a wholly different kind of engineer, as by now James Gosling and Chris Warth, another Oak old-timer, were the only Green team members still working on Java). One of the engineers' big remaining design objectives was to make Java secure (Kim all but insisted on this over the objections of some others on the team). As they went about this and their other frenetic tasks, Kim recruited several more companies to experiment with Java so that she could later cite them to potential customers as references. This group included mainstream service companies like Morgan Stanley and Arthur Anderson, as well as leading-edge Internet companies like HotWired. All of these early users turned out to be ecstatic about the language, so in the late winter, Kim and Sun's PR group decided that it was time to arrange a press leak to prime the market.

The PR people targeted *The San Jose Mercury News* (or "the *Merc*," as it is called) because it was popularly read among the Valley's executives and engineers. Before the article ran, Kim decided to tell Marc Andreessen about the team's technology and plans. "We had a browser and Netscape had a browser, and I was concerned that the press would view this as a competitive thing, or position it that way," she explains. If that in fact happened, she certainly didn't want Marc to learn about Java through a speculative piece in the local press. So she sent him E-mail, he downloaded the software, and soon wrote back that it was terrific stuff (although as it turns out, he probably knew plenty about it already; see below).

Kim and her PR contacts didn't really have executive approval to talk to the press. But at Sun, "it's kind of easier to get forgiveness than permission," explains Lisa Poulson, who helped place the article. So they called the *Merc*, spent some hours with its reporter, referred him to their users and to Marc Andreessen, and then informed Eric Schmidt that (*Oh my God!*) there was some journalist stomping around the office who wanted to talk to him. Ambushed, Schmidt graciously forgave, as planned. The following morning Kim anxiously scanned the front page of the *Merc*'s business section. *Nothing*. Then she fretfully skimmed the second page, the third page, the rest of the section. *Nothing!* Then she noticed the front-front page—*the front-front page!*—and there it was, the lead story above the fold-line: "Why Sun thinks Hot Java will give you a lift." At least as shocking as this prominent placement was that the article ran with a enlarged quote from Marc Andreessen ("the God of the Internet!" Kim later gushed) saying "What these guys are doing is undeniably, absolutely new. It's great stuff." Kim later had a poster-sized enlargement of the historic front page installed on her wall, and can still rattle off its date (MARCH 23, 1995!!!) like it's her mother's birthday. In retrospect, she says that "that was when we turned the corner. That was it. The defining moment, if I could say that there was one. When we knew we had made it."

Things went instantly crazy. Java's Web site was buried in traffic. Kim's phone began to ring constantly ("I'd put it down, and it would ring again"). And from that moment onward, "it was just relentless," she remembers. "It built and it continued building. I basically lived at the office from March through May." Soon she was "learning all of the different functions of a marketing department by doing everything by myself." There were branding issues to deal with, data sheets to write, journalists and analysts to prebrief, early users to nurture, even T-shirts to produce. And there still remained a big, burning, overriding issue—Java needed a customer. This was one of Schmidt's imperatives (along with ship dates), and was one that Kim and the rest of the team were more than bought in on.

The list of potential customers was not especially long. With everything free to most end users, the only way to generate revenues would be to license the language to somebody who wanted to integrate it into their products. Potential licensees included vendors of programming tools and developers in the nascent "plug-in" market (see Chapter 2). But far more attractive than any of them from a ubiquity standpoint was Netscape. Sun and Netscape's seniormost people had been discussing Java off and on (more off than on) for some time by then. Schmidt recalls that back before the very first beta version of the Netscape Navigator was even posted to the Internet, he and others had a meeting with Jim Clark at which the possibility of "sell[ing] the entire Java team to Netscape" was raised. This idea was never considered very seriously. But Schmidt believes that "one of the positive benefits" of the discussion was that "we were able to imprint within the young mind of Netscape, a small company at the time, the virtues of Java."

Those virtues were of course far more evident by the spring of 1995. So in the weeks leading up to the May announcement, Kim, Eric Schmidt, and others had a relatively easy time persuading Netscape to integrate Java with the Navigator. Kim recalls that Marc gave "the technical thumbs up" and exited pretty quickly, but it took a while to come to a final agreement. That agreement's terms have never been publicly disclosed. But *Wired* magazine has speculated credibly that Netscape paid a $750,000 flat fee for the right to build Java into its products. This would not have been a great deal of money in light of Java's since-inception development budget, or of the value that the language added to the Navigator. But the Sun team reckoned that a Netscape deal would touch off an avalanche of other licensings (and it did). They also knew that only ubiquity could make Java truly relevant. And in the spring of 1995, nothing was more ubiquitous on the Web than the Netscape Navigator.

The negotiations with Netscape went late into the night before Java's debut at SunWorld. Schmidt recalls that "the pressure point was that we wanted Andreessen to be on stage" to announce the deal and his support of the language as it was introduced. Eventually the two sides reached terms and Marc agreed to speak. This dramatically raised Java's profile in the conference agenda, which had originally been limited to "perhaps a minute and a half," Schmidt recalls. But since Marc was a keynote, not a soundbite, Java moved to center stage. And from there it stole the show.

Kim recalls that it was almost like the thousands packed into San Francisco's Moscone convention center were "seeing TV for the first time." The new *TV-like* Web had Duke somersaulting and waving from its pages. It had crossword puzzles and Hangman games. And it had pragmatic features, like a stock portfolio monitor that displayed a streaming ticker tape. This was an early hint that powerful financial tools of the sort that had long existed on expensive closed networks might soon come to the masses on the openest network of all. Kim had championed this particular demo because she "thought we needed a real-world application," and nothing was realer-world to most people than their finances. "Imagine, a spreadsheet that was calculating your net worth *at this second*," she thrills. "That's *really* cool." SunWorld immediately became a giddy de facto JavaWorld. The conference's attendees couldn't hear enough about the new language, and every vendor on the trade-show floor (most of whom had nothing to do with the Web) seemed to be begging the Java team for copies of its HotJava browser (as WebRunner had been renamed) to display in their booths.

And so Java was out of its skunk works for good. And although the language was virtually inaccessible to most people (for now HotJava worked only on systems running Sun's Solaris operating system, and on the yet-unreleased Windows 95), the tightly-coupled community of serious Internet users was almost universally aware of it within days. A cacophony of press coverage meanwhile brought the message to the rest of the world. Lisa Poulson had worked in technology PR for years before landing in the midst of the Java furor, and had never seen anything like it. "Normally as a PR person," she explains, "you try to flog a product in an established product category. You try to try to flog your product's differences. . . . you try hard to think of something new and different. You get *no* consumer and business media attention." But with Java, "there were literally months when I did nothing but answer the phone, which never ever happened to me as a PR person." The Java story seemed to cross all lines. Soon, even consumer media like *Newsweek*, *Time*, and the major broadcast networks were calling about it.

An especially important article appeared in August of 1995, when George Gilder discussed Java in *Forbes'* technology supplement *ASAP*. Gilder was one of a small group of writers with both a loyal technical audience in the Valley and a wide readership in the general business community. His article prophesied that "To the extent that Java or a similar language prevails, software becomes truly open for the first time. The Microsoft desktop becomes a commodity; the Intel microprocessor becomes the peripheral . . ." These were bold statements. Intel had invented, and was virtually synonymous with, the microprocessor, and Microsoft was the most powerful entity in the software industry (*if not the world*, many whisper darkly). Lumping these giants in with joystick makers and pork belly futures just a few months before would have left readers searching for the telltale April 1 publication date.

But only a hundred days on the scene, Java was making notions like Gilder's very credible. The specter that the language raised over the industry's landed gentry was on its simplest level one of a suddenly flattened competitive playing field. For years, this field had been tilting increasingly and precipitously toward the vertical with the *Wintel* biumverate (named for Microsoft's *Win*dows operating systems and *Intel* microprocessors) perched triumphantly at the top. One dynamic behind this was a self-feeding cycle in which Wintel's larger user base attracted the support of a majority of software developers, whose labors gave Wintel a more diverse and competitive selection of software, which in turn made the platform even more attractive to computer buyers, which increased its share even further. This cozy cycle, combined with other factors (including scale economies in the PC hardware market), was threatening to push non-Microsoft operating systems into oblivion.

But in a world of Java applications, proprietary platform advantages would erode, because if the applications that users valued ran identically on all platforms, people would presumably care far less about what operating system their computers supported. In a maximum scenario, Java could make the operating system a *who cares* adjunct to the running of productive applications, much as PC hardware had largely become a *who cares* adjunct to the running of the Windows operating environment. The notion of applications residing on the Internet rather than in hard drives also had ramifications for ownership and usage models in another Microsoft bastion, the application software market. Because if applications really came to flit in and out

of computers as needed and when summoned, people might stop buying shrink-wrapped software from retail stores. They might stop paying for preloaded software on new computers. They might indeed stop
buying software at all. They might instead start paying for it on a per-
use basis, in effect *renting* it. Possibilities like these were innately
threatening to a company that had, like Microsoft, built an unassail-
ably dominant presence in the traditional software distribution channels. In light of all this, nobody was surprised when Microsoft
chairman Bill Gates started harumphing that *Java is there to over-
throw what we've done,* and other such things.

But all worried harumphings aside, the Java of mid-1995 was still
far from toppling any prevailing orders. It was not yet implemented on
most computer platforms, it ran slowly and often crashed, and it had
only a tiny cadre of developers supporting it. And while these facts
would presumably change with time, Java also had some defining limitations that could hobble it badly in the there-and-then world, however
liberating they might become in George Gilder's *Abracadabra!* future.
One of Java's greatest shortcomings was that it lacked *persistence.* This
meant that once an applet had run through its little tricks or had been
dismissed by its user, it was *outtathere,* gone from the system, leaving no
trace on the hard drive. This meant that applets had to be downloaded
fresh whenever they were needed. And since there was a limit to how
much downloading users would sit through for applications that would
go poof the moment they were done with them, there was a corollary
limit to how big and functionally ambitious applets could really be.

Java's lack of persistence stemmed from the fact that the language's
security model banished it from the hard drive (if applets couldn't
touch the disk, then malevolent applets couldn't erase it . . .). Connected to this was the fact that Java could not access a user's local file
system. This meant that applets could not interact with spreadsheets,
creative work, or any other files developed with traditional desktop
software. Such a limitation would not of course matter in an imagined
future in which every bit and byte *lived on the network* and spoke fluent Java. But in the boring old here-and-now, people were interested in
linking their personal finance software directly to their bank accounts,
in connecting their schedules and calendars to those of distant coworkers, and in other such things. This kind of melding of the island personal computer's doings to the global network was one of the
Internet's great promises—although for the moment, it was a promise
that Java itself could not help deliver on.

But despite its launch-time limitations, Java had truly fired the industry's imagination. And Gilder's notions were widely accepted as being as credible as they were startling. Eric Schmidt indeed discovered that many people responded to them in the realest way they could. On one dramatic day in August he was out of town for a meeting when Sun's stock price started going up. "So I called up my broker," he recalls, "and I asked, what the hell is going on? He said it was this article by Gilder. I said I couldn't believe it. He said he'd gotten three calls about it!"

Things like this just kept happening. Java excitement was credited with much of the over 100 percent appreciation in Sun's stock price between the language's May debut and the end of the year (a march that represented over $4 billion in market value). Many of the companies that licensed Java after Netscape also fell under its happy spell. Browser distributor Spyglass's share price shot from $35 the day before it announced its licensing agreement to $41.75 the day after. Not long afterward, Macromedia jumped from $30 to $37, and development toolmaker Borland from $13.25 to $18.625 (a 40 percent surge) during the days surrounding their announcements.

These were just a few of the companies that announced their support for Java in the months following its debut. By the end of 1995, Eric Schmidt and a small business development team got over a dozen licensing arrangements *signed* (not just announced). This tally tripled during the first half of 1996. Every browser company of consequence was among the early signatories, guaranteeing that Java would become as ubiquitous as the Web itself. Every desktop computer operating system company of consequence was among the later signatories (Schmidt largely credits Bill Joy with this second-phase strategy), which hinted that Java might soon become as ubiquitous as computing.

Kim did not get involved in many deals after Netscape's, as she was busy managing almost every other Java-related matter that wasn't connected to engineering. The frantic time that led up to the May announcement (branding! positioning! users! press! analysts!) turned out to be a mellow test-drive, a dress rehearsal for the rest of the year. From May onward Sun's sales force buried her with requests to tell The Java Story to innumerable deep-pocketed customers, even as a steady stream of wide-eyed journalists and sharp-eyed analysts filed through her office. She meanwhile had trade shows to manage, developer conferences to organize, and (oh yeah) a product to manage.

Kim could keep up with all of this only by delegating. And this was problematic, because she had no staff, no budget, and no power to delegate. She worked around this by becoming "very clever in getting others to leverage the work," Schmidt recalls. She seemed to know everyone in the company, especially down in the trenches, where it mattered. Soon local sales offices were running "Java Days" seminars at which thousands of potential customers heard the Java story, Sun employees throughout the world were making Java pitches, and almost every Sun executive was moonlighting as an ardent Java evangelist. Sami Shaio chuckles about how "you would see small companies complaining about, 'how can we ever match Sun's marketing budget for Java?' " But for months after Java's release, there weren't many items in that budget other than Kim's salary.

One of Kim's unexpected allies in spreading the Java message turned out to be the language's once-unloved new name. *Java* was different from the names attached to so much of the Web's other fauna (*Hypertext Transfer Protocol . . . Virtual Reality Modeling Language . . . Plug-in Application Programming Interface*), in that it was not offputtingly technical. Instead it was wholly memorable, *mainstream*, energetic, and fun. In this it struck an immediate chord in millions of nontechnical Web users. This served Java's mandate tremendously well, as it needed to be much more of a consumer product than any programming language before it. After all, nobody hyped word processors based on the fact that they *had lots of* C++ inside them, but Sun wanted millions of people to know that they liked Java in their Web pages. The accessible *Java* name made it easy to build this popular affinity.

By fall, Netscape's new betas supported Java in their Unix and Windows 95 versions (other platforms followed later). Navigator product manager Alex Edelstein estimates that seven to eight million Navigator users had became Java users by the end of 1995. And by then, the Web was already twinkling with interactive elements. Decorative animations quickly became widespread. Many sites also enlivened themselves with little freestanding games, like Hangman and Asteroids. Others featured bits of content that melded art and programming, like The Impressionist (created by Paul Haeberli of Silicon Graphics), whose users scrubbed a blank Java "canvas" with cursors to coax out images that had the muted look of impressionist painting. Publishers like CNET meanwhile started experimenting with "interactive features." One early CNET Java piece recommended system configurations and brands to computer buyers based on their price, performance, and feature preferences (see Chapter 8).

None of this came close to rivaling the power or functionality of traditional desktop software. But while Java's early instances were indeed baby steps, they showed that the language could deliver on its core agenda. They showed that Java programs were secure, that they ran on multiple platforms, and that they could travel and install themselves seamlessly across networks. They also showed that Java could become a democratic phenomenon, because suddenly, millions of people were regularly downloading code written by unidentified strangers without worrying about its origins or destructiveness. This did not stem from a spontaneous welling of brotherly, sisterly, and nephewly trust, but from Java's tremendous embedded security. Security bred trust, trust bred usage, and usage created a global showcase for innumerable weekend hackers who never before had had access to a distribution channel. Suddenly, anybody who could assemble some inventive code could aspire to have it running on countless thousands of desktops (and on several different operating systems) in days, even hours. Nothing remotely like this could ever have happened through the traditional software distribution channels. And while the earliest Java consisted mainly of trinkets and toys, it was easy to imagine that its more evolved descendants could one day make that circumvented channel squirm. In the face of all this grassroots mayhem, the old order indeed seemed to buckle.

Much of the resulting giddiness dissipated on December 7, 1995, when Microsoft's enunciation of its Internet strategy brought the old order surging back into the game (see Chapter 1). Among the many things announced that day was the company's licensing of Java. Many observers heralded this announcement as a triumph for both Java and Sun (*BusinessWeek* referred to it as a "capitulation"). But while licensing the language to the world's most powerful software company was in fact essential to the goal of ubiquity, Microsoft's announcements made it clear that the company intended to both embrace *and extend* Internet standards like Java. That notion of *extension* set off some serious alarms in the Java community. Java was fundamentally, nay, *ideologically* committed to treating all computer platforms and operating systems identically. But if Microsoft successfully *extended* Java's functionality on its own platform in unique and meaningful ways, the language could well bifurcate into Microsoft and *un*-Microsoft Java, sundering this commitment.

Also in December, Microsoft announced a technology called ActiveX, which seemed to compete with Java head-on. ActiveX was an older technology called OLE (Object Linking and Embedding) that Microsoft had decided to "tweak about five degrees," according to the company's ActiveX Marketing Guy, Shawn Morissey (yes, that's an

official title). OLE had long made it possible for applications to interoperate on the Microsoft desktop. OLE could, for example, allow a
user to place an Excel spreadsheet into a word-processing document. If
somebody later manipulated the spreadsheet while reading the document, OLE could summon Excel to perform its calculations.

In creating ActiveX, Microsoft made OLE Internet-aware. The
newly-*tweaked* technology was immediately labeled as a Java competitor because like Java, it enables Web site developers to attach functional
code to their pages that can be downloaded and run in Web browsers
(these pieces of code are called "controls" rather than "applets"). But
beyond this, ActiveX and Java are fundamentally different. Unlike Java,
ActiveX is not a language. It is an infrastructure for communication
and collaboration between pieces of software. Its controls can be written in any language, including Java. But in practice, ActiveX controls
have traditionally been written in platform-specific languages like C++.
Also unlike Java, ActiveX is not inherently secure. Its controls are not
sequestered from the hard drive and file system, and as such have the
potential to be biblically destructive. And also unlike Java, ActiveX traditionally runs only on Microsoft platforms. In this its announcement,
like the notion of a Microsoft-only strain of Java, raised the specter of a
bifurcated Web of Microsoft and *un*-Microsoft content and sites.

Microsoft later quelled some (certainly not all) concerns by announcing in October of 1996 that it would cede control of the ActiveX
technology to the Open Group, an independent standards body (Microsoft did not surrender the right to make its own enhancements to
the technology in doing this, however). By then Microsoft was also
making arrangements to expedite the technology's migration to other
operating systems (this transfer was still pending as of this writing).
But since almost all ActiveX controls were written in operating system–specific languages, transferring the ActiveX *infrastructure* to non-
Microsoft operating systems would do nothing to transfer the
controls, the content. In short, most ActiveX controls were likely to
continue coming in Microsoft and *un*-Microsoft versions—wherever
the infrastructure resided. And in light of the history of the desktop
software market, it was easy to imagine that this could foster the emergence of a Microsoft Web. For this and other reasons, many viewed
Microsoft's December announcements as less of an embrace, and more
of a call to arms against the cross-platform, secure, and democratic
precepts of Java computing. *Embrace and extend*, Gosling later
quipped, meant "swallow you whole."

All of this made for gripping drama in the Java team's trenches, and it was exciting to watch from the outside too—although Jonathan Payne (who had followed Patrick Naughton to StarWave in February) found Seattle's distant sideline to be a poignantly less thrilling vantage point than Silicon Valley. By then Jonathan had sacrificed countless evenings, weekends, and holidays at Java's hungry altar. He had even written the first working version of the HotJava browser, for crying out loud. But now it seemed that everybody was turning into a rock star over this thing but him. Back home people were closing book deals, fighting off journalists, and hanging up on venture capitalists. Sun's stock price was meanwhile bizillion-tupling, and here he was, unhounded for autographs, untrailed by paparazzi, unlinked to Madonna and Keanu by even the faintest of rumors, and just *watching* everything from the socked-in shadows of Seattle's eternal mist-bank. By November of 1995, Jonathan decided that enough was enough; it was time to go home.

The first person he called was his old friend and coworker Arthur Van Hoff. Jonathan first met Arthur in 1993, shortly after Sun's talent scouts plucked him from a university functionaryship in Scotland. Arthur found his way into First Person almost immediately after that, and was soon famous for his thick Dutch accent, his mighty intellect ("the best programmer I have ever worked with," Jonathan says), and his at times devastating candor ("He didn't bear fools lightly," shudders a former teammate). Arthur zealously promoted Jonathan's cause with Sun's recruiters. But things did not go as quickly or as smoothly as they had hoped. Sun was of course eager to get Jonathan back. But aware of his own market value, Jonathan requested a compensation package that fell north of the norm for young nonmanagers. As the HR people scratched their heads and counted their beans, Jonathan grew impatient.

Eventually he hit Arthur with an idea that he had been nurturing for some time; why not start their own Java company? Arthur liked the notion. He had thought about leaving Sun several times before, mainly because recruiters were continually calling and asking him to. But he had never taken any of those discussions very seriously, because, like Kim, he had long toyed with the idea of starting his own company. Arthur floated the idea by his officemate, Sami Shaio, and Sami liked it, giving their maybe-startup three of the sub-dozen best-qualified Java engineers in the world. This was a good start, but they still needed something else. They needed more business-sense balance.

They needed a Rolodex the size of Montana. They needed a person "who will check us against reality," as Arthur put it. In short, they needed a *B team*; they needed Kim.

Kim was at first torn by the idea. "It was a difficult decision because [Sun] was fun," she remembers. "I was working on what I loved. It was Java. So it was part of me." But she had wanted to start a company since high school, and that was starting to seem like a long time ago. She also knew that life on the Java team was going to change. Up until then there had been "no parental supervision," she laughs. But it was clear "that all of Sun was now going to be galvanized behind Java, which was good. But it was also kind of sad, because I realized that the corporation would now take over." This was a necessary and expected step, as Java had grown far too big for the tiny team that had created it. But Kim had grown fond of her autonomy. So after agonizing for a while, she realized that "You've got to know when to leave the stage, and it felt like this is the time, if there ever was one. I can leave now on a high note." She reached this conclusion at a restaurant near her home called Café Marimba—quite a funny coincidence, as it later turned out.

The future Marimbans spent the Christmas week of 1995 considering their possibly-maybe startup. Because they were all still employees of other companies, they weren't comfortable discussing product plans in much detail. So they spent a lot of time figuring out if they had enough money, guts, and energy to proceed. Cases of cold feet broke out, grew contagious, were eradicated. Then finally, not long after New Year's Day, the team decided to go for it. With that agreed upon, it was time to start worrying about how Sun would react to their plans. They were all eager to be viewed as alums of the company, not defectors; so they fretfully planned out every detail of their resignations. Kim and Arthur ended up breaking the news to Sun CEO Scott McNealy together. At the same moment, Jonathan gave notice to Patrick Naughton up at Star-Wave. Sami was meanwhile assigned to "hold down" the main building in Palo Alto, in case Microsoft attacked while everyone was out or something. All of this choreography turned out to be unnecessary. McNealy's reaction "was typical Scott," Kim recalls. He was "very controlled, didn't freak out, didn't get mad." His only message was "Don't hire my people, don't compete with me, and . . . don't steal my intellectual property."

The YAJSU moniker came almost immediately. *Some*body leaked word of the group's departure to the Internet's scarily plugged-in id, *suck.com* (see Chapter 7), and *Suck*'s daily column christened their company with the wryly-concocted name (*YAJSU* was a deliberately kludgey play on *Yahoo!*; see Chapter 6). This was all very clever. But *USA Today* soberly reported the name as fact, and the company was pelted with YAJSU inquiries for months afterward—starting before they even wrapped things up at Sun. "It was horrible," now Kim shudders. It seemed like every venture capitalist in the Valley wanted to give them money. One company even offered to take them public straightaway. Kim was sure that one was a crank call, but it turned out to be "a semireputable investment bank."

Everybody was relieved to leave Sun for the silence of un-YAJSU's nonphones (it took weeks to get lines into the ex-warecloset). After fitting out their humble digs with some cut-rate furniture that they hauled up themselves, the soon-to-be Marimbans settled down and brainstormed about what to do next. They knew they wanted to create products that would make Java fundamentally more powerful or easier to work with. They also wanted to help silence the critics who were starting to dismiss Java as a lightweight novelty. A leading complaint at the time was that the language hadn't yet produced any truly compelling applications. Who cared about waving Dukes and demo-ing stock tickers, this argument went, where were the word processors? The spreadsheets? The gory cartoon dungeons?

The Marimba team knew that most Java content was still functionally modest for several reasons, and that other companies and the market's natural evolution would take care of most of them. One issue was simply that Java still lacked developers. Programmers need to learn a language before programs can be written in it, and as a new language, Java still had few native speakers. But Java was a close cousin of C++, was the Portuguese to its Spanish, and as such was very accessible to the vast community of C++ programmers. Between this and the Internet's fiscal glitter, it seemed that there would be plenty of Java programmers by the end of 1996.

Another issue was that early Java was slow—up to 30 times slower than native C++. This was because its existing implementations ran in an interpreter, which meant that commands had to be translated by the interpreter into the host computer's native tongue before they could be processed. Just as communicating through a translator is slower than chattering with someone in his or her native tongue, this process takes longer than managing a computer directly. But the slowness issue would also soon be resolved, as a number of companies like Borland, Microsoft, and Asymetrix were already developing *just-in-time com-*

pilers for Java. These are tools that speed the interpretation process by anticipating the commands that a Java program will issue, and pre-translating them into the host computer's lowermost language. The team was confident that other companies' just-in-time compilers would have Java running at near-C++ speeds by the year's end.

A third issue was that Java needed development tools. This was a significant matter because programmers need tools for writing, debugging, and compiling programs even more than writers need word processors to process their words. At the time, Java developers had only the most rudimentary sketch pads to work with. Market forces were sure to at least partly take care of this issue as well, as all of the leading development-tool companies (e.g., Borland, Symantec, Metrowerks) had already announced support for Java. But development environments in other languages had evolved over years, not months. It seemed that this area might therefore offer Marimba some opportunities.

The Marimba team considered this and soon hit upon an interesting product notion. It was clear to them that while all Java applets were unique, many of them were built from similar components. Innumerable applets drew little windows on their users' screens in which content or data were arranged, for instance. Many also used buttons, or scroll bars. It seemed that Marimba could make life easier for developers by preassembling commonly-used "widgets" like these, and making them available in a library. Developers could then pull their widgets from the library rather than developing them all themselves. This would let them focus on more interesting matters than widget reinvention, like what to draw in those little windows, and what to do with those little buttons. There were lots of "builder" tools like this for other languages. But as far as the Marimba team knew, nobody was developing a Java builder.

Such a tool could easily find a large and lasting market, and was an interesting product idea for that reason alone. But it also suggested an intriguing follow-on deployment that could help with another of Java's core weaknesses: the fact that accessing truly ambitious Java content could involve interminably long downloads. This problem stemmed from the fact that Java lacked persistence; that it vanished from a computer moments after it was used, since the language's security model didn't allow it to touch the hard drive. Marimba's widgets alone would not make Java a persistent language. But if they could somehow be loaded onto end users' computers, the applets that used them would not have to bring them along on their sluggish journeys across the Internet. They could instead travel light and summon Marimba's buttons, windows, and scroll bars from their users' hard drives as needed. This would let applets download far more quickly. For this system to really work, Marimba would need to distribute its widgets widely among end users. This dissemination could perhaps be accomplished through relationships with browser or operating system companies.

Marimba got off to a fast start. Within days the engineers were hacking, and Kim was sketching out some early marketing plans. Everything went great for weeks. Then in March, Netscape announced that it was acquiring a tiny company called NetCode that was developing a tool that Netscape believed would advance its Java strategy considerably. That tool was a Java builder. It was designed to save developers time by making libraries of widgets available to them. Those widgets would soon be built into the Netscape Navigator, which would speed the download times of the applets that used them considerably. In the wake of this announcement, the Marimba team was forced to ask itself "who would write anything to our tool kit," Jonathan remembers, "when that tool kit would have to be downloaded along with every applet, so it would take forever, when they could write it to Net-Code, which was going to be bundled with Netscape?"

The inevitable answer to this was, *perhaps nobody*.

What followed was "kind of a hard period," Sami remembers. Everybody was "completely bummed out, because we thought, 'it should have been us,' or something. . . . We went through about three or four weeks after that announcement kind of examining our navels, and figuring out, 'What are we going to do next? Should we even continue?' " Everybody was irritable. "We were arguing all the time about what the right thing to do was," Arthur remembers. "We just kept going around in circles." But luckily there was "one person [who] really kept her feet on the ground," Jonathan recalls, and that was Kim. "She said, 'this is totally to be expected,' " he remembers. " 'We'll just have to figure out something else to do.' " So the team brainstormed. They came up with a few ideas that were pragmatic and feasible, but most were mind-bendingly boring. Suddenly self-conscious about the fact that the industry was expecting *something interesting* of them, they shelved the yawners and continued to think. The days ticked by, and things started getting a little desperate. Then somebody saw PointCast.

Essentially a cross between a Web site and screen saver, PointCast was a then-new service that had taken a pioneering look at the way the Internet distributed information. When a PointCast-enabled computer wasn't being used, its screen would fill wholly with dynamic and fast-changing displays of text, graphics, and (inevitably) advertisements. This information would be continually refreshed with current head-lines, sports scores, and stock prices from PointCast's servers if the computer was online. If it was off-line, it would display recycled infor-mation from its last online session. Even if a computer had not been connected to the Internet for weeks, its PointCast screens would al-ways appear lively, engaging, and ever-changing.

PointCast was all about persistence. It carried the online experience off-line, and replenished it when it reconnected. In doing this it showed that even a very dynamic online environment could be preserved and ex-perienced at any time. It also showed that not all Internet content had to be framed by a Web browser's scroll bars and buttons. It could instead seize the entire screen, could *take over*. The PointCast example inspired Marimba's founders to view their own mandate more broadly. Perhaps they could free Java of the Web browser's constraints as well? More dra-matically, perhaps they could give it the enabling power of persistence? Persistence was a thorny issue, because it cut so close to Java's security model. But it was also an exciting issue, because bringing persistence to Java would open whole new classes of much, much larger and more am-bitious applications to the language. Marimba's engineers also knew a thing or two about Java's security model, and they believed that they could extend it to the hard drive without compromising it.

In late March, the Marimbans decided that they would build an entirely new framework for distributing and managing Java. Their Java would be able to run outside the browser's framework. This meant that it would live on its host computer's desktop and in its file system as well as on the network. It would also be accessible without a Web browser's intercession, and indeed without an open Internet con-nection. The company's founders got excited again. This was no wid-get library; it cut to the language's soul. Winning here therefore not only meant securing a market niche, but advancing Java's own agenda.

The language certainly seemed primed to take the step that they were proposing for it. Its applets had by then wowed millions and en-livened countless Web sites. In this they had made Java a success, a ubiquity, while also helping to expand the Web's own popularity. But impressive as all of that was, teensy applets were never Java's end goal. They were at most an intermediate step, a way station. And with millions of users, thousands of developers, and a fast-expanding arsenal of tools to speed its performance and development, Java was ready to move closer to delivering on the maximum promise that Gilder and others had enunciated. Achieving this demanded certain fundamental capabilities from the language that applets themselves did not require, and persistence was foremost among them.

Marimba's engineers dove into their work, and by the late spring, their "Castanet" system was taking shape. At Castanet's core is Marimba's "tuner," a piece of software that sits on a user's computer and manages the "channels" that the user subscribes to. Channels are buckets of Java content and code that are broadcast across the Internet (or corporate intranets) by publishers using Marimba "transmitters," or servers. Some channels are like PointCast, in that they feature lively displays of up-to-date information or content (e.g., HotWired uses Marimba to transmit news stories—see Chapter 7). Others are more like traditional computer applications, in that their users summon them to perform specific functional tasks (e.g., a developer at NASA created an application-like channel that employees can use to track their work hours. It launches from a computer's hard drive like any other application).

A channel's underlying code can be very dynamic, changing daily, hourly, even by the minute. Updates are effected by broadcasts of fresh code from a channel's transmitter. These can be frequent and regular, or very erratic. A news channel, for instance, might receive small, almost continual updates consisting mainly of new stories, whereas an application-like channel might receive irregular broadcasts consisting mainly of software revisions. When users are online, their channels can update dynamically and automatically whether they are using them or not. Users can also summon and interact with their channels when they are off-line, although their content might be somewhat outdated (e.g., a news channel cannot of course display stories that are any more recent than the computer's last online session).

Once its product plans were in place, Marimba began cohering in other ways as well. The company was finally named in the late spring. Kim had wanted to call it something that would convey vitality and liveliness, like *Java*. Since she was (incredibly) still dancing three to four times a week (she had joined a highly-regarded local dance company called Zohar in 1987), dance names were inevitably among her candidates. She researched the status of several of these—Tango, Mambo, Cha Cha Cha—and discovered that most were already trademarked. But Marimba was available, and she liked its sound, its medial accent, its vowels. She also liked the fact that the marimba was an instrument as well as a dance (it's a xylophone-like contraption), as well as the rather cool coincidence that she was sitting in a Café Marimba when she decided to leave Sun. She and her cofounders considered several other names (*Casbah*, *Senteo*, and *Kashmir* were all finalists), but in the end, *Marimba* carried the day.

Not long after Marimba's christening, Kim officially became its CEO. This title was not formally designated to anybody back when the company was being formed. But Kim had tended to most of its business affairs since its inception, and had tended to them remarkably well. She had sustained the venture capital community's engagement through countless power breakfasts and lunches, even as she kept its courtship on hold. She had also turned the extraordinary network that she had developed as Java's product manager into an invaluable asset for the company. "She knows every company doing Java anywhere in the world," Arthur points out. "We can phone up. You want a contact in Borland? We can talk to the VP of engineering there, or the CTO, or whoever we want, because we have his private phone number. If you want to talk to anybody, there's always a way in. Other small companies have a very hard time even getting somebody on the phone."

Marimba started edging into public view in May of 1996, at Sun's Java One conference in San Francisco. At Kim's urging, the company rented a "whisper suite" at a hotel near the event in which it briefed dozens of analysts, journalists, and potential customers on its technology. These briefings were given in strict confidence, as Marimba had decided to buck industry tradition and not announce its products until they were actually ready. Java One drained roughly half of the company's scant remaining funds. But Kim understood the value of recruiting early users and partisans from her experiences in launching Java, and insisted that it would be a good investment ("I was like, 'this is such a waste of money,' but it wasn't at all," Jonathan remembers).

Java One helped Marimba recruit more than 20 active users to test its products by the summer's end. These included prominent Web content companies like HotWired and Dimension X, educational institutions like Open University in the United Kingdom, and old service sector friends from Kim's Java days like Arthur Anderson. Marimba also formally announced its name and formation at the conference.

Unexpectedly, Java One's first day was met with a $3.25 slide in Sun's share price (this represented a roughly $600-million decline in the company's market value). It was strange that the wildly successful opening of a sold-out Java love-in would coincide with this, the biggest drop in Sun's share price in over four months. But analysts attributed the slide to the news of the Marimba team's departure from Sun's Java team, according to *The Wall Street Journal*. It seemed from this that Wall Street was not yet compulsively reading *Suck* (nor perhaps even the *Journal*, which had announced the team's departure quite clearly back when it actually took place).

Marimba closed its first round of venture financing not long after the conference. The company had its pick amongst some of the Valley's finest funds, and in the end went with Netscape's elite backer Kleiner Perkins. KP had offered to invest in part because of Marimba's obvious sizzle and promise. But partners Doug MacKenzie and John Doerr (who previously funded both Netscape and Sun; see Chapter 1) also saw terrific value in its products. MacKenzie, who directly managed the investment, viewed Castanet as "NTSC for the Internet," or as a new kind of "virtual permanent connection" between clients and servers. This struck him as very powerful, as he had long believed that the Net needed to transcend its traditional "search and find browser metaphor."

He and Doerr also believed that Kim had great potential as a chief executive, despite her relative lack of managerial experience. Her poise in the public spotlight had impressed them, as had the way she conducted Marimba's search for financing. Throughout that process, it seemed clear to them that "she was coached by a lot of advisers," MacKenzie remembers, "and you could see that she was paying attention, and she wasn't letting her ego get in the way." This was significant to him, because in his experience, a CEO's ability to accept criticism, be coached, and listen could have an enormous impact on a startup's performance. For his part, Doerr was particularly impressed by Kim's market savvy. "I've seen more companies with great technology fail because they can't seem to hit the marketing strike zone," he explains. "I think Kim was very much not just in tune, but ahead of where the Web was headed."

Marimba became one of the two maiden investments in KP's Java Fund, which was announced in the summer of 1996. With corporate backers like Netscape, IBM, Compaq, USWest, Oracle, and (of course) Sun, this $100-million fund invests only in early-stage companies that are building their businesses around Java technology and content. The raising of the Java Fund was a remarkable event by any measure. Funds of its size are still relatively unusual in the venture community (although by no means unheard of). Funds of its size that are wholly dedicated to single markets (including relatively broad ones like the Internet, or even software) are scarcer still. And funds of its size that are wedded to single programming languages are unheard-of (no, there was never a $100-million C++ *Fund*). But of course, that's the whole point: Java is much more than a language and the Java Fund's scale and backing testify to the technology industry's extraordinary, even unprecedented commitment to Java's success. So does the tremendous enthusiasm that it has met with. Doerr estimates that within two days of the fund's announcement, KP had received roughly 500 calls from entrepreneurs with business plans, would-be investors, and the press. "That's not a case of wondering if the dogs are going to eat the food," he points out. "That's a case of the dogs ripping the bag open to go get at this opportunity."

With KP's backing secured, Marimba was finally in a position to bring on some more people. The first new hires came aboard in July of 1996, and soon the tiny ex-warecloset office was straining to fit everybody. The company finally moved to more spacious quarters in late September, but by then everyone was so frantic about meeting Castanet's October 7th launch date that the move was more of a burden than a relief. Castanet's debut turned out to be at least as enfrazzling as Java's own launch 17 months before. No Marimban slept much during the weeks leading up to it. And Kim, now with a business development "staff" of only one to help her with all of the attendant marketing chores, at times felt particularly overwhelmed.

The night before the launch she didn't get to bed until 3:00 A.M. Three hours later she was awakened by a call from a local radio station. She gamely yawned and murmured her way through the interview. Then after hurriedly showering, dressing, and breakfasting, she hopped into her car to race off to the local CNN studio for what she thought would be a taped interview. Heading northward toward San Francisco, she switched on the radio and heard a familiar voice murmuring about Marimba. It was shaping up to be a surreal kind of day. At CNN she learned that tape, *shmape*; this baby was going to be broadcast live to several million dressing and breakfasting Americans. Startled only briefly, she managed to "walk through the fear" and addressed the masses without a hitch. Next came a photo session at *The Red Herring*, a leading Valley insiders' magazine (she ended up on the cover of the December '96 issue). Later that day she read long articles about Marimba, Castanet, and Bongo (as the builder had been named) in *The Wall Street Journal* and *The New York Times*. No less satisfying, *The San Jose Mercury News*, which first broke the Java story, favored Marimba with an enormous front-page article in its business section. The whole sprint ended the following evening with a fancy launch party at a chic San Francisco restaurant. John Doerr of Kleiner Perkins, a veteran of many such events, found this to be "just electric." He indeed detected "that same kind of excitement and enthusiasm that we felt around Netscape's launch."

Marimba gathered enough early momentum during the subsequent weeks to affirm its launch-day promise. Over 50 thousand copies of its tuner had downloaded within 20 days of its debut. This compared well to the early download traffic of RealAudio Player, the first VRML browsers (see Chapter 4), and even the Netscape Navigator. Dozens of new customers meanwhile entered Marimba's pipeline, and the media's interest in the young company continued unabated (e.g., *Newsweek* covered Marimba with a full-page article the week following its launch).

Marimba remained a very young and unproven company as of this writing, and it already faced competition from rival startups (e.g., BackWeb and Intermind), which had released Marimba-like tools. But those tools targeted content delivery almost exclusively, and as such lacked the broader focus that Castanet has on both content and applications (the latter being potentially the far greater market). So at least on the surface and for the time being, a greater threat to Marimba than another startup seemed to be that an established company working close to the Web's foundations might encroach on Castanet's functional space. The risk of side-on competition always lurks on the Internet (see Chapter 2). It looms particularly large when companies play close to the Web browser's core functionality, and persistent Java happens to be a very browserlike matter in that most Web browsers cache (or temporarily save to a user's hard drive) almost everything that they touch. This is done to make recently-visited content more accessible (e.g., if a user wants to revisit a Web page that was downloaded five minutes ago, it can be summoned much more quickly from the hard drive than from across the Internet). Caching Java is not such a big step away from caching HTML. For this reason, longtime Marimba friend Karl Jacob of Dimension X has worried that "any time you solve a problem that close to the bone . . . you are potentially competing with very, very big players. Potentially competing with Microsoft, or Netscape, or whoever. Because that's squarely in their turf."

Marimba is of course aware of this. The company is likewise

Jerry Yang and David Filo, founders of Yahoo! *Jerry compares the
newness of business on the Web to "being dropped off a helicopter,
and you're the first guy skiing down the hill. You don't know where
the tree is, you don't know where the cliff is, but it's a great feeling."*

Halsey Miner, founder and CEO of CNET. *If his bet pays off, Halsey could one day blossom into the Web's own Ted Turner.*

Kim Polese, president and CEO, and the team at Marimba, Jonathan Payne, Arthur Van Hoff, and Sami Shaio. *Talking about Java's power, Kim could light up like a missionary recalling a particularly tough convert.*

Ariel Poler, founder of Internet Profiles Corporation (I/PRO). *I/PRO is making a bid to become a cornerstone, perhaps the cornerstone, upon which advertisers could rest their faith in the Internet as a medium.*

Jim Clark, Mark Andreeson, and Jim Barksdale of Netscape. *The Netscape Navigator became the preferred portal to peering into Web's ether, the preferred joystick for steering its traffic.*

Mark Pesce of VRML. *Mark's vision is to "bring the Web out from the flat text and images and into a new sensibility that would be more fluid, expressive, and emotional."*

(top left) Andrew Anker, CEO of HotWired. *Andrew believes that HotWired's free form culture is essential to its content's sensibilities.*

(top right) Louis Rosetto, founder of Wired Ventures. *Louis sees HotWired as being muscle for the Web's garage bands.*

(left) HotWired's old office, the "Grotto", was designed for ten and held fourteen.

(bottom left) HotWired's new office, a more spacious and less quirky home.

PHOTOGRAPH BY DAVID A. JOHNSON

Rob Glaser, founder and CEO of Progressive Networks. *Rob antici-pates a "transformative event" when the signal clarity of Net-based audio exceeds that of FM radio.*

aware that as Netscape, Progressive Networks, and others have demonstrated, an overwhelming market presence during a technology's emergence on the Internet can generate a durable (although certainly not insuperable) market lead. Considering this issue as Marimba prepared for its launch, Arthur predicted, "Our only advantage is going to be market penetration, and time to market." For this reason, secrecy and speed were the company's prelaunch watchwords. And whatever becomes of Marimba now that its products have shipped to a contestable market, its speed, and perhaps its secrecy as well, have allowed the company to play a historic and pivotal role in Java's development. Because Marimba was the first company to ship a comprehensive persistence framework for Java content and application developers alike. And this was significant, because there are three broad ways for developers to harness Java's functional power, and Marimba's persistence framework can play to all of them. First, developers can create entertaining, informative, or educational Java content and distribute it over the Internet. Second, developers can use Java to simplify information and software management within corporations, potentially saving vast amounts of money. Third, developers can use Java to develop commercial application software, which can then be distributed and updated over the Internet (or corporate intranets) rather than through traditional distribution channels. These areas will be considered in order.

For content developers, Castanet has the potential to deliver on a promise that Kim and Patrick Naughton once imagined that Oak might deliver on. While researching their business plan for First Person, they envisioned hybrid CD-ROM/online systems in which images, video content, and audio files would be shipped to users on disks, to later be integrated with online experiences. Hybrid delivery systems like these made sense because media files are big. They consist of vast amounts of data, and download ploddingly. A single detailed image can take minutes to download, and until recently there was no way to have a meaningful online interaction with video content. But content that would take hours to shoehorn through a modem can be summoned quickly if it is already available on a user's system. Large media assets that are preshipped to users can therefore be integrated with online experiences relatively easily.

In First Person's day, CD-ROMs were the only realistic way to deliver and store bulky media. Hard drives weren't big enough to quarter it, modems weren't fast enough to download it directly, and online services charged by the hour, which would have made users reluctant to download large content files anyway. But CD-ROMs turned out to be poorly suited to the needs of many online content categories. As prerecorded media they lack the immediacy and spontaneity of online content. CDs also have to be burnt, packaged, and shipped. Their users have to organize, install, and swap them. All of this involvement and complexity incurs costs and further reduces the immediacy of content.

The infrastructure for online media delivery has since become significantly more robust. Hard drives are now bigger, modems are faster, and Internet service providers now typically charge flat monthly access fees. It has therefore become far easier for content providers to send bulky media directly to users' hard drives, a simpler, more immediate, and of course less expensive channel than shipping disks. Castanet can enhance the immediacy and simplicity of direct delivery further by managing and integrating content updates in an automated and highly granular manner.

Bulky media drawn over the Internet can then be integrated into lively and timely Java-powered environments. Like the PointCast system, Marimba content channels can take over and fill the screen. But they can also draw on far richer assets than PointCast's ampules of headlines and statistics in that content creators can integrate megabytes of media files or thousands of lines of Java code into a Marimba channel if they choose. This content can slip onto users' hard drives at night, or in the background when they are working on other things on their computers. Once downloaded, large media files and content can be immediately accessible to their users. This can allow for a far richer media experience than a Web site's, whose content has to be dribbled through a modem in real time. Placing lively content directly on users' hard drives also forges more direct and powerful links with them than just posting it to the Web. HotWired, for instance, used Castanet to build a news channel. Because it is hosted on their disk drives, the channel's subscribers can always summon its news immediately, without having to launch a Web browser and navigate to the HotWired site. They can also access it when they are off-line, and receive continual updates from HotWired when they are online.

Search engine Excite, meanwhile, has used Castanet to build a Marimba "channel guide." Emceed by the voice of Barbara Feldon (Agent 99 on "Get Smart"), this provides a comprehensive, multimedia listing of the Marimba channels currently available over the Internet, as well as reviews and previews of them. Executive Producer Stacey Jolna, who built the channel guide, believes that "the media richness that Castanet brings to content, by allowing digital audio and video to download gradually in the background, is helping to bridge the gap between a still-hoped-for interactive television experience and today's Web."

The fact that Castanet transmissions can alter the content stored on user's disks in a very granular manner allows content like Excite's to be updated in a highly efficient manner. Jolna points out that when a new channel is added to the guide, "we just have to push out the content and code corresponding to its listing, rather than an entirely new version of the channel guide itself." This feature can reduce data traffic dramatically when the subtleties that a publication (e.g., the Excite channel guide, or a movie listing, or even a news channel) reports on change, saving connection time and reducing administrative loads on end users' systems. Advantages like this have drawn many companies like Excite and HotWired to experiment with persistent Java, and to build outposts for their brands and media assets directly onto their audiences' hard drives. In this they are starting to build distribution networks for their franchises that are far more immediate and simple than traditional physical channels.

Java-enabled immediacy and simplicity can also benefit any company struggling with the demands of today's enslavingly complex PCs. Traditional PCs are complex in part because they presume no network connection. They are instead built as island-states, roundly outfitted with all of the intricate resources and infrastructure they need to tough it out alone. They have their own hard drives for storage, their own copies of several applications, and millions of lines of OS code (11 million in the case of Windows 95) tending to their underpinnings. Maintaining the PC's go-it-alone complexity demands continuous diets of disks and downloads to keep software current, and regular tut-tuttings from network overseers after disk crashes and other tantrums. All of this care and feeding inevitably gets expensive. The average corporate desktop system now costs almost $12,000 per year just to maintain, according to a study by the Gartner Group. This cost can best be reduced by taming rampant complexity, which itself can best be reduced by heightening the PC's network orientation. Networks can ease complexity by allowing resources and chores to be shared rather than replicated. They can also allow complexity to migrate inward, toward the professional MIS staff, and away from the less initiated end users on the network periphery.

Java abets both the easing and the centerward migration of complexity. Unlike traditional software, Java does not travel to the network periphery via disks or careful downloads, but finds its own way there. Also unlike traditional software, Java programs do not have to be regularly updated at the periphery, but exist in only one version: the current one. And also unlike traditional software, Java does not have to be surgically targeted to the periphery's various platforms and operating systems, but targets only one platform: the ubiquitous virtual machine. A computer that grows reliant on Java for its applications becomes dependent upon the network for its currency and functionality. This dependence reduces complexity and thus ultimately cost. The notion of *independence* is of course always appealing. But network independence in a networked environment is a staggeringly expensive anachronism that corporations can ill afford.

By reducing network complexity, Java can lighten the tactical administrative burdens (e.g., helping hundreds of individual users update their word processing software) that now claim up to 80 percent of the time and attention of corporate MIS staffs. This can give MIS professionals far more time to write customized productivity-enhancing software for their companies—a far more leveraged use of their talents than, say, grappling with software version management issues. The software that they develop, particularly the applications that are distributed to many different groups and departments using (presumably) many different types and configurations of computers (e.g., applications to administer expense reports, 401(k) accounts, and so forth) can also be developed far more quickly if it is written only once for the Java virtual machine, rather than several times for every operating system on the network. Here-and-now benefits like these had drawn more than 60 percent of Fortune 1000 companies to use Java for internal development within a year of the language's release, according to a survey by Forrester Research.

In an imaginable longer-term maximum scenario, companies could also one day withdraw almost all complexity from the periphery by equipping their desktops with hard disk-free systems loaded up with the Java virtual machine and little else. These diskless systems could turn to the network for applications and storage alike. Sun estimates that such "thin" terminals would cost only $2500 a year to maintain, or roughly $9000 less than the average PC (Sun is only one of many companies, including Oracle, IBM, and Microsoft, that are maneuvering to play in this "network computer," or NC, market). But tantalizing as these savings may be, thin client networks will take time to arise and become widely relevant. For now, many important office productivity applications have yet to be written in Java. Also hard disks exist for a reason—they're fast. The SCSI connections that tie hard disks to computers are many times faster than most corporate networks, and they are not dense with the traffic of hundreds of other users.

So for now, hard drives are better places to store large applications than the more sluggish and crowded networks that they connect to, and Kim accordingly sees a big market for Marimba on the intranet. Marimba channels can bring the same benefits of immediate and simple distribution to corporate software that they bring to Internet content. But instead of news stories and sports scores, the broadcasts supporting them contain tiny bits of code that fix bugs and add new features to applications. Entirely new versions of applications, or indeed new applications, can be shipped to thousands of users without a single disk changing hands. And because applications reside on users' hard drives, they can always be summoned immediately, without straining network resources. This is an economically and logistically appealing way to distribute any software, regardless of its language. For this reason, Marimba is tuning its tools to deliver and update applications written in C, C++, COBOL, and almost any other digital tongue—although since other languages lack Java's dynamism, applications written in them cannot be updated as granularly as Java applications.

Marimba can also imaginably help deliver on certain aspects of the diskless dream without actually requiring computers to shed their speedy and useful disks. This is because disklessness is all about cost savings. And while the not-buying of hard disks does save some money, the real bonanza lies in the not-administering of them. Disk administration is very expensive on the operating system level in that it consumes millions of lines of OS code. It can be even more expensive on a care and feeding level because files and applications are often toted to and from hard drives via sneakers and floppy disks. Castanet might be able to obviate these costs by making it possible to maintain and administer hard disks from the network. A computer that had all of its software piped in and managed by Marimba transmitters would need very little hands-on administration and could probably run on a very slender OS; but it would still provide the speedy access to content and code that only a hard disk can offer. Marimba-administered networks could therefore conceivably let companies cash in on most of the savings that disklessness theoretically offers, without having to await the rise of Tomorrowland networks that can spirit code around the enterprise as fast as a SCSI cable can firehose it from a hard drive to a motherboard.

The application accessibility that only disks can offer becomes an even greater asset when software distributors and end users are not all sitting on the same fast corporate network. For this reason, persistence is making Java a far more viable choice for commercial software developers of all kinds. The spread of Java development within this community could have a tremendous leveling impact on the all-important operating system market, where Microsoft's OS's have long enjoyed their tremendous popularity in part because the vast selection of software that they support runs nowhere else. Apple Computer, the most famous casualty of this popularity, for years offered what was widely viewed as the most viable alternative to Microsofts OS's. But with Apple's new system market share now standing well below 10 percent, most developers face strong disincentives to port (or translate) their software to the Macintosh. Eric Dunn, the senior vice president of the consumer/international division at personal finance software giant Intuit, estimates that developing a new application for both Windows and Macintosh requires roughly 75 percent more effort than just developing it for Windows. This is a large incremental investment to make on behalf of the Macintosh when scarce development resources could otherwise be used to build additional products.

However, if applications could be written once in Java and deployed to all platforms, developers could imaginably face no opportunity costs in supporting non-Microsoft operating systems. This would absolutely benefit developers, who could then target even larger markets than Windows' with single versions of their applications. It would also of course benefit Microsoft's competitors. For this reason, Apple chief scientist Larry Tessler believes that Java will put competition in the OS market on a much more even footing. "The playing field today is almost vertical," he points out. "If you try to climb up on it you fall off, unless you are the guy sitting at the top. . . . What Java will do is tilt it down to a more reasonable angle."

But Tessler does not think that "anyone in their right mind will say the playing field is going to be flat." And he is right for several reasons. Products in many important software categories will take time to migrate to Java, if they even migrate at all. Translating the giant personal productivity applications that dominate much of today's software market into Java would be a particularly onerous chore. Intuit's Eric Dunn is skeptical about the prospects of a single code base supporting truly competitive versions of Quicken for the Mac and PC platforms. And in any event, he points out that Intuit's flagship Quicken product already has hundreds of engineer-years invested in its code base, "and it's virtually inconceivable that we would rewrite it in the next five years." Products like Quicken also demand highly evolved development environments that Java currently lacks. "To adopt Java for a core product," Dunn says, "we would have to be sure that we could be as productive in Java as we are with our existing development environment. And that requires a lot of sophisticated tools that have not yet released for Java. We couldn't accept anything more than a 5 percent penalty on our development time for the Windows platform, if that."

This reluctance indicates that many traditional bastions of desktop software might for now be closed to Java. But it does not mean that Java will not become an important development language. Indeed, new computing models never rise to prominence solely by mimicking the traits and functions of their predecessors. PCs did not arise by being better mainframes; they arose by performing functions that fell far from the mainframe's purview. Java will likewise take root first on the market's periphery, on uncontested land. It will pioneer and dominate new application categories that are native to the Internet and intranet, its own native platforms. And as the importance of these platforms expands, the Java periphery will grow in importance and move toward the center. The software vendors now dominating the center will take note of this process. Many will find that Java's development and distribution models are relevant to their own core businesses, and will migrate toward them (indeed, many already are).

But for now, most post-applet Java programs tend to be small, far smaller than traditional desktop applications. They also tend to turn to network connections for the data, content, or dialogue that make them interesting. These characteristics are related. Internet applications are small because they can get away with it—like the network-aware computer, they don't have to be embedded with everything that makes them useful. This lets them function as slim infrastructures that draw the content and features that make them whole from the network, instead of from their own code. Wall Street Web, a product of BulletProof Corporation, is representative of this. It tracks users' stock portfolios and can calculate and display their performance in sophisticated ways. HotWired's JavaChat is also typical. It is a simple interface that gives access to HotWired's "chat rooms" (environments in which visitors conduct dialogues by swapping text messages in real time; see Chapter 4). Both BulletProof and HotWired are now using the Marimba system to distribute their wares. Persistence adds value to their products because small as they are, they do require significant download times (e.g., Wall Street Web can take a half hour or more to stream through a slower modem). But as Marimba channels, they can be summoned as quickly as anything on the hard drive. This lets users check their portfolios or chat up other HotWired denizens impulsively, rather than just when they have several minutes to spare for a download.

Dimension X is also using Marimba to distribute applications. The company produces a line of tools for creating Java and VRML content that are themselves written in Java, and is distributing them over the Internet. Unlike a lot of early post-applet Java, Dimension X's tools are not especially small. But like Wall Street Web and JavaChat, they are refreshed regularly by their network connections, in that Dimension X broadcasts periodic feature upgrades and bug fixes to them through its Marimba transmitters. This makes its tools evergreen applications—applications that are always updated, upgraded, and complete. CEO Karl Jacob believes that the freshness and flexibility that persistent Java can bring to applications is especially valuable in his market. "Internet software," he points out, "is constantly morphing and trying to address all the new pieces of technology that come out. How many times does a Netscape user install Netscape? If it was the [3.0 version], *seven times* you had to reinstall a piece of software [i.e., there were six beta versions before the code was finalized]. Normal people just don't do that." And normal people won't have to, as persistent Java and their network connections start doing it for them. Computers filled with evergreen applications and content will eventually never require the installation of updated software by disk, or even by deliberate download. Patches and updates to software and media will arrive continually, and will install invisibly. At night as their owners sleep, thousands of engineers will in effect go to work on their machines, leaving them updated, upgraded, and more functional in the morning.

While word processors and spreadsheets may not cycle through as many versions as the Navigator or Dimension X's tools, updating is a major issue in traditional software markets, too. Most desktop software developers rely on disks and physical channels to reach the majority of their customers, which makes pushing out updates a logistically taxing and expensive proposition. Developers accordingly try to address many issues (whether they are bug fixes or small functional improvements) at once, with a single patch to their software. These patches are often quite large, as C++ code is much harder to alter granularly than Java code. It is in fact not unheard of for patches to be as large as the programs that they update. All of this means that administering updates is a real headache for users and developers alike. It is also a frequent headache; Intuit's Eric Dunn notes that "it would be very rare not to have at least one maintenance release" for each major version of Quicken, and Quicken is not at all unusual in this regard (e.g., Microsoft commonly slips two or three minor maintenance releases of office productivity applications like Word and Excel into its sales channel every year). Product versions themselves also cycle frequently—annually in the case of Quicken and many other packages. End users and developers alike must therefore walk an endless administrative treadmill just to keep up with the tremendous churn in the industry's code base.

Developers in even the least Net-oriented desktop software markets could therefore make their products easier and less expensive to own by adopting the evergreen model. They could also move to a pattern of fixing bugs as they are identified and adding features as they are completed, rather than in erratic cycles dictated by constricted physical channels. This would certainly please customers, whose software would become more reliable and fully-featured that much faster. On its surface, the evergreen model could seem dangerously dislocating to developers who have grown accustomed to annual harvests of upgrade revenues from their installed customer bases. But evergreen software won't drive maintenance-related annuity revenues out of the industry. It will rather make software maintenance a matter of seamless ongoing subscription rather than one of annual physical upgrades. In this, it could actually lure many software users who are put off by the current model's hassle and all-at-once expense to enter the upgrade market.

Java also offers another, perhaps even greater benefit to less Net-centric developers in that it is a simple and speedy language to program in (Gosling has called it "C++ without the guns and knives"). Devin Breise, a lead engineer at Intuit, has noticed that Java can at times double a programmer's productivity. People at Sun have heard of many other dramatic improvements, ranging in some cases as high as five times (which Gosling himself modestly dismisses as "sort of incredible"). As its development tools mature, Java's productive power will only rise, making the language an increasingly compelling option for developers facing schedule and resource pressures in any market.

These advantages should allow persistent Java to gradually infiltrate more and more traditional software markets. As this happens, the language's blessings of network-enabled simplicity and smallness could begin to revolutionize even such desktop-centric products as word processors, spreadsheets, and presentation graphics packages. For now these products are anything but simple and small. They are indeed quite unsmall, and are getting unsmaller at such an alarming rate that many now sneeringly refer to them as "bloatware" (the "fatso" of the industry's schoolyard). Microsoft's gluttonous Office '97 suite, for instance, weighs in at 120 megabytes, or three times the disk capacity of many new computers at the start of the decade. And it is no outlier (e.g., Corel's WordPerfect 7 is a tubby 68 megabytes in most installations).

Traditional desktop software bloats because it is designed for the un-networked island PC. Unlike the ectomorphic Wall Street Web, it must therefore carry along everything that makes it functional. Like a Sunday newspaper, it also has to satisfy all the needs of a diverse constituency with a single package that it delivers to everybody. Newspaper publishers cannot very easily deliver the Automotive section to only those who want it, so forests topple and everyone gets it. It is even trickier to put NINE POINT BOOKMAN SMALL CAPS on only the disks of people who will switch them on, so word processors bloat and disk drives buckle. Java alone can't do much about the forests. But it can liberate desktop software from its enbloating urge to be all things to all people all at once. In this it can help liberate hard drives from their sprawling squatter colonies of unknown and unwanted files and features. Like Wall Street Web, much of tomorrow's desktop software will be built around slender infrastructures that meet their users' needs by drawing code in from the Internet. Feel like writing in the `Courier font`? It's on its way. Sick of all those tips and help messages popping up on your screen? Flush them from your disk; you can always draw them in from the network if you find that you miss them. Aware of the relevance of Java to its markets, aggressive young Corel (which acquired the WordPerfect business in 1996) hopes to build a big business around new office productivity applications written in the language.

As persistent Java gradually infiltrates the application software industry, the language itself will inevitably undermine many of the software industry's traditional barriers. This could throw open the market to new entrants of almost all conceivable sizes and mandates. Newly-opened and democratized, the software industry could then sustain patterns of competition and cooperation that have no real precedents. This new openness would benefit consumers and software vendors alike, and can be enabled by certain of Java's defining traits.

Java's network orientation can lower barriers by making it easy for software vendors to market, sell, distribute, and maintain their products over the network, rather than through retail stores, catalogs, and other distributors. This practice can improve margins, and of course eliminate the costs related to physical materials and shelf space acquisition. In this, Java can reduce the market's cost-of-entry barriers, making it far more accessible to new and smaller players. Java's security can meanwhile lower barriers by making it possible for users to trust software created by remote and unknown parties as much as they trust branded retail software. Retail software is trusted implicitly because its shelved and shrink-wrapped form indicates that it is backed by a going economic concern with strong vested interests in its hygiene. No company with a physical address and bills to pay will maliciously ransack a customer's hard drive with viruses, so such companies are deemed safe to deal with. But software from a stranger on the network may or may not originate with an identifiable, trustworthy, and suable party, and is therefore inherently suspect. It can therefore be hard for tiny players without trusted (and costly) physical distribution channels to engender confidence in their products and develop markets. But Java itself is virtually impervious to viruses, a trait that lets users trust Java code implicitly, allowing even the least-known players to distribute software to a confident clientele.

Finally, Java's various enablements of smallness lower barriers because they reduce the minimum economic scale of commercial software projects, further reducing the market's de facto cost of entry. Small, inexpensive applications that would never pay the freight in a costly physical distribution channel can be distributed profitably over the network. Code that does not even constitute a complete application can also find a market. Software chunks known as "components" could particularly thrive in the open, trusted, and mobile world of Java computing. A component is a piece of software that performs a discrete function and has an accessible interface that enables it to interact with other components. Groups of components can be integrated together to build applications. A lone developer with a world-class understanding of Swahili fonts might for example build a Swahili font component that other developers could then integrate into page-design tools, multimedia titles, Swahili spreadsheets, or any number of other products.

Components are intriguing because they can be combined and leveraged in ways that even their makers cannot foresee. Combined with Java's embedded trust model, this can allow developers to create code that embodies their best efforts in their most unique area of expertise, and deliver its benefits not just to one product or company, but to the entire community of software developers and an unlimited number of products. This can allow the formation of de facto global teams of world-class developers who can collaborate, share, and build on each other's work without even knowing one another. *Dream teams* that could never be recruited, nor even identified by single companies, can then effectively form, reconfigure, and disband around thousands of innovative products.

This sort of innovation could never be orchestrated by individual companies with clear product mandates, because, as Sun's lead Java evangelist Miko Matsumura points out, "the smartest programmers are distributed planetwide. And they're hacking on everything. They're hacking on NT device drivers, they're hacking on cell phones, they're hacking on ten thousand million different projects. But all of those innovators can only leverage what they do themselves. What Java can do is it can bring them all under one roof. And what that means is that when one person innovates, another person can then leverage that person's innovation into an entirely different domain. So we're talking about giants standing on the shoulders of giants, rather than side by side." Secure and therefore trusted, mobile and therefore accessible, the innovation of a giant in a Slovenian physics lab can be leveraged by another giant in a Malaysian semiconductor plant. A British software publisher might then combine the results into a product with the work of 10 giants from other domains. In this model, innovators and their output alike become free agents, combining in unforeseeable, efficient, and market-driven ways.

In the fall of 1996, Sun's JavaSoft division (the multihundred-person heir to the dozens-strong First Person company and the half-dozen strong Green team) released the specification of an infrastructure called JavaBeans that will help enable all of this. Stated simply, JavaBeans makes it easy for Java components (or *beans*) to "talk" to one another and collaborate. JavaBeans is also compliant with a broader component infrastructure called CORBA (Common Object Request Broker Architecture), which runs across many major operating systems, languages, and platforms, including the Netscape Navigator. CORBA can allow components to interoperate even if they are residing on computers across the planet from one another. This could allow a Java component running on a PC in Minneapolis, say, to summon the help of a component written in native C++ code on a Unix server halfway around the world. The C++ component would not have to travel across the network to interoperate with the code residing on the Minneapolis PC (indeed it couldn't, because as Unix code it wouldn't run on the PC). In this manner, millions of computers throughout the world could come to collaborate and interoperate by offering the code they host and their processing power as resources for other systems, much as hundreds of thousands of computers now share the contents of their hard drives over the World Wide Web.

All of this could prove to be enormously liberating for developers. Java has already freed them from the need to target particular operating systems with their output. Marimba has freed them from the need to confine their output to teensy applets. JavaBeans can now free them from the need to build large, ambitious applications in order to have commercially viable code, and CORBA can enable them to leverage some of the world's vast base of non-Java code, as well as the work of its millions of non-Java developers—while also (ideally) making it irrelevant where code resides. Combined with the barrier-lowering power of Java's security provisions and network friendliness, all of this could bring software authors and integrators of almost any scale into the promised land of *Asymptopia*, as James Gosling likes to call it. This is a favored term of an old professor of his (Jon Bently of Carnegie-Mellon). Products enter it when their unit volume is high enough to spread their fixed costs so thinly that a unit's effective total cost approaches its variable cost (see Exhibit 3.1).

For example, imagine that a chair manufacturer needs to invest $100 to open a factory and that chairs subsequently cost $10 each to build. If only one chair is built and sold, it alone must cover all of the factory's bills, so its effective total cost is $110. If 10 chairs are sold and the factory's fixed costs are allocated evenly across them (at $10 each), their effective average cost is $10 + $10, or $20 apiece. If 5000 chairs are sold, their average cost is $10.02. If 10,000 chairs are sold, their average cost is $10.01. At these higher volumes, the manufacturer is deep into Asymptopia, because the up-front cost that a chair has to help cover is triflingly small compared to its marginal cost. Companies that make it to Asymptopia compete not on the basis of scale, but on their ability to build and distribute chairs efficiently. They can also underprice and annihilate those unhappy non-Asymptopians who have to cover their up-front costs on much lower volumes (Asymptopia itself, incidentally, takes its name from the asymptotic relationship between the average total cost curve and the variable cost line. And Bently, its progenitor, uses it to describe mathematical situations, not software economics—but it's a great word, so we'll go with it).

Exhibit 3.1

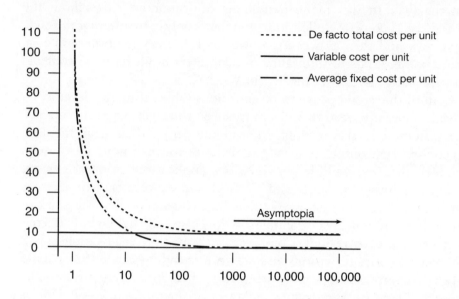

Gosling notes that in software engineering, up-front costs can be vast (particularly when channels and brands must be built), but per-unit costs are vanishingly small. This can make Asymptopia an elusive realm, as it is hard to spread large initial costs down to a trifle of marginal costs when marginal costs verge on zero. But by lowering so many barriers for developers, Java and the Web together can throw wide the gates of Asymptopia. And as that privileged land starts filling with Matsumura's small-scale yet towering giants, waves of unimaginably innovative havoc could start crashing upon the software industry's landscape.

None of this is necessarily good news if you're Microsoft. After all, Microsoft does rather well by Asymptopia's current depopulation. In fact, in at least one key software market (the keyest) it is arguably its only citizen. However, Microsoft also stands to benefit from anything that invigorates its industry and aggrandizes its role in the broader economy. And this seems to have made the company deeply ambivalent about Java. On the one hand it has thrown its desktop open to the language, aiding and abetting its spread to the large majority of the world's computers that it holds in its dominion. Yet it has also taken steps that effectively alter Java's capabilities when it runs on the Microsoft platform, which is contrary to the language's tenet of treating all computers, operating systems, and toasters equally. Some of these steps genuinely enhance the language's power. Others just make it different. Together, they could imaginably give rise to a strain of de facto Microsoft Java, a strain distinct from the *un*-Microsoft Java running on *un*-Microsoft computers. And should the Microsoft strain then proliferate and grow dominant, Java's flattening impact on the industry's playing field could be muted, even obviated. In all of this, Microsoft is both *embracing* and *extending* Java, just as promised back in December of 1995. And whether its delicate dance with the language is being driven by ambivalence or by some fell and hidden design, its impact will linger in the software industry well into the next century.

For now there is relatively little confusion about Microsoft's *embrace* of Java. By all accounts it has been firm and unabashed. The company has built a world-class virtual machine and just-in-time compiler, and is embedding them in all relevant products. As a result, the old maximum fantasies about its operating systems vanishing beneath a Java tidal wave have been shelved by the more levelheaded. Because attractive as some may find that notion, it is hard to deny that Microsoft is now well equipped to rise with the Java tide.

But while Microsoft's embrace of Java has been open and well-publicized, one could question whether it is a gesture of tender infatuation or a black widow's duplicitous squeeze. Many accusations of Microsoft's veiled hostility toward Java have centered upon its ActiveX technology. ActiveX has been widely portrayed as a direct competitor to Java. And it is, to the extent that developers can use ActiveX to distribute non-Java code over the Internet. But Java and ActiveX fundamentally solve different problems. And at least on the Microsoft platform, they can be entirely complementary technologies (and this is where *extension* begins to enter the picture). ActiveX makes it possible to run code written in almost any language in a Web browser. This code is most frequently written in platform-specific languages like C++. In embracing traditional languages, ActiveX makes it easier for developers to Internet-enable their existing code bases, as programs already written in C++ (or most other languages) can be plugged into the ActiveX infrastructure far more easily than they can be translated into Java. In light of the countless thousands of engineer-years already invested in platform-specific software, it would be hard for any sincere supporter of the Internet's proliferation to argue that this is contrary to the Internet's interests.

But distributing code written in traditional platform-specific languages can be risky, because languages like C++ lack Java's robust security provisions. ActiveX partly makes up for this by passing all code through a "trusted" system. This system can verify a download's point of origin (e.g., *It's coming from Intuit*). It can also ensure that software arrives precisely as it was sent, so if a malevolent party hijacks it en route and implants it with a virus, it will not be installed. All of this greatly reduces the risk of infection. But the downfall of trusted security is that it indeed requires *trust* in the party sending the software. Anybody would accept verified code from Microsoft, IBM, or Sun. But many would think twice about accepting code from Goran Radosavljevic of Ljubljana, Slovenia. After all, we don't know Goran as well as we know Bill Gates. So even if ActiveX can verify that his C++ code was unhijacked en route, for all we know it might be destructive by design. But Bill will never send us deliberately destructive code, because we know where he works and can sue him. And so we reject Goran's code. And we tell him to go build a *retribution channel* as reassuring as Bill's before he comes calling again. And in this we boot him out of Asymptopia, even though he might just be a giant upon whose shoulders we should stand. For this reason, commercial software does not get created by *planetwide networks of innovators leveraging their work into different domains* when security models are based on trust. It rather gets created by managed professionals working for companies with Dun & Bradstreet ratings.

This does not mean that ActiveX lacks positive potential. As noted, it makes it easier for developers to introduce their existing code bases to the Internet. It can also enable very robust interactions between the network and the desktop, which is something that straight Java (even persistent Java as enabled by Marimba) cannot yet do. This is possible because ActiveX software can communicate directly with almost anything on the Microsoft desktop (and perhaps all desktops, once the infrastructure's transfer to other platforms is realized; see above). Banks can therefore create ActiveX software that interacts directly with their customers' personal finance packages. Game companies can create ActiveX software that accesses 3-D accelerator cards and other performance-boosting peripherals on their players' computers. ActiveX can also open all of these desktop services to Java, because ActiveX code can be written in almost any language. This means that through ActiveX, a piece of Java software can access services and files on a computer that are normally inaccessible because of Java's security strictures. Put simply, Java can *take over* a computer more thoroughly through ActiveX than it can on its own. But when Java interacts more intimately with a computer, when it manipulates its peripherals and engages the other software it is running, it inevitably becomes platform-aware Java. And once Java becomes platform-aware, it almost inevitably becomes platform-specific. Because if a Java program is written to interact through ActiveX with a software application (or peripheral, or operating system service) that exists only on the Microsoft platform, it is de facto Microsoft-only Java.

ActiveX's potential to tie Java to the Microsoft platform in this manner has inevitably set off alarms in the Java community. But unless one is willing to say that—*Abracadabra!*—now that Java is here, the countless thousands of engineer-years invested in proprietary platforms no longer matter and should be discarded, it is hard to fault Microsoft for integrating its desktop more tightly with the Internet. For Microsoft to do otherwise would withhold much of that vast investment from the Internet. And while Microsoft's offering of that investment should by no means be confused with altruism (it helps the company extend its traditional proprietary advantages to a generally platform-neutral medium), the union of network and desktop it helps foster can only aggrandize the Net. Even arch Microsoft bogey-company Netscape acknowledged ActiveX's positive value by announcing support for the technology in October of 1996. In light of all this, while ActiveX does present challenges to some of Java's precepts, it is unfair to dismiss the technology as a cynical and valueless attempt to subvert Java's philosophy.

The jury is still out, however, on Microsoft's efforts to extend Java itself.

Like all Java licensees, Microsoft is contractually bound to support the language's "portable API." This is the set of core commands and calls that developers make when writing programs in the language. Developers who write only to the portable API can be assured that their code will run on any platform with a Java virtual machine. But licensees can also extend the language unilaterally, in that they can create additional libraries of commands to work in concert with their virtual machines. A Java program that relies on one of those commands might not work in another licensee's Java implementation. This means that if Microsoft (or any other licensee) adds a set of new commands to its Java implementation and attracts a large cadre of developers to use them, the content they create will run on its browsers and computers alone. Should this happen, Java could subsequently balkanize and fracture, lose its platform neutrality, and effectively become one more reason to avoid *un*-Microsoft computers.

For now there is some risk of this happening, as the portable API needs work. Java is still a new language, and is not as functional as anybody would like it to be. For this reason, Gosling's team is working furiously to "make sure the portable API is at least as powerful as any sort of kitchen sink–worth pile of stuff that Microsoft throws in," Gosling says. Whenever Microsoft adds functions to its Java implementation, it must (and does) duly notify Sun of its additions. "And then we have to decide, on a sort of case-by-case basis, whether those are important enough, or causing enough trouble to put those into the portable core," Gosling explains. Microsoft made its first of (no doubt) many extensions to its Java implementation in the summer of 1996.

The system of notification that Sun has established with the Java community protects it from being blindsided by licensees secretly adding features to their Java implementations. But it leaves open the danger that Microsoft could start leading the dance by swamping Sun with extensions and improvements for consideration. Sun would then either have to add them all to the portable API, effectively surrendering the language's agenda to Microsoft, or reject some of them, permitting the dreaded strain of Microsoft-only Java to start taking root. The risk of this will be most acute while the portable API still has significant functional holes that Microsoft could plug faster than Sun. And for now this risk seems dangerously real, because the API does have holes, and "we're too small, alone," Gosling worries. "Last time I asked, they had like twenty-two hundred engineers in the Internet division. Big number. We don't have 10 percent of that here. In this building we have maybe 5 percent of that. But we're working with a lot of outside companies." And the roster is an impressive one, including such industry giants as Silicon Graphics, Adobe, Apple, IBM, Netscape, and others. All of this of course has the potential to degenerate into another case of Microsoft vs. The World. There have been a few of these already. And so far Microsoft has done rather well.

But while Java may face significant challenges from Microsoft and other quarters as it seeks to deliver on its maximum promise, it does have a tremendous set of advantages behind it. It has its wild popularity, which is perhaps without precedent, and is backed with hundreds of millions of dollars in investments. It has its enormous user base, which could soon include almost every heavy computer user in the world. It has dozens of inventive young bet-the-company supporters like Marimba. And perhaps most importantly, it has the *periphery*. It has that new and (for now) undercontested land of Internet computing where its native strengths are most needed. It has new evergreen content categories of the sort that Marimba is helping to enable. It has emerging evergreen application categories that Marimba is likewise helping to enable. It may even have the old Green territory of embedded microprocessors in everyday devices. Sun now hopes to build a huge business from Java chips—microprocessors that are physical implementations of the virtual machine. Native speakers of Java, these can roost in devices far too small for Windows 95's heaving girth. Java chips could give rise to new classes of dedicated computing devices—user-friendly tools that keep calendars, manage recipes, or track golf scores. Such devices could well grow up outside the framework of traditional computing to become an enormous category in their own right, much as the PC largely grew up outside of the mainframe's purview.

All of this is going to make for a wild ride for those already on board, and Kim is certainly game for it. And of course, the Java Express has already taken her a long way. It has brought her to a commanding front-row seat at what could be the most dramatic changing of the guard in the history of computing: that between the proprietary desktop monolith and the open, networked, virtual *something else*. It has also helped her become an entrepreneur—something that she has had her sights on since high school. And, because of her very public role in Java's rise, it has brought her to be labeled in certain circles as *one of the most capable women in the technology industry*. This is of course meant as a flattering description, and it is wholly accurate. But it begs a reference to something that Esther Dyson, one of the technology industry's finest thinkers, once said when asked about Ann Winblad, one of its finest investors. "You *can't* quote me as saying she's one of the most influential women in computing," Dyson was quoted as saying, but "you *can* quote me as saying she's one of the most influential people in computing."

Kim has likewise proven herself to be *one of the most capable people* in technology. And this is how she likes to frame her own work—in a broad context. In professional settings she tries "to not focus on the fact that I'm a woman, as opposed to the fact that I'm doing this job, or playing this role," she explains. But while her professional settings have "almost always" made it easy for her do this, she acknowledges that she has encountered her share of discrimination over the years. Usually, this has been "very subtle," she says. "It's men not taking you seriously, or saying belittling things about you when you're not around. Or even not wanting you to succeed because you're a woman." But none of this has held Kim back. Nor will it, she believes, because in the end, "It's all about your attitude. With the right attitude you can blast through any of this. Because the attitude that you have affects the way that you're treated, and this means that you have power." Kim also points out that the gender issue is "a very complex one, because being a woman in this industry, or any industry, isn't all drawbacks." She acknowledges, for instance, that at least some of the public and press attention she has received "has something—or maybe a lot—to do with the fact that I am a woman in an industry that consists mainly of men." Her appearance in a December 1996 *Forbes* cover story about women in technology is one obvious example of this kind of attention.

But Kim generally doesn't spend much time thinking about broad issues like the role of gender in the workplace, because she frankly doesn't have much time to spare. And "this is the one drawback, if I had to list one, about all of this," she says, which is that life in the Internet vortex can be beyond all-consuming. The pace of the last few years has obliged her to put almost all of her many interests on hold, other than dance and (of course) work. Forgoing the balance that she'd like to have in her day-to-day life, Kim instead thinks in terms of achieving balance *sequentially*, over spans of years, rather than spans of weeks or months. To this end she talks about leading "many lives"—with this Java, Silicon Valley stint being just one of them. When (and if?) it has run its course, she's sure she'll be ready for the next one. She guesses it could be in Europe. One of the Old Countries perhaps (more likely her father's Italy than her mother's Denmark). Or maybe Southern France. Dance may be integral to the coming life. Computers (let's face it) almost certainly will be too.

But for now, Kim doesn't worry much about Phase Next—because things are plenty busy with Phase This. And they will be for a while yet. At least until this Java thing has played itself out.

Make that quite a while yet.

CHAPTER 4

MARK PESCE VRML

The Web in 3-D

WebInnovation, a conference–*cum*–summit meeting arranged by Silicon Graphics, first convened in San Francisco in December of 1995. The fully-booked event drew a thousand key influencers from throughout the Web community. Though growing fast, this community was still nascent and finding its leaders, its forums, and its voice. WebInnovation was loosely meant to hasten all of this. Attendees networked, debated, and socialized. They were also treated to conventional conference distractions like tracks of seminars and a trade showlike floor.

The first general session featured a rock festival-like lineup of opening acts designed to whip up the crowd for the headliner's entry. And this headliner—the Green Day of that Woodstock II—was none other than *The Marc* himself. Marc Andreessen's address brought the program to a satisfying climax, as planned. But while his talk was a treat, the treat was no surprise; by then everyone knew what they were getting into with an Andreessen speech. And so to many, a far more surprising and arresting speaker was a wholly intent, wholly articulate, wholly bald young man whose talk preceded Marc's by a half hour or so. This was another Mark—Mark Pesce. Although an *opening act*, this Mark was no local garage band getting a rare break on the big stage. He was instead impressively credentialed as the originator of the Virtual Reality Modeling Language (or VRML; pronounced *VERmal*

by some, *veeyaremel* by others, *verMAL* by none). VRML is a language that makes it possible for three-dimensional scenes to be distributed over the Web. By then, hundreds of thousands of people were
already using it to create, share, and view models of objects, buildings,
and wild imaginary vistas.

Like Marc, Mark has become something of a celebrity for his contributions (although the magazines that put him on their covers have
names like *Web Developer*, rather than *Time*). And like Marc, Mark is
tall, and no toothpick. His physical stature certainly didn't hurt his
stage presence that day. Neither did the striking baldness, which was a
fashion, not genetic thing. But Mark's real magic was in his delivery.
As usual, he was funny, getting the morning's biggest laughs. As always, he was lucid, uttering not a single *um* in his 20 minutes on stage.
And as no one else, he spoke with enough conviction to make Web-
Innovation feel briefly like an evangelical congress. In this, Mark's
speech was so polished that it almost seemed manipulatively re-
hearsed. But it was largely ad-libbed. He was in fact still outlining
the thing two minutes before he stepped onto the stage. His cheat
sheet was no bigger than a business card. He covered it with impossibly tiny words. He did carry it up to the podium for some reason.
But he hardly glanced at it during his speech. Not bad for a guy who
had hustled almost directly to the stage from a sleepless flight from
Amsterdam.

Exciting as it was, Mark later confided that the high point of his
busy morning was not his own talk. Instead it was a press conference
that shortly followed it. There, Silicon Graphics, Netscape, and Sun
Microsystems jointly endorsed VRML as a means of distributing 3-D
environments over the Web. It was further announced that Silicon
Graphics, Sun, and multimedia software giant Macromedia would
work together to build 3-D capabilities into Sun's Java language (see
Chapter 3). Mark was not in on the talks that led to those announcements for a variety of reasons. He had also been out of the country
for well over a month. As a result, the whole event caught him completely unawares. On stage before the press were Andreessen, SGI
president Tom Jermoluk, and Sun chief technology officer Eric
Schmidt—a very unlikely trio. Netscape and Silicon Graphics were famously friendly, as were Netscape and Sun. But Silicon Graphics and
Sun were known to have their differences. The two companies produced wholly competitive product lines, and squared off in countless
sales situations every quarter. Their joint briefing left Mark more stag-

gered than even his nine hours of jet lag and his straight-from-the-airport speech. The whole production was entirely unexpected. It verged on surreal. But above all, it was an unadulterated delight. Mark later designated that day as *Day One* in VRML's history (and yes, it was preceded by an equally momentous *Day Zero*, and was shortly followed by a *Day Two*). He later said that it all felt "like a gift." Coming just four days before his thirty-third birthday, the timing seemed almost deliberate.

Anyone proclaiming Days Zero, One, and Two had better be a protagonist in the history he landmarks. And Mark is indeed central to the VRML story. But he is not alone behind the language's development and growing popularity. In his own words, VRML "comes from and belongs to the communities which have given it shelter—the Web community, the graphics community, and the simulation community." A product of community, the language represents "the Web's shining example of a grass-roots effort that works." Mark originated the notions behind VRML in late 1993. Working with an engineer named Tony Parisi, he codeveloped its first working prototype, named *Labyrinth*. He and Parisi then shopped their vision and their prototype around. *The community* was running with the ball almost immediately thereafter. The language's name was coined by Dave Raggett, a key figure in the HTML language's development. Most of its underlying code was written by engineers at Silicon Graphics. Untold thousands meanwhile discussed, monitored, and debated its development through *www-vrml*, an E-mail list that Mark and others set up in mid-1994 (the "agora of our *polis*," as he has called it).

Dozens of companies, most of them startups, now comprise VRML's private sector. Together they are creating the tools and much of the content that give the language life. For his part, Mark has yet to turn a corporate profit from VRML. In fact, he does not even have a formal job. But while not an entrepreneur in the strictest sense, Mark has worked to build the VRML community with all of the zeal and focus of a founder-CEO. As its most tireless organizer, most public face, and sometimes conscience, Mark is arguably its "leader." But this role is not easy to exercise, as *the community* lacks the economic links that make private organizations cohere. It can be fractious, and at times deeply political. Almost all of its leaders are controversial with at least some of its blocs, and Mark is certainly no exception to this. He furthermore has no organizational mandate, no corporate power base to draw upon, and certainly no capital to fund his interests or campaigns.

His influence springs solely from his ability to persuade, inform, organize, and, occasionally, shame. But so far, this has proven to be plenty
for him to draw upon in the *ad-hocracy*, as he calls it, of the VRML
landscape.

The scene description language that so fires Mark's pro bono loyal-
ties joins the Web's collaborative power to the representational power
of 3-D graphics. Here, *3-D* does not refer to the pop-up-book effects
viewed through polarized paper "eyeglasses" in cinematic efforts like
Friday the 13th Part 3-D. It rather refers to computer-based representations of physical spaces or items. Computerized 3-D models are almost always displayed on flat screens, and they are not meant to
envelop their users or make them flinch. They are instead meant to enable interaction, exploration, and query. It is this that distinguishes
3-D models from 2-D imagery. A photograph, a painting, or a static
image on a computer screen is just one image, however lush and realistic it might be. But a 3-D representation can put forth infinite numbers
of faces, enabling intimate and intuitive understandings of the scene it
represents.

A robust 3-D model of a chair, for example, can be examined from
any angle. An observer can rotate it, enlarge it, view it up close or
from far away. Aware of the x, y, and z coordinates of the chair's ver-
tices, the computer draws them on its screen in a way that is consistent
with the chair's notional positioning. On a powerful system, the chair
might be mapped with textures to represent wood (or steel, or barna-
cles, or whatever). It might be "lit" by several digital lamps, each with
a different intensity and color of light. If lit, the chair might even cast
shadows and reflections in its environment. Physical processes and
properties can also be modeled. How will the chair break if it's
dropped? Where will it buckle if the wrong person sits on it? How will
water run across its surface in a rain, and where will the puddles form?
Complex *what if* scenarios like these, as well as simpler ones like color
scheme testing, can be modeled almost instantly, saving designers from
the arduous (and expensive) process of physical prototyping.

3-D visualization has become a very serious business. Almost
every industrial product of consequence is now designed in a CAD
(computer-aided design) environment. Non-CAD uses of 3-D technology include flight simulation, oil field mapping, digital special effects,
and *blowing shit up*. This latter market emerged in the early 1990s,
when the wild popularity of the game Doom anointed 3-D as the preferred display mode for advanced video games (and, incidentally,

helped validate the Internet as a distribution channel for commercial software).

Mark was not thinking of *blowing shit up* when he conceived of the notions behind VRML back in 1993. He was instead thinking in downright gentle terms, specifically, of the need to "teach [computers] to speak to our hearts," in order "to make [them] clear to our minds." He believed that as a uniquely accessible and natural way to represent information of all kinds, 3-D visualization could enable this. And so when he first saw the Web (bringing on "an epiphany that has never really ended") he "immediately sensed that [it] needed a three-dimensional interface," one that could "bring the Web out from the flat text and images into a new sensuality that would be more fluid, expressive, and emotional." This would require "a sensual interface," one that could enable people to organize information as they organize their homes and workplaces: intuitively, visually, humanly. Mark writes:

> Imagine an Internet interface where data sources—books, sounds, movies, could be represented naturally, as they are in the real world, with real-world metaphors. People *can* remember real-world metaphors, because they make sense. . . . We organize our lives sensually—think of your record collection or your books—and need to bring that same technique to the Internet if we ever hope to be able to use it to our fullest capacity.

VRML has not since become the Internet's main interface; far from it. HTML is still the Web's lingua franca, and perhaps it (or its 2-D successors) always will be. But VRML has become one of the Web's dominant media types. And as the specification becomes more robust, its capabilities will expand, as will its usage. VRML is already commonly used to represent and distribute 3-D models, abstract data sets, and complex, navigable environments. Visual simulation, *blowing shit up*, and much, much more are not far behind.

All of this got started long ago in North Kingstown, Rhode Island, where Mark first started dabbling with computers ("I've really never done anything but work on *micros*," he says, dropping the Olde English word for "PC", which shows that he was pretty much onto this thing from the start). Mark's circumstances in North Kingstown were comfortable but modest; his father was an insurance inspector, his mother an executive assistant. Ever since those earliest days, he has viewed himself as a very "integral person," one who harbors "a real love for literature, for poetry, for various other arts" in addition to *micros*. Given his diversity of interests and aptitudes, he might have done better than to choose a college known for the raw intensity and focus it demands from students. But Mark of course lacked the hindsight to make that call at age 18. And so, with high school awards in both science and English putting wind to his sails, he confidently trooped off to MIT in the fall of 1980. Today, while he does not seem to be genuinely bitter about what came of that, he will point out that he found the Institute to be a "profoundly dehumanizing place." His time there wasn't lonely, as he did encounter his own kind ("I managed to find the *freaks*," he confides). But that didn't do much for his academic standing. Mark barely lasted three semesters as a student.

"Washing out of the Institute" was no fun, but it did not sour Mark on Cambridge or its *freaks*, and he ended up lingering in town for the better part of a decade. Local lore had it that "if you get thrown out of MIT, that's your first step in your career as a programmer" (Mark cites a long list of legendary hackers that supports this proposition). So in a sense he was off to a roaring start. Mark stayed connected to MIT through lecture series, events, and social circles for years, and he found this to be very stimulating. Many of his friends also ended up working with distinguished or soon-to-be-distinguished researchers, which brought him into the orbit (or at least within a handshake) of the likes of Danny Hillis, the parallel computing pioneer who later founded Thinking Machines, and "this weird guy named Nick Negroponte."

Negroponte is now widely-known for his role in founding MIT's celebrated Media Lab, and for funding HotWired's parent, *Wired* magazine (see Chapter 7). But back then, he was still cutting his teeth on something called the Architecture Machine. Although not personally acquainted with Negroponte, Mark had friends who were helping with the *ArcMac*, as it was known. He now describes this as "one of the prototypical instances of a VR [virtual reality] system." In it, "you . . . sat in front of this huge monitor, and you saw an office in front of you, with a file cabinet that you could open up and get files out of." Tame stuff by today's standards, but very innovative in its time. It was also very influential to Mark, whose later fascination with virtual reality heavily informed VRML's development.

Also on the scene in those days was Eric Drexler, the father of nanotechnology. Drexler would hold periodic *salons* at his home at which "some of the more interesting geek types at MIT" would hang out and discuss ideas (and this was "back when being a geek was still a bad thing," Mark points out, clearly proud to have been *fashion-forward*). Mark got to know Drexler well enough to get an early-access draft of his seminal book *Engines of Creation* (which included "a chapter or two on the reanimation of *dead* people, which did *not* make it into the Random House version," Mark gossips, his voice conspiratorially low). But more influential to Mark than this was the writing of Ted Nelson. Although wholly lacking the power to raise the dead, Nelson lay the foundation of Mark's thinking about networked media.

Mark first encountered Nelson's thoughts through a conference called Xanacon, which was held at MIT during the summer of 1982. This and Nelson's book, *Literary Machines*, constituted "epiphany number one" in his intellectual life. Nelson was then in the midst of his decades-long pursuit of a dream called Xanadu. In the words of *Wired* magazine's Gary Wolfe (who wrote a powerful retrospective on the project), Xanadu "was supposed to be the universal, democratic hypertext library that would help human life evolve into an entirely new form." It instead evolved into "a 30-year saga of rabid prototyping and heart-slashing despair." Xanadu sought to bring a vast expanse of published documents together into a hyperlinked whole, which would be made accessible throughout the world by a distributed computing network (sound familiar?). It never quite *got there*. But Nelson did enlist many hardworking disciples to his vision during its rabid and heart-slashing years. And while Mark never joined their ranks, the notion of Xanadu seduced and inspired him from the moment he first learned of it. It haunted him for years after.

In addition to reading out-there technical tracts and chitchatting at *salons geeks*, Mark had to make ends meet, so he worked. The country was going through tough economic times when he left the Institute, which drew him to the communications industry ("recession-proof," he reasoned). Within it he moved from job to job. Eventually he landed at an innovative networking company called Shiva. It was while he was at Shiva that he first read a science fiction novel called *Neuromancer* by William Gibson. *Neuromancer* introduced him (and the rest of us, as it is Gibson's term) to the notion of *Cyberspace*, which is described therein as "a consensual hallucination experienced daily by billions. . . . A graphic representation of data abstracted from the banks of every computer in the human system" (this, incidentally, is one of the most quoted passages on the Web. Type *consensual hallucination* into any good search engine and brace yourself). At roughly the same time Mark encountered a magazine interview with Jaron Lanier ("it was issue #2 of *Mondo 2000*," he points out, characteristically precise). Described by some as a "Rastafarian hobbit," Lanier was a famously dreadlocked inventor and the nascent virtual reality industry's most public face. He had in fact coined the term "virtual reality," and was at the time running VPL, the first virtual reality company to really matter.

Very loosely, VR is meant to involve an encompassing interaction with a computer-generated world. Its main interface device as conceived by Lanier and others is the "head-mounted display," or HMD. HMDs are meant to fill a user's field of view with 3-D graphics. But unlike the 3-D on computer screen, this stuff is ideally meant to have enough stereoscopic depth and grab-your-nose reach to make *Friday the 13th Part 3-D* look like a ho-hum Viewmaster disk. HMDs are powerful largely because they can track and respond to a user's head movements. This means that if somebody wearing a good HMD glimpses a building to the right and turns to face it, the imagery it displays will shift in sync with the user's neck motion. At the end of the gesture, the building will fill the user's field of view head-on, just as happens when we turn to face a building on a street corner.

Mark was familiar with the notion of virtual reality by the time he encountered Lanier's *Mondo* interview. But as an engineer with a networking, not graphics background (and one who is, he insists, "functionally handicapped as a 3-D designer"), he did not see himself fitting into the field. But in *Mondo*, Mark recalls, Lanier said that VR was not meant to be the television of the future (then a popular presumption), but the *telephone* of the future. The *telephone*? The telephone! "There is a structural divide in my life around me reading that phrase," Mark now says. "There is before, and after." Suddenly it was *after*; it was *epiphany number two*. And it was time to move to California.

The San Francisco Bay Area at that time "was the nerve center of all things VR," Mark says, and he arrived in the summer of 1991 with a handful of "core people" from his Boston crowd. After a few months of brainstorming on back porches and looking for a market opening, he cofounded Ono-Sendai and brought his group on board. Self-consciously named (with the author's permission) after the manufacturer of the cyberspace "decks" in *Neuromancer*, the young company hoped to design the first $300 HMD. Today Mark's simplest advice for young entrepreneurs is to "[n]ever name your company after something in a Gibson novel; it's bad karma." Ono-Sendai grew to 14 full-timers and briefly looked like it would deliver on its ambitious goals. But then the money got tight. The early enthusiasm went missing, and he and his cofounder started disagreeing violently. Among the indignities that Mark eventually suffered was termination (Him! A founder!). Ono-Sendai did not long outlast his departure.

Mark soon found work as a contract engineer and started marking time, vaguely awaiting *epiphany number three*. This luckily came quickly, and it came via *Fringeware*, an E-mail list which he describes as "dealing with the obscure, the weird, and the marginal from the fringes of Cyberspace." In the early autumn of 1993, a perplexing series of references to "URLs" began to crop up in the *Fringeware* mailings. You are *what*s? Mark did some digging and discovered that these were "Uniform Resource Locators," or addresses in a new area of the Internet called the World Wide Web. Mystified, he downloaded Mosaic and there it was—*Xanadu!* Soon he was strutting around with an Hallelujah grin that "did not go away for two *weeks*!" Every night he came home directly from work and surfed the Web for hours. Within a few days, he reckoned that he had seen the whole thing (you could do that back in 1993). And already, he was thinking of that *sensuous interface* that would later become VRML.

New Year's Day of 1994 found Mark visiting an engineer named Tony Parisi and his wife, Marina Berlin. Tony and Marina were new arrivals from Boston, and he shared several mutual friends with them back in the old country. He didn't know them very well yet, and as a result had "stayed away from talking the geek stuff with them." But by then, Mark was becoming a familiar face at Tony and Marina's place, and the young couple felt that the time had come to politely ask him what he . . . *did*. A four-hour conversation followed. To Mark's surprise, Tony turned out to be very interested in his notion of creating a 3-D interface to the Web. And since Tony was a "languages geek," his skill set happened to complement Mark's networking background nicely. Mark and Tony began meeting regularly at a café called Jumping Java, where they fleshed out VRML's earliest prototype (score one ironic point for the Java language, which has no *Jumping VRML* in its past). By Valentine's Day their work was ready. "Preferring a poetic name to a functional one," Mark remembers, they christened it *Labyrinth*.

Within Labyrinth, Mark could build three-dimensional "worlds" (or gatherings of polygons and objects that users could navigate through). He could link objects within his worlds to Web pages (click on that blue sphere, say, and find yourself at Netscape's home page). He could likewise link into Labyrinth worlds from Web pages (click on that highlighted word, say, and the Labyrinth browser would launch and draw the world you selected). In this, Labyrinth was similar to the early "helper-apps" described in Chapter 2. But it had many limitations. It pretty much just ran on the old Unix workstation that Mark wrote it on, for one thing. It also could only support relatively small worlds, and was not thoroughly "debugged" (i.e., rigorously tested and patched by a quality assurance team). In short, Labyrinth was a proof-of-concept piece, one that could evangelize the notion of a 3-D interface to the Web and frankly do little else. But in this, it worked very well.

Within a few weeks of Labyrinth's completion, Tim Berners-Lee himself invited Mark and Tony to present at the First International Conference on the World Wide Web in Geneva. Mark later breathlessly compared that event to "training at Starfleet Academy—with all the races, all the cultures, collaborating to create a global infrastructure for human knowledge, a restoration of the library of human knowledge lost when the Romans burned Alexandria, two thousand years ago." Only a few hundred people attended, but the trappings of momentous beginnings (many of them self-conscious) were everywhere. Tim Berners-Lee lectured on "the need for a constitution for Cyberspace" ("for the first time we had something worth protecting!" Mark explains). David Chaum gave the maiden demonstration of his DigiCash system. And Mark presented Labyrinth (Tony did not attend, as they only had enough money between them for one plane ticket). In retrospect, Mark marvels that "the one thing that absolutely no one said" throughout all of this "was that the Web was going to change the world. It was *just understood*."

The name VRML (then for Virtual Reality *Markup* Language; "Modeling" was swapped in later) was coined by David Raggett in a discussion session which preceded Mark's presentation of Labyrinth. An important pioneer of the HTML language, Raggett thought Labyrinth "was very simple but nevertheless a sign of things to come." His own conception of VRML was more complex. But, he recalls, he was "too busy in late '94 on HTML-related work to build a demo or write the detailed specs" for it. So he and Mark powwowed, and Mark ran with the ball. Already sensitive to *the community*'s will, Mark hung onto the popular VRML name, despite reservations about its *unpoetic* ring. *The community*'s infrastructure arose quickly after that. Brian Behlendorf, then the systems administrator at *Wired* magazine (*Unix Sherpa* was his official title), attended Mark's presentation. Behlendorf recalls being impressed, not so much by Labyrinth itself as by "the ideas it embodied." He soon offered Mark some *Wired* bandwidth and disk space to host an E-mail list. *www-vrml*, itself the catalyst of the broader VRML community, was born. Over a thousand people subscribed almost immediately.

Behlendorf was a valuable ally for Mark's cause, because he was everywhere on the early Web. He was the founding chief engineer at HotWired (see Chapter 7). He was a cofounder of agenda-setting Web site designer Organic Online (see also Chapter 7). He also created Hyperreal, one of the first and (certainly) best early Web sites that was not devoted to a wholly technical topic (Hyperreal was and remains an information clearinghouse for the Bay Area's rave scene, as well as for a certain segment of youth culture in general). Even the Apache freeware Web server, a democratic hodgepodge of "patches" (or impromptu enhancements) to the NCSA Web server, was among Behlendorf's brainchildren (by the summer of 1996, this pro bono gift of his to the Internet was running roughly 33 percent of the Web's servers. This was twice Netscape's share, 10 times Microsoft's, and substantially more than that of first runner-up NCSA). Mark was of course delighted to affiliate VRML with such a tenured Internet old-timer. And since Behlendorf had finally reached California's drinking age just a few months before the conference, he could even take the guy out for a beer to say thanks once they were home.

VRML's next big outing was SIGGRAPH '94 in Orlando. The summer SIGGRAPH sessions (shorthand for the Special Interest Group on Computer Graphics) are the computer graphics industry's annual family reunions. Hoping to recruit some more supporters in this community, Mark and Tony went to the show and set up a Labyrinth demo in "SIGKIDS," an exhibit area that caters to SIGGRAPH's youngest constituents. The demo was popular with SIG's kids as well as with at least a few of its grownups, some of whom were on *www-vrml*'s now 2000-strong subscriber list.

Somewhere in the midst of SIGGRAPH's chaos, Mark came across Rikk Carey. Bespectacled, ponytailed, and frank, Rikk was a key engineering manager at Silicon Graphics, a company so monolithic within the computer graphics community that some had come to refer to SIG-GRAPH as SGI-GRAPH ("SGI" being Silicon Graphic's stock ticker symbol and its preferred nickname in the United States. Abbreviating Silicon Graphics to *Silicon* marks a clueless outsider about as quickly as calling San Francisco *Frisco*). Silicon Graphics had pioneered and largely created the commercial 3-D market, building a once-narrow niche into a multibillion-dollar business. Its hardware was behind the dinosaurs of *Jurassic Park*, the Boeing 777, the Nintendo 64, and countless more humble special effects, designs, and products. The company also had an interesting Internet credential in that it was founded by Netscape founder Jim Clark.

For his part, Rikk led the team that developed and maintained a programming environment called Open Inventor (which is almost universally abbreviated to *Inventor*). Rikk had come to interest Mark considerably by then, as a well-regarded 3-D designer named Clay Graham had recently suggested that Inventor might be a good basis for VRML. Mark knew he needed something, as Labyrinth was a *demo*, not the foundations of Cyberspace. And Inventor seemed like it could be up to the task.

Inventor is a tool kit that can greatly speed the development of 3-D scenes. (Rikk describes it as "an infrastructure for building Cyberspace applications"). In simple terms, it is a series of shortcuts, or building blocks. To get a sense for its simplifying power, consider the commands an engineer might write in an Inventor-compliant environment to draw a cube with a texture mapped to its surface:

```
root = new SoSeparator;
camera = new SoPerspectiveCamera;
light = new SoDirectionalLight;
texture = new SoTexture2;
cube = new SoCube;
root->addChild(camera);
root->addChild(light);
root->addChild(texture);
root->addChild(cube);
texture->filename = "brick.rgb";
ra.setSceneGraph(root);
```

Compare this to the commands that would generate the same cube in OpenGL (usually abbreviated to GL, for graphics library), a lower-level 3-D engine which is a standard throughout the computing world:

```
float tVec[4];
float tMat[16];
/* glGetIntegerv(GL_DEPTH_BITS, . . .);*/
glViewport(0, 0, 400, 400);
glClearIndex(0);
glClear(0x4000);
glEnable(GL_DEPTH TEST);
glClear(0x100);
glDisable(GL_DEPTH_TEST);
/* glGetIntegerv(GL_DEPTH_BITS, . . .);*/
glViewport(0, 0, 400, 400);
glClearColor(0, 0, 0, 0);
glClear(0x4000);
glEnable(GL_DEPTH_TEST);
glClear(0x100);
tVec[0]=0.2;tVec[1]=0.2;tVec[2]=0.2;tVec[3]=1;
glMaterialfv(GL_FRONT_AND_BACK, GL_AMBIENT, tVec);
tVec[0]=0.8;tVec[1]=0.8;tVec[2]=0.8;tVec[3]=1;
glMaterialfv(GL_FRONT_AND_BACK, GL_DIFFUSE, tVec);
glPolygonMode(GL_FRONT_AND_BACK, GL_FILL);
tVec[0]=0;tVec[1]=0;tVec[2]=0;tVec[3]=1;
glMaterialfv(GL_FRONT_AND_BACK, GL_EMISSION, tVec);
/* glGetBooleanv(GL_RGBA_MODE, . . .); */
glEnable(GL_LIGHTING);
glDisable(GL_LINE_STIPPLE);
glLineWidth(1);
glEnable(GL_NORMALIZE);
glPointSize(1);
glDisable(GL_CULL_FACE);
glLightModeli(GL_LIGHT_MODEL_TWO_SIDE, 0);
glMaterialf(GL_FRONT_AND_BACK, GL_SHININESS, 25.6);
tVec[0]=0;tVec[1]=0;tVec[2]=0;tVec[3]=1;
glMaterialfv(GL_FRONT_AND_BACK, GL_SPECULAR, tVec);
tVec[0]=0;tVec[1]=0;tVec[2]=0;tVec[3]=1;
glTexEnvfv(GL_TEXTURE_ENV, GL_TEXTURE_ENV_COLOR,
   tVec);
glTexEnvi(GL_TEXTURE_ENV, GL_TEXTURE_ENV_MODE, GL
   MODULATE);
glTexParameteri(GL_TEXTURE_2D, GL_TEXTURE_WRAP_S,
   GL_REPEAT);
glTexParameteri(GL_TEXTURE_2D, GL_TEXTURE_WRAP_T,
   GL_REPEAT);
glDisable(GL_POLYGON_STIPPLE);
glDisable(GL_TEXTURE_2D);
glDisable(GL_POINT_SMOOTH);
glDisable(GL_LINE_SMOOTH);
glViewport(0, 0, 400, 400);
glScissor(0, 0, 400, 400);
glMatrixMode(GL_PROJECTION);
   tMat[0] = 2.414;tMat[1] = 0.000;tMat[2] =
      0.000;tMat[3] = 0.000;
   tMat[4] = 0.000;tMat[5] = 2.414;tMat[6] =
      0.000;tMat[7] = 0.000;
```

```
    tMat[8] = 0.000;tMat[9] = 0.000;tMat[10]=-
        2.414;tMat[11]=-1.000;
    tMat[12]= 0.000;tMat[13]= 0.000;tMat[14]=-
        8.363;tMat[15]= 0.000;
glLoadMatrixf(tMat);
glMatrixMode(GL_MODELVIEW);
    tMat[0] = 1.000;tMat[1] = 0.000;tMat[2] =
        0.000;tMat[3] = 0.000;
    tMat[4] = 0.000;tMat[5] = 1.000;tMat[6] =
        0.000;tMat[7] = 0.000;
    tMat[8] = 0.000;tMat[9] = 0.000;tMat[10]=
        1.000;tMat[11]= 0.000;
    tMat[12]= 0.000;tMat[13]= 0.000;tMat[14]=-
        4.182;tMat[15]= 1.000;
glLoadMatrixf(tMat);
/* glGetIntegerv(GL_MAX_LIGHTS, . . .);*/
glEnable(GL_LIGHT0);
tVec[0]=0;tVec[1]=0;tVec[2]=0;tVec[3]=1;
glLightfv(GL_LIGHT0, GL_AMBIENT, tVec);
tVec[0]=1;tVec[1]=1;tVec[2]=1;tVec[3]=1;
glLightfv(GL_LIGHT0, GL_DIFFUSE, tVec);
tVec[0]=1;tVec[1]=1;tVec[2]=1;tVec[3]=1;
glLightfv(GL_LIGHT0, GL_SPECULAR, tVec);
tVec[0]=0;tVec[1]=0;tVec[2]=1;tVec[3]=0;
glLightfv(GL_LIGHT0, GL_POSITION, tVec);
glLightf(GL_LIGHT0, GL_SPOT_EXPONENT, 0);
glLightf(GL_LIGHT0, GL_SPOT_CUTOFF, 180);
glTexEnvi(GL_TEXTURE_ENV, GL_TEXTURE_ENV MODE, GL
    MODULATE);
tVec[0]=0;tVec[1]=0;tVec[2]=0;tVec[3]=1;
glTexEnvfv(GL_TEXTURE_ENV, GL_TEXTURE_ENV_COLOR,
    tVec);
glEnable(GL_TEXTURE_2D);
glGenLists(1);
glNewList(1, GL_COMPILE_AND_EXECUTE);
    glPixelTransferf(GL_RED_SCALE, 1.000000);
    glPixelTransferf(GL_GREEN_SCALE, 1.000000);
    glPixelTransferf(GL_BLUE_SCALE, 1.000000);
    glPixelTransferf(GL_ALPHA_SCALE, 1.000000);
    glPixelTransferf(GL_RED_BIAS, 0.000000);
    glPixelTransferf(GL_GREEN_ BIAS, 0.000000);
    glPixelTransferf(GL_BLUE_BIAS, 0.000000);
    glPixelTransferf(GL_ALPHA_BIAS, 0.000000);
    {
    gluBuild2DMipmaps(GL_TEXTURE 2D, 3, 64, 64, GL
    RGB, GL_UNSIGNED_BYTE, b);
}
glEndList();
glFrontFace(GL_CCW);
glEnable(GL_CULL_FACE);
glLightModeli(GL_LIGHT_MODEL_TWO_SIDE, 0);
tVec[0]=0.8;tVec[1]=0.8;tVec[2]=0.8;tVec[3]=1;
glMaterialfv(GL_FRONT_AND_BACK, GL_DIFFUSE, tVec);
tVec[0]=0.2;tVec[1]=0.2;tVec[2]=0.2;tVec[3]=1;
```

```
glMaterialfv(GL_FRONT_AND_BACK, GL_AMBIENT, tVec);
tVec[0]=0;tVec[1]=0;tVec[2]=0;tVec[3]=1;
glMaterialfv(GL_FRONT_AND_BACK, GL_SPECULAR, tVec);
tVec[0]=0;tVec[1]=0;tVec[2]=0;tVec[3]=1;
glMaterialfv(GL_FRONT_AND_BACK, GL_EMISSION, tVec);
glMaterialf(GL_FRONT_AND_BACK, GL_SHININESS, 25.6);
glBegin(GL_QUADS);
        tVec[0]=0;tVec[1]=0;tVec[2]=1;
        glNormal3fv(tVec);
        tVec[0]=0;tVec[1]=0;
        glTexCoord2fv(tVec);
        tVec[0]=-1;tVec[1]=-1;tVec[2]=1;
        glVertex3fv(tVec);
        tVec[0]=1;tVec[1]=0;
        glTexCoord2fv(tVec);
        tVec[0]=1;tVec[1]=-1;tVec[2]=1;
        glVertex3fv(tVec);
        tVec[0]=1;tVec[1]=1;
        glTexCoord2fv(tVec);
        tVec[0]=1;tVec[1]=1;tVec[2]=1;
        glVertex3fv(tVec);
        tVec[0]=0;tVec[1]=1;
        glTexCoord2fv(tVec);
        tVec[0]=-1;tVec[1]=1;tVec[2]=1;
        glVertex3fv(tVec);
        tVec[0]=0;tVec[1]=0;tVec[2]=-1;
        glNormal3fv(tVec);
        tVec[0]=0;tVec[1]=0;
        glTexCoord2fv(tVec);
        tVec[0]=1;tVec[1]=-1;tVec[2]=-1;
        glVertex3fv(tVec);
        tVec[0]=1;tVec[1]=0;
        glTexCoord2fv(tVec);
        tVec[0]=-1;tVec[1]=-1;tVec[2]=-1;
        glVertex3fv(tVec);
        tVec[0]=1;tVec[1]=1;
        glTexCoord2fv(tVec);
        tVec[0]=-1;tVec[1]=1;tVec[2]=-1;
        glVertex3fv(tVec);
        tVec[0]=0;tVec[1]=1;
        glTexCoord2fv(tVec);
        tVec[0]=1;tVec[1]=1;tVec[2]=-1;

glEnd();
```

Both command sets would create substantially the same cube, but the first is obviously faster to enter and easier to architect. The difference is that GL is geared toward drawing, spraying, fire-hosing pixels on the screen ("it's the best thing in the world at that!" Rikk gushes), but there is no such thing as an *object* within it. Inventor, on the other hand, is object-aware. It understands notions like *cube* and *texture*.

This understanding makes it concise, and more approachable to people who are not graphics experts. Inventor, then, can be thought of as a higher-level abstraction of the 3-D programming process. It translates between a more accessible language (its own) and a deeper one that operates closer to the metal (GL). GL is itself one of the most important programming layers in the world. It too was developed and propagated by Silicon Graphics (long before Inventor). Licensed by innumerable companies including IBM, Hewlett-Packard, Sun, and Microsoft, it is all but ubiquitous in computing today. GL's ubiquity has enabled Inventor to itself become a cross-platform tool kit, which means that something written in it can be made to run on a PC, a Macintosh, or a Unix workstation with minimal heartache. This is clearly an essential feature for a content language on the cross-platform Internet. Combined with the language's many other strengths, it seemed to make Inventor an ideal foundation for VRML.

Mark and Rikk were already acquainted by SIGGRAPH as Brian Behlendorf (here he is again) had arranged their meeting back in July. After a quick talk in the conference's corridors, they agreed to reconvene once they were back in the Bay Area. Shortly afterward, Rikk made the Inventor file format available to the VRML community royalty-free. His rationale for doing this was that "a rising tide floats all ships," and as the 3-D tide went, so would go SGI.

A consensus supporting Inventor as VRML 1.0's basis soon built within *the community*. This process began at SIGGRAPH with the first of many VRML "BOFs" (or Birds of a Feather meetings) under Mark's direction. It continued throughout the late summer and early fall in the *www-vrml* forum. Eventually Mark arranged a vote in which Inventor was the most serious (but not sole) candidate (Mark's own Labyrinth scripting language was among the other contenders, as was an entry from CAD software giant AutoDesk). Inventor won. This left only one small remaining "t" to cross in VRML 1.0's development, which was that somebody had to write the actual specification. Gavin Bell, one of Inventor's lead engineers, ended up with the job. It took him only three days to assemble the first 1.0 proposal, because "Inventor already had many, many man-years invested in it," he explains, which he just had to "reapply" to VRML. In the end, about 90 percent of the 1.0 specification was taken directly from Inventor, which was itself largely written by Rikk and an engineer named Paul Strauss.

Once the specification was in place, somebody needed to create a VRML browser, and Silicon Graphics again volunteered its engineering team for the heavy lifting. Soon, Bell and co-Inventor inventor Paul Strauss had created "QvLib." QvLib is a "parser," or an engine that can read (in this case) VRML files and produce sets of manipulable objects from them. SGI made it freely available to the rest of *the community*, which meant that anybody willing to create a user interface and the other features essential to a browser would now have their parser built for them ("another major gift from SGI," in Mark's words). SGI did not initially plan to do this itself ("we had pans in lots of fires," Rikk recalls). But some weeks after QvLib was posted to the Internet, Rikk decided to have his team finish the job. Soon after, the WebSpace browser was ready.

VRML content viewed through WebSpace (or any of the other early VRML browsers that followed it) was displayed in a helper-app mode. In practice, this meant that when a user clicked on a hyperlink to a VRML model, a new window would appear on the computer screen in which the model would then be drawn (this new window would be the VRML browser). The user would then be able to navigate the model at will; to zoom in for close-up looks at objects, to spin and manipulate them, to examine them from many angles. Objects could be hot-linked back to Web pages or to other VRML worlds.

WebSpace was ready for beta testing in early April of 1995. Its public debut and the announcements surrounding it became *Day Zero* in Mark's nomenclature (although this term originated with Kevin Hughes, another VRML pioneer. Days *One*, *Two*, *Three*, and *Four* are all Mark's). Mark remembers local papers like the *San Francisco Chronicle* and the *San Jose Mercury News* breaking SGI's press embargo and scooping the news. *Newsweek* was on the story too. For the first time since the disappointing collapse of Jaron Lanier's company VPL, Cyberspace was reentering the popular consciousness. When the third World Wide Web Conference was held later that month in Damstadt, Germany, visitors to SGI's booth could see VRML for the first time through WebSpace's portal. After little more than a year of development, the technology had been realized.

A number of other browsers soon appeared. All were based on Silicon Graphics' QvLib parser. But unlike WebSpace, which was originally written (logically enough) for Silicon Graphics machines, these were targeted at democratic platforms like the PC and Macintosh. Most were released by tiny startups that were staking their futures on VRML. These included Chaco Communications, Paper Software, and InterVista. InterVista was Tony Parisi's company. Mark did not join him in the venture ("Now I can go off and be a kook [without] injuring his business," he explains). Instead, he set to evangelizing VRML's message, building its community through *www-vrml* and other forums, and encouraging every tiny browser company he came across. He also started work on his first book (*VRML: Browsing & Building Cyberspace*). With a foreword from Tim Berners-Lee, more than 50,000 copies were quickly sold.

Long before the book's publication, VRML content of all kinds started seeping through the Web. Some designers were drawn to VRML as much for its newness as anything else. The Web's Joneses move fast, and the Webmasters keeping up with them will use any trick to stay current. Decorative and flashy instances of VRML therefore became (and remain) common.

Others were drawn to VRML because it was accessible across such a wide variety of computer platforms, which was unusual in the traditionally proprietary realm of 3-D graphics. By the time VRML appeared, almost all 3-D authoring had long been done in software environments that had to be present (in at least in some scaled-down form) for their creations to be viewed. In practice, this often meant that the best way to see a piece of 3-D work was to walk over to the workstation it was designed on ("downloading through the sneakernet," as it is said). When geography made this impossible, 2-D printouts or even faxes were (and certainly still are) used to show off 3-D work. VRML is rendering such meager substitutes unnecessary by making 3-D designs as portable as E-mail messages. It is also making 3-D content as broadly accessible as E-mail, because once a model is translated into VRML, it can be viewed on any computer with a VRML browser, regardless of its operating system.

Some companies soon began experimenting with VRML as a design-sharing medium. VRML seemed especially well-suited to aiding engineer-to-nonengineer communication, as engineers with high-end hardware and software are often unable to share their output with co-workers who have humbler gear on their desks. Because of this, senior executives, sales and marketing staffs, and even some engineering management often have no easy access to their design staff's output. VRML over a corporate intranet can change this by enabling the distribution of robust, interactive views of almost any 3-D work throughout the enterprise.

VRML also won early enthusiasts in areas far removed from to-be-expected markets like design, as professionals in many different fields have come to use 3-D visualization as an analytical tool but lack an easy way to share their work with distant colleagues. For instance, research chemists commonly use 3-D visualization packages to model molecular structures and valences. Electronic journals can now at least consider distributing the output of these tools, enabling much richer communication between publishing chemists and their audiences than ink on paper. A noted VRML user in this field, Omer Casher of Imperial College, London, points out that "A molecular model in [a] printed journal provides only one perspective," that of the author. But a "3-D model in an electronic journal allows for user interaction. Perhaps the user may come up with another viewpoint that the author hadn't originally considered." This, Casher postulates, "may ultimately foster future collaborations" between contributors to online publications and their readers.

VRML's native advantages helped it spread quickly after Web-Space's release. There were several early experiments in design sharing and publishing. Many companies also used VRML to enrich their Web sites in ways that went beyond simple decoration. British Telecom posted an innovative application in which VRML was used to identify errors in a phone network. Intel used it to heighten the draw and effect of its Pentium showcase. Several ambitious efforts were meanwhile made to represent "real world" physical spaces. Mark was involved in a project that created a detailed VRML model of San Francisco's South Park area. Another effort modeled the layout of a multimedia festival in Los Angeles. The number of VRML-presenting sites linked out of directories like the VRML Repository at the University of California at San Diego numbered in the hundreds, then thousands. Millions of people meanwhile downloaded copies of the many VRML browsers that were made freely available over the Internet (Mark estimates that there were 20 to 25 such browsers within a year of *Day Zero*).

But despite the excitement it caused, VRML 1.0 had limitations.

For one thing, it was static; objects did not move in its worlds. It was also silent, as the specification had no provision for sound. And there was nobody there, as "entering" a 1.0 world meant downloading it across the Web and viewing it alone. *Cyberspace* may have hinted at the virtual throngs and mayhem found in speculative novels like *Neuromancer* and *Snow Crash*. But in its first release, it was a still and very quiet place. VRML would clearly have to do better than this if it was ever to become a mass phenomenon within a society hooked on flashy media.

A second hurdle was that VRML could be sluggish, and downright cartoonish in look. Viewing VRML on older (and still very common) systems like 486 PCs could be especially unrewarding. Scenes moved jerkily, and often slipped in and out of "wireframe" display mode (in which objects are represented as 3-D meshes without surfaces mapped onto them to save computing cycles). Poor scene design was to blame for some early performance problems, and this issue would gradually obviate as VRML designers got better at their art. But the quality of the VRML experience was inevitably tied closely to hardware capabilities. And much of the world was still accessing the Internet from systems that simply couldn't keep up with VRML's demands.

A third hurdle was distribution. The RealAudio Player and the first VRML browsers were posted to the Web at roughly the same time. But a year later, far more RealAudio Players had been downloaded. One reason for this was that the VRML community was a *community*. It was comprised of many different companies that were posting browsers for a variety of reasons; not of a single company with a unified marketing message and strategy. This led to the fourth, and perhaps most troubling hurdle, which was lingua franca. Because of VRML 1.0's functional limitations, many of the browsers that appeared after WebSpace implemented their own "proprietary nodes." These typically added flashy features to scenes that VRML 1.0 lacked, such as motion, movies, or even multiple-user interactions.

The danger in this was that the various VRML browsers generally could not read one another's proprietary nodes. And there was meanwhile no Netscape Navigator equivalent which could create a de facto standard node set through sheer market domination. This meant that some of the most functional VRML sites charged steep "admission prices" in that they required their visitors to download *yet another*

VRML browser in order to enter. For instance, visiting the San Francisco Opera House model, the "Point World" chat space, and Chaco
Communications' "Pueblo" world (all described below) required three
separate browsers. Together, they swallowed many megabytes of disk
space, and each alone required up to 30 minutes of download time using a 28.8 modem over a good Internet connection. Such high demands of user intent, disk space, and idle time were anything but the
ingredients of a budding mass medium.

By the summer of 1995, Mark had suggested to several other community leaders that they "get like thirty people together for a day or
two to figure out what should be done," he recalls. But then "Rikk
[came] to me and said, you know, Mark it's a good idea, but why don't
we do something a little more permanent?" The two drew up a list of
10 people, and the VRML Architecture Group (VAG) was created.
The group was chosen "with the intent of getting all the technical areas covered, and then as many companies as possible as well," Rikk
remembers. It included Rikk, Tony Parisi, and Gavin Bell, as well as
representatives from companies including Microsoft, Netscape, and
World's Inc. (which had created a popular multiuser environment
called "Alpha World").

The VAG charged itself with creating VRML 2.0, which would be
a new and far more functional version of the specification. It was a
product of Mark and Rikk's initiative, not of a spontaneous movement
on the *www-vrml* list. Asked if this didn't make it a kind of . . . self-appointed body, Mark answers that "There was no 'kind of' about that!
We were self-appointed, and whenever people ask I say 'yes, we're self-
appointed.' And so far, only a few people have seemed to really get upset about that. Someone had to do it. And really, frankly, most people
are not upset with the results because the VAG tends to not act auto-
cratically. That's one of the things we *don't do*."

The VAG was announced at a VRML session at SIGGRAPH 1995
in Los Angeles. Only a year after Labyrinth had debuted at the influential conference before a curious handful in a children's exhibition hall,
there was suddenly an astonishingly large SIGGRAPH constituency
(Rikk estimates that at least 500 attended) who cared enough about
the specification to join its *ad hocrats* in debating its future. This made
it a very "seminal meeting," Rikk recalls. "It really felt almost like a
Declaration of Independence sort of a meeting. There were representatives from all across the industry. Virtual reality, visual simulation,

artists, animation, networking, Cyberspace, Internet. These people were all mixed together in this big room with Mark up there trying to control it."

The meeting (and much of SIGGRAPH) was dominated by "this raging debate that was going on as to the future of VRML," Rikk remembers. The big question was, "Is the next step a small incremental improvement [on] VRML 1.0? Or is it . . . radically major?" To most people, *Radically major* meant supporting "behaviors" within VRML. This was a broad notion, as depending on whom you asked, behaviors could mean anything from simple animations, like spinning chairs, to "a walking, talking duck that follows you around and helps you out whenever you have problems," Rikk explains.

It didn't take long for the raging debate to move from SIGGRAPH to the newly-formed VAG. Rikk and Gavin Bell were both in its conservative, un*radically major* camp at first. But despite that, they turned up at the second VAG meeting with a new VRML proposal that had some "really interesting behavioral capabilities," Rikk recalls. They ended up "switching sides" like this because while "everyone with their rational side agreed" that a small step forward was appropriate, "the irrational side, and the VRML community itself, would not shut up about behaviors on the mailing list, and in private," Rikk remembers. After a while, he "started realizing we're not winning this discussion. People are not listening, and maybe they're right." So about a month before the VAG meeting, he and Bell decided to do something about it. The result was that "A bunch of people were *furious*," Rikk recalls. They were skeptical about the sudden change of heart, particularly in light of the fact that all of the VAG members had agreed to come the meeting with only un*radically major* proposals for an incremental "1.1" specification. SGI's work looked suspiciously like a full-blown "2.0" proposal, which left a lot of people feeling ambushed "because we came to the VAG meeting with a proposal in hand, and didn't give it to them ahead of time," Rikk remembers. And the awful truth of it is, we didn't have time." By the end of the VAG meeting things were just "chaos."

Much of what came next was influenced by another VRML-related effort that SGI already had under way—one that lay far from Mark's purview. At the heart of it was an SGI marketer named John McCrea, who had coincidentally been an MIT classmate of Mark's during those three fleeting semesters. John and Mark hadn't known each other in college (John too was a bit out of the mainstream there—he was a creative writing major). But they knew each other well through VRML circles, as McCrea was heading up the marketing team behind WebForce, SGI's popular line of Web authoring and serving products. Since the spring of that year, the Webforce team (and McCrea in particular) had a gnawing pet peeve, and its name was *Java*. Not the language itself, but the misperceptions that an excited but puzzled public held about its relationship to VRML. "Customers, partners, the press; everybody seemed to think they were competitive technologies," McCrea remembers, "which was fundamentally untrue."

The confusion had many sources. Both Java and VRML were brand-new technologies for one thing. Both also played in a new medium that was not yet widely understood. But perhaps most significantly, Java's Sun ties and VRML's SGI ties affiliated them with two of the Valley's most famously rivalsome rivals. It also didn't help that they were both widely associated with *decorative stuff* in their earliest days. Never mind that VRML's decorations were all about visualization, and Java's were all about *interpreted, object-oriented, multithreaded, garbage-collected, safe, and robust alternatives to* C++. The irony in this was that "VRML and Java were if anything great complements, rather than competitors," McCrea says. And it seemed to him that if Sun and SGI could get this message out to the public, both languages would benefit. So in August he called Kim Polese at Sun, and soon he and Rikk held a meeting with her, James Gosling, and others.

A few months later, SGI, Sun, and Netscape were ready to make their joint announcements supporting Java and VRML at WebInnovation. During the press conference that followed the opening session, Sun and SGI announced that they would work together to extend Javas portable API (see Chapter 3) in a way that would build a bridge between it and VRML. Startlingly to many, the companies also indicated that the underlying logic that would enable behaviors in SGI's VRML 2.0 proposal would be based on the Java language. This fact was not formally noted in the day's press releases. But it was evident to anybody who attended the press conference itself ("the word 'integration' was used," Rikk recalls). *Day One* had arrived. As mentioned, this caught Mark unawares. He had been writing in Holland during the prior month, and when in Europe, "I'm able to answer E-mail," he says, "but I'm not able to know what's really going on." But even if he had been at home, SGI's talks with other companies were SGI business, and Mark would not have been party to them. *Community* or no, this is the reality of the private sector. For these reasons, the revelation was a shocker to him—and a good one, as he had long believed that Java and VRML would make an excellent team.

A still bigger shock came three days later, when Microsoft announced a technology it was calling *ActiveVRML* (or AVRML) as part of the sweeping Pearl Harbor Day announcement of its Internet strategy (see Chapter 1). To the mainstream press, AVRML was just a small sideshow to Netscape and Microsoft's dramatic showdown. But the fact that the world's most powerful software company suddenly cared enough about VRML to put forth an alternative to it (and to appropriate its name) was big news in the VRML community—big enough to make it *Day Two* on Mark's calendar.

Some brief inspection made it clear that AVMRL was nothing to dismiss with a sniff and an eye roll. Its roots dated back to an advanced development project called "TBAG," which began at Sun Microsystems in 1990. The TBAG team had migrated en masse to Microsoft in 1994, where it "worked on a project with similar goals, but which had a much stronger productization focus and corporate support," according to its leader, Salim AbiEzzi. The Microsoft project was called RBML (for "Reaction-Based Modeling Language"). The AVRML moniker was a very recent innovation. AbiEzzi's team had plenty of technical smarts and accomplishments to recommend it. Its halo glowed all the brighter for its affiliation with Andy Van Dam, the man who *wrote the book* on computer graphics (quite literally; *Introduction to Computer Graphics*, which he coauthored with James Foley and three others, is one of the industry's canonical texts). A Brown University professor, Van Dam was also a consultant to Microsoft. He recalls that the company's initial intention had been to release AVRML as a mature specification in 1996. But he urged AbiEzzi's team to enter the VRML 2.0 process, warning that Microsoft "would be seen as the heavy if they, after VRML 2.0 had been ratified, then came out with an alternative proposal. A lot of people would take umbrage, no matter how good of a proposal it was."

AVRML's sudden appearance created a dilemma for the VAG. There were now two credible de facto proposals on the table for VRML 2.0 and no designated process for anointing the better, as the VAG had originally intended to (*ooops*) develop the one-and-only proposal itself. So what's a VAG to do? "We screamed at each other for a couple of hours," Mark recalls sheepishly. Most of its members then went to a briefing (which Van Dam presided over) at which Microsoft discussed AVRML's features. Afterward, in the face of "two reasonable candidates for VRML 2.0," the VAG members agreed that they needed "a *process*," Mark remembers. Specifically, an RFP, or Request For Proposal would be made. This meant that any party—Silicon Graphics, Microsoft, Apple, the City of Milwaukee—would be welcome to submit a VRML 2.0 proposal. Some yet-to-be-defined mechanism would then anoint the victor. The SGI team was unable to attend the Microsoft meeting, and learned about the decision shortly afterward. Mark recalls that they weren't pleased ("I had to scrape Rikk off the ceiling with a *spatula*," he shudders).

Rikk leaves the spatula out, but otherwise tells a similar story. "We had a bad attitude" about the RFP, he confesses. Among other things, he worried that "We were gonna be spending six to nine months evaluating this stuff, and trying figure out what an RFP looks like, what are the rules for proposing, how do we decide which ones are better," he remembers. He was also skeptical about the role *the community* could play in an engineering design process, even after all those months of hearing Mark effuse about its wonders. "Any dimwit and their brother who has an idea can disrupt your discussion and disrupt your spec by asking dumb questions and just saying, 'I disagree,' " he fretted.

But as December wore on, "Mark kept on saying, 'Rikk, if you're so confident your stuff is good, why can't you be confident in an open forum,' " Rikk remembers. And this point hit home, because Rikk was terrifically confident. He was also afraid that fighting the RFP would make it look like SGI had "some private secret agenda" to take over VRML. So in the end he decided that the best approach was to "work with the community, and be as open, and have as many alliances as we possibly could, and win it that way."

The RFP was officially announced in January with a February submission deadline and a March voting deadline. Entries from Sun Microsystems, Apple Computer, and others were submitted along with SGI's proposal and AVRML. Mark decided to open the vote not only to the VAG, not only to subscribers to the *www-vrml* list (both of these had been considered as possibilities), but to the entire planet. Anybody who felt strongly enough about the process to examine the proposals and cast a vote was entitled to do so.

SGI christened its proposal "Moving Worlds" and openly engaged the VRML community in its development. Although most of the spec's design was done by Rikk's team, outside engineers from Sony and elsewhere were also involved. The team meanwhile kept an active and open channel to the rest of *the community* through regular postings and discussions in the *www-vrml* forum. They also created an online Moving Worlds "polling both" where *community* members could vote their preferences on different design decisions. And this "actually made a difference in what we did," Rikk recalls. "Whenever we would have a split decision on what to do, the vote would always push us the right way."

Rikk and his team duly examined AVRML to see if there was any way to create a "compromise" specification incorporating the best ideas from both candidates. But unfortunately, "the proposals were so far apart, there was no place in between," Rikk says. He found their differences to be like those between Russian and English, in that "They both work, but there's no way to create a Russian-English mixture. It would be worse than either." Fundamentally, Rikk characterizes AVRML as a "programming language," and Moving Worlds as a "content language." A good programming language can tell a computer to do almost anything, and this made AVRML an enormously flexible tool. But "to do anything in ActiveVRML you have to write a program," Rikk points out, which "is not something that content-creative people are going to be able do." Since the best 3-D work in SGI's other content markets (e.g., Hollywood and the video game industry) was invariably created by artists, not engineers, Rikk felt that Moving Worlds' artist-friendly (or at least artist-friendlier) approach was the right one for the job.

Whatever AVRML's technical merits, Microsoft did a poor job of campaigning for the hearts and minds of the AVRML community by almost all accounts. Mike McCue, the founder of an influential VRML browser company called Paper Software (which Netscape was to soon acquire), remembers that "there was zero [Microsoft] presence on the mailing list and suddenly boom—it was like an onslaught. . . . Post after post was from Microsoft explaining why ActiveVRML was great and why everything else was screwed." Some of those who had been pouring their pro bono energies into VRML for over a year at that point not surprisingly viewed Microsoft's sudden fascination with the language skeptically (Microsoft also invited trouble by appropriating the VRML name, as this tends to be "a particularly good way to piss people off," in Gavin Bell's words).

All of these issues concerned Mark. But what really informed his own view of Microsoft was its decision to withhold its "Direct 3-D" rendering software from SGI (rendering software draws 3-D images on computer screens). Rikk and his team wanted to experiment with Direct 3-D because it ran well on PCs, and they were starting to build a PC-based Moving Worlds browser. But because Direct 3-D was only available as beta software at the time, Microsoft was able to control its distribution very closely. Rikk recalls that he was informally told that he could have a Direct 3-D beta license sometime in December of 1995. But Microsoft soon reversed this position because "the VRML work we were doing [was] considered competitive."

This infuriated Mark because however logically, legally, even ethically sound Microsoft's position was from a strict business standpoint, it clashed badly with his own notions of the VRML community's cooperative ethos. It also convinced him that AVRML "was never going to be open," that "regardless of how good the technology was, it was all going to end up being in Microsoft's pocket." Since in his view "it takes an industry to build Cyberspace, not a company," this meant that making Microsoft's technology the foundation of VRML 2.0 could only be a recipe for Cyberspace's failure. In a retrospective on the matter, he wrote that "Watching Microsoft bungle its relationship with the VRML community is a case study in how to be heavy-handed, ham-fisted, and woefully arrogant." Asked about Microsoft some months after that, he summarized that their "products are Internet-ready, but their culture is not." Ironically enough, Microsoft did eventually reverse its position on Direct 3-D ("they were unbelievably helpful, and they really wanted us to be a beta site," Rikk recalls). But by then Rikk's team had already adopted a rival technology.

Moving Worlds got a big leg up in February of 1996, when Netscape announced its public support for it along with more than 50 other companies, including IBM, Sony, Informix, and video game giant Sega. Also applauding Moving Worlds that day was Mark himself, who was quoted saying that "Silicon Graphics, Netscape, and their many partners are to be congratulated on developing a community-driven consensus process, which led to the current proposal. It is an endorsement of the open exchange of ideas which is the core tenet of the VRML community. Moving Worlds accurately reflects the needs of the VRML community, both as a content delivery vehicle and as a new platform for development." The final vote in March favored Moving Worlds overwhelmingly.

The Microsoft side was of course not happy to lose, and took exception to Mark's endorsement of Moving Worlds. AbiEzzi believes that the selection process "got started on the right track." But when Mark "put his name on the [Moving Worlds] announcement," it "for all practical purposes preempted the RFP process." Van Dam also thinks Mark's statement "distorted impartiality" in the vote. He believes that "there may be a perfectly reasonable explanation, but . . . on the surface of it, it looks like he bypassed [the] process." Mark's simple answer to these complaints is that "I'm allowed to have an opinion too." In making the February announcement, he says, he "was trying to reflect the fact that one party was open to the process and the other one was not. SGI was listening to its users and the community, and Microsoft was not."

In the end, even Microsoft lined up squarely behind Moving Worlds when it announced that it would integrate a VRML 2.0 browser with Internet Explorer at SIGGRAPH '96. And so, by the fall of 1996, Moving Worlds, a.k.a. VRML 2.0, ruled the VRML landscape. And this made that landscape far livelier than it had been, because comparing Moving Worlds to VRML 1.0 is like comparing color television to AM radio.

The most powerful new features that Moving Worlds brought to VRML were *sound, scripts,* and *sensors. Sound* is sound. Unlike the silent VRML 1.0, Moving Worlds can tie audio to objects and support background soundtracks. Sounds can also be "localized," meaning that they can be made to (apparently) emanate from the objects they are tied to. Navigate toward an eggbeater in a VRML scene, for instance, and its sound might get louder and move to the foreground. Startle the eggbeater, and its sound might follow it leftward as it scurries away.

Scripts enable animations and behaviors. Animations are predetermined movements, much as they are in cartoons, while behaviors allow objects to react to their environments dynamically according to rules. A VRML ball, for instance, might be given behaviors that teach it how to bounce. Once it "knows" how to bounce, it can bounce in anywhere. It can bounce outside on the ground, or it can ping between the floor and ceiling of a VRML hut. If the hut's ceiling starts sinking downward toward the floor, the ball might "know" to ping faster.

Sensors, finally, are like trip wires, in that they trigger actions in response to other actions. If a user navigates into a VRML room, a sensor might tell the room's lights to switch on. If the user then pushes a blinking red button, another sensor might tell a nearby artillery gun to start *blowing shit up*.

Silicon Graphics's creative engineers designed a number of refined VRML 2.0 scenes while the spec was being finalized in the summer of 1996. The canonical one features a red ball, a green cone, and a blue cube that bounce about, each emitting its own noise upon hitting the floor. More elaborate is a palm treed and pyramided oasis whose sun rises and sets, and whose objects squawk and morph when clicked. More elaborate still is a world known as Aztec City, whose visitors can navigate about a *templo mayor* area and find smoking urns, drumming drummers, and maybe even a gory sacrificial rite.

By bringing VRML far beyond static hyper-linked polygons, Moving Worlds helped it over one of the major hurdles separating it from widespread use: its initial lack of flash, motion, and excitement. The distribution and lingua franca hurdles were also effectively cleared on February 12, 1996 (while the RFP was still in process), when Netscape announced its acquisition of tiny Paper Software, a company that had developed a remarkably popular VRML 1.0 browser called WebFX (WebFX already had two million users at the time of the acquisition, according to Paper's founder, Mike McCue). WebFX would soon be integrated with the Netscape Navigator, and would later be replaced by a VRML 2.0 browser.

This amounted to a tremendous benediction of VRML technology by the Web's then-undisputed arbiter of relevance. It also meant that the audience for VRML content would soon increase dramatically, as by the start of 1997 substantially all serious Navigator users would also be de facto VRML users. An explosion of VRML content was almost sure to result, as almost all content people are drawn to large audiences, and VRML would soon have one of the largest audiences on the Web.

VRML's lingua franca issue was meanwhile about as dead as its distribution problems, because Paper's VRML browser would almost inevitably become the de facto 1.0 standard. And when Netscape (through Paper's engineering team) developed a 2.0 browser, it would be a standard too. To the extent that non-Netscape browsers appeared, they would have little cause to introduce proprietary nodes, as the 2.0 specification was not stifling. VRML 2.0 is indeed so rich that it is difficult for browsers to implement all of its features. Non-Netscape browsers were therefore more likely to differentiate themselves with fuller implementations of the specification than with extensions to it. This clean lingua franca situation was later partly muddied when Microsoft's belated embrace of VRML 2.0 and the rising popularity of Internet Explorer brought a second VRML browser into broad distribution. But as of this writing, that browser, like Netscapes, was compliant with the 2.0 specification. For all of these reasons, Mark urgently designated the date of the Netscape-Paper acquisition as "The Day the Universe Changed"—or *Day Three* (*Day Four* came in August of 1996, when the completion of the 2.0 specification was announced at SIG-GRAPH).

SGI released the first beta version of its VRML 2.0 browser (the Cosmo Player) early in the summer of 1996. By then, VRML 1.0–enabled copies of the Netscape Navigator were being downloaded at a rate of thousands per hour. Netscape's own implementation of VRML 2.0 was slated to be integrated with the Navigator by early 1997, and, by most estimates, release versions of VRML 2.0 browsers were expected to approach ubiquity amongst Web users by the summer of that year. As this ubiquity is achieved, and as designers become more expert in creating VRML 2.0 scenes, the Internet's *sensuous interface* is finally leaving its dress rehearsal.

VRML's new ubiquity means that VRML content can reach all of the Web's users, not just a subset of them. Its integration with the major Web browsers and the rise of technology like Netscape's plug-in API (see Chapter 1) also now lets VRML display in an "in-line" mode, meaning that VRML models can be integrated as seamlessly with Web pages as images or pieces of text. This is causing both decorative and professional uses of VRML to expand. Budget-sensitive Web site designers and publishers are more likely to invest in 3-D content if all of their visitors can appreciate it, rather than just a few. And designers can more easily use VRML to share work with clients, since anybody with Web access now also has VRML access.

Some believe that the rich representations of physical spaces that VRML enables have particularly great business potential. In the summer of 1996 a Web-based Yellow Pages service called BigBook launched an ambitious VRML effort that uses satellite imagery to create 3-D models of major U.S. cities which it links to its database of business listings. BigBook debuted this service with a model of its hometown, San Francisco. The model's visitors can fly through the city, click on a building, and see all the businesses that are located within it—or ask to see all of the restaurants in a particular section of the city, with flags marking the buildings in which they are located. BigBook CEO Kris Hagerman says that "People navigate a city based on landmarks—such as streets, buildings, bridges—even the city's skyline. VRML provides a level of realism that no other medium can match, by allowing us to take all the information in a flat, two-dimensional street map and extend it vertically into 'real' space." He believes that this not only provides a more compelling and intuitive user experience, but can at the same time offer marketers a differentiated and powerful advertising vehicle.

VRML stadiums and theaters might also soon populate the Web, as sales tools for online ticket vendors. James Waldrop of VRML design shop Construct Inc. ("the premier VRML user," according to Gavin Bell) estimates that an application that would let theatergoers explore 3-D representations of the views from different seats in a venue could cost as little as $25,000, provided that blueprints were available and that the underlying technology was already developed. San Francisco's Planet Nine Studios has already developed an application like this in its model of that city's opera house. Waldrop believes that VRML trade show spaces and shops supporting multiple simultaneous users could also become popular. His company created the first such trade show site for NTT, Japan's telecom. In it, visitors found booths staffed by live "avatars," or 3-D representations of other people with whom they could discuss products by rattling messages back and forth on their keyboards.

Avatars, the colonists of the VRML frontier, are becoming common on the Web. A "real" person's proxy, puppet, or delegate to an online environment, an avatar can be a faithful representation of its master or (more commonly) a fanciful one. Avatars mark presence. As in NTT's online trade show environment, users typically navigate their avatars around 3-D spaces in which they encounter other avatars and engage them in conversation. Mark describes avatars as "essential to an interactive 3-D experience—without them, you're lost and alone in a world of disembodied spirits."

The most obvious and (for now) common use of avatars is in "chat" environments. These are gathering points where visitors exchange typed messages in real time. Text-only chat has been popular since the early eighties, accounting for up to 30 percent of user time in the commercial online services. This is an impressive figure, considering how limiting a medium text is for conversation. Consider the little punctuation packets ("smileys" or "emoticons") that chat room regulars use to emote glowers, winks, and embraces (rotate this page 90 degrees clockwise to see :-) a friendly smile from the author). Clever but blunt instruments, they themselves emote a need for a richer medium. Chat environments that truly harness the expressiveness and sensuality of 3-D space should therefore blossom into truly evocative alternatives to their text-only ancestors.

Chatting avatars are already common on the Web. Black Sun Interactive (which takes its name from *Snow Crash*, an important Cyberspace novel *not* by Gibson) built its CyberGate browser around VRML 1.0 extensions. It enables multiuser avatar interactions, and was adopted early on by sites including the Lycos search engine (Lycos's chat area is called *Point World*—which ironically suggests zero dimensions rather than three). Other early multiavatar sites included MTV's Tikki Land. Match.com, an online dating service, has even hosted avatar-based "singles parties."

Early avatar environments are low in detail and offer only sluggish motion. But they hint at the power that visually-rich chat spaces will acquire. Even the most primitive avatars reveal something about the people who design or choose them. In this they can allow for richer first impressions than even the cleverest "screen names" (the online aliases of text-only chat-ers). Avatars also provide visual anchors for the personalities behind them, making the chat experience more natural to visually-oriented people. Such anchors can also build a sense of personal continuity among those who encounter one another in chat spaces regularly over time (although this of course doesn't happen when people change their avatars like socks). Some early avatars can communicate with rudimentary gestures as well as words. These do not, of course, make them even remotely as expressive as the human face, but avatar gestures should eventually evolve into something more expressive than typed "smileys." A company called OnLive! is making avatars even more capable of nuance by connecting them to their masters' voices, and even synchronizing their lips to their masters' words. Mark writes that the first time he saw an OnLive! demo "I couldn't break eye contact with the avatar. Simultaneous vocal and visual connection are the two elements which propel you through the critical suspension of disbelief and into the virtual world."

Avatar technology will not stop at the chat room. VRML 2.0's (and 3.0's, and 4.0's . . .) proliferation will place increasingly lush, realistic, and complex shared environments within the equivalent of a short stroll of tens, and eventually hundreds of millions of people. There is no reason why these environments can't support as much diversity and depth as the shared spaces of equally large (and diverse) societies. Forerunners of what might result from this can be found in MUDs, MUSHes and MUSEs. MUDs (Multi-User Domains, or Dungeons) and their ilk are shared online fantasy realms. Their users log in regularly, and at times for very long periods. Inside, they converse, build complex personae, and forge friendships, rivalries, and sometimes even marriages. Over time they acquire greater powers, and may learn how to affect their MUDs structures, or break, or even change their rules. MUDs are intensely seductive environments for many of their users. In her 1995 work *Life on the Screen*, MIT sociology of science professor Sherry Turkle writes of users spending tremendously long hours in them, at times logging into several at once. Some even come to think of reality (or "RL" for *real life*) as "just one more window" among the many that divide their screens ("and it's usually not my best one," a student confides).

But despite this almost frightening power, traditional MUDs draw relatively few people. Construct's James Waldrop, a dedicated MUD user for many years, estimates that by mid-1996 there were roughly 150 MUDs of scale, each with roughly 200–300 "day-to-day" users and perhaps 2000–3000 more casual ones. Assuming (as Waldrop does) that there is significant user overlap across MUDs, this indicates that serious MUD users number only in the tens of thousands. Traditional MUDs have small populations because, like the early Internet (see Chapter 1), using them requires some real technical acumen. The fact that they are almost invariably text-based furthermore limits their popular appeal. But advanced VRML can change all this by putting highly accessible, visually-rich MUDs within the reach of millions.

Chaco Communications, the maker of a popular VRML 1.0 browser called "VR Scout," created the earliest VRML MUD-like environment (called "Pueblo") using VRML 1.0 extensions. Waldrop, for one, believes that MUDs will "absolutely" go mainstream as they take on 3-D interfaces.

The result could be a growth in MUDs or other complex online social environments comparable to that which computer gaming enjoyed after it adopted visual interfaces many years ago. The gaming world's giant was once Adventure, a majestic, almost lyrical text-based piece. In its day, Adventure mesmerized thousands. But the multibillion-dollar game industry that now far outgrosses the first-run movie market didn't really take root until games started engaging their players eyes, ears, and tripwire reflexes. Nintendo's flashy Donkey Kong Country game (itself now a primitive golden oldie), which racked up over a half billion dollars in retail sales, no doubt accounted for more player hours in its first weekend on the market than Adventure has in the decades since its release. The appeal of games like it is rooted in a raw craving for realism in media that crosses ages and cultures. This craving added pictures to broadcast media and sound to movies. It causes screen sizes, sample rates, and dots-per-inch counts to increase inexorably every year. It will just as inexorably drive the lushness of networked 3-D forward as quickly as processor speeds can sustain its march.

And this, of course, is that one hurdle to VRML's market acceptance that neither the 2.0 specification nor Netscapes acquisition of Paper Software could resolve. Three-dimensional representation taxes computer systems terribly. This can make VRML sluggish, jerky, and cartoonsome. VRML 1.0 can be agony to browse on a PC running on an older Intel 486 microprocessor. VRML 2.0 can be far worse. But computer software and content are almost always designed for current and coming platforms, because the installed hardware base is on its way out the moment it is plugged in. Countless 486-based PCs have already joined their 286 grandparents farming dust in attics, propping open doors, and sailing off cliffs. The P-90s (i.e., PCs with Pentium chips running at 90 megahertz) that will for now survive them can do a fine job of displaying well-designed VRML. And P-90s have themselves long been as rare in new computer stores as expired medicine on a responsible pharmacist's shelf. The installed base of computing hardware will continue to churn as furiously as it has in the past. P-90s, their heirs, and theirs will farm dust and fly off cliffs before today's sixth graders are through with high school. And as they do, the VRML (or its replacement) of the masses will become increasingly fast, lush, and real.

One hint of where this could all lead can be found in the Montreal headquarters of Softimage. Softimage creates sophisticated 3-D authoring software that runs on high-end graphics workstations like Silicon Graphics'. Now a division of Microsoft (it was acquired in 1994) Softimage employs hundreds of people. Its director of visual research is Char Davies, an accomplished artist who has been with the company almost since its inception. One of Davies' most powerful works is called "Osmose." Osmose is an immersive virtual-reality piece of the scale, nature, and realism that the public once expected from VR pioneers like Jaron Lanier. It runs on a $280,000 graphics supercomputer that directs its full fury at a lone user wearing a head-mounted display.

Mark considers Osmose to be the first instance of VR as art. In it, visitors explore a majestic, translucent representation of a forest clearing. Osmose is not a linear story with beginnings and closure, nor is it a game with opponents and points. It is rather a piece to explore intuitively and languidly. With neither joystick nor keypad, Osmose has a user interface built around balance and breath. Breathe in, rise up; breathe out, sink down. Lean back, drift backward; lean left, drift leftward. Davies says that Osmose borrows its navigational metaphor from Scuba diving, the one realm in which people truly operate in three dimensions. Its content, she says, is "affected by a painterly sensibility" that she developed during her years as an artist. In describing Osmose, Mark echoes Davies' words about painterliness. But at times he accidentally describes her as a sculptor, perhaps because she has so mastered the *sensuality of space* that he sees at the heart of 3-D design. Of Osmose, Mark has said that it "could only have been designed by a woman," because it is about being and intuiting, rather than battling and overcoming.

Perhaps he is right. But let's face it—some of us are guys. If you're one of these, you too might feel yourself connecting to that guy zeitgeist even as the straps of Osmose's breath monitor tighten on your chest and its machine-head slides onto your shoulders. As the adjustments are made, your right hand might—just might—clutch involuntarily for a gun. And if it does—admit it—you're gonna want grenades in that forest. You're gonna want M-16s. You're gonna want rabid bears, trees you can blast at, and trees that'll blast you back. And you're gonna want to beat those trees. And then you're gonna want to claw your way to Level Five and get blown to kingdom come yourself. And when it's all over, you'll want a score. You'll want a *high* score. You'll want the highest damn score on the board, so you can call up Mark Pesce and let him know that you *kicked his ass* at Osmose.

And this will last for a good eight seconds. But after growing accustomed to Osmose's interface, almost any visitor will start feeling weightless, and soon, wholly of the environment. All notions of Bonus Rounds will fade (don't worry, guys—this will pass) as Osmose itself kicks in. Osmose's center is a tree in a clearing. All is translucent and most is still. Everywhere pulse bright corpuscles of light. They surge through the translucent earth to the tree's roots, then pulse through them and upward through its trunk and beyond. The light flows into the forest. There are rivers, roots, and ponds to explore, and leaves as well. And everywhere shine the bright corpuscles of the forest's life while a set of seductive, ambient sounds echo and shift with a visitor's proximity. Breath in, rise slowly through the forest's roof, and enter a place of light and verse. Scrolling lines of poetry in French and English float about the visitor in this cloudy realm. Exhale, sink past the roots through the forest's floor, and enter the substrata. This is the 20 thousand lines of C-code that programmer John Harrison wrote for this world; they surround the visitor here. Somewhere is the code that connects to the breath monitor. Find it, and watch the values surge from 0 to 255 as Osmose attunes itself to its visitor's life. Everything in Osmose is displayed with full stereoscopic depth. Its illusions are made complete by the sophistication of its head tracking gear. Turn to the right, and the displayed images shift just as they would if you were really in that clearing, under that pond, on that leaf.

Sure, sure, sure; *try doing that on your Pentium 90*. Clearly, Osmose is not consumer electronics. But inevitably, the horsepower it harnesses will be. Greg Estes is the director of marketing in the Silicon Graphics division that designs the Onyx, the computer system that Osmose runs on. He estimates that Davies' Onyx would have listed for roughly $280,000 when new. But it is not new. Indeed, the configuration she owns has not even been available since June of 1995, when it was superseded by faster gear. A year later, Estes estimated that the same amount of money could buy a system which ran roughly 10 times faster than hers. A year after that, it would buy a lot more.

And as Davies' budget buys more and more, the performance she acquired in 1995 inevitably sells for less and less. To get a rough sense for how quickly this process is moving, consider the Nintendo 64, Nintendo's third-generation TV set-top gaming platform. The Nintendo 64 first shipped in the United States in September of 1996. Its real-time 3-D graphics capabilities were designed by Silicon Graphics engineers. In very rough terms, Estes estimates that the 3-D graphics performance found in it would have resided at the top of the Silicon Graphics product line as recently as 1990 (although the top SGI systems of that day of course had many features that Nintendo machines lack).

Does this mean that technology which listed at the Osmose price-point just six years ago is available at Wal-Mart today? Not exactly. Estes points out that "graphics performance is a very complex characteristic which can't possibly be measured with a single metric. In many meaningful ways, 1990's high-end systems outperform the Nintendo 64 significantly. In some others, the Nintendo 64 is actually more capable. But in terms of those performance traits which are most pertinent to navigating, not creating 3-D worlds [which is what the Osmose end user experience involves], the high-end system performance of 1990 is largely present in the Nintendo 64." And with those caveats, could we expect to see playback performance of the sort that powers Osmose at a consumer price-point in 2002? "With those caveats," Estes answers, "absolutely. SGI's strategic mandate is to migrate the levels of digital realism found at our top end into consumer hands. Weve been doing that for years. And we're not slowing down. So I definitely expect that Osmose-like realism will be accessible to consumers within a few years."

Osmose is not written in VRML. But there is no reason why experiences as powerful as the one it offers cannot be, after the language has matured further and PCs have caught up with 1995's Onyxes. And when that inevitable day comes, environments as rich as Osmose's can become available in the home, and can be shared over the network. Avatars and their environs could then become dizzyingly realistic. Whether the network protocol of that day is called *VRML*, *AVRML*, or *Fred* is almost irrelevant. And whether the day actually comes in 2002 or 2006 is likewise irrelevant. What is relevant is that the long-term significance of 3-D graphics over the Web is indicated by pieces like Osmose, not the Lego Land animations of yesterday's VRML 1.0. And that significance will become manifest not only within our lifetimes, but within a single-digit span of years. When it does, ever-heightening processor speeds and network ubiquity could truly turn VR into *tomorrow's telephone*, just as Jaron Lanier once predicted.

These days, Lanier himself is more of an observer and commentator than a pot-stirring catalyst in the technology world. His company collapsed a few years ago in an ugly episode that ended with a French corporation seizing its patents (some felt the affair smacked of French industrial policy). These days he lives in a spacious and sunny loft in Manhattan's TriBeCa neighborhood. His life is more filled with headphones than head-mounted displays. Always an accomplished musician, Lanier now records for Sony, plays jazz at the Knitting Factory, and has even had a symphony commissioned. But he still keeps his technical riffs honed. Among other things, he heads up a research team at Columbia University which is developing a visual programming interface for the Java language.

Lanier believes that Osmose-like immersiveness could be networked over the Internet (whether using VRML or another medium) and made available in homes within five years. Of VRML itself, he says he was "a little disappointed" at first. He initially felt the language should have been named something like "Geometry Environment Markup Language" because "it only cared about this external environment, this fixed geometry." But now that the language is growing more robust , he finds its name more appropriate.

Lanier believes that VRML's architects (or those of its successors, or replacements) play an important role, because "there's this way that the quality of underlying standards percolates up to the end results. If you look at a world that's built with GL [the Silicon Graphics graphics library; see above], there's something that looks good about it, because GL has a really solid, well-thought-out underlying philosophy." This means that "one of the most fundamental duties of computer scientists is to build underlying layers that will lead to beautiful culture," because they are "building the fabric of which culture is sewn together."

If this is true, the man who has devoted his last three years to VRML's layers has some important work ahead him. But Mark certainly does not face it alone. Rikk Carey and Gavin Bell, who are now departed from Silicon Graphics and building their own VRML company called Wasabi, are among those who have worked just as hard to advance VRML's agenda as he has. Also on the case are countless engineers at Silicon Graphics, Netscape, Sony, and many other companies, as well the thousands of contributors and subscribers to www-vrml. The community, then, is huge—bigger than most companies—and the commitment among some of its members is extraordinary.

Talk to Mark of his own future, for instance, and it is rare to hear mention of anything other than VRMLs. It was largely in service of the languages agenda that he astonished roughly everybody by moving to Los Angeles in the fall of 1996. "LA is where the content will ultimately come from," he explained to the slack-jawed, "not South Park." Mark's mission then became playing a role of "diplomacy and facilitization" in bringing VRML to Hollywood. Also high on his list was helping to drive the VRML Consortium's development. The Consortium's charter was agreed upon at SIGGRAPH '96, and Rikk Carey was later chosen to be its first president in the fall. The VAG's heir, it was to be financed by a group of dues-paying corporate affiliates (Mark ultimately distanced himself from the Consortium in December of 1996, citing concerns about the heavy representation of multi-billion dollar corporations on its board of directors and other matters).

Although he is often as flustered about VRML's state and well-being as any doting father (or Godfather, or uncle, or whatever the appropriate relationship may be), Mark usually seems to be confident about VRML's future as a robust and independent specification. He has not worried that the integration of VRML into the leading Web browsers would let Netscape or Microsoft control the specification as thoroughly as Netscape once controlled de facto HTML (see Chapter 1). Shortly after the Paper Software acquisition, he wrote that such an outcome was "unlikely" because "VRML is several orders of magnitude more sophisticated than HTML and won't withstand willy-nilly changes or improvements that have been commonplace with HTML." A greater risk than VRML's domination might therefore be of a rival specification, perhaps even a proprietary one, eclipsing it. After all, the simple fact that networked 3-D has an awesome maximum potential does not mean that only VRML can deliver it. On this subject, Mark's crystal ball is no clearer than anybody's. Although with regard to proprietary standards, he is likely to repeat his admonition that Cyberspace is too big a project for any one company to handle.

Of VRML's maximum promise, Mark wholly believes in the notion of immersive virtual worlds networked over the Internet. But his vision differs from Lanier's in that he, the onetime would-be mogul of the $300 head-mounted display (HMD), now considers the devices to be downright dangerous. "They can cause binocular dysphoria," he warns—a potentially dangerous condition that he says HMDs can bring about by displaying everything in maximum focus at once. This, Mark points out, is just not the way we are wired to see things. Hold your thumb before your nose. Gaze at it, and the wall behind it blurs. Gaze at the wall, and there goes your thumb. But both thumb and wall can remain in constant sharp focus in an HMD. When faced with a uniformly-focused world, the brain can retrain itself, Mark warns. Depth perception can suffer. Minds can *rewire*. Mark's vision of tomorrow's immersive VRML is now that of "the Cave," a notion first developed by Carolina Cruz-Neira at the University of Illinois at Chicago. Mark believes that in tomorrow's Cave, users will enter rooms built around display screens— fore and aft, up and down, left and right. The screens will fire and synchronize to create adequately immersive virtual spaces that will rewire no brains. Mark predicts—perhaps a little bullishly—that widespread *home* deployments of the Cave will appear within 10 years, obviating the dangers of HMDs (for the record, many people, including Jaron Lanier, do not wholly share Mark's concerns about HMDs).

But this would not necessarily make immersive VR wholly benign, because Mark sees risks in the technology that go far beyond its treatment of depth and focus. He often cites Osmose creator Char Davies as a worthy guardian of potentially dangerous technology, because he feels that her work embodies much of what is frightening about VR, even as it exemplifies its beauty. In Osmose, he says, Char "is breaching the walls of your ego, and using that breach to fill you with something that you didn't have before. She's changing your perception of the world." Given this, "It's a good thing that Char is a very ethical human being. Because when you're open that wide, who is to stop someone from putting in all sorts of messages that you might not want there? That's the other side of this coin. Because if we can develop techniques that are really very simple for breaching your own natural, innate sensibilities, we have a mechanism for mind control that Joseph Goebbels would have died for." For this reason, Mark expects that "within three years, we will see systems like this that understand your biology and your ontology to a degree that they can produce mutations that are *addictive.*"

Despite this inclement forecast, Mark remains VRML's biggest and most public booster. He explains this dichotomy by saying, "I am both excited and mortified by this technology. I see both sides of it. Because anything that is powerful expresses both natures. You can then become entranced and enslaved by that power, or behold it, step back, and put it to use. If networked VR becomes a new form of drug, there will of course be addicts. But there will also be miracle cures. And remember, any trajectory is highly sensitive to initial conditions. So if we can create healthful initial conditions today, we increase the chances of healthful outcomes."

And so Mark pours much of his professional life into fostering those healthy outcomes. To this end, he now spends a lot of time *teaching* VRML. He does this in one-off seminars on the road, and in full-blown courses at institutions like San Francisco State University. Most of his students are practitioners: graphic designers, Internet consultants, and the like. Mark also teaches VRML over the Web. In this, he can hope to reach thousands of people, rather than the handfuls he can reach in person. His forum is called VRML University, and it debuted in December of 1996 at Howard Rheingold's Electric Minds site (see Chapter 7). Another learning tool that Mark is developing is "WebEarth," a VRML model of the planet whose face is mapped with up-to-the-hour imagery from weather satellites. Mark hopes his students and others will take WebEarth as a starting point and "fill in its blanks" with VRML models of their own countries, cities, neighborhoods, homes, bedrooms, desktops, pencil cases, and so forth.

Mark also *writes* VRML. He spent much of the fall of 1996 working on his third book, his most ambitious to date, and maintains a weekly online column. Mark also (of course) *organizes* VRML. The most public of his many activities in this area are the conference-initiated VRML "Birds of a feather" meetings (BOFs) that he (let's be honest) often runs. At these, people line up to make announcements. Debates are urged. Companies demo products and answer questions. The BOFs are packed with competitors, yet their atmosphere is usually collaborative and cocreative. Attendees have compared them to New

England town meetings—something that Mark has in fact idealized in his writing.

But Mark serves his mandate most dramatically by *speaking* VRML. Oratory is his greatest strength, and is perhaps his most natural domain. Almost every one of his speeches is memorable, even moving in some way. One Friday evening in San Francisco, he gave a particularly evocative lecture on what might be summarized as his worldview. It was accompanied by eerily appropriate ambient sounds generated by a . . . call him a *deejay*. Attend more than one Pesce talk, and it becomes tempting to tally his *um*s, as they are very few and conspicuously far between. That night, after almost 90 minutes of nonlinear lecturing, Mark's *um* count had reached one. Like most of us, Mark does *um* when he converses. But he simply doesn't when he addresses. It's impressive and at times unsettling.

Mark is paid for some of the work he does on VRML's behalf. But in light of all of the hours and efforts he pours into the cause, his material compensation is modest. His sacrifice is all the more remarkable for the opportunity costs that it could be incurring. During one of the greatest of periods of wealth creation in the world's history, Mark has taken a seat that is on the pitch of the battlefield, yet on the fiscal sidelines. The Web has made his professional acquaintances into millionaires by the dozens, yet he is taking no equity stakes, and is placing no financial bets. He lives in an extremely modest one-bedroom apartment. Its corners and crannies are piled high with papers and books. "I'm *sorting them*," he tells a visitor, hinting at great industry caught midstride. But the sad fact is that there's nowhere to put them. See him on TV, know his role, and it's easy to imagine that he has his own late-model Onyx, and perhaps an engineer or two to cluck over its every bleep and whir. But the man who originated the notion behind today's implementation of Cyberspace beholds this realm through the cramped portal of a 14-inch screen patched to (you guessed it) a Pentium-90.

Mark has no plans to change this any time soon. Of the notion of joining a hot VRML startup, he shrugs. "I'm not easy to work with," he admits simply. Of the idea of starting another company of his own, he declares that "catalysts don't make good CEOs." Besides, he will tell you, he enjoys what he's doing too much to give it up. "Stopping to make money on the way," he says, "is something I'm too impatient to do." Some might dismiss this as the sound-bite bravado of a prima donna waiting for the right moment to sell out. But don't count on it. If Mark had a mind to sell out, he never could have held out this long.

This is not to say that he will never again be an entrepreneur. Mark is a reflective person, and his reflections have brought him to reinvent himself more than once. The guy who moved to Los Angeles in the fall of 1996 was probably Mark Pesce 7.1 or 7.2. Perhaps Mark Pesce 8.0 will trot out a white-hot business plan and become the darling of Sand Hill Road. Should this happen, and should the champagne corks pop on the day of his IPO as the Street initiates coverage with *Strong Buys*, few would deny that the man had earned it.

CHAPTER 5

ARIEL POLER
I/PRO

Advertising on the Web

It was foggy, damp, and well after dark, and Ariel Poler was vague on the details. It had been a long day for him. A long couple of years, if you really wanted to get into it. And to top it off he was fighting a sore throat. "I think Lycos was supposed to come out already," he mused, making his way down a long and particularly bleak block of Mission Street in San Francisco. Lycos was one of three Internet search and directory services slated to go public in the next few days (see Chapter 6). "Close to two hundred million," he guessed of their forecasted market value. "But they delayed it by a day or two. I'm not sure why. Then Excite, they were going to go out today or something, right?

"We'll have Yahoo! in another week or so," he continued with a Venezuelan lilt. "But it will be a while before we see InfoSeek." *Eenfo-Seek.* "They're taking a private round of financing for now." He nodded slowly, as if preparing to sum it all up. "Soup," he said. *Soup?* "Soup," he repeated. "Some soup with dinner should definitely help my throat."

Soup. The market seemed like it was ready to value the Internet search services at some three-quarters of a billion dollars (and as it turned out, Yahoo!'s value alone surged far past that on its IPO day). These services were relying on ad sales for substantially all of their revenues. And Ariel's company, I/PRO, was making a credible bid to become the auditor of record for the Internet advertising marketing (among many other things). In this, it had a shot at becoming a cornerstone, perhaps *the* cornerstone upon which advertisers could rest their faith in the medium. Considering all of this on the eve of that validating flurry of IPOs, it should have been easy (even forgivable) for a guy in Ariel's position to become a little self-consumed, maybe just a bit noisy about historical missions and mandates. But self-consumption just isn't Ariel's style. Low-key and down-dressing, he's more inclined to talk soup than historic mandates in almost any circumstance. He also knew that while Lycos's (and Yahoo!'s and everybody else's) IPO validated the market that he had targeted as his own, it wasn't yet champagne corks for I/PRO. After all, the Web still had a long way to go before it would become a mainstream advertising medium. And I/PRO likewise had a long way to go before it would really secure the role that it sought to play within that medium. Maybe its rankings and reports would one day pack all the wallop of a Nielsen ratings sweep. But a lot would have to happen before that. Dinner, for instance. And perhaps some soup.

The industry that Ariel's company is helping to bring to the Internet is one of the world's most sophisticated, glamorous, and (certainly) biggest. Over $150 billion is spent annually on advertising in the United States, and over $350 billion worldwide. This fiscal flood subsidizes all manner of paid-for media, including magazines, movies, and even video games. It also almost wholly funds most of the broadcast content that our media-rich society widely regards as free. But however *free* TV shows and radio songs may seem to be, we do enter into an economic relationship when we consume one, and advertising is the currency of the deal. We at least notionally "pay for" 22 minutes of sitcom by (oh, al*right*) putting up with the eight minutes of salesmanship that comes with it. Our attention to the appeals of soap, beer, and noodle makers is likewise our favorite radio stations' lifeblood. But while hard dollars may not pass between us and the staff at WLIR, they certainly fly between the station's managers and its sponsors. Underpinning this trade is of course a consensus on the value of ads. And underpinning that consensus is an army of trusted third parties whose measurings and auditings price advertising time and space. The most popularly recognized player in the traditional media measurement market is TV audience tallier Nielsen Media Research. And in both its early market dominance and (it turns out) its name, Nielsen's closest analog on the Web is Ariel Poler's I/PRO.

After months of inhaling talented people, I/PRO (shorthand for *Internet Profiles Corporation*) was past making its hundredth hire by the summer of 1996. Perched high above San Francisco's seedy but colorful

Market Street, the company's main lobby had the feel of a law or consulting office's entryway. Its spacious waiting area bordered a still more spacious glassed-in conference room. Its windows peered out at downtown towers. But get past the receptionist and the office was a young and relatively free-form place. Scattered reports and files cluttered desks, bookshelves, even the floor. Boxed stacks of computer gear lined the walls, awaiting new hires. A white board was overwritten with the word *Dork* and an arrow pointing toward a senior manager's office.

The covers of the reports stacked in the office crannies denoted one of I/PRO's claims to fame. *Nielsen I/PRO I/COUNT. Nielsen I/PRO I/AUDIT.* Nielsen I/PRO. The branding reflected the fact that in September of 1995, Nielsen Media Research, the granddaddy of 'em all, had squarely partnered with (and invested in) its industry's young upstart. I/PRO's kitchen was for a long time the seat of the partnership's catalyst. There, with their power and data cables snaking scarily past the dishwasher and sink, sat the humming Unix workstations that ground countless gigabytes of data from client Web sites into I/PRO's commercial reports and statements. This was a lot of data, as any one of those gigabytes could cover the pages of a 10-story stack of standard office paper with text (20 stories single-sided).

As I/PRO grew, this hardware inevitably left the kitchen for a fancier, more sterile, and (let's face it) fairly boring room on another floor. There it continues to hum and process—a vivid sign of how sophisticated media auditing has become since the start of Arthur Nielsen's pioneering career. Back then, advertisers commonly compared the popularity of radio shows by literally weighing the sacks of cards that listeners mailed in to them. Heavy sack, popular show; the method had a certain folk elegance to it. But mailroom scales turned out to be blunt instruments for the task. Today, most media auditing is segmented into two broad activities: audience profiling and audience sizing. Profiling involves measuring an audience's psychographics (*How rich are they? How old are they? How healthy, holy, or left-handed are they?*) Sizing involves establishing and verifying audience sizes. In some media (e.g., periodicals), companies tend to specialize in one of these two areas. In other media (e.g., broadcast television) a single organization (e.g., Nielsen) does it all.

Sophisticated as traditional media advertising and its auditing infrastructure have become, the system faces its challenges. Among them is the fact that consumers are all too inclined, and increasingly well-equipped, to duck marketers' messages. Broadcast advertising is especially unpopular, as it stands between audiences and the content that they really show up for. And with at first several, now dozens, and perhaps someday hundreds of channels on the dial, TV viewers have many sanctuaries to flee to when ads take over the screen. Growing arsenals of remote controls and mute buttons meanwhile make fleeing all the easier. Radio advertising is even easier to dodge, because most radio content is broken into small, modular bursts (three- to five-minute songs or news stories). Once one of these bursts is over, switching stations is not a wrenching process—we never have to sit through a commercial to hear how a song ends. Advertising in media that are not truly interrupted by their sponsors is even easier to avoid. We can read our favorite periodicals from cover to cover without even noticing their advertisers' names, if we choose.

None of this means that the traditional mass media are ineffective channels for reaching consumers. It rather means that marketers need to buy far more air time and print space to get their messages across than they would if audiences were more attentive to them. Attentiveness is not out of the question, as consumers do not find ad content to be universally distracting, uninteresting, or dull. Every one of us would in fact inevitably find a certain small subset of the existing body of ads to be exceptionally timely, useful, or entertaining. The problem is that this subset of "intriguing ads" varies dramatically from person to person. And since one-way media must by their nature present the same message to all comers, the odds that a particular ad will resonate with any given viewer, listener, or reader is typically low. Marketers are of course aware of this, and try to target their ads to the media that most closely maps to their core markets. A holy grail for advertisers, content providers, and consumers alike is advertising so targeted that it becomes part of the media's draw. Some content achieves this. Many people read style magazines or their industries' trade journals as much for their ads as for their articles. Some financiers likewise read the Money and Investing section of *The Wall Street Journal* as much to monitor its paid-for announcements of new underwritings as for its articles and market summaries.

But there is a limit to how targeted advertising can be in traditional media. Because any audience that is larger than one, even a fairly small and targeted one, will inevitably have its diversity elements (certain readers of the *Journal*'s C section surely do not care about new bond issues, while certain readers of *Field and Stream* surely do). The Web has the potential to let marketers overcome this, because as an interactive medium, it can enable them to target their messages with surgical precision. Database technology can allow entirely unique Web pages to be generated and served in moments based upon what is known about a viewer's background, interests, and prior trajectory through a site. A site with a diverse audience can therefore direct one set of messages to high-school boys, and a wholly different one to retired women. Or it could go further than this—after all, not all retired women are interested in precisely the same things—and present each visitor with an entirely unique message or experience.

This could potentially make the economics of the content provider/advertiser/audience relationship far more attractive to all parties. Because whereas "In traditional media you are subsidizing the content with ads, and they are often not particularly relevant ads," Ariel points out, content on the Web can be subsidized with ads which are uniquely relevant to each audience member, giving them "the best of both worlds"—subsidized content and highly relevant ads. Audiences can gain from this as advertisements start benefiting them rather than burdening them. Marketers can gain as their messages fall on increasingly receptive ears. And content providers can gain as their more potent ad space starts commanding higher prices.

It was the Web's potential to redefine the meaning of targeted marketing that inspired Ariel to establish I/PRO in the spring of 1994. The company later almost stumbled into the auditing business that it is now best known for. But it was able to redirect itself quickly, as it was still a lean and agile organization at the time. It was in fact every bit as lean and agile as Ariel himself, because for much of its early history, I/PRO *was* Ariel. I/PRO did well in its Ariel-only phase, and was later able to outgrow it and start dominating its important market because Ariel was almost ideally equipped to pioneer the field of Internet auditing. As a Stanford MBA, he had business smarts and credentials. As an MIT engineer, he had his digital wits about him. Auditing is of course all about measurement, and Ariel was an established expert in measurement science (okay, that's a stretch—he invented a postage scale once). But perhaps most importantly, Ariel was a proven entrepreneur.

Ariel started his first successful business at age 13, shortly after his bar mitzvah left a few thousand dollars in his care. A new media pioneer even then, Ariel bet it all on *deesko*, which was about to become as hot on the Caracas teen party circuit as the Web later became in Silicon Valley. He joined forces with a kid who really knew stereos (Ariel was the *content guy*, as he knew the music). Soon they were raking it is as

DJs. Ariel sold his stake in the business after graduating from high school and headed off to MIT, where he studied computer science and math. Intense as that was, Ariel thrived. He may not even have gotten his fill of intensity, because when he decided at graduation that it was time to go off and "experience a foreign culture" (the United States was no longer foreign enough to count toward that goal) he blew off the customary two-month swing through Europe, and instead signed up for a full-time hitch with a construction company in Japan.

Ariel packed lightly for his foreign year, bringing only some clothes and a flute. He couldn't play the flute. But he wanted music in Japan, and his stereo was too big to pack. So he brought the flute—figured he'd make it up as he went along—and headed East. In Tokyo he lived in a spartan company dorm with 48 fellow workers. His job was demanding, and he filled up his spare hours working on his Japanese and playing music. After over a year of this, with foreignness now roundly experienced, he returned to Venezuela.

Ariel then spent some time working in his family's hotel business. This was definitely a good experience, but before too long he was restless to go to business school. He applied, and was admitted to several programs. But Harvard and Stanford said no, and they were the schools that really interested him. So Ariel tossed the dice and got serious. He turned down the schools that accepted him, and dove into the Harvard and Stanford applications again. He worked on them carefully for months, while also keeping up with a few business obligations and (what the hell) inventing his postage scale. He was trying to get a patent for the scale when Stanford saw the light. And so in September of 1992, Ariel, now married, moved to California.

Ariel entered Stanford openly intent on becoming an entrepreneur again. He had no idea of what his company would do, but business school seemed like the right place to figure that out. While his classmates enjoyed the posh courtship of consulting firms and investment banks, he led the campus's entrepreneurship club and hammered out a series of business plans. *Museums on CD-ROM. Photo album transfers to videotape.* The ideas came and went. Ariel first glimpsed the Web in December of 1993, when it was still but a tot. Intrigued, he started dabbling in Web publishing. First he posted a site detailing the agenda and offerings of a manufacturing conference that he was helping to organize. Next he developed a Web-based guide to local restaurants with some classmates. Through this and other work, Ariel started getting pretty good at authoring Web sites. But then "after like two months of fooling around with this and that," he remembers, he began to get "concerned." Graduation was suddenly looming. Most of his classmates already had a job offer or nine. All he had was a vague sense that "the Web was it," and that sure didn't come with a signing bonus.

Then one night he was brainstorming with some classmates about marketing issues on the Web, and one of them mused that "what the Internet needed was the equivalent of supermarket scanners to track everything," Ariel remembers. And that was it—*scanners!* The moment he got home Ariel called his wife Cindy (who was then living in Los Angeles and working on a Ph.D.) and breathlessly told her that he *had* it. The core concept behind I/PRO was born. Ariel drew up his business plan quickly. His company would present the demographic profiles of people to Webmasters as they entered their sites, while safeguarding their anonymity. This would let sites tailor the experiences that they offered their visitors, without compromising their privacy (Ariel almost called his company PIC, for *Privacy in Cyberspace*). Ariel took his business plan around for feedback and found that everywhere "people were questioning the Web as a business domain." He often found himself dedicating half of his pitch to explaining what the Web was and why it mattered. *But what about interactive TV*, investors would challenge. *What about video-enabled arcade games?*

Right after graduating from Stanford in June of 1994, Ariel tapped into the last reserves of his *deesko* plunder and started funding the development of I/PRO's early software. His outside financing amounted to an unsolicited $20,000 check from his mother (an investment which "is hopefully going to pay off very nicely for her," he points out pragmatically, as it was converted to stock). He hired contract engineers to write his code, offering them a choice between I/PRO stock and a $25 hourly fee as compensation. This was a reasonably generous wage for the young grad student engineers that he hired (although it was probably the wrong choice, as one early contractor's stock was already worth some $700 for every hour that he put in by the time of I/PRO's second round of financing). Two of Ariel's best early contractors were fellow Stanford graduate students Jerry Yang and David Filo, who by then had already established their renowned Yahoo! directory service. Jerry and Dave took the cash (but nobody's calling them stupid; see Chapter 6).

As the autumn began, Ariel found himself with an evolving product strategy. Netscape was by then preparing its Navigator's first beta release. The Web's population was doubling every several weeks. New Web sites were appearing at a rate of scores, then hundreds per day.

But most of the "dot-com's," or private company Web sites (so named because of the *.com* designation at the end of their addresses) were still taking their babiest baby steps. Servicing their needs clearly represented a vast and immediate market opportunity. But the days when their masters would fret about tuning their content to each visitor's unique psychographics were still distant. Most were still struggling just to master the basic art of Web authoring while keeping up with exploding traffic. The more advanced among them were only beginning to ponder the aggregate scale and composition of their audiences. Ariel began to suspect that his most immediate business opportunity would lie in helping them do this, and that his entrée lay in their *log files*.

Not cabinets for classifying or storing firewood, log files are the raw tools for tracking Web site traffic. All Web server software, from NCSA freeware to the most sophisticated Netscape products, record in their log files some baseline information about each "hit," or discrete request for information, that they serve. This includes the precise time of the hit, and the requesting client's *domain* (which usually identifies its corporate point of origin). A day's log amounts to an immensely rich trove of information about a site's constituents and their paths through its pages. But log files are ungainly veins to mine for high-level insights, because individual visitor behavior is extremely difficult to deduce from them. The problem is that the Web is built upon a "stateless" protocol, which means that every site's every hit is a freestanding event (rather than part of an extended on-line session). As a result, a standard log file won't trace a visitor's route from pages A to B to C. It will rather note three (or more) apparently unrelated requests for information. Each entry will look something like this:

```
machine2.ipro.com - - [10/Dec/1996:11:54:56 -0700]
"GET /cgi-bin/ic_gencustom?GEN=custom" 200 1040
```

Not even the most log-savvy Webmaster can sift through a megabyte of that and come away with anything more meaningful than a headache and a blown evening or two.

Standard log files don't track the number of unique visitors that their sites receive, the average duration of their stays, or even the number of pages that are served to them (every media file associated with a served page is recorded as a discrete hit, so if a single page of text adorned with two images is requested, a log file will record three separate events, not one). This makes it all but impossible for the uninitiated to detect any detailed traffic patterns from raw log file. And traffic patterns hold the answers to some intriguing questions. For instance, are visitors being entertained, or are they leaving after a handful of page-views? Where are they coming from? Is the site successfully driving them to the product pricing pages? The Web has the power to give marketers and publishers detailed insights about their constituents' interests and attention spans, something that no newspaper or TV broadcast can do. But this power can be tapped only through a highly informed reading of the log file's tea leaves.

Another problem with log files is that they can be *biiiiig*. Standard entries include roughly 100 bytes of information. This means that a million hits of traffic (high-traffic sites can draw this in hours, a privileged few in minutes) will generate 100 megabytes of log data. Ten million hits (some sites serve multiples of this every day) will generate a gigabyte. Going back to analog terms, Netscape could churn out a 10-story stack of log file entries (20 stories single-sided) in a couple of hours. Storage costs have been in free fall for years. But a gigabyte of disk still costs hundreds of dollars. Acquiring and administering database software to manage this kind of information is likewise a nontrivial (and expensive) proposition.

Around the time that Netscape posted the first beta version of its Navigator to the Internet in the fall of 1994, Ariel directed his contract engineers to tackle some of the more bedeviling problems associated with log files. He wanted to create a product for those Webmasters who were curious about their log files' contents, but were too busy or resource-constrained to analyze them. The solution he envisioned would involve customers sending their log files to I/PRO every night over the Internet (or perhaps via portable media like digital tapes). A series of proprietary algorithms would then tease distinct visits from each vast set of apparently discrete hits. This would be quite a task, not only because of the statelessness issue but also because most visitors from corporate networks (a huge proportion of total traffic) sit behind digital buttresses that protect their internal webs from outside snooping. These software shields (or "firewalls," as they are called) can cause all of a company's employees to appear as a single entity. The combined meanderings of five hundred Bell Atlantic employees at Netscape's site, for instance, could well appear in its log files as the work of a single restless soul named *proxy.bell-atl.com* (this being the name of a Bell Atlantic Internet gateway computer). To resolve this problem, Ariel planned to create algorithms that would apply behavior observed in individual visits to corporate traffic to infer its component structure.

Once their log files were digested, Ariel imagined, customers would be able to query I/PRO about their particulars through a simple interface over the Web. What proportion of traffic hails from the East Coast? From manufacturing companies? How many visitors to page A went on to page B? How many people from Kentucky saw image C? Did they react by leaving the site or moving on to page D? I/PRO would answer these questions by connecting its clients' log files to a database of public and private company profiles (visitors' corporate affiliations are indicated by their Internet addresses; the database eventually came from I/PRO partner Dun and Bradstreet). After a while, I/PRO would be able to apply lessons learned from its aggregate collected data to any one customer's query (e.g., it would be able tell a car company how its site traffic compared to that of others in its industry.) Today I/PRO does offer these services, and its total log file archives are measured in terabytes, or thousands of 10-story stacks (20 stories single-sided, to flog the dead horse).

By late autumn, Ariel was ready to present a refined business and product plan to private investors. Although he had an extensive network in the venture community by then, he "had absolutely no expectations" that a venture capitalist would invest in him. "I didn't quite fit the mold," he recalls. "VCs want experience, they want patents, they wanted all sorts of things that I didn't have." But seeking expert advice on his plans, he did show I/PRO's term sheet to a partner at Sutter Hill Ventures that he had gotten to know while at business school named Tench Coxe. Within a half hour of receiving it, Coxe astounded him by offering to fund I/PRO's first round of financing.

Sutter Hill is a top-tier, technology-oriented venture fund, and as such rarely doles out money to newly-minted MBAs with little more than South American hospitality companies and Japanese construction firms on their resumés. But Coxe viewed Ariel as a "brilliant guy," he remembers, one who was "intellectually honest [and] mature." More importantly, he thought that the business opportunity that Ariel had identified was vast. He and his partners were by then believers in the long-term potential of electronic commerce and marketing. They were therefore intrigued by I/PRO's endgame promise to play in those areas. Coxe saw I/PRO as perhaps becoming "the Switzerland" of the electronic marketplace; the "trustworthy arbiter" between buyer and seller in perhaps billions of dollars' worth of transactions. The financing was completed in December of 1994.

In March, I/PRO's log file analysis system, by then named I/Count, was just weeks from release. But although Ariel was now keeping several cash-compensated contractors busy (Coxe had made quick work of Ariel's practice of paying the help with equity), he remained I/PRO's sole employee. It was clearly time to change this, so in early April, he hired a Stanford classmate named Tina Lin to be his marketing department, and one of his contract engineers, Mike Wolfe, to be his engineering staff. A good-natured debate still simmers between Wolfe and Lin about who was first in the door (his tenure as a contractor preceded her start date, but she became an official employee before he did; take your pick). But nobody debates the fact that April of 1995 was a hectic time. Early in the month *The Wall Street Journal* ran its first article about I/PRO, in which the then-trio was ascribed with the potential to become "what A. C. Nielsen is to television [*sic*] and what Arbitron is to radio." From that time forward, Lin recalls, "the phone just didn't stop ringing." Some weeks later the tiny, months-old company (make that *The Next Nielsen!*) attended its first Internet World show and came home with hundreds of leads. And that's when things really started getting busy.

I/Count's May launch attracted great industry interest, and soon dozens of customers. Ariel's old contractors at Yahoo! wrote I/PRO its first customer check (although this was almost a cash-negative event, as the dinner celebrating its deposit cost close to its face value). Some early competitors were starting to emerge by then. But I/PRO had beaten all of them to market by months, and just weeks after I/Count's release, the company's second product was nearing launch. Named I/Audit, this was developed to serve the infant market for Web advertisements that was just then taking form. The emerging standard format for these advertisements was the "banner," which first appeared on the HotWired site in October of 1994 (see Chapter 7). A banner is typically a rectangular inset placed toward the top of a Web page that features a sponsor's name, message, or product. Clicking on it whisks a visitor to its sponsor's site.

Banners are powerful because they can effectively deliver an unlimited amount of marketing material to their audiences, despite their small surface areas. They can do this because unlike traditional media advertisements, which can only say their piece in the space (or air time) allotted to them, banners can transport audience members wholly to their sponsors' worlds. Once someone has responded to a banner's *come hither*, its sponsor can use every tool in the Web's arsenal to get its messages across. Banners are also powerful because their effectiveness can be gauged cheaply, accurately, and immediately. Banner performance is typically measured with *click-through* rates. As the name suggests, a click-through is counted whenever somebody clicks on a banner and lands at its sponsor's site. A 1996 survey conducted by I/PRO and its partner DoubleClick indicated that roughly 2 percent of all banners are clicked. But well-designed, -written, and -targeted banners can do far better than this (in some rare cases attaining click-through rates exceeding 50 percent).

Click-through performance can be tracked in real time, and sites and services that do this can help advertisers refine their messages in ways that are not possible in traditional media (CNET is particularly good at this; see Chapter 8). Ineffective banners can be swapped out of campaigns in days or even hours. This is not even remotely possible in a print campaign, in which millions of pages are commonly inked at once. Subtle variations in layout and messaging can also be experimented with quite easily. One widely-known mail order merchant was astonished to learn that including the word *free* in a particular banner increased its click-through performance by roughly 1700 percent. The company subsequently adjusted its messaging, greatly enhancing its banners' effectiveness. Compared to this, ad effectiveness measurement in traditional media is matter of imprecise, expensive, and (certainly) ex post facto speculation.

Web-savvy marketers were excited about the banner's native power from the outset. But early banner buyers and sellers were forced to do business in an unsettling vacuum, as there were no standard systems for tallying and verifying banner performance, nor even standard banner prices. I/Audit sought to dispel some of this confusion by providing Web advertisers with an unbiased source of traffic sizing and audience demographic information. The product consisted of two component reports. The first was a certified traffic summary. A pre-sales tool, site managers could use this to showcase the size and quality of their audience bases to potential advertisers. It included the site's gross traffic tallies (e.g., number of visits per day and number of pages accessed), as well as geographic profiles of its audience and a list (by company) of its biggest traffic sources. I/Audit's second standard report was an ad performance summary, which tabulated the number of times that particular ads were viewed, as well as their click-through rates. Site managers could present this to customers as evidence that their ads had run, reached audiences, and achieved responses.

I/Audit quickly dominated its market. Its early subscribers included prominent sites like Yahoo!, ESPNET, *USA Today*, *Playboy*, and AT/T WorldNet. By November of 1996, Ariel counted 9 of the

Web's 10 top ad revenue-generating sites among its customers (as well as roughly 70 percent of the top 30 sites). Given this huge market lead, a big question for I/PRO quickly became whether I/Audit's market could one day become as big as the $100-million-plus TV measurement market that Nielsen Media Research dominates. The answer to this will of course ultimately depend on secular growth rates in the banner market, a market which is still nascent by any measure. One widely-cited source (WebTrack—a division of market researcher Jupiter Communications) estimated that quarterly spending on banners and other links was running at a meager $12.4 million by the end of 1995 (an annualized run-rate of only $50 million). But Jupiter also estimated that 1996 spending would exceed $300 million, and that the market would expand to $5 billion by the decade's end.

The growth implied by Jupiter's estimate, while impressive, has of course not yet been realized. And even if it is realized, the resulting market will still be a small fraction of the $35+ billion American TV advertising market that Nielsen referees. But TV advertising took 40 years to get to where it is. And the Web offers marketers powerful native advantages that TV—that indeed all traditional media lack. These advantages could fuel its growth beyond even Jupiter's projections.

The power of banners derives from the power of the sponsoring Web sites that they direct people to. Web-savvy marketers can turn their sites into highly customizable, interactive, media-rich forums in which to prove their cases to customers. Banner advertisements are but distribution networks for these forums; but especially when their performance is closely measured (and audited), banners can be powerful marketing tools in their own right. Banners are powerful in part because they can allow marketers to track the bottom-line performance of their advertising dollars with unprecedented accuracy. For instance, if I/PRO verifies that one million people see a certain banner and that 2 percent of them click on it, the banner is known to have delivered 20 thousand people to its sponsor's site. That site can then track those people closely. If it is a commerce site, sales to them can be tallied, and margins on those sales can be compared to the advertising costs that enabled them. If it is a marketing site, the advertising costs incurred in bringing the company's message to 20 thousand *attentive* listeners can be compared to the costs of achieving this through other channels like direct mail. All of this can lead to a credible, verifiable return on investment (ROI) estimates of a banner campaign's performance.

No traditional advertising medium offers anywhere near this level of accountability—and accountability has become very important to the marketing community. In the 1980s and early '90s, countless marketers indeed reduced their advertising budgets drastically in favor of trade promotions and couponing, precisely because these measures impact sales in highly detectable ways. David Williams, a brand manager at Cadbury Schweppes, notes that while traditional advertising is his preferred long-term, strategic means of promoting his wares, "if you mark a $1.29 product down to $0.99 in a particular market, the results are immediate, quantified, and verifiable." His own need for such results eventually led Williams to spend more than half of his budgets on sales promotion rather than advertising. He characterizes this allocation as typical in a company (and an industry) that not long ago directed almost all of its budgets to advertising.

Unlike traditional media auditing (which can verify the number of people *exposed* to ads, but which can never truly verify the number that pay attention to them, let alone actually react to them), Web auditing is furthermore a refined, rather than a blunt instrument. This means that "for the first time," Ariel says, "advertisers [can] pay for precisely the kind of interactions they want to have with customers. They can also closely measure the results of those interactions. And over time, they can even pay on the basis of those results." This could potentially be very powerful, as not all marketers try to achieve precisely the same things with their advertising campaigns, and should therefore not all measure, nor pay, by precisely the same metrics. For instance, certain marketers sell largely on the basis of image and brand equity. Their campaigns seek mainly to get their names out in front of the public. Their ads are often more geared to reminding people that they exist (and to perhaps assert affiliation with broad concepts like *youth* or *the competitive spirit*) than they are to listing detailed selling points. Cola vendors and athletic shoe makers are among those that fall into this category. Such advertisers are impression-driven, and might therefore wish to track and pay for the gross number of banners that are placed before consumers' eyes. I/Audit measures this. And indeed, almost all banner pricing is now done on this basis. Prices at most sites range between $15 and $75 per 1000 banners delivered, or 1.5–7.5 cents per banner (although HotWired continues to impress all of us by maintaining a $150-per-thousand rate).

But the sale of some products commonly involves the careful study of marketing messages, product specifications, and the like. Marketers of products like these (or "considered purchases," as they are sometimes called) might be more interested in bringing customers to their sites, where product advantages can be presented in depth. Such companies might be more interested in click-through performance than impression deliveries. And other advertisers, Ariel points out, "may only care if a visitor gives them their name," and want to pay on that basis. Still others might only care "whether a banner leads somebody to click through and then actually buy something from their site." On the Web, advertisers with diverse objectives can track (and in theory pay by) those metrics which most closely tie to their marketing goals. Traditional media cannot enable this. Its limited auditability forces payment by a single metric (generally impressions delivered), which for many advertisers is at best a rough proxy for their business objectives.

Surprisingly, some in the Internet ad community seem to be more inclined to reject than embrace this unique power of their medium. In April of 1996, *Advertising Age* reported that Procter and Gambler had cut a deal with directory service Yahoo! whereby P&G would shatter the Web's tradition (an 18-month-old tradition at that time, which made it Mayflower ancient) by paying for its banners on the basis of click-throughs rather than impressions. Many Internet ad vendors howled at this; one complained that "The advertiser should and will pay for every time your [*sic*] name or your product is seen by a consumer. This is how TV works—this is how radio works." The click-through pricing model that P&G and Yahoo! pioneered in fact has its philosophical weaknesses. Among them is that it gives sites financial exposure to the effectiveness of their banners' creative content, content that the advertisers, not the sites, control. Still, rejecting new models on the Web because they are *not how TV works* amounts to rotely shackling the new medium to the constraints of the old.

It also amounts to rejecting a source of potentially powerful competitive differentiation. For its own reasons, P&G decided that its campaign's objective was to draw customers into a dialogue, rather than to deliver impressions to them. In the click-through, the Web had a metric that let P&G pay Yahoo! on the basis of meeting this objective. No other media offers such a metric. Magazines, for instance, cannot possibly charge advertisers based on people responding to (or even reading) their ads because they have no direct way of measuring that. In this, P&G's move therefore indicated that it valued one of the Web's unique native powers. And as it and other major marketers come to value (and exercise) these powers more, the Web's ad revenue base can only grow. For this reason, Yahoo! sales director Anil Singh reasonably describes click-through pricing's knee-jerk opponents as "in the dark ages," because "The key to the Web is to use the flexibility of the medium to meet advertiser goals. And if you try to impose the blueprint of other media on it . . . you just constrain what it can do, and we're all going to fail."

Other worries about click-through pricing focused on its revenue ramifications. The fear seemed to be that if ad rates were expressed in dollars per click-through, advertisers would find them excessive and revenues would plunge. Some have in fact argued that de facto click-through rates (and therefore ad rates on the Web in general) are unjustifiably high. In an article delicately titled "It's the Click-Through's, Stupid!" industry commentator Rosalind Resnick made this point, citing as proof an instance in which HotWired effectively charged a company $4.76 per click-through by delivering a 2.8 percent click-through rate on its $150 cost-per-thousand banner charge (a 2.8 percent click-through rate on one thousand banners means that the banners delivered 28 click-throughs; since each thousand banners cost $150, this means that each click-through cost $150÷28, or $4.76 to generate). Resnick argued that because the advertiser "could have taken everybody [who clicked on a banner] out for a burger and fries" for that money, HotWired was "threatening to sink" Web advertising as we know it. She concluded that "Web publishers will soon have to drop their rates or come up with other ways to give their advertisers value."

Resnick's reckonings sounded grim on the surface, because a $4.76 *impression* would indeed be laughably expensive in most media. But it is important to remember that a click-through is *not* an impression. And a banner is fundamentally different from a newspaper, TV, or radio ad, because it is "not an ad, it's an *entrance*," as Ariel often says. This fundamentally gives a click-through a different kind of value than an impression which has been pushed, unrequested, before its viewer's eyes. Because once a banner delivers somebody to its sponsor's world, the sponsor gains an *attentive* audience to its message (the audience has come deliberately, after all). The Web can then nurture that attentiveness in ways that traditional media cannot match. Unlike print, TV, or radio ads which are out of tricks once they have persuaded someone to sit through their every word and visual, messages on the Web are not constrained by the bounds of expensive advertising real estate. A Web site's visitors can request and receive enough information to fill an entire newspaper page, or indeed an entire newspaper. A well-designed site can also learn a tremendous amount about its visitors from the information they request and from the facts that they reveal about their own backgrounds and motivations.

For these reasons, click-through costs might be more fairly compared to those of direct-mail campaigns than to those of impressions in magazines or other media. Direct marketing has enjoyed tremendous growth in recent years as marketers have come to demand greater accountability from their channels, as described above. Billing statements and stand-alone mailings are now popular tools for reaching consumers. Like the Web, these are targeted routes to them, as direct mailings are typically guided by demographic profiles. Also like the Web, they are auditable routes, as most direct marketing campaigns are embedded with feedback mechanisms that enable their organizers to track results (e.g., recipients are often asked to call an 800 number or send in a card requesting more information).

But unlike the Web, traditional direct marketing is a very expensive way to engage customers. The fact that the market bears its expense indicates how greatly it values targeted, auditable communication. Mark Hodes, vice president of measurement technologies at True North Technologies (which was recently spun out of another True North holding, advertising giant Foote, Cone, & Belding) came to new media advertising from direct marketing. He notes that direct mailings typically cost from one to two dollars per address reached (mailing list acquisition, production costs, and of course mailing costs must all be borne). Each expensively-shipped piece then needs to be noticed, opened, and then read before it can have any impact on its recipient. Hodes reports that 1 percent response rates are common for direct mail, 2 percent quite respectable, and 3 percent outstanding outcomes. Direct-mail campaigns might therefore easily spend $30 to $200 to generate a single response, to bring a single attentive party into a marketer's audience. Such budgets could allow direct marketers to treat their each and every respondent to a fine meal and perhaps a night on the town, burgers and fries be damned. But direct marketing is still an economical way to promote certain products.

Web sites and the banner ads that serve as their distribution networks therefore surely are as well, particularly if they are monitored and tuned by a set of carefully-chosen and reliably-audited performance metrics. This would indicate that Ariel chose wisely when he made Web ad auditing I/PRO's second market. But obvious as his choice may seem now, it was downright avant-garde at the time. When I/Audit launched in June of 1995, only eight months had passed since the appearance of the Web's first banner ad. Most of the tiny and close-knit market's buyers and sellers knew each other well enough to make audits seem unnecessary at that point, and industry sales were still running at a trickle. But I/Audit's market grew quickly. And as it did, so did I/PRO. By September of 1995, I/PRO had 20 employees and its Unix kitchen was getting crowded. It was then that the company's partnership with Nielsen was announced.

Nielsen's courtship of I/PRO was by then a long-running item. Ariel and the auditing giant first discussed a partnership back in December of 1994. Their talks didn't come to immediate fruition, but Nielsen became very interested in I/PRO and its markets. Tom Dubois, a Nielsen business development director involved in the deal, estimates that he encountered at least 20 potential I/PRO competitors in the subsequent months. In the end, he and his team decided to invest in I/PRO because the company had a good balance of engineering and marketing talent, a comprehensive business plan, and a huge market lead. Ariel himself was also an important factor. He was "a straight shooter," Dubois thought, "not at all pretentious," and generally an attractive CEO to work with.

I/PRO's biggest period of growth and change followed the Nielsen deal by a few months. Between January and April of 1996, the company's head count exploded from a few dozen to almost one hundred. New hires were still ritually required to assemble their own chairs. But there was no denying that I/PRO had left its early startup phase. In light of this, Ariel and his backers agreed that it was time to bring some more seasoned management on board. I/PRO had acquired an entirely new executive team by May of 1996. Mark Ashida, a onetime consultant who had worked in three technology startups, came on as I/PRO's new CEO.

Ariel's succession had been in the cards for a long time. His willingness to contemplate it from the outset was in fact important to Sutter Hill when it made its original investment decision. Still, Ariel remembers many friends and associates telling him that they thought it was *admirable* of him to make room at the top. To this he would chuckle that "there was nothing admirable about it—it was a relief. . . . I was in over my head." Ashida's arrival freed Ariel to focus on managing I/PRO's relations with other companies, spreading its message through speaking engagements, and arranging financing. This latter activity kept him particularly busy during the early part of 1996. Softbank (which also holds major stakes in Yahoo!, PointCast, InterVista, and many others; see

Chapter 6), announced an investment in I/PRO in May of that year. Hearst New Media, a major I/PRO customer, quickly followed suit.

All of this expansion was exciting for Ariel and his company. But it also presented challenges. Because while rapid growth is common in Internet companies, I/PRO, which went from Ariel-only to 100 people in an office tower in scarcely more than a year, seemed to move at a particularly headlong pace. This was all part of what Sutter Hill's Tench Coxe describes as "a mini-Netscape strategy." Coxe credits Netscape's own aggressive growth with being "what really allowed them to take Microsoft by surprise," while making the company look like "a safe choice" to customers. He, Ariel, and the rest of I/PRO's management felt that their market opportunity called for a similar strategy. This strategy is perhaps the best-proven one on the Internet so far. But it can bring an awful lot of new people, managers, and products into a company in very short order.

The most ambitious new product that I/PRO rolled out in the months following the new management team's arrival was I/Code. I/Code took on the mandate that Ariel originally identified as the company's own: that of delivering uniquely-tuned content to Web site visitors based on *who they are*, while preserving their privacy. It was designed to serve "two key constituents," Ariel says, "the consumers on one side, and the sites on the other." Site visitors "want to get the most relevant content from a site, which is driven by their interests and backgrounds," whereas site managers want to "customize the experience of the visitors, in terms of the content, ads, and other things" so that they can market more effectively to them. Both ends can be achieved through "an efficient market for information" between visitors and sites that "gives sites the information they need to customize experiences, while rewarding visitors for their disclosure with more relevant experiences," while also preserving their anonymity.

I/Code's design objectives were not entirely unique, as many Web sites have long tried to make personal background information their price of admission. Visitors to such sites are typically asked to fill out registration forms before entering (a password and user ID are then issued to save them from going through this hassle again). But registration systems have not been very popular, because filling out their forms can be a time-consuming hassle. Many people are also reluctant to pass out personal information to strangers over the Internet. The result is that however much value they purport to return to visitors, registration systems almost invariably reduce traffic at the sites that implement them. HotWired found that it was losing as many as 80 percent of its visitors at its registration screen before it made registration optional early in its history (see Chapter 7).

I/Code presented an integrated solution to this problem. I/Code users would fill out a single form with I/PRO to obtain a user ID (their "I/Code") that could then be used at all I/Code-enabled sites. When an I/Code user logged in at an affiliated site, I/PRO would pass its administrators the information they needed to customize the user's experience in a meaningful way, while withholding identifying personal information (name, E-mail address, and so on). This, it was hoped, would benefit users by giving them more relevant experiences at many sites without forcing them to fill out countless forms or compromise their privacy. It would meanwhile benefit site administrators by helping them communicate more directly with their visitors.

I/Code's potential was extraordinary, even in the fairly limited realm of targeting banner advertising. Consider the record of DoubleClick, a Web media buyer that brokers banner sales on behalf of a large base of Web sites (including American Airline's Travelocity, Intuit, Sportsline, Access Health, and search engine Excite). DoubleClick uses database technology to match banners to visitors at the sites that it works with. It targets its banners based on a number of specifications, including the geographic locations of the people receiving them, and, if they are logged into the Web from work, their employers (visitors' companies are usually indicated by their Internet addresses).

When a Web page tagged with a DoubleClick ad is requested, two servers respond; the site hosting the page serves its content, while a DoubleClick server in New York sends the ad. Ad and content are then integrated seamlessly on the visitor's screen. This means that a single Web page can carry different ads based on who is looking. DoubleClick might send somebody hitting Intuit's Web site from Merrill Lynch an ad for a financial newspaper, say, and somebody hitting the same page from the University of Washington an ad for a Seattle coffee house. DoubleClick's rates vary with the number of filtering specifications that are used to target its ads. The company's network manager, Jeff Dickey, reports that one thousand untargeted impressions cost $12 to $20 and get a median click-through rate of 1.5 percent. Two specifications cost $24 to $40 per thousand and get a 3.5 percent click-through rate. Costs and response rates go up from there. In experiments with highly refined targeting, Dickey has seen click-through rates as high as 20 percent.

If consistently attainable, these numbers represent very powerful economics. For ad buyers who are principally interested getting in click-throughs, impressions are just a means to an end, and effective click-through costs drop as more specifications are applied (from an average of $1.07 per click-through for untargeted ads, to an average of $.91 when two specifications are used). But a site's raw advertising real estate is measured in impressions, not click-throughs. And these generate more revenue as specifications are added (from an average of 1.8 cents per impression for untargeted ads, to an average of 3.2 cents when two specifications are used). This means that sites can in effect sell their inventory for more money, even as their customers are buying it for less. Measurable economic value can thereby be created for both parties through effective targeting—targeting based only on (for now) fairly blunt metrics. Targeting should of course become far more effective as sites become more intimate with their visitors. If DoubleClick knew the musical tastes, marital status, favorite colors, and current buying needs of the people receiving its banners, it could imaginably create far greater value for the ad buyers and sellers that it brokers between than it can from just knowing their points of origin. For this reason, I/Code, which was all about heightening the intimacy between sites and their visitors, had the potential to change the economics of banner placement dramatically.

But powerful as this promised to be, Ariel has always believed that "the *real* ads on the Web are the sites, not the banners." He therefore felt that I/Code's greatest promise lay not in targeting banner ads, but in tuning the content *within* Web sites to visitors. This was certainly where Webmasters invested most of their money and attention. David Carlick, an I/PRO (and onetime DoubleClick) board member, estimates that corporate spending on site content was already running at a multibillion-dollar annual rate in 1995, a year in which scant millions were spent on banners. This reckoning begins with an estimate of roughly 50 thousand active .com sites on the Web at that time. Assuming that 40 person-hours per month were on average devoted to maintaining those sites (a conservative estimate), and that talented Web developers and administrators cost roughly $100 per hour to employ and equip, roughly $2.5 billion was spent on site content. This is several dozen times the size of the banner market in that year.

It was this market of *real ads* that most interested Ariel when I/Code debuted in the spring of 1996. This was in a sense the product's second launch, as it had made a brief appearance as pilot project back in the spring of 1995. In that maiden run, I/Code was used in conjunction with a CompuServe giveaway contest on the Web. After that, still-tiny I/PRO put I/Code on the "back burner," Ariel recalls, to focus on I/Count and I/Audit. But the I/Code system remained in development ever since, which had given Ariel plenty of time to consider what it might be capable of.

In the months following its full release in the spring of 1996, he optimistically described I/Code as "clearly the aspect of our business that has the highest potential upside." But he also knew that the system faced many hurdles. One of these was that its value to end users ultimately came not from I/PRO, but from site developers who had to learn how to reward its use with tailored and interesting experiences (ones going beyond the Publishers' Clearinghouse school of customer intimacy—*Hello ROBERTREID   welcome to our site!!!*). Another was that many Webmasters saw as much value in their visitors' demographic information as I/PRO did, and to them, the notion of making a third party responsible for gathering that data and doling it out in sanitized clumps was a tough sell. A third problem was that many Web users simply shunned registration forms categorically.

In the spring and summer of 1996, I/PRO hired, heavily by startup standards, to swing at its home-run pitch. Over a dozen people were soon working on the I/Code project. But while this was a big team for I/PRO, the market challenge they faced was even bigger. At its heart was "a fundamental chicken-and-egg problem," Ariel says, as "the sites wanted to see a big population of I/Code users before signing up, but the users of course wanted to see a lot of sites using the system." Since people in both populations had some natural reservations about I/Code for the reasons described above, this chicken-and-egg problem was a particularly hard one to crack. Another problem was that I/Code needed to succeed with a mass market of consumers, and I/PRO was at its heart a business-to-business, not consumer marketing company. But perhaps the biggest problem, Ariel believes, was that I/PRO, larger but still small, older but still young, and pioneering at least three infant markets, was "getting overextended."

Despite all of this, the I/Code team managed to sign up over a half million users within months of their product's release. They also recruited dozens of high-profile sites to their system, including *USA Today*, Visa, *Playboy*, and The Sharper Image. But by late summer, the total number of I/Code sites still just numbered in the dozens. This was such a small base that even heavy Web users could go days, weeks, even forever without encountering a site that recommended or required the use of an I/Code number. In light of this, Ariel and his management team began to reexamine the system and its basic premise. They decided that the premise itself was sound, but that the Web's rapid evolution had rendered certain aspects of its architecture obsolete. "When we started working on the I/Code system in 1995," Ariel recalls, "we had to develop all the components in order to provide a workable solution to our customers. That meant a consumer registration system, a consumer incentive program, a consumer identification mechanism—including a cross-site infrastructure for transferring such information, and, of course, the back end for analyzing all the information." This was a lot to build. But on the mid-1995 Web, there was nowhere to buy it, so I/PRO built away.

Things changed quickly, however, and "by the summer of 1996," Ariel explains, "there were several startups going after every one of these components. For us to continue trying to do them all was crazy. So we decided to focus on the component that was key to our core—the measurement and analysis of all the data. Something else that we realized was that the system needed to be more open—a big hurdle had been [its] proprietary nature." To redress all of this, I/PRO identified several potential partners with whom it could create "an open system in which each company would focus on their strength," Ariel says. After some progress had been made in these talks, I/PRO restructured the I/Code team (and some other parts of the company) and laid several employees off. This was a "very unhappy decision to make," Ariel says. But I/PRO was fortunately able to provide its dismissed employees with good outplacement services, and with severance packages that included I/PRO equity.

The resuscitated I/Code (which will be marketed under a different name) was still in development as of this writing, and I/PRO's new partners in developing it had not yet been announced. But there was plenty of excitement in I/PRO's other product areas to keep management from getting bored. Much of it was coming from competitors—a remarkable fact, given that Ariel's target market had been very much of a *huh?* concept just two years before. Most of I/Count's competition came from off-the-shelf software rather than rival centralized services. The off-the-shelf model became popular with many Webmasters because it lets them retain control over their log data, while also saving them monthly service fees. I/PRO's advantage over this is that it can save companies from having to analyze log files (a complex chore, even with the best off-the-shelf software). I/PRO is also able to tell its clients how their traffic compares to general patterns within their industries by querying its terabytes of historic log file data.

In November of 1996, I/PRO relaunched I/Count as NetLine. Net-Line has a far more robust user interface than its predecessor, one which runs outside of the Web browser and takes over the entire computer screen. It also lets its users download data and reports and store them on their own hard drives—something which I/Count did not do. NetLine's more user-friendly technology should help I/PRO maintain a strong position in this market, which it briefly had to itself. But the market will in all likelihood remain crowded. It will also continue to offer its players ample opportunity to differentiate themselves, as customers within it report that no product yet comes close to wholly satisfying their needs.

This is not an indictment of NetLine or its competitors, as the technical challenges facing them are enormous. Firewalls bedevil anyone trying to extrapolate discrete visits from log file data. The distortions caused by a practice called "caching," which has become very widespread since I/Count's first release, are if anything even worse. Caching involves storing frequently-requested content nearer to its audience, thereby speeding its delivery. Large networks (e.g., those of universities, corporations, or Internet service providers) often do this by saving copies of the Web pages that they deliver on local servers (usually called "proxy servers"). When a cached page is requested, it can then be served quickly over the speedy internal or local network, rather than through the Internet's slower circuitry. This means that not all requests for a given page are necessarily recorded in its server's log file. For instance, CNN's commonly-accessed front page might be requested by hundreds of people in General Electric's headquarters, but only receive a single hit from a GE proxy server. This makes it hard for products like NetLine to really understand the shape of a site's traffic. This and other problems related to firewalls and corporate networks make it unlikely that anyone will truly master the black art of log file analysis for many years. As a result, neither I/PRO nor anyone else is likely to run away with the market.

Things may go very differently in I/Audit's market, as media auditing is almost invariably dominated by monopolies or duopolies. This is because ad buyers and vendors alike constantly benchmark performance and prices across their markets, and therefore need standards. For this reason, a single (or perhaps a dual) audience measurement standard will likely emerge on the Web. Since monopolists (and duopolists) tend to lead rosy economic existences, it is not surprising that there are now several pretenders to I/Audit's early throne. Los Angeles–based NetCount offers NetCount AdCount and has been aligned with financial auditor Price Waterhouse. Periodicals auditors the Audit Bureau of Circulation (ABC) and the Business Publications Association (BPA) have also started auditing Web sites, and radio auditor Arbitron has rumbled about doing the same. None of these competitors can be dismissed lightly. But a month is a long time on the Web, and I/Audit beat almost all of its rivals to market by at least 12 of them. Because of its early lead, the product has been able to seize extraordinary market share (9 of the top 10 ad revenue–generating sites, and 70 percent of the top 30 by November of 1996, as described above).

I/PRO is now parlaying its early lead into key partnerships that can further it more. One of these is with NetGravity, a leading purveyor of software for managing ad inventory. NetGravity's AdServer is designed to place, target, rotate, tally, and otherwise manage a site's banners. AdServer users include Netscape and Yahoo! In June of 1996, NetGravity and I/PRO announced plans to integrate their products and align their marketing and sales efforts. NetGravity's president, John Danner, predicts that the companies will together "provide a solution with ad serving, targeting, and auditing capabilities to produce one of the most advanced online advertising packages available today." Another important I/PRO partner is Internet service provider UUnet Technologies. One of the country's leading ISPs, UUnet hosts over 12 thousand Web sites on behalf of its customers. Its partnership with I/PRO (which was announced in July of 1996) lets it resell products like I/Count and I/Audit to its customers.

Because auditing markets are so standards-hungry, I/Audit's early lead might prove to be quite self-perpetuating. And while it is still far too early to characterize I/Audit as an entrenched standard ("the sense in the marketplace is not that we've 'won,' " Ariel points out. "We're definitely not there yet") the product's market share and customer list and I/PRO's partnerships will serve it well as it seeks those distinctions. An interesting question, then, still concerns the eventual size of the market that I/Audit serves. Some argue that the Web will never draw the ad revenues that traditional media like television pull in (and therefore, its auditors will never prosper like Nielsen Media Research) because while the medium is very useful to marketers of complex or expensive products, it seems to have appealed little to those who sell more on the basis of impression and brand equity. The small-ticket consumer products that so dominate big-budget TV advertising are almost never marketed in direct-mail campaigns, after all. And for now, such products are likewise relatively rare on the Web. WebTrack's survey of 1995's top 15 Web advertisers in fact included no major consumer goods companies (although consumer service companies like AT&T and MasterCard made a good showing)—and by the time a follow-up survey was taken in spring of 1996, little had changed.

One person who feels strongly that the Web does in fact matter to consumer product marketers, however, is Rob Holloway, Levi's senior vice president for worldwide marketing. Few companies have commanded greater brand premiums more consistently across time and cultures than his, and few are more active buyers of traditional media advertising. This gives Holloway a rare intimacy with the strengths and limitations of the Web's alternatives. Levi's site first launched in mid-1995, and has since attracted millions of visitors. It conveys a general affiliation with global youth culture, while perhaps seeking to make something of a contribution to it. Puzzles, games, articles on art and entertainment, as well as links to sites dealing with such topics as rave culture and in-line skating are presented. Woven in amongst them are a "denim dictionary," a company history, and other such content that at most amounts to extremely soft selling. In this, the site conveys attitude and affinity far more than *buy me* logic. The same thing can also probably be said of most of Levi's traditional media advertising. The difference is that visitors to the company's site spend minutes or even hours actively connecting to its brand, whereas viewers of its TV commercials more typically spend just a few moments passively tolerating its message.

Holloway ties his site's strategy to the most basic objectives of any brand marketer. Brands are built upon brand equity, which in turn commands price premiums. To be sustainable, premiums have to be supported by some kind of added value, which can either be tangible or emotional in nature. And "if you have a media that allows you to add a richness around products and the brand," he says, employing it is an obvious choice. Holloway believes that the Web "provides advertisers with an opportunity to communicate in a depth that they could never reach" with conventional media. The product affinity imparted by Levi's site could cost "hundreds of millions of dollars" to develop using conventional media. But annual spending at even the top-budgeted commercial Web sites rarely exceeds two to three million dollars. This indicates that the Web can offer consumer product companies immense marketing leverage if they can learn to truly enlist its native advantages. Holloway's commitment to the Web is clear from his own schedule. Although less than 1 percent of the company's total marketing budget goes into it, there have been periods when he has devoted up to a quarter of his time to the Levi's site's development.

This is not solely due to his excitement about the Web's potential, great as it is. Holloway also believes that the Web will inevitably draw consumer attention away from traditional media, which behooves established marketers to invest in it. "A challenge for a company like Levi's," he points out, "which has built itself on the back of conventional media, is that when consumers are looking at the Internet, or when they're playing around with the Web, or with E-mail, or newsgroups, or whatever, they're not looking at the television." Holloway believes that the Web is already starting to have "a real impact" on media habits, and as such "absolutely" poses a threat to traditional media. Signs of this threat are already there. A 1996 Nielsen Media Research survey indicated that children, long among the most voracious and least abashed consumers of broadcast content, had reduced their television intake by about 18 percent since 1984. Tellingly, Nielsen also noted that 33 percent of children surveyed had used a computer "some" or "a lot" on the previous day. If consumer attention is indeed migrating away from mass one-way media like television, more and more impression-driven marketers like Levi's might begin to bring their mighty budgets to the Web. This should in theory be great news for auditors of Web advertising. However, unless this migration sparks a banner bonanza, its revenue impact on products like I/Audit will be minimal.

One schooled and thoughtful observer of all this is True North Technology's David Clauson. Clauson measures his industry tenure in decades, and has run practices as big as Foote, Cone and Belding's West Coast technology group (which included such companies as Hewlett-Packard, National Semiconductor, and Adobe Systems). Clauson is no fan of the banner, and is anything but ardently bullish about its future. He believes that banner advertising and hit auditing amount to "using the scorekeeping mechanisms of the one-way media and applying them to digital media." But in the digital media "you cannot be intrusive . . . you have to be attractive." And the banner, which is pushed, uninvited, to its viewers in a pulled medium, is an inherently intrusive device. Clauson argues that the Web demands a "fundamentally different way of marketing than a generation of marketers have grown up understanding." And the banner, he feels, is a product of the old mindset, not the new. He believes that marketers cannot ultimately succeed on the Web by planting themselves between another site's content and its audience. A brand must rather seek to "create itself as a destination" in its own right.

Brands that in fact become destinations on the Web can limit their exposure to *avoidant behavior*, as marketers chidingly call it, or the dodging and ditching of advertising in sponsored media. Such behavior is already cropping up on the Web, as the first of new medium's *mute buttons* has already been released. This is Fast Forward, the product of a tiny North Carolinian startup called PrivNet. Fast Forward is a tool that strips banner advertisements out of Web pages before they are downloaded, allowing the "real" content to stream in more quickly. Some have complained that products like it could undermine the Web content community's willingness and ability to create free content. If people will not deign to view advertising along with their news and entertainment, the argument goes, they might soon find themselves supporting it with subscription fees.

PrivNet's James Howard's retort to complaints like this is that his product is every bit "as American as getting up and going to the bathroom when a commercial comes on." And perhaps he is right. After all, interactivity is about empowering audiences. It is about handing them the wheel. And as Clauson argues, if advertisers are not truly welcomed, they cannot in the end thrust themselves between content and a wheel-wielding audience. The fate of the commercials that inadvertently get recorded on VCRs demonstrates this. TV commercials are anything but *destinations*. They gain audience attention only by staging periodic coups on the screen. Their medium's one-way nature then lets them sustain their fleeting dictatorships. But when a VCR hands its owner the wheel, the intruder is shown the door. *Fast Forward*. Perhaps it is very American after all.

None of this means that banners are necessarily doomed. For now they cannot possibly be as invasive or as annoying as bad TV commercial (although reckless uses of Java, RealAudio, and other technologies could change this). Banners can indeed be entirely good citizens, if they are targeted to their audiences' interests well enough to blend with and enhance the content they sponsor. But the best bet for inventive marketers on the Web will ultimately lie in becoming *destinations*, as Clauson suggests. Levi's (one of Clauson's clients) seems to be taking the "destination Web site" strategy seriously. It sells no banners itself and buys them in only modest numbers. Levi's Holloway has in fact mused that banners might already be "old hat" for companies like his.

If this is true, it is not necessarily devastating news for one like

Ariel who has always believed that *the sites are the real ads*, and therefore sees a greater opportunity in enhancing the destination's appeal than in erecting the billboards that point to it. But Ariel also absolutely sees a bright future for Web advertising of the nondestination sort—although he does expect that the banner's form will eventually evolve. Today, he points out, when an ad "succeeds" (i.e., when somebody responds to it by clicking on it), the site hosting it loses a member of its audience. Many sites are as eager to change this as TV stations would be if their ads caused interested viewers to switch channels (along with the disinterested ones). For this reason, Ariel expects Web advertisements to become more informative and freestanding (perhaps by using Java technology), so that people will not have to leave for a sponsor's site in order to learn more about its products or messages.

Ariel also expects banner pricing models to evolve. He was "very surprised that the cost-per-banner delivery model became a quasi-standard" pricing metric, he says, because pricing models should "depend on what [advertisers] are trying to achieve." In the future he expects the Web to sustain a diversity of payment models, from which advertisers will choose based up their business objectives. Maybe "you're gonna have a cent an impression, ten cents a click, one dollar whenever somebody leaves their name, and ten dollars when they go on to make a purchase," he speculates. I/PRO client Yahoo!, one of the Web's most successful ad sellers with over 300 paying sponsors, is one influential player that is planning for just such a future. Its sales director Anil Singh says his company expects "to have programs for tiny, big [or] small advertisers that want awareness. Traffic. . . . Measure cost per order. Generated cost per inquiry. . . . So we'll have a whole à la carte pricing model. No matter what your needs, or how you want to measure it."

As for the relationship between content and advertising, Ariel believes that most Web content will remain advertiser-supported, although he expects "a spectrum" of models to exist between the ad-only approach and a strict subscription scheme. He even expects the spread of an "off-the-scale ad-supported" model, in which "the advertiser will pay you to go spend time" looking at their content. "Not only will the ad subsidize all the costs, but you will end up receiving money for it," he predicts. The logic behind this is that there is real economic value in the information advertisers gain from observing consumer behavior. They already pay for this kind of information from market research firms that conduct focus groups. So why not "hire" their own customers now that technology enables it? There is also, of course, economic value in booking sales, which capable marketers may be able to do after luring customers to their sites with some kind of low-cost lollipop. This *off-the-scale* model interestingly appeared on the Web just a few weeks after Ariel predicted its rise, when a new venture called CyberGold announced its service. CyberGold's users enter their profiles into its database. They are then routed advertisements that they are asked to read and assess. Users are rewarded for their troubles with CyberGold Dollars, which can be invested in goodies like online subscriptions.

Things are changing so quickly in the Web advertising and auditing markets that it is hard to predict exactly what other *on-* and *off-the-scale* models will emerge within them. But even in the face of their rapid evolution, some generalizations can be made safely. First, the Internet advertising market will continue to grow at a tremendous clip, particularly if one assumes, as Ariel does, that the *real ads are the sites*. The economics of the Web as a communications channel are simply too powerful for marketers to ignore, especially when their messages are complex or customizable. Second, the Web will support an increasingly sophisticated array of performance and payment metrics. The *impression* is such a distant proxy for most marketing objectives that it cannot possibly remain the sole metric by which marketing time and space is tallied and priced, now that a new medium has arisen which makes more sophisticated measurement possible. Third, those who reject change and innovation in the Web advertising marketing because it is *not how TV works!* are simply doomed.

The fact that the market it referees is growing quickly and becoming more complex should be good news for I/PRO. And while it faces competition in all of its product areas, the company's early lead has been enviable. In this, its *mini-Netscape strategy* of rapid claim-staking growth has served it well—although the I/Code stumble should (and no doubt will) serve to caution management when it next puts its foot to the accelerator. To hang onto its for now dominant position, I/PRO will need to continue to drive, rather than react to change in its dynamic market. It will also need to recover from its early overextension. To this end, the company was retrenching—significantly—throughout late 1996. By December of that year, lay-offs and departures had brought its headcount down below 70 from a peak of over 100, according to industry chronicler CNET (see Chapter 8). Also in that month, CEO Mark Ashida announced that he would step down by

March of 1997. As of this writing, it was unclear how I/PRO would weather these changes, or the financial adversity that brought them on. But the fact that the company had over $8 million in the bank, and that its monthly sales were up 500 percent since the start of the year indicated that it had a lot of fight in it.

I/PRO will also need to focus on delivering products and services that lie within its core competencies as a technically-driven business-to-business marketer. To this end, the company started a research and consulting practice in the summer of 1996 that leverages its tremendous archive of log file data to help clients understand their sites' traffic. This is a business that lies well within I/PRO's core expertise, and could become a major growth area for it.

Wherever I/PRO goes from here, it will go without Ariel's day-to-day involvement; because in the fall of 1996, he decided it was time to move on. It had been a very long two and a half years with the company, and he and his wife were expecting a baby in February of 1997. Ariel had also concluded that "for me, it's very important to be deeply involved in key issues and decisions. And I realized, I couldn't do that and let management do their job. It was hard to draw the line at the right place." He remained an active I/PRO board member. He also remained bullish about the company's prospects, as he felt it was "an execution game from here, and they've got a lot of talent." He was looking forward to taking on something new soon, and speculated that he would "most likely be an entrepreneur in this space again."

But for a while, he was really looking forward to *not* being an Internet entrepreneur. He had always been a person of many interests: foreign travel, sailing, *deesko*, even postage scales. As a result, he was excited to finally take on some non–work-related projects—one in particular. Because MIT, Japanese construction, inventoring, entrepreneurship—all of these had been relatively simple stuff. But parenting, now *that* was going to be a real challenge.

CHAPTER 6

JERRY YANG
Yahoo!

Finding Needles in the Internet's Haystack

It was just Jerry, Dave, four walls, a shut door, and a dictionary that night.

"Ya—"

"Ya . . ."

"YA—"

"Ya—, Ya—, Ya . . . Yataghan!"

"Yataghan?"

"Yup. *A type of Turkish short saber with a double-curved blade and a handle without guard.*"

"Hmm. Yet Another . . . T-A-G-H-A-N's an awful lot to work with."

"Yeah. How 'bout . . . Yankee?"

"Yapok."

"Yardbird?"

Dave and Jerry were trying to christen this . . . *thing* that they had created, and it seemed like it had been going on like this for hours. So far they hadn't gotten much further than deciding that the new name would start with Y-A. You'd think that would have narrowed it down a bit.

"Yauld."

"Yammer?"

"Yardage."

"Yang!"

"Ha ha. *Yang.* Very funny. Heh."

Yang was Jerry's last name. Dave's last name (Filo) had of course been out of the running since they decided on the YA- thing. This prefix (at least) seemed obvious to them, because the names of several software tools that they had used as computer science students began with it. YA- names were usually acronyms, and the Y-A denoted *Yet Another.* The best-known YA- tool was YACC (pronounced *yack*), or "Yet Another C Compiler." YACC was an awesome name. YACC was the role model. It kind of sucked that YACC was taken. Jerry and Dave were determined to come up with something that was every bit as good. They'd figure out what it stood for later.

"Yawn, yawp, yaws, *yaxis.*"

"Yaxis?"

"Oh, sorry. *Y-axis.*"

"Y-axis. Like you said, *yawn.* . . ."

Finally somebody hit on it.

"How's this? *Yahoo.*"

"*Yahoo?*"

Webster's traced *Yahoo's* roots to Swift's *Gulliver's Travels.* Therein, a Yahoo was *any of a race of brutish, degraded creatures subject to the* HOUYHNHNM *and having the form and all the vices of man.* Yahoos, it seemed, were rude. They were unsophisticated. And perhaps above all, they were vulgar. Jerry and Dave looked at one another. *Rude. Unsophisticated. Vulgar.* Well, none of the above, frankly. But self-effacement was always welcome on the (then) egalitarian Internet. So *Yahoo* it would be. Yet Another . . . *Hierarchical!* (gooood) . . . Officious . . . *Oracle.* Whatever. They threw in a ! for good measure, and Yahoo! it now is.

Yahoo!, then, is pronounced *YAHHH*-hoo, not *Yaaaaa*-hoo, and it has nothing to do with yelping hicks out on the town. The Yahoo! service itself predated its now-famous name by several months. It started out as a humble little Web site called "Jerry's Guide to the World Wide Web." For a while, this understated name seemed just fine for the idle, spare-time student project that it was. But then the project became a bit less idle. And the time it took up stopped being entirely *spare.* Eventually Jerry decided that he'd had enough of Dave doing half of the work and taking none of the blame. So he unilaterally changed the name to "*David and* Jerry's Guide to the World Wide Web." He did this mainly to "frustrate David so he'd think of a better name," Jerry recalls. And "Of course, it worked. He said, 'I'm not putting *my* name on this.' " The shut door and dictionary followed shortly.

Although it has since evolved significantly, Yahoo! is still, as it was then, a guide for needle-seekers in the Internet's haystack. And as its reverse-engineered name suggests, it is *hierarchically-organized*. At its pinnacle sit 14 broad categories covering such subjects as BUSINESS AND ECONOMY; ENTERTAINMENT; HEALTH; and (inevitably) COMPUTERS AND THE INTERNET. Beneath each of them lurks a group of subcategories that Yahoo! users (or *yoozers*, as it's tempting to call them) can access with the click of a mouse. Clicking on ENTERTAINMENT, for instance, summons a page full of listings like AMUSEMENT/THEME PARKS; HUMOR, JOKES, AND FUN; and MUSIC. These all lead to other things—MUSIC, for instance, to categories like KARAOKE, CHARTS, GENRES, and ORGANIZATIONS. ORGANIZATIONS then leads to BELL RINGING, DRUM AND BUGLE CORPS, CHORAL, and more. Users click down through the hierarchy until they hit the floor, where categories link to actual Web sites instead of further subject areas. This can lie a dozen or more levels below the surface (although it's not usually that far down). Yahoo!'s hierarchy is deep because of its tremendous scope; the 14 top-level categories trickle down to over 400 thousand unique Web sites, and thousands of new sites are added every week. Users who don't want to dig through all of this can type the subjects or names that interest them into a search window, and receive a list of links to relevant Web sites immediately.

The Yahoo! hierarchy is a handcrafted tool in that all of its over 100 thousand categories were designated by people, not computers. The sites they link to are likewise deliberately chosen, not assigned by software algorithms. In this, Yahoo! is a very labor-intensive product. But it is also a guide with human discretion and judgment built into it—and this can at times make it almost uncannily effective. The experience of an archaeologist whose maiden journey through the Web began at Yahoo! was not atypical. Within minutes of glimpsing both the Netscape Navigator and the Yahoo! hierarchy for the first time (and with little guidance), she had drilled down through SOCIOLOGY, through ANTHROPOLOGY, through ARCHAEOLOGY, through FIELDWORK AND EXPEDITIONS, to a site that included several pictures that she herself had taken on a dig (and yes, they were appropriately attributed). This was a remarkable find. It may well have been the most personally relevant site on the Web to her. But she hadn't deliberately set out to find it, because she hadn't even known that it existed. Despite this, and despite the fact that Yahoo!'s architects never anticipated her (nor indeed anybody's) interest in the site, the hierarchy's installed wisdom created a path to it that to her was as obvious as a well-marked interstate highway.

This is the essence of Yahoo!'s uniqueness and (let's say it) genius. It isn't especially hard to point to information that many people are known to find interesting. *TV Guide* does this. So do phone books, and countless Web sites that cater to well-defined interest groups (*Links to the seven most vital Web sites for Northern California's Windsurfers!*) But Yahoo! is able to build intuitive paths to information that might be singularly, or even temporarily important to the people seeking it. And it does this in a way that no other service has truly replicated. Because while the Web has many other powerful and well-regarded search sites, all of them have highly automated underpinnings compared to Yahoo! Most take key words as input (e.g., *Windsurfing*, or *Ashkelon*), and identify sites and pages that contain them in a relatively rote manner. While the better key word search services have refined this process with proprietary techniques, they remain in their essence *machines*. Yahoo! alone is a carefully-architected edifice.

Its uniqueness has made Yahoo! one of the most powerful franchises on the Web. Scarcely two years after Jerry and Dave shut their dictionary, their site was serving almost a hundred million pages to millions of distinct users every week. This was more than double its closest competitor's traffic by some estimates, and far more than half of mighty Netscape's. Yahoo! had meanwhile attracted over three hundred paying advertisers. Fueling this explosion in usage and sponsorship was a dramatic expansion in Yahoo!'s service offerings. From its roots as a simple Web directory, Yahoo! had flowered into a nexus of information of all types, including news stories, stock quotes, weather reports, phone listings, and interactive maps.

All this robustness and growth have turned Yahoo! into the Web's *seismograph*. By executing more searches than anyone else, the company is uniquely well-positioned to listen to the Web and to learn about its users' interests and fancies, and this helps it develop new sites and services that cater to emerging trends and interests long before they become widely evident. Yahoo!'s proprietary view on the Web's evolution has already prompted it to launch several affiliated sites targeted at specific interest groups and geographies. The company is meanwhile leveraging its enormous position on the Web into other media. There are now Yahoo! books, a Yahoo! magazine, and regular Yahoo! appearances on several TV programs. All of this leads Jerry to describe Yahoo! as a *media company*, not a technology company.

But this doesn't mean that he and Dave were necessarily thinking *Viacom* back when they started building the humble list of hyper-links that (*ooops*) became an empire. Far from it. They were instead thinking more along the lines of how hard it was to find anything on the still-teensy Web. About how nice it would be to fix this little problem for themselves, and (*maybe*) for a few of their friends. Then later, about how cool it was to have something to focus on other than school for a change. In this, Yahoo! is the happy fallout of a hobby, not the calculated product of a business plan—although Jerry might have been thinking vaguely (*very* vaguely) about business and economic opportunity when he first came to Silicon Valley. But that journey wasn't really his idea. And it happened a good 15 years before Yahoo! was formed.

Jerry came to California from Taiwan, where he spent his early childhood. His father passed away when he was just two. His mother, a professor of English and drama, raised him and his younger brother Ken alone after that. She ended up moving her young family to the United States because her sister lived there, and it sounded like a good place for the boys to grow up. "There was always talk about opportunities here," Jerry remembers, although nobody was thinking of anything quite as big as Yahoo! Jerry was just 10 when his family settled in San Jose, California. Hardly an energetic organizer and categorizer in those days, he was "*lazy*," he insists, and had "a very short attention span." But *lazy* as he might have been, Jerry did well in his studies. From humble beginnings (his English vocabulary consisted solely of the word *shoe* on his first day of school in America) he built an academic record that earned him a place in nearby Stanford University's class of 1990.

Jerry liked the rigor of the engineering classes that he took early in college, and was also intrigued by "the fact that the Valley was built on engineers, and Stanford was a big part of that." Soon enough he registered as an electrical engineering major. Despite the heavy academic demands that this entailed he was always very involved in his dorms and eating clubs. He also joined a fraternity, and sat on a few university committees which dealt with labor issues and other such matters. He spent most of his social time with the guys in his fraternity. But he also kept up with his brother Ken, who matriculated two years after him. Like Jerry, Ken became an electrical engineer. The two of them eventually enrolled in precisely the same Ph.D. program as well. But despite their similar trajectories, Jerry and Ken are very different people. Unlike Jerry, Ken is a vegetarian, "and he's got hair down to *here*," Jerry says, pointing below his neck. "Basically, he hikes and camps in the High Sierras a lot," he explains. He's very Zen. He's not a Buddhist, but he believes in a lot of Buddhist values." But while they have always moved in different social orbits, Jerry and Ken are close. To this day, they convene weekly in San Jose to spend time with one another and their mother (and to enjoy some fine cooking).

Despite his nonacademic distractions, Jerry managed to complete both a bachelor's and a master's degree in just four years. He dutifully met with a few suited recruiters when graduation loomed; but he quickly realized that he "wasn't really ready to work yet. I had the degree of a Master's," he recalls, "but I didn't have the experience or the maturity. I was twenty-one, barely. Actually, not even. So I looked for ways to stay in school." Turning over all stones, he eventually found his way over "to the research side of it." And luckily, perhaps inevitably, *the research side of it* was where Dave Filo's bid to stay in school had recently landed him.

Jerry and Dave were acquainted by then, as they had been in the same academic department for a couple of years. Dave was a bit further down the road than Jerry, having graduated from Tulane in 1988. He had in fact served briefly as Jerry's teaching assistant ("he gave me a *B!*" straight-A Jerry still grumbles). But they still found themselves in a number of classes together. They ended up doing a class project together in one of them. And Dave, God bless him, "basically wrote the whole program," Jerry remembers. "I didn't do *anything*. So I knew then that I was going to have to work with this guy more often."

Jerry did of course end up *working with this guy* plenty, and he and Dave quickly became a remarkably balanced team—so balanced that it is almost tempting to think of Dave as Dave *Yin*, as he and Jerry (*Yang*) complement and contrast each other in so many ways. Jerry is gregarious, a ringleader. Dave is reserved, a thinker, not talker. And while Jerry is technically solid, Dave is technically brilliant. He certainly is the organized one *on the screen*. Whether it lurks in the Internet's crannies or deep in his own system's files, he can generally find it, process it, perhaps control it (it's "that *I'm at my terminal and I can rule the world* kind of a feeling," Jerry explains). But walk into his cubicle, where he still sleeps most nights, and it's cyclone city, baby. Jerry is the opposite. His physical space is tidy (well, kind of). But he is less sorted and in control than Dave when he is on the computer. Jerry says that Yahoo! in fact got started partly because he was always "about a half step behind" Dave in online and other technical matters. "Because of his knack of being able to find things," Jerry explains, "I was always trying to figure out how in the hell he *knew* everything." And since so much of Dave's wisdom seemed to flow from the Internet, Jerry became eager to build a map of it. A guide. A *hierarchical oracle*, if you will.

Different as they were, Jerry and Dave found that they had plenty in common from the outset. They held similar views on matters like the classes they had both taken, technology, and certain people. They also shared the same dissertation adviser and narrow technical specialty, which meant that they were often grappling with the same academic questions (like *what the hell are we going to do with this* DEGREE?). Their cubicles adjoined, so they literally worked shoulder to shoulder. But close as their quarters were, they always got along well. These days Jerry figures that he and Dave "probably couldn't have found two better partners [than] each other in the business sense. We're both extremely tolerant of each other," he explains, "but extremely critical of everything else. We're both extremely stubborn, but very unstubborn when it comes to just understanding where we need to go. We give each other the space we need, but also help each other when we need it. We've been through some rough times [but] we've never had rough times together. Which is unbelievable to me. I look at my girlfriend, I look at my mom, I look at my family. We've had rough times all over the place. With Dave and I, we've always kind of shrugged it off and moved on. There was hardly ever any tension between him and I. It's just a fantastic relationship, and I hope it's a lifelong one."

Dave echoes all of this, characteristically reserved. "Jerry's cool," he says.

At the start of their doctoral programs, Dave and Jerry had both decided to focus on design automation software. This "was a pretty big industry at the time," Jerry recalls, with "lots of startups." He and Dave looked forward to joining startups themselves after they graduated. Then in the early nineties, a small number of aggressive companies began to dominate the market, and soon enough, the industry was "so consolidated that there weren't that many startup opportunities left," Jerry sighs.

As this unhappy development unfolded, one of them stumbled across a teaching opportunity at a Stanford program in Kyoto, Japan. Neither of them had been to Japan before, and this seemed like a particularly cushy way to get there, so they both signed up. It was in Japan that their friendship really solidified, "because you go through so much there together," Jerry recalls, "just being foreigners." They taught, worked, drank lots of Sapporo, and watched hours of sumo wrestling. Sumo soon became a minor fetish for both of them. "It was an explosive sport, and we just thought it was the coolest thing," Jerry explains. Somewhere in the midst of all this, Jerry met a young Costa Rican woman of Japanese descent named Akiko. Akiko was also in Kyoto with Stanford (although as a student, not a junketing teaching assistant). She and Jerry started dating shortly after their return to the United States, and were engaged in the summer of 1996. It was also in Japan that Dave and Jerry met Srinija Srinivasan, another Stanford student. Srinija—Ninj for short—was to figure prominently in their lives, as she became their first *ontological yahoo*. But that wasn't for a while yet.

Back at Stanford, Jerry and Dave set up a tiny office in a university trailer (they also had homes, but spent little time in them). They named their workstations after their favorite sumo champions in commemoration of their cool journey (Jerry's was Akebono, Dave's Konishiki). But other than this nostalgic nod, they were back to their full-bore existences as Ph.D. students out on the periphery of a fast-consolidating industry. Things got back to normal dismayingly quickly. But then after a few months, *something happened*—Dave discovered Mosaic. Keeping to custom, he nonchalantly paraded his new find before Jerry straightaway, and things haven't been quite the same since.

Jerry and Dave quickly became Web aficionados. They posted their own home pages (Jerry's included vital information like his golf scores). They surfed the Web for hours. And hours. At some point their Ph.D. work started falling by the wayside. But their adviser was conveniently out of the country on sabbatical, so they got away with it. Somewhere in midst of all of this, Yahoo! took root. It began when Jerry and Dave started building little lists of links to their favorite Web sites. Jerry was of course very interested in Dave's links, as he suspected that they were the source of his omniscience. And Dave was interested in Jerry's links because, well, Jerry always found some neat stuff too. Soon they were passing links back and forth daily, then hourly, then continually. Eventually they decided to pool their links together in a "more digestible form," Jerry recalls. And so their little private lists of links became a rather unlittle shared list of links which they christened (gotta call it something) "Jerry's Guide to the World Wide Web." And when the unlittle shared list became unwieldy, they broke it into categories. And when the categories got too full, they broke them into subcategories. The core concept behind Yahoo! arose in no time, and it hasn't changed much since.

The need that Jerry and Dave were addressing for themselves was apparently widely shared, as it wasn't long before dozens, then hundreds of people were accessing the Guide from outside the trailer. This was a surprise, as their Guide wasn't really designed with an external audience in mind. But there was no real reason why it couldn't support one. After all, it was a Web site like any other. And Akebono (Jerry's system) sat on an open part of the Stanford network. This meant that anybody who knew the Guide's address could access it almost as easily as Dave could from the adjoining cubicle. Dave and Jerry E-mailed this address to just a few friends at first. But their friends were wowed, and word can travel fast when messaging moves at light speed and postage is free. Jerry's Guide acquired a broad and loyal following almost overnight.

And so without really meaning to, Dave and Jerry quickly had—*ooops!*—an audience. And without really knowing why, they soon found themselves responding to its needs. At first they accepted, then started soliciting site submissions from their users. Then they started to expand their Guide with little featurelets, like "What's New" and "What's Cool" listings. The Guide's audience cheered every embellishment with a trickle, then a torrent of encouraging E-mails—digital applause that Jerry and Dave found to be enormously gratifying. Much of this applause came with constructive advice, so it also helped shape Yahoo!'s evolution. Today, Jerry believes that "if there was no feedback, if it was in this dark secret lab, we wouldn't have done it."

An unspoken understanding quickly arose between Jerry and Dave that more attention and traffic were somehow better, more fun, and *cooler* than less. And so they started bidding for more traffic by continually providing more and better service for free. They got so good at this that by the winter of 1994, Dave remembers that he was "kind of hoping it wouldn't grow so quickly." It was getting hard to find time to eat or sleep. And oh yeah, they still had their Ph.D.s to worry about—at least for another year or four. But the Web was just entering one of its fastest periods of growth. And Netscape, its mighty catalyst, was just getting started. This made for a lousy time to rein in a service that was fast acquiring a secular exposure to the Web's expansion. By the time of their summer naming session, Jerry and Dave had effectively hoisted the white flag and become full-time Yahoos (or rather *Chief Yahoos*, as Jerry's business card now reads—or perhaps *Cheap Yahoos*, as Dave's reads). And as their traffic surged and the digital applause roared louder, they both began to think seriously about turning Yahoo! into a business.

On the surface this was a sketchy proposition. The two of them had about 17 years of higher education and little else in the way of resumé credentials between them. Yahoo! also lacked an obvious revenue model. Charge the users, it seemed, and they'd go elsewhere. Charge the listees, and they'd shrug and pay nothing. Sell advertisements, and incur the wrath of Internet old-timers who were still adamant about keeping the Web free of commercial taint. But despite all of this, the notion of a commercial Yahoo! still made a great deal of intuitive sense. It seemed that any large, loyal audience had to be worth *some*thing to *some*body. And Yahoo! was certainly drawing the faithful crowds. By the summer of 1994, Jerry reckoned that their site was logging tens of thousands of visitors daily. And the traffic just kept building.

Equally validating, there were competitors out there. Dave remembers WebCrawler at the University of Washington; Lycos, a project at Carnegie-Mellon University (Lycos later incorporated and went public); and World Wide Web Worm, which came out of nowhere, then "died off really early on." There was also a paid-access service called InfoSeek, which was started by a seasoned entrepreneur named Steven Kirsch (Kirsch's prior successes included Frame Technologies, which Adobe Systems eventually acquired in a $500 million merger). Most of Yahoo!'s competitors maintained indexes of Web sites, which they scanned for search terms that their users typed in. These indexes were built and refreshed by "spiders," or programs which scoured the Internet and sent back detailed reports on their findings. Spiders can run through a lot of sites quickly, and of course they work for free. For this reason, the index search services tended to be far more comprehensive than Yahoo!

But Yahoo!'s hand-built hierarchy had its own advantages, because key word searches often betray their mechanical roots. An index

search for information on the band Oasis, for instance, can easily generate as many references to Egypt's lovely Siwa Oasis as to the British
quintet. A search for information about the Olympic games could likewise end at a site promoting Olympic Paint. The power of indexes naturally grows with the range of content that they cover. But so do their
native pitfalls. Almost every imaginable English word and name now
has countless roosts throughout the Web. This makes it all too easy for
index searches to be comprehensive beyond the point of usefulness. A
recent index query to a fine search service called Excite yielded
115,396 references to the word "Oasis," while a query to Yahoo!'s
database produced only 151. The far more manageable and (it turned
out) relevant list of Yahoo! results was also framed in the hierarchy's
context, which made it easy to sift through them. A hierarchy category, ENTERTAINMENT: MUSIC: ARTISTS: BY GENRE: ROCK: OASIS in fact
appeared at the top of Yahoo!'s list of links, and it was plenty obvious
that all of the 23 sites attached to it (*Fowzry's Oasis Tribute*, *I Hate
Oasis Anti-Fan Club*, etc.) dealt with a band, while the sites listed under REGIONAL: REGIONS: AFRICA: SOCIETY AND CULTURE dealt with
patches of water in dry, dry places.

Even in Yahoo!'s earliest days, the better index search sites of
course offered tools to make their output more meaningful. Boolean
logic was (and remains) a popular method for narrowing searches
(e.g., Olympic AND Sports; Oasis NOT Desert). Most index services
also ranked the apparent relevance of the results that they returned to
the user's query. But Boolean queries are far less accessible to novices
than Yahoo!'s intuitive hierarchy, and their syntax varies from service
to service. Also, relevancy ranking systems commonly tally the frequency with which search terms appear in the "header" files and bodies of the sites that they scan. Aware of this, index-savvy page
designers have developed arsenals of tricks to heighten their sites' apparent relevance to common search terms (e.g., many header files have
the word *sex* written in them dozens of times). None of this means the
index search services are useless, or even necessarily less useful than
Yahoo! Index searching is rather an undeniably powerful tool, and
many Yahoo! loyalists indeed turn to other sites for this service regularly. But a well-ordered hierarchy offers distinct advantages of its
own, and by creating the Web's best hierarchy, Yahoo! laid early claim
on a niche that it now largely has to itself.

But Yahoo!'s hierarchy was not alone on the Web in the early
days—not by a long shot. Dave and Jerry remember a number of close

competitors, including one called EINet Galaxy, and another called the
World Wide Web Virtual Library. But since "there was no gain from
being the coolest directory out there at the time other than [that] you
can go out and say, 'I created a cool directory,' " Jerry remembers, the
competition was hardly savage. Perhaps because of the lowness of the
stakes involved, most of it also faded out fairly quickly. By late 1994,
Jerry estimates, Yahoo! had become the de facto leader in the hierarchy space.

This success was sweet. But it had its downside. By the autumn,
Jerry and Dave's every day had become a headlong rush of categorizations. Their E-mail accounts were meanwhile filling up faster than they
could empty them, and their phones were ringing constantly. Their site
had its first million-hit day in the fall of 1994, which translated to almost 100 thousand unique visitors. But while they were excited about
this milestone, Dave and Jerry knew that things couldn't go much further without snapping. "That was the point," Jerry remembers, "at
which we said, we've got to do something about this, or we're going to
shut it down."

Luckily, the time to *do something about this* was ripe. Netscape
had just released the first beta copy of its Navigator. HotWired had
meanwhile launched the first ad-supported Web site. The popular
press was starting to clamor about the Internet Phenomenon, and the
venture capital community was *all over* the Web. Dave and Jerry may
have been overwhelmed, underresourced, and unpaid. But their service
was already legendary in Internet circles. With Net mania building as
it was, this made Yahoo!'s iron very hot. And so, almost as soon as
they decided that they were ready to meet with them, a long procession of corporations and financiers began to march on Dave and
Jerry's humble trailer.

The first major media company to come calling was Reuters.
Reuters is a $5-billion purveyor of general news and financial informa-
tion services headquartered in London. Although it is less known in
the United States than some of its rivals like the Associated Press,
Reuters' scale and pedigree (it has been in the news business for more
than 150 years) place it in its industry's top echelon. Reuters discovered Yahoo! through the initiative of a marketing vice president named
John Taysom, who had transferred from London to its Palo Alto office
largely out of a fascination with the business possibilities that the
emerging Web might offer. He read about Yahoo! in the local press
shortly after his arrival, and was soon a regular visitor to its site.

Taysom recalls that it quickly occurred to him that "Yahoo! was all about lessening the distance between information and the people seeking it." The information in this equation was strictly Web-related at the time. But it seemed to him that integrating Reuters' news feeds with the Yahoo! service could "both draw repeat viewers and add context to the news." Affiliating with Yahoo! could also help Reuters start building a distribution network in an important new medium.

Taysom worried that his idea might be ahead of its time. It seemed that all of the major search services were still sorting out their content and business models (InfoSeek was still charging for access, and nobody was selling advertisements). But Yahoo! seemed like an inventive site, so Taysom tried his luck and called. "And the first thing Jerry said to me," he remembers, "was 'if you hadn't called me, I would have called you.' " Jerry *got* the news feed vision. He had been thinking about it himself for months. He further surprised Taysom by informing him that as far as he was concerned, Yahoo! was "not just a directory, but a *media property*." And so almost a year before it logged its first nickel of revenues, Jerry had already started to view and position Yahoo! much as he views and positions it today.

Yahoo! and Reuters remained friends, but not partners, for months after that. Reuters was willing to offer its content in exchange for a share of the ad revenues it generated. But Yahoo! had no revenues to share just yet. With this and other business matters starting to loom large, Jerry realized that it was time to solicit some business-savvy help, to perhaps even write a business plan. At the time, an old college friend of his, Tim Brady, was in his second year at Harvard Business School. *Business school* shared an awful lot of syllables with *business plan*, so Jerry put Brady to work over his Christmas break. Partly using HotWired's first media kit as a reference (see Chapter 7), Brady quickly produced a five-page snapshot of Yahoo!'s business prospects for Jerry and Dave to present to venture capitalists. Thus armed, Yahoo! began making the rounds on nearby Sand Hill Road, the epicenter of the American venture capital community.

Jerry and Dave met with dozens of VC funds during the first months of 1995. This required them to become instantly fluent in the ways of some of the world's most sophisticated financiers, even as they continued to keep up with a growing daily deluge of site categorizations. On top of this they were now managing more Web traffic than all but a few people in the world had ever faced. There were no ready rule books to follow in this, and Yahoo!'s servers required constant tending. Soon days, then entire weeks slipped by in which Jerry and Dave barely saw their homes. There in their trailer, "Dave and I would sleep in the same spot," Jerry recalls. "He would sleep for about four hours, and then I would work. And then he would get up and work and I would go to sleep." They played music continually, but there never seemed to be more than one CD in there (for months it was Hootie and the Blowfish, then somebody mercifully brought in the Counting Crows). Draining as all of this was, they were having a blast. "It's just one of those things where when you were doing it, you just thought it was the coolest thing," Jerry recalls. "There was nothing else in the world like it. You were doing it, and there was such cama- raderie, it was like driving off a cliff. Like *Thelma and Louise*. You just don't know what's going to be out there. There might be a net to catch us, and there might be nothing. But we didn't care. We had nothing to lose."

Before they really sailed into the void, Jerry and Dave found their way to Sequoia Capital. One of the Valley's best-regarded venture funds, Sequoia counts among its investments Apple Computer, which launched the personal computing revolution; Atari, which created the video game industry; Oracle, which has pioneered and dominated the database industry for years; and network hardware giant Cisco Sys- tems, which is said to have been the single most profitable investment in the history of the venture capital industry. These are just a few leg- endary companies that Sequoia can boast about having seeded and nurtured to success. But these days, it's a Yahoo! poster that hangs be- hind its receptionist's desk.

Mike Moritz, the partner who led Sequoia's eventual investment in Yahoo!, vividly remembers his first visit to Dave and Jerry's trailer. When he arrived, the *Chief Yahoo*s were "sitting in this cube with the shades drawn tight, the Sun servers generating a ferocious amount of heat, the answering machine going on and off every couple of minutes, golf clubs stashed against the walls, pizza cartons on the floor, and un- washed clothes strewn around," he recalls. "It was every mother's idea of the bedroom that she wished her sons never had."

Moritz wasn't planning to stand in for anybody's mother, so the mess didn't particularly worry him. Other aspects of Yahoo!'s chaos, however, did. For one thing, it was still "very unclear who really cared about this," he recalls, and "very unclear what the business was." Ya- hoo! also had no seasoned management, and "one of the craziest names around. Why would anyone ever back anything called Yahoo!?" But more than anything, Moritz was troubled by the fact that he could think of no instance in which "the venture community [had] ever invested in anything that gave a service or a product away for free. And people talk[ed] about Netscape giving its product away for free . . . but that's a lot of hoo-ha!"

Moritz's concerns were of course quite legitimate. Yahoo! was a goofy name, Jerry and Dave were anything but a proven management team, and their business model could be best summed up as *giving away service over the Web*. The popular notion that Netscape had already proven that this model could work was also, indeed, *hoo-ha*. The Navigator had never been de jure free for most people. And while its price tag was a de facto fantasy for the majority of its users, Netscape was known to be generating most of its revenues from client software sales. Yahoo!'s model at the time, such as it was, was far closer to HotWired's. HotWired's "product" was entirely free, and was supported by a well-defined ad revenue model (see Chapter 7). But Yahoo! was never designed to be a vehicle for advertising. Jerry and Dave were only considering an ad model in reaction to an unexpected opportunity—and they were still anything but committed to selling ad space at all (Moritz recalls that they were in fact "very apprehensive . . . and justifiably, about adding a commercial taint to the Yahoo! service" for fear of turning off their existing users).

None of this meant that Yahoo! lacked commercial potential. The *giving away service over the Web* model turns out to be a very powerful one, and Jerry and Dave were fast becoming masters of it. Fortunately for all parties, Moritz saw this quickly. A former journalist, he was already convinced of the Internet's communicative power. His first visit to the trailer also made it clear to him that "these guys were sitting at a very interesting position on the Net that could, if developed properly, be reasonably strategic."

But while Moritz was quickly sold on Yahoo!, others soon were too. America Online was the first to make an interesting rival overture. AOL was then about to eclipse CompuServe as the world's largest commercial online service, and was in the midst of a major push into the Internet market. The company felt that it needed a search engine, and made Yahoo! an offer that, Dave recalls, would probably have made him and Jerry into millionaires fairly quickly. AOL's alluring carrot also had a fairly menacing stick lurking behind it, in that the online giant warned Jerry and Dave that if they didn't sell, they'd soon find themselves competing with a deep-pocketed AOL-sponsored rival.

This was no idle threat, as AOL clearly had the resources to build its own Yahoo! It could also jump-start that process by buying one of Yahoo!'s competitors (as it eventually did).

Dave and Jerry considered AOL's offer closely. But in the end they chose to build rather than sell. AOL was mainly offering stock for one thing, and the structure of the deal would have tied them to working there for years. But a bigger issue than money or liquidity was that "we still wanted to do it ourselves," Dave recalls. Building Yahoo! was *fun*, particularly without adult supervision. He and Jerry were also worried that selling to AOL would have "most likely killed" Yahoo! in the end.

A procession of other corporate suitors soon followed. Dave and Jerry held at least exploratory talks with MCI, Microsoft, and even CNET (see Chapter 8). But the only other formal offer they received came from Netscape. Netscape first contacted them when Marc Andreessen learned that they were planning to move off the Stanford campus. He soon arranged for Netscape to host their site for a couple of months. Some weeks into this arrangement, Jerry and Dave were invited to "just come on board as Netscape employees and do this," Jerry recalls. This offer was in essence quite similar to AOL's. Like AOL, Netscape wanted to take their service in-house, and sign them on as employees. Like AOL, Netscape also mainly had stock to offer. But unlike AOL, Netscape had not yet gone public, and its stock was still valued at an almost sarcastically low price. Netscape also seemed like a far better cultural fit than AOL, and the threat of it creating a rival directory if they said no was much scarier. All of this made turning Netscape down "a harder decision than anything else,' Jerry recalls. But in the end, he and Dave decided to go it alone. Sequoia financed their company in April of 1995 at an assessed valuation of $4 million.

Luckily, Netscape never did introduce its own directory service. It instead gave Yahoo! a tremendous boost by linking the "Internet Directory" button on its Navigator's toolbar directly to the Yahoo! site throughout most of 1995. This link amounted to a ringing endorsement from the world's most powerful Internet software company. It also made turning to Yahoo! a natural, easy, and *preprogrammed* action for everyone in the Navigator's vast user base. The timing of this could not have been better, as millions of people were then discovering the Internet (and the notion of Internet directories) through the Navigator. In this, Yahoo! became the default entry point for countless maiden explorations of the Web.

For its part, AOL eventually purchased WebCrawler, one of the better early index search services. WebCrawler went on to draw tremendous traffic, as subscribers to both AOL and GNN (an Internet service provider that AOL bought during its acquisitions binge) were given browsers that pointed directly to it (much as Netscape pointed to Yahoo!). But compared to Yahoo!, whose form and features subsequently evolved dramatically, WebCrawler remained very much of a no-frills service. In this, Dave was probably right to worry that Yahoo! would have suffocated as an AOL property.

Yahoo! did anything but stagnate in its makers' hands, however, as Dave and Jerry threw their company into high gear as soon as Sequoia's money was in the till. The first people they hired were Tim Brady, who had helped with the business plan, and an engineer name Donald Lobo. Srinija Srinivasan, whom they had met in Japan, then became Yahoo!'s first "surfer," or site categorizer. She went on to "single-handedly build the surfer and editorial department that Yahoo! has today," Jerry says. Her arrival (and that of the other early surfers) finally freed Dave and Jerry from the frenetic and at times tiresome job of site categorization.

With so many new people to train, deploy, and motivate, a new CEO quickly rose to the top of Yahoo!'s shopping list. This wasn't because Jerry and Dave planned to reduce their own involvement in Yahoo! They rather knew that their company had the potential to get big fast, and neither of them felt fully equipped to run a giant Yahoo!—a sentiment that was no doubt shared by their backers at Sequoia. They hired an interim CEO to fill in while they looked for a full-timer. Within a few months, they met Tim Koogle, and their search was over.

Like Jerry and Dave, Koogle was a product of Stanford's engineering department. Also like them, he began dabbling in entrepreneurship while still a graduate student. His company "rebuil[t] engines for wealthy Stanford undergraduate students whose cars were always breaking," he recalls, and was not *quiiite* as successful as Yahoo! So after completing his studies, Koogle established a more substantive enterprise, a contract engineering firm that Motorola later acquired. Koogle remained with Motorola for several years after that. He worked in its Japanese operation, ran one of its Canadian divisions, then did some corporate venture capital work. Eventually he left to run a large division of Litton (later Western Atlas) called Intermec.

Jerry and Dave liked Koogle because they sensed that he "was willing to put up with a lot of change," Jerry recalls, and there was cer-

tainly going to be plenty of that at Yahoo! It also seemed that Koogle's
background had prepared him well to see the company through many
stages of growth, which meant that they could get "a great CEO for a
long time to come" in him, Jerry remembers. Once Koogle started,
Jerry and Dave were both happy to hand over the managerial reins to
focus more deeply on other matters. Dave remained on the engineering
team, while Jerry started working more on business strategy and outside relations.

Koogle recalls that his first order of business was to "put meat on
the bones in terms of our vision." Yahoo! needed to start producing
revenues. It also needed to prepare for battle, as competition in the directory space would no longer be of the mellow, everybody-wins,
EINet Galaxy sort. It was in fact likely to become quite hotly contested
and lavishly funded, as Netscape's August IPO had made it clear that
winning on the Internet meant winning very, very big. A number of serious competitors were by then on Yahoo!'s horizon. InfoSeek had
stopped charging admission at its site, and was already selling ads. Lycos had split off from Carnegie-Mellon University, and was looking
very commercial, hungry, and tough. So was McKinley, a company
that had recently published a successful *Internet Yellow Pages* book.
The jilted AOL was meanwhile starting to promote WebCrawler, Microsoft was almost by definition a potential competitor, and there was
a pending dark-horse entrant to the race in a company called Architext. Dave and Jerry had had one close brush with Architext already
during their swing through Sand Hill Road, when Netscape's backer
Kleiner Perkins tried to talk them into merging with the company.
They refused. Now they knew it was only a matter of time before Architext came after them (Architext is now called Excite, and its search
service debuted in the fall of 1995).

Yahoo! met its competition with an entirely new look in August of
1995. A number of major additions were introduced to the site that
month, the most obvious being advertising. Tim Brady recalls that the
company "went out meekly" with that change. Just as feared, it was
greeted with "a lot of E-mail saying, 'You sold out. I can't believe you're
doing this,' " Brady recalls. This criticism stopped after just a few days,
however. And if anybody actually abandoned the service for having the
nerve to make a living, their boycott never dented its traffic. Along with
advertising, Yahoo! rolled out a major overhaul of its hierarchy in which
the original 19 top-level categories were pared back to today's 14. At the
same time, the news service that Yahoo! first discussed with Reuters in

late 1994 finally debuted. Accessed through a "Headlines" button on Yahoo!'s front page, this featured news stories in several topical categories (e.g., Business, Entertainment, Politics, Top Stories).

Although it had been almost a year in the making, the Reuters debut was the first public indication of a new and deeper level in Yahoo!'s functional strategy. Yahoo! had traditionally delivered service to its visitors by literally sending them elsewhere. In offering news, it was now becoming a *destination* as well as a hub. This shift might have been viewed as simply an extension of the site's new revenue model, since now that Yahoo! was affixing its pages with banner advertisements, every page it served represented advertising real estate. Destination services like news that generated more traffic would therefore also generate more salable ad space.

But there was more to the Reuters' launch than this, as adding news was just the first of several major bids that Yahoo! has made to not only become a greater generator of traffic, but to also become a broadly useful tool. News was followed by weather information in December. Weather was followed by stock quotes in the spring of 1996. Stock was followed by a blizzard of new sites and services in the summer and fall of 1996. Through all of these additions, Yahoo! has been bidding to integrate itself with its users daily media habits, and more generally, to aggrandize its role in their lives. And within a year of the Reuters' launch, the site had succeeded in redefining itself and much of its market (as all of its major competitors followed its lead). No longer just a gateway to the Web, Yahoo! had become a nexus of information of all types. If it continues on its trajectory, it could well grow into a service that millions turn to daily as they now turn to their newspapers, phone books, and more.

The revenue implications that this could have are for now unclear. But the value in out-executing EINet Galaxy and the World Wide Web Virtual Library was no clearer back in the days of "Jerry's Guide," and if Jerry and Dave had stopped then to ponder their *revenue model*, they never would have started again. But they didn't stop, because they have always understood intuitively that more traffic and attention is better than less. The market value that Yahoo! attained scarcely a year after its first round of venture financing indicates that their early instincts were good. Not ones to fix unbroken things, Jerry and Dave are still essentially following the same strategy that they have been following since Yahoo!'s inception—that of continually bidding for more traffic and attention by continually providing more and better service for free. They are now among the best people in the world at doing this. And they will almost certainly continue to be, because it turns out that *giving away service over the Web* has a real first-mover advantage to it. This is because success in this model is measured in traffic, and traffic on the Web begets more traffic.

As an early and successful player in this game, Yahoo! has always had a tremendous traffic base compared to almost anybody else. This makes it easy for it to stay ahead by continually parlaying its traffic into still more traffic. Yahoo! traffic begets more Yahoo! traffic because first-time Yahoo! users almost invariably find the site to be accessible, friendly, and useful. The service works for them, so they come back. Regular users become traffic annuities, and Yahoo! now has millions of them. Heavy traffic also makes for an ideal platform for launching new destination services, which can themselves generate still more traffic. For instance, Yahoo! became one of the Web's leading news providers the day it switched on its Reuters service. Many other sites had been providing news on the Web since long before that. But Yahoo!'s enormous daily audience provided its new service a vast ready constituency which soon eclipsed the readership of many longer-established news sites. Today, Yahoo!'s news service draws plenty of its own distinct and loyal traffic. This traffic can itself now help to launch still more services.

Once the August, 1995, makeover was complete, management turned its attention to the more mundane, and suddenly more pressing matter of funding the company. Yahoo! actually turned a profit shortly after it started selling ads. But profitability does not always translate into positive cash flow, and even if it did, Yahoo!'s market opportunity warranted far more aggressive growth than its meager income could sustain. For this reason the company lined up a second round of investment in the fall of 1995. Management asked for a $40 million valuation. This seemed adequately audacious, given that Yahoo! had only been making money for a few weeks, and had been assessed at $4 million just seven months before. But when the investors heard the figure, "nobody even blinked," Jerry recalls, which left him and his slack-jawed team thinking, "*Shit, it should have been higher!*" Still, everyone was happy just to have the money in the till, particularly in light of its sources. The financing's strategic investors were Reuters, which had long been an important friend, and a fast-growing Japanese conglomerate called Softbank.

Softbank was founded in 1981 by Masayoshi Son, a Japanese entrepreneur with an American education and Korean family roots. By the early 1990s it had become Japan's dominant computer software distributor (it now claims a 50 percent market share). Softbank first attracted considerable American attention when it acquired Ziff-Davis's trade show operations in 1994, gaining title to such properties as the enormous COMDEX computer conventions. It gained even more notice the following year when it acquired Ziff-Davis's publishing properties for $2.1 billion, a transaction that closed just a few weeks before the Yahoo! investment.

Masayoshi Son learned of Yahoo! through Sequoia—he sat on the board of Cisco Systems with Don Valentine, a Sequoia partner—and became intrigued with Yahoo!'s business. His Ziff-Davis link immediately made him an attractive potential investor, as Yahoo! was already talking to ZD about partnering on a magazine at that point, and it seemed that this project could only go more smoothly if the publisher's new owner acquired a stake in Yahoo! as well. Jerry was also excited about Softbank's potential to help Yahoo! establish a presence in Japan. Japanese Web traffic was just starting to rocket at that point, which made it look like a great time to start a Japanese Yahoo! And since Jerry considered Yahoo! to be a media property, and therefore a cultural product, he believed that a Japanese Yahoo! would have to be locally grown in order to succeed. Softbank ultimately acquired 5 percent of Yahoo!'s equity in its second round of financing, which closed in November of 1995. The two companies quickly established a joint venture to develop Yahoo! Japan, and not long afterward, the first issue of Ziff-Davis's *Yahoo! Internet Life* hit the newsstands.

Yahoo!'s second round of investment funded the development of several second-generation Yahoo! services, as well as the hiring of several seasoned managers. This new team was put to its first real test in December, when Netscape made it clear that the Internet Directory button on its Navigator would soon point to rival directory service Excite (formally Architext). This button had been pointing to Yahoo! for almost a year by then, and had brought the service considerable cachet. It had also at times fed it up to 20 percent of its traffic directly—a significant proportion which if anything understated the button's significance, as many (perhaps even most—there was no way to tell) of the people who came directly to Yahoo! had originally discovered it through the button. Jerry recalls that there had been talk about reallocating both of the Navigator's buttons (a second button, "Internet Search," had long pointed to InfoSeek) since the summer. Nobody had a problem with this, as the buttons had turned out to be very valuable real estate and it was quite reasonable for Netscape to want to start charging rent for them. But the process, Jerry recalls, had been "a long and tortuous road.' At one point, Yahoo! had been asked to submit a bid for its button. At another, there had been talk of connecting the buttons to an alphabetic listing of links to several search services (which sucks if your name starts with "Y"). But all had been quiet for some time when Netscape suddenly called with the news about Excite in mid-December. "We were like, shit, merry Christmas to you guys too," Jerry remembers.

The change was implemented almost immediately, and everybody held their breath over the holidays. Then in January, Yahoo! was still one of the Web's biggest draws, having lost less than 10 percent of its traffic. Tim Brady now looks back on the button calamity as "a turning point for us as a company, mentally," because "it was like the floor was pulled out in a matter of two days, and we were still standing. We were looking around, waiting for things to collapse in a lot of ways. And we were just like, I guess we're on our own now. It was that kind of feeling. And bad as it was at the time, it was a good feeling like. . . . OK, we're our own business, you know, love to be there but we're not there, so let's deal. And it really gave us this feeling of independence, and made us think about how we're going to do things and approach markets outside the confines of Netscape."

Bigger, older, better funded, and still standing, Yahoo! entered 1996 ready for the mantle of autonomy and stability that an initial public offering could give it. The timing for this seemed perfect. Netscape's August IPO had shown how hungry, nay, *ravenous* the investing public was for exposure to the new medium, and few business seemed to offer more direct exposure to the Web's growth than the search services. After all, the more people use the Web, the more they needed to search. So as Web usage went, so should go the directories (or at least their traffic). Yahoo!'s own traffic history certainly supported this notion. By February of 1996, the company was serving over six million pages to its visitors every day. This was double September's traffic, several times the previous February's traffic, and growth wasn't slowing. Yahoo! had also already signed up more than 80 paying sponsors in less than six months, indicating that it was highly capable of converting its traffic into revenue.

Long before finalizing its IPO plans, Yahoo! got another call from

Softbank. It turned out that Masayoshi Son wanted to up his stake in the company. And this time, he wanted to acquire enough of the companys equity to make his holding one that he could deem "strategic." Yahoo! CFO Gary Valenzuela recalls that Son "made a very specific point of saying, the way I look at investments, there's a line [at] 30 percent" ownership, which to him meant the difference between being a financial investor and "a real partner." Being above that line was very important to him.

Jerry and Dave agonized over Softbank's offer. They knew that Son was the gateway to Japan. Between that, his Ziff-Davis properties, and his expanding interests throughout the Internet, he could clearly become an outstanding partner to their company. But Yahoo! would have float at least 10 percent of its equity in the IPO to make its stock adequately liquid in the market. Selling Son enough of the company to leave him with 30 percent of it afterward would therefore require that both Jerry and Dave sell off large pieces of their own holdings. Jerry recalls that neither he, nor Dave, nor Sequoia particularly wanted to sell anything. So in the end, they all sold in equal parts and made the deal work. Jerry, who like Dave was left with just over 15 percent of the company after the IPO (to Sequoia's 17 percent and Softbank's 37 percent) knew it was the right thing to do, but it still upset him to sell off such a big piece of Yahoo! "It's like giving part of your kid away," he now says. "It really feels like that. Nobody believes me, but that's basically what it feels like." Still, the kid did all right from the deal, as Softbank's investment put over $60 million into Yahoo!'s coffers.

Softbank has since embarked on an aggressive campaign to expand its Internet holdings. Ziff-Davis Publishing CEO Eric Hippeau (Son's "right-hand man" in the United States, Jerry says), says that Son "got so excited [about] Jerry's vision as to what could happen, not only to Yahoo!, but what was likely to happen on the Internet" that his investment in Yahoo! became "a catalyst" to his subsequent buying spree. By the fall of 1996, Softbank had acquired all or part of dozens of Internet companies. Among them were I/PRO (see Chapter 5), InterVista (Tony Parisi's company; see Chapter 4), PointCast (see Chapters 3 and 8), Agents Inc. (now Firefly; see Chapter 2), Electric Minds (Howard Rheingold's new company; see Chapter 7), Freeloader (see Chapter 8), and OnLive! Technologies (see Chapter 4), as well as E*Trade, US Web, and CyberCash.

Yahoo! filed to go public on March 7, 1996, and the frenzy for its shares started building immediately. *The Wall Street Journal* dramatically billed Yahoo!'s debut as a "Wall Street Event." A clerk at Yahoo!'s lead underwriter, Goldman Sachs was soon getting over 100 Yahoo!-related, phone calls per hour—the most he had ever received for an underwriting in his four years on the job (and the most he will ever receive, as he was summarily fired for blabbing this fact to a reporter). Two Yahoo! competitors, Lycos and Excite, went public a few days before Yahoo! (InfoSeek went public some months later). But this did nothing to reduce demand for Yahoo!'s stock. Yahoo! CFO Gary Valenzuela recalls that the ratio of orders for Yahoo! shares to the number that were actually offered on the morning of the IPO was far higher than he had seen in an IPO before—and he had been through a few.

Yahoo! went public on April 12th, a Friday. Its shares priced at $13, but the extraordinary demand for them drove the first trade to clear at $24.50. Yahoo!'s shares then changed hands an average of over six times each during the frenetic hours that followed. The stock peaked at $43 before ending the day at $33, giving Yahoo! a market value of almost $850 million—over two hundred times the valuation that Sequoia had granted it roughly a year before. It was a good day.

As the frenzy subsided over the subsequent months (and as share prices throughout the technology sector deflated), Yahoo!'s stock settled back toward (but never below) its $13 offering price. This decline did attract some attention ("Yahoo! more like boo-hoo" sniffed one particularly memorable headline in *The Orange County Register*). But it never elicited real acrimony. Because although the company had reacted to a market opportunity in going public, it had in no way acted opportunistically. Yahoo! had in fact left a great deal of money on the table. Analysts at Donaldson, Lufkin & Jenrette (DLJ, a Yahoo! counderwriter) and at Hambrecht & Quist (a close Yahoo! watcher) have reckoned that based on the overwhelming demand for its shares, the company could have gone public at $25 or more. This indicates that Yahoo! may have effectively transferred over $30 million in value to the investing public that it could have directed to its own balance sheet.

Yahoo's restraint allowed it to "[make a lot of friends in the community," Jerry believes. "They got a good deal, and a lot of them made money, and we didn't need the cash." It also helped the company keep its stock trading above its IPO price throughout the unfavorable technology equities market of mid-1996, something that none of its competitors could claim. In this, Yahoo! was helped not only by its modest

IPO price, but also by a significant premium that the market was granting it. By late summer, it was trading at roughly eight times its expected 1998 revenues, while its rivals were trading closer to one to two times their 1998 revenues. Analyst Sue Decker of DLJ partly attributes this to Yahoo!'s superior branding. Yahoo!'s management "understands that success in this market is about brand differentiation, not just greater traffic," she believes, which sets the company apart. Danny Rimer of Hambrecht & Quist echoes this notion. "Yahoo! is *cool*," he says simply. "It's not a technology company. It's a brand, it's an article of culture. This differentiates Yahoo!, makes it cool, and gives it a market premium." Fundamental investors might be reluctant to pay a premium for *cool*. But intangible advantages are the hardest ones for competitors to replicate. And within its market, Yahoo! is, without doubt, inimitably *cool*.

Yahoo! is cool largely because Jerry and Dave are cool. Their trailer-to-riches story is the stuff of legends. It is a familiar piece of Internet lore, and the company is not shy about retelling and promoting it. Jerry and Dave's PR value has earned them coverage on countless TV shows and magazine covers (including those of *Wired* and *Forbes ASAP*). Through these channels, they can reach Yahoo! users off-line, and reaffirm their company's youth, sense of humor, and up-from-the-trenches credibility.

Yahoo! is also cool because Jerry and Dave have built their company in their own image. Yahoo! is a young, unpretentious, twentysomething place. Its dozens of surfers (full-time Web categorizers) can and do help Jerry and Dave extend the company persona in many forums. Yahoo! surfers now appear daily on TV shows like MSNBC's "The Site," where they kick back and anoint with-it Web sites. The plugged-in-but-unsnooty ethos that they project ring true because they are a sincere reflection of their company, not a marketer's fabrication. And those ethos are always evident at the Yahoo! site. There Yahoo! continually affirms its identity, uniqueness, and *cool*ness through devices like lively contests, inventive new services, and of course its ubiquitous big, red name. In this, it's a good thing that Dave and Jerry passed on *Yataghan*, *Yapok*, and *Yardage*, because Yahoo!'s name is one of its greatest assets. Something wryly billed as an *officious oracle* is almost inevitably fun and eminently brandable. Something soberly billed as *Latin for Wolf Spider* (Lycos) might also be a lot of terrific things (and it is—Lycos is a fine service). But no way is it *cool*.

Yahoo! is now pushing hard to extend its brand, name, and image off-line as well as on-. TV shows and tellings of the Jerry & Dave saga support this. So do several recent publishing efforts. *Yahoo! Unplugged*, the first Yahoo! book, has done well in its first printing. *Yahoo! Internet Life* is meanwhile bringing the Yahoo! name and logo out of the ether and into newsstands, airports, and other *real world* places. This early fruit of Yahoo!'s partnership with Ziff-Davis Publishing could well be followed by other titles (Son's ambitious plans for ZD include expanding its magazine offerings from 80 to 1000 titles in 10 years, and he will no doubt be looking to leverage every brand that he can). Although Yahoo!'s staff makes only minimal editorial contributions to it (see below), Ziff-Davis CEO Eric Hippeau says that the company's name alone almost immediately "galvanized the magazine," which had previously existed as plain old *Internet Life*. His staff reports that its circulation doubled to 200 thousand shortly after its reflagging.

Yahoo! also extends its brand through traditional advertising. It was the first Internet company to launch a TV campaign, and is now buying time and space in a variety of media. Guiding these efforts is Karen Edwards, the Yahoo! name's full-time keeper. Significantly, Edwards' background is in consumer marketing and media, not in software or engineering (she previously worked at Clorox and 20th Century–Fox) The Yahoo! brand's success has already earned her a slot in *Advertising Age*'s 1996 "Marketing 100" (its "salute to the people who represent the very best in brand building." Marimba's Kim Polese was likewise honored). One of Edwards' earlier projects was to develop a "Big Idea" tag line, which she describes as "the one idea that really encompasses, or makes a statement about a company." For now, Yahoo!'s answer to Nike's "Just Do It" and Burger King's "Have It Your Way" is "Do You Yahoo!?" Edwards now features this phrase in almost all Yahoo! advertising. Her long-term goals for the brand include making it "a thing of popular culture," not just online culture, and making the Yahoo! name recognizable to at least half of all Americans.

This might seem like an excessively ambitious, even messianic, goal for Yahoo! to have while the proportion of Americans with Internet (and therefore Yahoo!) access is closer to a tenth than a half. But Yahoo! is investing ahead of the curve. The company thinks of the audience for its promotional campaign as consisting of "Near Surfers," "Non-Surfers," and "Current Surfers." The Near Surfers are a vast and growing group of people who "look at the Net in the same way as a lot of current surfers do," Edwards explains. They are familiar with what it is and with what it can do, but "what they don't know is how do I get on, how do I sign up, where would I start?" Yahoo! management has faith that the Near Surfers will continue to get their acts together and come online in record numbers. And as they do, "if you're the brand name that people know, [your site] is where they're going to go first," Edwards points out. By buying time and space in the off-line media, Yahoo! can therefore start winning over the Near-Surfers before they come online. This could prove to be a powerful strategy, because when markets grow as quickly as the Internet, new customers are more relevant to market share than old ones, as even monolithic installed bases quickly become rounding errors when user populations quadruple regularly.

Yahoo! is also eager to reach Current Surfers with its marketing. It is of course already a big hit with this crowd—but the company doesn't believe that it is a big-enough hit yet ("We think we have about 50 percent of all the people who are on the Web," Edwards explains, "and so I want the rest of them"). To this end, Yahoo! has spent lavishly to rebuild its position in the Navigator's buttonry, shelling out some $5 million to end its exile shortly before its IPO. Even this regal sum didn't wholly regain it its once uncontested throne, because four other services paid up as well, earning rights to equal billing. But Yahoo! also has a link on Microsoft's Internet Explorer browser all to itself, as well as tens of thousands of other links scattered about personal home pages, corporate sites, and other corners and crannies throughout the Web. All of this together gives Yahoo! a tremendous distribution network for reaching Current Surfers.

This leaves only the Non-Surfers unaccounted for. But even those people, with their smoke signals, their stone implements, their simple grunt-based languages—even they interest Yahoo! "Maybe they'll buy merchandise for their kids to wear," Edwards speculates. "Maybe they'll invest in the company." It is partly with the Non-Surfers in mind (along with their Near- and Current- cousins) that Yahoo! promotes its "Do You Yahoo!?" Big Idea so aggressively on radio, on television, and in print.

Yahoo!'s traditional media campaigns are doing a lot to build its name and business. But much as TV ads and Dave and Jerry's *cool* halo help to give it a unique image, Yahoo!'s true seat of competitive differentiation still lies in its hierarchy. This is maintained by a staff of over fifty surfers whose collective efforts are needed for the job that Dave and Jerry handled alone on the smaller, simpler Web of 1995.

The surfer staff carefully screens each of the thousands of site submissions that Yahoo! receives every week. Almost all are placed in the hierarchy, although sites that seem to lack original content, or which look like they're just components or repetitions of other sites are rejected. Multilevel marketeers sometimes fall into this category (although most franchisees seem to pass the screen). The hawkers of something called *Super Blue Green Algae* are especially legendary among the surfers ("It'll change your *life!*" they bellow ritually when the product is mentioned).

But while Yahoo! occasionally excludes sites to keep its hierarchy free of redundancies, it never does this to serve a moral or political agenda. It rather links to sites created by every imaginable group and arguing every conceivable viewpoint, and its staff takes real pains to avoid implicit editorial pronouncements in its category titles. For this reason, Ku Klux Klan–related sites, for instance, are listed under SOCIETY AND CULTURE: ALTERNATIVE: WHITE POWER, instead of HATE GROUPS, FASCISTS, or TROGLODYTES.

Yahoo! surfers start as generalists, but most take on specialties over time. They're a young group; their average age is somewhere in the mid to upper twenties. They are also a smart group; all are college-educated, many have master's degrees, and some are, not surprisingly, professional librarians. Surfers are expected to process at least 100 sites per day, but the experienced ones can make it through significantly more than that without breaking a sweat. This doesn't mean that 5000 sites are added to the main hierarchy every day, as a lot of energy is directed to keeping things current (e.g., weeding out sites that have switched off) or working on regional Yahoo! properties (see below). Certain categories, like ENTERTAINMENT: MUSIC, are popular with many surfers. Certain others, like BUSINESS AND ECONOMY: COMPANIES: SEX, are popular with none ("I guess it's not that bad, but you just burn out," one woman explains). For some reason, several surfers seem to find REGIONAL: US STATES: FLORIDA: REAL ESTATE to be the all-time creepy category.

The surfers are a tremendous resource for Yahoo! They have of course brought the hierarchy further than Jerry and Dave ever could have alone, and have meanwhile become a flexible resource for the company to draw on as it extends its brand off-line. As noted, they work regularly as TV fillerpeople for Jerry and Dave. They are also an invaluable source of "Yahoo! recommends" fodder, which the company feeds to a variety of media. Among those now turning regularly to the surfers for pointers are the *Yahoo! Internet Life* folk (the surfer maintaining the college football category can be quite the resource if you're writing a survey of sites dealing with that subject), as well as the editors of non-Yahoo!-branded periodicals like *Buzz* magazine and *USA Today*. Also, Granite Broadcasting, which has TV stations in nine markets, has been integrating Yahoo! site recommendations with features and stories in its local nightly news broadcasts since the summer of 1996. Collaborations like these provide cheap sources of off-line presence for Yahoo!, and it is the surfing staff that largely makes them possible.

One obvious question that the surfer model raises is, *Does it scale?* Its predecessor, the Jerry-and-Dave Do Everything model, worked fine for over a year. But in the end, it didn't scale. It could only go so far without breaking. So Jerry and Dave incorporated, took their company public, hired 50 surfers, stopped doing everything, and Yahoo! subsequently kept up with the explosive growth of the Web and the 25-fold surge in submissions that it generated. But if the next 18 months brings another 25-fold surge, and the next 18 months yet another, Yahoo! will either have 31,250 surfers on staff at the end of the decade or it will be on to a new model. The surfer model is in fact already pushing some limits today. As late as the fall of 1996, all of the surfers were reporting directly to the same Ontological Yahoo (an official title meaning roughly *hierarchy keeper* or *surfer foreperson*—this was still Srinija Srinivasan, whom Jerry and Dave first met in Japan). This managerial model clearly will not scale, as having 31,250 direct reports to manage (or even a mere 1250) would probably be the end of any yahoo. But these projections may be misleadingly gloom and doomsome. After all, the Web was already a big place when Yahoo! hired its fiftieth surfer. And once big, even the fastest-of-growing places tend to expand geometrically or arithmetically, rather than exponentially. This should give the surfer model some breathing room.

It is certainly in Yahoo!'s interests that the surfer model endures, because the hierarchy that the surfers maintain is a marvelous, carefully-written and intelligently organized edifice of human judgment. As such, it certainly is *content* in every meaningful sense of the word, however devoid it may be of subplots, heroines, and foreshadowings. And content, particularly powerful and functionally unique content like Yahoo!, can form the foundation of a highly defensible business. This aspect of Yahoo! is often misunderstood, because its content is very subtle. Its subtlety leads many casual observers to mistake the site's underpinnings for a proprietary software tool, or yet another high-output organizer.

But Yahoo!'s hierarchy is built from many surfer-years' worth of thoughtful attention. So while it may not qualify as *editorial* content, the hierarchy could no more be replicated by a clever software algorithm than tomorrow's edition of *The New York Times*. This means that until the artificial intelligence community delivers on the brave promises of the early 1980s, the only way to build a hierarchy like Yahoo!'s will be through a large staff of educated surfers. And for now at least, the only such staff is at Yahoo! Some of Yahoo!'s competitors do offer hierarchies of their own. But they are not the products of large dedicated staffs, and are comparatively halfhearted affairs as a result. Few go more than two or three levels deep (compared to Yahoo!'s occasional 15). This effectively makes Yahoo! a near-monopoly provider of in-depth hierarchy-driven searches. In this, Yahoo! is like the sole table of contents in a book with many indexes. People searching the Web face many substitutable choices and options when they need a good index service. But the Web has only one true table of contents in the Yahoo! hierarchy. The traffic that hierarchy-driven searches generate at Yahoo! is therefore highly defensible. And this is a staggering amount of traffic, as Jerry estimates that roughly 60 percent of the pages that Yahoo! serves are responses to hierarchy-related queries. This amounted almost 10 million pages daily by September of 1996—more than the total traffic of any other search service at that time.

This is not to say that Yahoo!'s competitors lack differentiation. All of the leading index search services have by now developed proprietary tools that make their automated searches more effective. Some, like Lycos and Excite, further differentiate themselves with proprietary editorial content of their own creation. Both of these companies are now well known for their vast libraries of subjective Web site reviews. The Lycos archive includes over 10 thousand entries and is maintained by a staff of roughly 50 writers and editors (including a two-time Emmy Award–winner). Lycos CEO Bob Davis describes site reviews as "a critical component of Web navigation." He compares their utility to that of movie reviews, which act as filters for people seeking good films. Davis believes that subjective guides are particularly important on the Web, because the Web's " 'film archive' consists of over seventy million entries," and this makes it "impossible to find the quality products without some assistance."

Yahoo! does not currently provide much in the way of site reviews (although it does flag the most comprehensive sites in many categories and maintains an extensive library of *cool links*). This may arguably leave a hole in its offerings. But the tradeoff that Yahoo! is making in devoting almost all of its internal content development attention to the hierarchy seems like a reasonable one for now. By mid-1996, Davis estimated that the Lycos reviews were drawing "in the neighborhood of several hundred thousand viewings" per day. This a great deal of traffic. Drawn as it is by unique content, it is also relatively defensible, and should grow with Lycos's reputation as a high-quality reviewer. But although Yahoo!'s surfer staff was about the same size of Lycos's reviewing staff, the content they created was drawing an order of magnitude more traffic. For this reason, Jerry is happy to turn to partners like Ziff-Davis and Reuters for editorial content as needed, and to keep his content development resources busy building *context*; context in which other content is framed, organized, and made accessible. The hierarchy is the hallmark example of this. It puts a coherent and navigable face to the otherwise dizzying jumble of the Web. Most of Yahoo!'s newer services function similarly, creating even more refined contexts that are native to national, local, or even individual vantage points (see below).

Yahoo!'s model succeeds because it focuses the company on providing *what's rare*. There has never been an environment as rich in content (both editorial and otherwise) and poor in context as the Web. The context market has accordingly never been quite so hot. DLJ's Sue Decker estimates that search services were in fact capturing over 70 percent of the Web's gross advertising revenues in 1996. Her statistics are remarkable, as guides, directories, and pointers-to-others have never had it this good. It is inconceivable that book cataloging would be a bigger business than book writing, or that *TV Guide* would ring up more revenues than the TV broadcast industry. But markets reward what's rare, context is rare on the Web, and Yahoo! and its competitors have fared well as a result.

Jerry does not expect the Web context market to cool any time soon. He in fact believes that "people's interest in the Internet is going to go from just browsing and looking at very high-level information to stuff that's very specifically interesting to them in some depth." This means that "we need to be able to have in-depth things as people grow and become more expert in the Internet." For this reason, Yahoo! will continue to invest its finite content development resources into building context like the hierarchy, rather than in creating traditional editorial content like reviews. And as Yahoo!'s context is embedded with more and more surfer years, decades, and centuries, it will become increasingly complete and defensible.

This does not, however, mean that it will be wholly irreplicable. After all, anybody with deep enough pockets and a few good pizzas could build an even bigger surfer force than Yahoo!'s. And this could eventually produce an even bigger hierarchy than Yahoo!'s. This may indeed happen as the growing value of Yahoo!'s franchise attracts more competitive attention. But surfer-years alone will never be enough to knock off Yahoo! The surfer system is fed by submittals for one thing, and the Web is now deeply into the habit of sending its best new bits to Yahoo! for categorization. A Yahoo! rival would have to get itself into that loop. And given the Web content community's vastness and fragmentation, that would not be an easy loop to enter.

The hierarchy also derives its commercial relevance from its traffic. Traffic begets more traffic. And by late 1996, Yahoo! was drawing more traffic than any site on the Web other than Netscape. This traffic was built up not overnight, but over dozens of months of careful nurturing. Wooing it away would therefore require a long, patient struggle against a very seasoned, focused, entrenched, and well-capitalized Yahoo! It would also require many more content services than just a hierarchy. Because central as the hierarchy is to Yahoo!'s traffic, the site's headline news, stock quotes, weather reports, events calendars, flight information, maps, ski reports, and other services are also popular and integral to it. Yahoo! also provides index searches of its own through DEC's outstanding Alta Vista search engine. All of these satellite services bolster the hierarchy by making Yahoo! more interesting, versatile, and generally worthy of visits. The hierarchy meanwhile bolsters the services by bringing its enormous audience to their doorsteps. And because the services' providers are compensated with shares of the ad revenues that their content generates, Yahoo!'s audience size makes it a particularly attractive partner.

Mimicking Yahoo!'s partnership portfolio would not be an impossible task, as most of its current competitors now offer their own suites of ancillary information services. But this is yet another hardly optional offering that a rival hierarchy would have to keep up with. Yahoo! is also expanding its content partnerships all the time. In doing this, it is creating a veritable engine of attention generation. This engine has become a powerful, self-feeding dynamo, in that "The more content we have, the more users we have," Jerry explains. "The more users we have, the more advertisers we have. The more advertisers, the more content we have. It's a positive feedback loop. And that positive feedback is magnified, so to speak, by the brand. The bigger the brand is, the more each incremental pop is. You don't have to spend as much money to get more content. You don't have to spend as much money to get more users. So it becomes more leveragable."

The dynamic that Jerry describes is very powerful. It could well turn Yahoo! into the most powerful media property in the world in a very small number of years. Not the most powerful media *company* (as many media companies own hundreds of powerful properties). But perhaps the most powerful media property. This may seem like an excessively bullish statement. But consider this: In the fall of 1995, Yahoo! was serving 3 million pages per day, or 21 million pages a week, to its visitors. By the spring of 1996, it was serving 42 million pages per week. By fall of that year, well over 100 million. It is safe to assume that virtually all of these pages were examined, as each of them was actively requested by its viewer. *Time*, the most widely read news magazine in America (and an enormously powerful media property by any definition) had a paid circulation of roughly 4 million at that point (this was growing at an annual rate of less than 2 percent). Issues of *Time* are typically around 100 pages long, meaning that it was then pushing out roughly 400 million pages per week to its audience. Assuming, rather generously, that half of all of the pages of each copy of *Time* are examined, this amounts to roughly 200 million viewed pages. Yahoo! will probably be serving more pages than this by the end of 1997, and several times as many pages by the end of the decade.

The question of whether Yahoo! will then be a *more powerful media property* than *Time* is one of definition. If power is a function of editorial influence, than Yahoo! will certainly be the lesser property, as it does not serve editorial content of its own creation. But if power is deemed to be a function of understanding and marketing to an audience, then Yahoo! will give *Time* a run for its money. This is because *Time*, like all traditional media, *broadcasts* to its audience, in that it pushes out the same signal to all comers (with perhaps some minor refinements based on regional distribution or subscriber demographics). These broadcasts are one-way affairs, in that *Time*'s audience does not really communicate back to it—save for the little white cards that are mailed in with checks every year or so.

But Yahoo! doesn't broadcast to its visitors. It instead engages them in dialogue. This means that unlike *Time*, it is able to target advertising and content to its audience in a very refined manner. Yahoo! has long based this targeting on its users' interests as expressed by their Internet searches, or by their queries to its Yellow Pages, its stock quote server, its news archive, and so forth. Single stand-alone queries like these can at times reveal quite a bit about the people making them. But Yahoo! is also now going beyond this by adding elements of *persistence* to its relationships with its visitors. This can let it start basing its understanding of them on hundreds of queries made over time. The heightened intimacy this allows will eventually let Yahoo! target its services and messaging in a far more refined manner than it can today. For instance, Yahoo! might deduce quite a bit about a visitor who searches for information about New York City sports teams, keeps abreast of the financial news, and regularly checks up on the Connecticut weather. Based on its deductions, it might tailor its marketing and services in ways that both the visitor and Yahoo!'s partners (be they advertisers, content providers, or merchandisers) would find valuable. But if the user's requests for information all come as separate, anonymous, and apparently unrelated transactions, Yahoo! can learn and tailor nothing.

A new product called "My Yahoo!" is designed to draw heavy Yahoo! users into mutually beneficial persistent relationships. My Yahoo! users enter their news, entertainment, geographic, and other interests into a system which creates personalized pages for them. Users can then visit their personal pages whenever they like. There, the up-to-the-minute sports scores, stock quotes, weather reports, and news headlines that interest them are always bundled together in one place. Users benefit from this in that it is a convenient way for them to get information that would otherwise have to be gathered piecemeal. Yahoo! benefits in that it gets to know its users better.

The most immediate material impact that My Yahoo! has had on the company has been in advertising revenues, as Yahoo! prices its ad space partly on the basis of targeting. Targeted banners command higher prices at the site because they reach more relevant audiences (see Chapter 5). Before it began to establish persistent relationships with its visitors, Yahoo! could target banners only on the basis of search terms. For instance, it could direct the banners of a technology company solely to visitors making searches in the COMPUTERS AND THE INTERNET category. But while this is a good way to reach a technically-oriented audience, a Floridian teenager digging around the category for the first time might respond to very different banners than a Seattle-based technology marketer searching it for the 2019th time. By knowing its visitors' backgrounds as well as the categories that they search, Yahoo! can target its banners in a far more refined and effective manner.

This is significant to Yahoo!, because the more targeted advertising space is, the more differentiated and salable it is to sponsors. And since Yahoo! serves so many pages that it can't possibly sell banners on all of them (roughly 75 percent of its total ad capacity was going unsold by mid-1996, according to DLJ's Sue Decker), the site's revenues are far more sensitive to the differentiation of its ad space than to its raw ability to generate it. Persistent relationships can make otherwise less-salable ad space (e.g., the pages served to people searching the SCI-ENCE: BIOLOGY: MOLECULAR-BIOLOGY: INSTITUTIONS category) highly salable, because they make it possible to target banners based upon who's looking, as well as on the basis of where they're looking.

As Yahoo! deepens its relationships with its existing users, it is of course always seeking to establish new ones. To this end, it is expanding its geographic reach rapidly. The first international Yahoo!, Yahoo! Japan, was launched in April of 1996. It has since been followed by several other national editions (including France, German, Canada, and the United Kingdom). All of these link principally to native language content, although they also tie back into the main hierarchy. Most operate as joint ventures between Yahoo! and a local partner (which is usually, but not always, Softbank). The international Yahoo!'s are bids to replicate the main site's success by seizing early share in growing markets. Yahoo! Japan's experience indicates that some of these markets could be vast. Just six months after its launch (in October of 1996) this site already had its first million-page-view day. This was as much traffic as all of Yahoo! was generating less than 18 months before.

Yahoo! is also drumming up new users (and winning even more traffic from old-timers) through a series of "community" Yahoo! sites. The first of these, Yahoo! San Francisco Bay Area, debuted in June of 1996. It was soon followed by Yahoo! products targeted at Los Angeles, New York, Chicago, Washington, D.C., and Boston. The metropolitan Yahoo!s place local information which is already scattered throughout the main hierarchy into focused hierarchies built around locally relevant topics like Transportation, Employment, and Sports and Recreation. This is rounded out with content like entertainment listings, local news, and traffic reports provided by local TV stations, alternative newspapers, and other local content partners.

Yahoo!'s community sites have become powerful vehicles for promoting and generating demand for several new Yahoo! services. Among these is Yahoo!'s national Yellow Pages directory, which itself links to another Yahoo! service that generates customized maps. Together these allow Yahoo! users to look up the address and phone number of almost any business in the United States, and also get a map to its doorstep. Yahoo! may not yet be the first thing that most of us think of when we need directions to the local hardware store. But the metropolitan Yahoo!'s are natural contexts for browsing, exploring, and learning about local services and enterprises of all types—exploration which inevitably generates demand for directions and phone numbers. In this, the metropolitan guides are natural gateways to these other Yahoo! services, which themselves represent interesting bids to further aggrandize Yahoo!'s role as an information provider. Yahoo!'s Yellow Pages service might eventually draw over a million queries per day (its stock quote service already does). And who knows—maybe it will one day become a more popular source of phone numbers than the phone book itself. As usual, it is hard to assess the revenue implications that this could have. But also as usual, Yahoo! is operating under the well-proven assumption that more traffic and attention is inevitably better than less. And since the Yellow Pages industry rings up over $10 billion a year in the United States alone, it safe to assume that *some* kind of revenue—maybe quite a bit of it—is out there.

Perhaps the most significant new listing business that Yahoo! has launched through its metropolitan sites is its classifieds service. Local Yahoo! classified listings cover such categories as real estate, automobiles, employment, and personals. Since Yahoo! does not have to fell trees, ink pages, and ship newsprint to create and distribute its listings, banner advertisements alone can make its classifieds highly profitable (and meanwhile create the rather odd phenomenon of ad-supported advertisements). This lets Yahoo! price its listings at their marginal cost. Rounding to the nearest fraction of a penny, that cost is roughly zero. Free listings have helped Yahoo! drum up a significant advertiser base very quickly. Ellen Siminoff, who runs the Yahoo! communities effort, reports that only four months after its debut, Yahoo! San Francisco Bay Area had already attracted 450 help-wanted advertisers, who were together running almost as many ads as the Sunday edition of the nearby *San Jose Mercury News*.

The advantages of online classifieds go beyond their freeness. Because they reside in databases rather than on pulp, they can be sorted quickly based on highly customized criteria. This means that perusers of Yahoo!'s car listings, for instance, can specify preferred price, year, and mileage ranges, and see only the listings that match their interests. Yahoo! classifieds can also be media-rich. Some already link to full-color images of the items, homes, or persons they promote. Some will no doubt eventually link to videos, RealAudio files, VRML models, and more.

Yahoo! is not the only online company that has identified local services as an attractive market. America Online's Digital Cities service, Microsoft's Cityscape, and an independent Web-based service called CitySearch have also entered this category. Not all of these services are necessarily wholly competitive to Yahoo!'s metropolitan sites. CitySearch, for instance, has a much stronger content orientation than Yahoo! It is now building a string of community media franchises around local writers and photographers, as well as its own content. Unlike Yahoo!, the company also builds and hosts sites for some of its content partners and others. Its business model and content ambitions differ enough from Yahoo!'s that the two services could become quite complementary to one another ("If it's great content, I'm thrilled to link with it, as that's just not our business," Siminoff says of it and the other local directories).

Whether they eventually become the twenty-first century's phone books, newspapers, and job markets or something entirely different, the metropolitan sites are giving Yahoo! a rich context in which to promote a variety of new information services. Through them, offerings like My Yahoo!, and the core hierarchy business, Yahoo! is steadily expanding its audience, its intimacy with it, and the scope of its interactions with it. Together this could create a media franchise whose reach and facility at dialogue with its audience has no precedent. Even Jerry finds it difficult to predict where all of this will lead. But he guesses that Yahoo! will grow to "maybe a couple or three hundred" employees by the beginning of 1998 (although he hedges that "it's still too early to tell" for sure). He expects that by then, Yahoo! will have long since entered the commerce arena with its partner Visa. He also expects that many new community Yahoo!'s will have launched, and hopes that all will have acquired "souls," or have become truly distinctive products of their communities.

For this to happen, Jerry believes that the services need to become con-
vening points, rather than just information clearinghouses. To this end,
they already host bulletin board discussion spaces. Jerry hopes that these
forums will come to draw large constituencies, and perhaps evolve into
robust and highly trafficked "chat" spaces.

Jerry doesn't speculate much about what will happen after 1998,
as he believes that the Internet is moving too quickly to see that far
out. Although when asked if Yahoo! will still be around at the end of
the decade, he is confident. "That's a no-brainer," he says. "It's just a
question of how successful well become." As for himself, he "absolutely" plans to be with Yahoo! for at least another five years. "I
love what I'm doing," he explains. "I don't even see it as a job." What
excites him most and keeps him around is "the integration of what traditionally has been a very techy, nerdy kind of a world to the mass media. I love the fact that computers are becoming more mainstream
rather than less," he says. "I think that we, Dave and I and the team,
are one of the first groups of people to literally take the two sides and
bring them together, along with Netscape and a couple of other companies. Us more than others, because we're in contact with people who
use Yahoo! every day. Marc [Andreessen] still has more corporate customers and techy MIS issues. We don't have any of that. Were a consumer brand, a consumer play, and were going to live and die on the
consumer end of it. That's exciting to me."

Jerry compares the newness of all of this to "being dropped off a
helicopter, and you're the first guy skiing down this hill. You don't
know where the tree is, you don't know where the cliff is, but it's a
great feeling. It's like being on the golf course, and being the first guy
to tee off in the morning, when there's still dew on the ground. The
ball mark is yours, and the footprint is yours. You're the first one to
screw up the sand trap. It's like landing on the moon. I don't know
what that feels like, but I'm sure it's just an exhilarating feeling. This is
a lot safer than all of those things. Including golf."

Yahoo! is a safer game partly because "We have nothing to lose.
We started this with nothing, and I can honestly say I don't mind if we
went back to nothing, because I had a great time. It might be different
ten years from now because I'll have a family and kids. But today, if
Yahoo! went away, we had a great time trying. So I think there's that
little bit of reckless abandon that makes this thing so exciting." And
just as rewardingly, "I've got a great team. Nobody has left Yahoo!
yet. That's a great statement of the people we've recruited."

For all of these reasons Jerry keeps coming back. And while the *Chief Yahoo* no longer subsists on four-hour catnaps next to his workstation, he still works hard, probably from 7 A.M. to 10 P.M., he estimates, "five days a week, and one day on the weekend I work about six or seven hours." For his part, *Cheap Yahoo* Dave is still known for camping out nights under his desk as often as not. Perhaps now finding it a bit lonely around the office in the wee hours, he frets that he's "always wanted to work in the startup environment, and now [Yahoo!] is becoming less and less of that." But despite that, he seems to be in this for the long haul too.

Outside of work, Jerry spends most of his time with his fiancée Akiko. "I couldn't have done Yahoo! without her or my family," he eagerly admits. Together, the two of them are "relatively boring," he says. "I'd like to say we have twenty different hobbies, but we don't." But in the fall of 1996, they bought their first house together, and that keeps them plenty busy. That combined with Yahoo! are probably hobby enough for almost anybody.

CHAPTER 7

ANDREW ANKER
HotWired

Publishing on the Web

The area south of downtown San Francisco's Market Street is a desolate place of warehouses, cyclone fencing, and broad, one-way boulevards. Converging interstates gouge its face with varicose strands of rumbling traffic. These turn First-thru-Eleventh streets and their more cleverly-named perpendiculars into a vast, gridded on-and-off ramp; a sprawling victim of muddleheaded planning shot through with rogue left-only lanes that abduct the unwary, shunt them onto freeways, and then dump them, dazed, in Oakland. South of Market; *SoMa*. Heavy with an air of menace and industry, for years it was avoided by all but the coveralled handful who happened to work there.

But eventually the place drew a new element, inventive folk who looked at warehouses and saw more than transshipment and storage. Artists' lofts appeared. Then dance halls, and high-ceilinged stores. Bits of the financial district slid from NoMa down to SoMa, and parts of the neighborhood became downright trendy. Among those who came to roost in this land of lowish rent and (once you learned the ropes) good highway access were a certain crowd of technology entrepreneurs. Particularly drawn were those from the *content side*: people merging bitstreams to artwork to create video games, CD-ROMs, Hollywood special effects, and other mayhem. The area loosely centered around SoMa's South Park (a tiny strip of struggling greenery) came to be known as "Multimedia Gulch." Black cloth replaced its coveralls.

Dimly-lit cafés appeared amongst its dive bars. Soon parking was a nightmare as the *cappuccino capitalists* moved in by the dozen. Culturally hip and technically literate, South Park was primed to pile the Web's yawning shelf with content when the fires started to build in 1994. Soon its renaissance was in full swing. Rents rocketed, housing lacked, and every few months seemed to bring word of another Web startup bursting out of its pack.

Beyond South Park, on the fringe of the *Gulch*, where both menace and industry are still amply present, lie many of the city's avant-garde night spots. On an evening in January of 1996, one of these played host to the *Night of the Innanet Kids*, as a grumbling cop on the beat described it. This was a party, an anniversary; and by midnight, they were lined up halfway to Mountain View. *Innanet Kids*—there were hundreds of them: artists, programmers, and black-jacketed entrepreneurs, impatiently queuing at the reception's door. Inside the place was packed to the rafters. There were countless dance floors, stairways, and catwalks, all of them dense with shmoozing and shimmying Innanet Somebodies. The main room hosted a World Beat act whose steady rhythms filled the building's every cranny. Its peaceful *thrum*s were punctured only by the crowd's hoots and hollers, plus some occasional explosions from a scary little room in the back.

These were the work of a "mechanical presentation" by Survival Research Labs. The scourge of fire marshals from California to France, SRL had created an installation out of animated mannequins and gaspowered butcher knives that battled to the death on roughly bi-hourly intervals. SRL's Barnums had billed the piece as *one in a series of* INCONSIDERATE EXPERIMENTS *to be performed on the public during the coming months*. Starring in the EXPERIMENT were a massive metallic arm with a whirling eggbeater-like fist (one built from blades, not comfy cookie dough–making paddles) and a wireframe scarecrow who lived in a shack with a noisy-ass shotgun and an electromechanical dawg. Electrified meshing above all this periodically built up charges that made the air taste poisonous, then purged itself with explosive CRACKS! and showers of sparks.

And so—happy birthday to *Wired*. The *Rolling Stone* of the Digital Revolution™ was turning three, and had put this celebration together along with its online cousin HotWired. In the scant years since its shoestring launch, *Wired* had already won several major awards, as well as hundreds of thousands of readers. It had meanwhile named, defined, then (literally) trademarked the Revolution that it chronicled, a revolution that by then was "whipping through our lives like a Bengali typhoon," in the ever-quotable words of the magazine's founder, chief architect, and vision-haver Louis Rossetto. Everybody from *Wired*'s inner and outer sanctums was on hand that night, and prominent among them was HotWired CEO Andrew Anker. *Innanet* yes, but *kid* no more, Andrew had just crossed the chasm to 30. He was dressed a couple of notches above the mean, and his dark hair was flecked with gray, not Day-Glo. This made him stand out just a bit in the crowd—but as a grownup, not as an obvious Boss.

Andrew had been running his agenda-setting company for just over a year by then, and it had already made plenty of waves during his tenure. HotWired debuted in October of 1994 as the Web's most ambitiously-funded and -staffed original content publication. It pioneered and soon popularized notions like site membership and weekly member E-mailings. Its *Wired*-inspired look and *attitude* meanwhile informed the content and presentation of countless Web publications that came after it. But of its many innovations, perhaps the most important were *suit* stuff; were business-related. Because even as HotWired helped set new standards for professionalism in a medium that was still dominated by part-time pioneers with day jobs, it also *broke the Web* as an advertising medium. The banner advertisement, which underpins the revenue hopes of almost every commercial content company on the Web today, was a HotWired creation. Using its banners as a wedge, HotWired also set an important early precedent by recruiting *real world* companies to use the Web to promote their goods & services. No usual-suspects list of disk drive makers and Star Trek memorabilia hawkers, HotWired's sponsors at its practically pre-Netscape launch included consumer brands like Zima, Volvo, and Club Med. By bringing such a diverse clientele to the party so early, HotWired made an unproven new medium look almost like a mainstream choice for levelheaded marketers. And in October of 1994, that was no easy feat.

Now as then, HotWired itself defies easy categorization. The site has often described itself in TV terms (arranging its content into "channels," later "programs"; today it calls itself a "network"). But it also has community elements that have no analogue in TV. It has chat rooms for real-time dialogues. Bulletin boards for asynchronous dialogues. It also sponsors several "auditorium"-style events each week at which notable notables lead discussions that dozens or (at times) hundreds attend. Traditionally posted in text, these events have also been held in RealAudio. Guest lecturers have included musical acts like King Crimson and the Cowboy Junkies, industry figures like Jaron Lanier (see Chapter 4), and many others.

But community spaces and TV jargon aside, HotWired is most frequently described as an "online magazine," and this label fits it well enough. Its content is mainly text, images, and graphics. It is arranged in subdivisions that suggest a magazine's departments. These include Webmonkey, which discusses technical matters for the Web developer or afficionado; Dr. Weil, which deals with health matters; and Netizen, which considers political issues. Like magazine departments, HotWired's content divisions (or *programs*, as they are called) post articles on their mandated subjects, which change daily or weekly. Asked about his site's (and the Web's) mix-and-match borrowings from other media vocabularies, Andrew shrugs that "We're still in horseless carriage days," referring to ye olde term for *car*. A more native, logical, and internally consistent industry vocabulary will arise once the dust has settled a bit. For now, the commercially sponsored Web is barely two years old, and we're still making it up as we go along.

HotWired's own horseless carriage has been on a fairly wild ride from the get-go, and it's been Andrew Anker's baby. Pretty much. But as Andrew himself always points out, HotWired is the product of many imaginations. And while one of them is certainly his own, he is not alone in HotWired's pantheon. Even more exalted within it is Louis Rossetto, *Wired*'s editor-in-chief (and HotWired's director of programming). Louis and his partner Jane Metcalfe created *Wired* from nothing—literally—other than a *vision* (the overused word actually fits here) and their relentless, courageous, almost comical tenacity. Scarcely a year after their company finally launched, they had the nerve to *bet* the thing on a new and underpopulated medium. It still isn't clear just how their bet will pay off. But now they have HotWired to show for it.

Also influential was a small clique of techno-idealists that formed in San Francisco during the Web's dawningest moments. Proximity and a shared passion for the new medium almost inevitably brought this group to *Wired*'s doorstep before HotWired even had a name or a business plan. Most of this crowd left within a few months of HotWired's launch. But their influence lived on in its code, in some of its interactive forums, and (until the company graduated to its third and most corporate home) its hot pink Ethernet cabling, which streaked throughout its office like the veins of some *live, twitching* Day-Glo beast.

But much as HotWired owes to all of these influences, Andrew has been running the place since Louis handed him the keys back in 1994. It has octupled or more in head count, content offerings, and traffic since its launch (much more in the case of traffic), and has done this on his watch. Andrew is not the original *net.visionary* behind the site. Nor is he the technical whiz who hacked together the code that now serves its content and runs its forums. But he has brought a lot of essential talent to the party. Though no Valley engineer, he has worked as a programmer, and has technical smarts that have served HotWired well. A photographer, musician, and (kind of) writer, he also has media instincts that Louis prizes. But most importantly, as a Wall Street veteran, Andrew has a business sensibility that HotWired and *Wired* needed acutely when he turned up.

It is this side of Andrew, Andrew the *suit*, that has added the most to the enterprise. It was a besuited and numbers-minded Andrew who first read *Wired*'s business plan back when Louis and Jane were still recent repatriates with big ideas and nothing to fund them with. Swayed by its logic, Andrew helped arrange for the $600,000 in financing that fueled the magazine's launch. It was Andrew the *suit* who, a year later, accepted Louis's invitation to mind the business side of *Wired*'s online effort. And by the time Marc Andreessen and Jim Clark tied the knot on Netscape in April of 1994, Andrew the *suit* had already run the numbers that gave Louis the last bit of confidence that he needed to bet the business he had (in a sense) spent decades launching on a crash-prone chunk of undergraduate code called *Mosaic*.

Andrew first became a programmer, musician, photographer, writer, and investment banker far from South Park, far from California even, amidst the flash and rumble of New York City, and in the far less flashy and rumblesome land of Pennsylvania (his childhood was divided roughly evenly between these two places). He began computer hobbying as an all-but-tot of 15, shortly after his dad bought the family its first Apple II. Andrew got his first formal computer training at Hotchkiss, a Connecticut prep school that caters to privileged New Yorkas and others. He became a *games hacker* soon after that, and a not-bad one. A magazine called *Hard Core* even offered to publish some code of his that let the players of a certain racing snake game break into the software and add "lives" to their rounds, speed up snakes, change blinking colors, and generally *take charge* (although the magazine vanished before it actually got around to printing it). The code that Andrew victimized may even have been that of Progressive Networks' Rob Glaser, who at the time was moonlighting as a racing snake game author across the state at Yale (see Chapter 2)—but Andrew unfortunately doesn't remember the game's title. It was also at Hotchkiss that Andrew began dabbling in media. He started out as a photographer for the school's weekly sports newspaper, then worked his way up until he was its editor-in-chief. Despite this position, Andrew says that he was never known for his writing. "I'm really good at writing one-hundred-and-fifty-word pieces," he explains. "Get me into three hundred words and I fall apart. That involves *actual writing*." His contributions to both *Wired* and HotWired (at least the ones that he signs his own name to) are still of a sub–*actual writing* length.

College was Columbia, coincidentally Louis Rossetto's alma mater. There Andrew studied economics. He also set his computer partly aside to get serious about music, mostly piano. Impatient with schooling, he also got serious about work. This was investment banking, "which is what you did in the eighties in New York," Andrew explains. By his senior year he was evenly dividing his days between Wall Street and college. Between that and moving in with his then-girlfriend-soon-wife Renee, he was deep into his *real life* before graduation came along.

Finishing with school did bring changes, however, as almost immediately afterward, Andrew and Renee moved to San Francisco—her hometown. There Andrew joined the corporate finance group at PaineWebber. Now among the *suited* masses, he at times showed his true colors by writing elaborate video games in Lotus 1-2-3, the financial modeling program (his best was a car-racing slalom). This was a pretty clear hint that dissecting balance sheets wasn't going to give him everything that he needed from his professional life. But Andrew ignored this cry for help and (oh, al*right*!) spent most of his hours building more mundane spreadsheets, mainly for the bank's local media group. Eventually that group defected to First Boston, taking him with it. Andrew then stayed with them until a promotion took him back to New York. There he worked on radio, newspaper, and magazine deals, and on a team that raised billions for cable television giant TCI. This was all very exciting, and the wages were good. But then the Eighties ended. And by then, Andrew the *hacker* had pretty much maxed out Lotus's possibilities. Hungry for something a bit more technical and entrepreneurial, he left investment banking in 1991 and took a job with a startup called Ad Express.

Ad Express was founded to help TV advertisers target their messages over cable networks by making it possible for them to "build a virtual network where you would buy Lake Forest in Chicago, and Marin in San Francisco, and Darien in Connecticut," Andrew explains—in other words, similar communities scattered throughout the country that might respond to ads in similar ways. Andrew traded in his *suit* for a keyboard and joined Ad Express's engineering team. He wrote software that would take an advertiser's *dream market* (e.g., 18-to-24-year-olds who are likely to buy imported cars), and target its ads based on a demographic analysis of the cable systems. His software was meant to work with a hardware infrastructure that would beam the commercials it targeted to the appropriate cable head-ends. But Ad Express never *got there*. "The cable companies never let them in," Andrew explains. He says that his code lives on, however, in that a second-generation version of it is used by Nielsen to measure and sell cable television demographic information.

Andrew lasted at Ad Express until January of 1992. By then, he and Renee (and their soon-to-be two children) were eager to return to the Bay Area. So Andrew started looking around, and soon had a job at Ad Express's financial backer, Sterling Payot Company. A tiny boutique investment firm, Sterling Payot was basically "whatever they want to be," Andrew explains. "The idea is, it's mostly ex-bankers, and they do whatever is enjoyable to them now." There Andrew worked mainly on media, telecommunications, and technology deals, including Pacific Telesis's spin-off of its cellular operations. He and Renee found a place in the suburbs and slipped into a comfortable routine fairly quickly. Then one day, Andrew came across the business plan of a possibly-maybe magazine that proposed to chronicle the, uh, "Digital Revolution." That magazine, of course, was *Wired*.

Black-jeaned, besneakered, and quotable almost to a fault, Louis Rossetto had been pounding the pavement for an awfully long time by then. His Columbia M.B.A. notwithstanding, he was no hard-core, nor even soft-core *suit*, nor had he been for any identifiable period since graduating from business school back in the early 1970s. He had instead been *on the content side*. He had written novels. He had worked on movies (including on the fleshy set of *Caligula*, upon which one of his novels is based). He had spent a decade in that least *suit* of Northern European capitals, Amsterdam. There he worked as editor-in-chief of *O*, a men's style magazine often compared to *Esquire*, and founded an innovative technology magazine called *Electric Word*. *Electric Word* made waves, captured imaginations, won awards, went broke. And so in 1991, Louis repatriated with his now-partner (in business as well as personal matters) Jane Metcalfe. Louis and Jane (who had worked together on *Electric Word*) left Holland armed with a plan, with a *vision* called *Wired*. With *Wired* on their minds, they figured that they would have plenty to do once they got home.

And they did. But for a while their timing seemed disastrous. The Gulf War had sapped investors' appetites for content ventures of all kinds. Magazines targeting *huh?* Revolutions fell off the bottom of almost every list. Louis and Jane knocked on doors, waited in lobbies, shook trees. There were countless *no*'s. But "every time we talked to somebody," Louis recalls, "the results of that discussion went into the plan." After a year and a half or so this left them with an "enormously evolved business plan," one that just *had* to wow somebody. Someday. Uh . . . right?

Finally, after an eternity of door knocking, lobby waiting, and tree shaking, it did when they met up with Nicholas Negroponte, the baron of MIT's celebrated Media Lab. Negroponte drank the *Wired* Kool-Aid and gave Louis and Jane enough money to assemble the magazine's prototype issue. But while no pauper, Negroponte was not a gazillionaire either, so this was a skin-of-your-teeth kind of deal. Louis and Jane had to rely on some inventive penny-counting to squeak through. At least one early *Wired* staffer jetted off to Boston once to use the Media Lab's color photocopiers because the plane ticket was cheaper than the copying bill would have been. Through financial *hacks* like this, *Wired* was able create its prototype issue and draw within the brink of a launch. But funding the launch itself called for truly deep pockets. Sterling Payot's pockets were Mariana-deep, and this eventually landed their door on the knocking docket. It was a Friday evening in the fall of 1992 when Louis and Jane came calling. They presented to Andrew and a few of his superiors and walked away, convinced that they had scored another miss, because they just "couldn't get any reaction from them," Louis remembers. Andrew's own (apparently well-concealed) reaction was that Louis had just presented "the most compelling business plan I had ever seen." The deal eventually closed, and in January of 1993, *Wired*'s arresting debut issue was on news-stands throughout the country.

Louis and Jane's disastrous-seeming timing suddenly proved to be impeccable. A global subculture of computer hobbyists and technology fetishists had been fermenting for years by then. And while countless periodicals had risen up to serve their interests in clock speeds and software bargains, they were ready for something more: Like a street, not a laboratory vocabulary; like a pantheon of contemporary heroes; like a mythology, an in-crowd chicness, an aura; a *look*. In delivering all of this, *Wired* struck an immediate chord in its core audience. It meanwhile spoke to a general population that was increasingly curious about the digital world. Its curiosity was fed by disparate things—by the spread of PCs in offices, by the rise of outlandishly powerful home video games, by the astonishing spectacle of digital effects in film and video. The digitally-aware now included millions who would never dream of building video games from spreadsheet software. There were artists who viewed digital technology as the new canvas and brush. Businessfolk who realized there was *gold* in them thar chips. Young people, exhausted by baby-boomer narcissism, who wanted something for their own generation to claim.

Wired wooed these groups and many others with a look and a voice that were all its own. They were lurid but chic, mass-market but aloof. *Wired*'s designers favor the Day-Glo over the earth tone; its editors, at times, the opaque over the accessible. Their efforts were anointed with a National Magazine Award for General Excellence (1994), the National Magazine Award for Design Excellence (1996), and many other major citations. Soon *The New York Times* had labeled *Wired* "the totem of a major cultural movement." But *Wired* drew its share of eye rolls and detractors along with its adherents. Some questioned the true technical acumen of its makers (the anti-*Wired* still chuckle about "Nicholas@Internet"—a pseudo E-mail address that accompanied a Negroponte essay in the first issue. This was printed, it is said, to save Negroponte from unwanted reader mail—but some interpreted it as a sign of cluelessness at the helm). Others dismissed the magazine as smug and self-involved. Attuned to this, *The New York Times* also characterized its *totem* as "inscrutable and nearly hostile to its readers."

But despite the controversy it stirred (and controversy is never such an awful thing in media) *Wired* connected to a remarkable audience from the outset. Its maiden issue reached well over 100 thousand people. Paid circulation expanded more or less steadily thereafter, and within three years exceeded 300 thousand—about a tenth the circulation of decades-old mainstream giants like *Newsweek*. But far more impressive than its composition was *Wired*'s audience's size. Overall, it was kind of young (37 on average), very well-to-do (over $600,000 in average household net worth), and extremely well-educated (almost 50 percent with *graduate* degrees). This attractive demographic helped the magazine develop a surprisingly diverse advertiser base early on. Full-page ads for Budweiser and Chrysler, surreal unlikelihoods in technology magazines for years, were soon par for the course in *Wired*.

Funded, extant, and finally read, *Wired* was looking to expand its reach even as it debuted. Louis started talking seriously about putting the magazine online within days of its ink-on-paper launch. And this wasn't just posturing, as he was soon hiring the people who made this happen. The first in the door was Jonathan Steuer. A young Harvard graduate, Steuer was then finishing up his Ph.D. work at Stanford, where his research focused on social interactions in online environments and interface design, among other things. Steuer was no *suit*—he'd never worked a corporate job, and had enough hair on his head to last Hotchkiss Andrew a good four or five years. But he was a damn good technician (although having been a philosophy major, he was a self-taught one). He was also a *pre-Mosaic* Web user. And in the end, he was the one who got *Wired* wired, in that he helped set up its internal network, and then got that network linked to the Internet.

Steuer did his first internal network project for *Wired* before its debut issue. A sporadic series of contract projects followed. Then in the summer of 1993 he persuaded the company to take him on as an official employee "to help them develop a real Internet product," he remembers. Steuer (rhymes with "lawyer," by the way) soon became a fixture at *Wired*. And once he was installed, it wasn't long before Jonathan Nelson started kicking around the office too. Nelson was a childhood friend of Steuer's from Milwaukee who had spent some time producing albums and shows in New York City. He had come West after determining "the club scene combined with the East Village is taxing," he explains, to de-*tax*, and to team up with Steuer in a new venture that was eventually called Cyborganic. Cyborganic's one-of-these-days plan was to open a café in which people could sample CD-ROMs, which were the new buzz at the time. They also later starting thinking about setting up an online space in which café regulars and others could convene. A core tenet of their philosophy, as it gradually developed, was that online and "real-life" interactions are mutually reinforcing, and together can build uniquely robust communities.

Steuer and Nelson were both very passionate about music (Nelson was still making his living as a producer), and this eventually drew them to the progressive fringes of the Bay Area's underground *scene*. It was there that they found Brian Behlendorf. Behlendorf was by then maintaining an electronic mailing list called *sfraves* which chronicled the happenings in San Francisco's rave scene (raves are all-night parties, generally held in warehouses or fields, which do get wild). *sfraves*, Behlendorf recalls, "developed this whole, real, solid community" very quickly because it was both an electronic forum and a *real-life* one, in that its "members met in person practically three or four times a week." This outcome gave Behlendorf a perspective on- and off-line community that was very similar to Steuer's and Nelson's then-evolving perspective, and which influenced their views significantly.

Steuer quickly discovered that Behlendorf was unbelievably Internet-savvy (see Chapter 4) and very accomplished technically. So it wasn't long before he recruited him to do some contract work at *Wired*. By then Steuer had already helped *Wired* set up an E-mail service through which anybody on the Internet could request and receive *Wired* articles. *Wired* was also maintaining an American Online presence, which offered more interactive and real-time access to the magazine's content. But AOL was "a really negative experience for a content provider," Louis says, "because we couldn't directly control the look and feel of our space. We had to do everything through them. It could take weeks for things to get changed on our site. It was like operating by remote control, with gloves on, in China. And then there was also the insulting revenue split that they were offering," which let AOL keep the vast majority of the billings its subscribers incurred while viewing *Wired* content. All of this made Louis eager to find a better way to distribute *Wired* online.

That fall, stable(ish) versions of Mosaic for PCs and the Macintosh were released. *Wired* on the Internet meanwhile became wildly popular. Within a few months, Steuer recalls, "we were serving like seventy thousand files a day, or some totally stupid tens of thousands of files a day, out of the mail server." Talk of building a *Wired* Web site started early. But "Louis didn't want to do anything graphical unless it was up to *Wired* standards," Steuer remembers. And this made sense, because *Wired* had already developed an enviable reputation for graphical excellence. Since the magazine was also still proving itself to the public, its reputation was its most precious asset. It was therefore imperative that the magazine's Web site build on, rather than undermine, its reputation. In light of this, everyone agreed that the site should not be rushed. Instead it should be developed methodically, and into a form worthy of the *Wired* name. But then somebody made the rather rude discovery that *Wired*'s Web site already existed. And boy, was it ugly.

As Steuer remembers it, "two nerds from a government computer lab in Singapore typed in all the text from the first several issues of *Wired*," and just kind of slapped it all onto the Web (or perhaps they pulled all the articles from the E-mail server—Steuer doesn't remember checking). The *Wired* staff discovered the *graphically unexciting* results in late 1993. The government nerds were quickly befriended, and amicably agreed to shut their site down. But the sting of its memory sent Steuer's group into overdrive, and soon they had all of the magazine's back issues accessible through a lovely little Web site. *Wired*'s Internet traffic exploded after that, and "it was clear pretty much immediately," Behlendorf recalls, that "this wasn't just going to be a tangential service." Ambitious talk began about making a *real* Web site, something that went far beyond *repurposing* the magazine's content. Julie Petersen, one of the fewish pre-launch HotWired employees who was still on board two years later, recalls that "one of the first decisions we made was not to do shovelware," as this was a new medium after all. It had native attributes that magazines lacked, and lacked native attributes that magazines had. So just as computer programs were written for the operating systems that they targeted (it was still that dark time before Java) all agreed that content should be—had to be—targeted to its medium. *No Shovelware!* became *Wired*'s World Wide Web rallying cry. And the magazine's seriousness about this dictum became one of the biggest distinctions between it and the other major periodicals that experimented with the Web early on.

By then, Andrew Anker was starting to become a familiar face around the office. As early as the summer of 1993 he had joined *Wired*'s "on-line brain trust"—an informal group that chitted and chatted about the Web, AOL, and other such matters. This gave him a ready excuse to set down his spreadsheets a little early on Fridays and head over to

Wired's South Park offices to loosen the ol' tie and do some blue-sky brainstorming. It wasn't long before Louis became keen to involve Andrew more directly in things. It was "his financial sensibilities which were something that we could really use at that point," Louis recalls, as well as "his solid technological sensibility." But beyond that, there was also "something about him as an individual. [Andrew is] just a very calm, reassuring, exceedingly balanced, even happy person," and this felt like the "right element to bring to the mix."

For his part, Andrew had been fantasizing about joining *Wired* since Louis first presented the business plan to him, but his growing family and his mortgage had ruled that notion out. Over a year had now passed, though, and his work at Sterling Payot "had built the coffers again." And while he hadn't yet tried to build a C compiler out of a PowerPoint, or piece together a modem from the office paper clips, he could feel his technical interests welling up just as strongly as they did back in his last days at First Boston. Andrew considered all of this and decided that he was done with finance. Again. So in March of 1994, he became a full-time *Wired*-ling.

Andrew was officially hired as the chief technology officer of *Wired*, which gave him over-arching responsibility for its yet-unnamed, non-*shovelware* online effort. By then the magazine had about a half dozen people managing its Web site, its America Online presence, the E-mail server, and so forth. Steuer was responsible for this group's day-to-day operations as Online Tsar. Technology and chiefdoms aside, much of Andrew's own initial mandate was to work on the *new Web thing*'s business plan (to which Steuer also contributed). Louis was adamant that one of these be written, as *Wired*-on-the-Web was a highly speculative proposition at best. *Wired* itself was still plenty speculative for one thing, and the Web was still a desolate frontier. Nobody knew exactly how many people were using it, although Louis figured it was maybe a few hundred thousand, tops. And most of its corporate and technical infrastructure still had yet to arise. Marc Andreessen was still working at EIT. Yahoo! was still *Jerry's Guide to the World Wide Web*. And Java was still called *Oak*, and was facing imminent extinction at First Person.

Wired was meanwhile in no position to be placing many big ol' long-shot bets. The magazine had not even released its 10th issue yet (it had only just become a true monthly, having spent most of 1993 as a quarterly, then as a bimonthly). It had lost over a million dollars in its maiden year, and was well on its way to trebling that in 1994. Louis estimates that he had 50-odd employees at the time, and making payroll was already plenty hard. And the standing (and, it turned out, accurate) presumption was that the new *Web thing* would require at least a couple of dozen new people—half the company!—to deliver on its mandate.

Groups that size were rounding error-small at media giants like Viacom, Disney, and Time Warner. But putting one together at *Wired* amounted to betting the company. And Louis understood just how quickly things could unravel, as he and Jane had gotten off to a good (although far more modest) start with *Electric Word*, only to watch it whither. This and all of those patient years of door knocking, lobby waiting, and tree shaking (both before *Wired* and *way* before *Wired*) made the company a rather precious thing to put on the table. But Louis was convinced that the Web would become everything it has since become, and more. He approved the business plan on April 1, 1994. Three days later, Netscape Communications, né Mosaic Communications, was incorporated.

At almost precisely the same time, another publisher was placing its own HotWired-sized bet on the Web. This was Time Warner, and its bet was called Pathfinder. Pathfinder was the brainchild of *Time* magazine's managing editor, Walter Isaacson. It was also the brainniece or -nephew of Louis, as its roots go back to a conversation that Isaacson and Louis had at the National Magazine Awards gathering in 1994 (where *Wired* received its prestigious award for General Excellence). There, Isaacson remembers asking Louis "what he thought would be the next big thing in new media, and Louis responded, 'the Web.' " Time Warner was already "talking about doing something with TelNet and Gopher [two other Internet protocols]" by then, Isaacson remembers, "but Louis was sure it would be the Web." Isaacson was soon convinced that he was right, and after some digging discovered that several Time Warner properties were onto this too. A marketer from *Vibe* magazine had set up a *Vibe* site in his spare time. Warner Books was thinking of doing some kind of Web-based catalog, and some people at *Time* itself were already talking about creating digital content for the Web. Isaacson considered all of this and decided that it made sense "to put all of these separate initiatives under one umbrella." Soon enough, the Pathfinder initiative was underway.

Nobody at *Wired* knew much about Pathfinder as their own online production went into overdrive. This was probably just as well, as they had little time to worry about rival projects during the giddy and grinding blur that followed. A number of new people soon turned up to help shoulder the burden. In June, Chip Bayers moved out to become HotWired's managing editor. A New York–based writer, Bayers had already coauthored a book called *Net Guide* for Random House. Not long afterward, Howard Rheingold came on as executive editor. Rheingold was the author of several books, including *The Virtual Community*, which discusses his experiences with online communities like the WELL (the Whole Earth 'Lectronic Link). A robust and deeply influential San Francisco–based online community, the WELL was a text-based world of "chat" areas, newsgroups, and other forums which arose years ahead of its time. *Wired* itself in fact existed as a restricted-access forum on the WELL before it took physical form. Rheingold's other writings include a number of novels, as well as a college thesis titled "On Mind Blowing and Its Methods." Decades after writing that one, Rheingold still had the countercultural edge that its title suggests.

Rheingold's right-hand intern during the summer of 1994 was one Justin Hall. Just 19 at the time, Hall was already becoming one of the Web's great guerrilla publishers. He taught himself HTML a few months after Mosaic was first released, and was soon plastering the Web with an outpouring that grew to thousands of pages. CNET CEO Halsey Minor hosted Hall's sprawling site for months, and estimates that his daily readers eventually numbered in the tens of thousands.

As HotWired was preparing to launch, experiences like Hall's were already demonstrating the Web's raw democratic power as a publishing medium. Traditional publishers had for centuries been obliged to overcome the costs of the physical channel and the constraints of the physical shelf. Dealing in a pushed medium, they also had to absorb the costs of many *misses* in order to get their content into the hands of those who really wanted it (see Chapter 1). All of these costs inevitably priced a great deal of content out of the channel. But now the frictionless, *practically free* ether and the Web's infinite shelf had dropped entry costs so low that almost any college freshman could tap into a distribution network that was already starting to rival any magazine's. Some had taken this to mean that since their economic and distributive muscles were no longer important, publishers themselves might not be needed in the new medium.

But publishers play many roles that go beyond simple distribution, and early online publishers imagined that these roles would secure them positions in the new medium, thereby opening its native power to them. One of these was that of *talent scout*. Publishers have always acted as talent scouts in that they place hurdles between writers and their audiences that hopefully screen the garbage *out* and the good stuff *in*. It seemed likely that this role would become important on the Web, because a great deal of low-rent garbage would inevitably enter the wide-open new channel along with all the worthy *new voices*. Respected publishers therefore stood to save the Web's users a lot of frustrating sifting by building shelves of high-quality content stamped with their branded seals of approval.

Publishers had also long played the related role of *aggregator*, in that they assembled both coherent sets of content for readers to access, and coherent audiences for advertisers to reach. This role is similar to that of talent scout in that it involves filtering content for readers, making it easier for them to find the things that interest them. But whereas talent scouting weeds out the garbage, aggregating involves placing like content next to like content. If the aggregator does a good job, the result is a blend of content that appeals to readers *as a whole*, as well as in its constituent parts. If the whole is coherent, readers don't have to work as hard to gather the content that interests them, because the publisher has done it for them. When the publisher of a local newspaper, for instance, aggregates coherent sets of articles, listings, and ads, they become valuable to readers as much because they are all in one place as for their contents. *Wired* itself was also an exemplary aggregator, in that it assembled a unique blend of content that as a whole was just as much of a *creation* as any of the articles it contained. It seemed to some that the Web's dizzying diversity of content would demand good aggregators, as it would become hard enough for most people to find one interesting drop of content out in the Web's vast ocean, let alone several. If they could find an aggregator that appealed to them, it seemed, their search could perhaps be largely over.

Even as the Web seemed to offer publishers many ways to continue differentiating themselves and justify their role in areas other than distribution, it also offered many new native capabilities that print lacked. Andrew lists the immediacy, ubiquity, and interactivity of content that the Web affords as being particularly exciting and promising to the *Wired* staff. Just as exciting, there was no rule book for a publisher tapping into all of this to follow. There were also very few tools to use, which meant that "this wasn't like a magazine where you go and get your printer to do something," Andrew remembers. "We wrote our own database software, our own threaded discussion [software]. We wrote a subscription system. We hacked the servers. We had to build it all."

Everyone involved in the venture was "excited about the fact that we didn't know what was going to happen, that we didn't know what our limitations were," Brian Behlendorf recalls. Not all people were excited about precisely the same things, however. "The biggest draw for me," Behlendorf recalls, "was the idea of community, the idea of being able to pull people together to the content, and provide *context* through their contributions. And to make people feel like they were empowered to actually be in control." Other people who were no less excited about building a community at the site included Howard Rheingold, who had of course *written the book* on online communities, and Jonathan Steuer, who was still dreaming of building Cyborganic's online/off-line communitarian café. Louis was interested in building an online community as well. But after almost two decades in publishing, he was also very, very focused, certainly more focused than many of the others, on the *content*, on the professionally talent-scouted and coherently aggregated words, images, and *whatever else*'s that would draw the community to the site. Everyone else, like Louis, believed that professional editorial content would have to be central to the site. But there was a great deal of disagreement, and ultimately division, on the question of how content and community elements should be balanced.

HotWired's first home a was an over-crowded little cubby hole called the Grotto. This was "a digital sweatshop," Andrew remembers, tucked into the most cramped and stuffy corner of *Wired*'s cramped and stuffy offices. "We didn't have a lot of money, didn't have a lot of space," Andrew remembers, and "people were working their asses off all night." But flat out as the pace was, the ambiance was wholly bohemian, because "If *Wired* was funky and grungy [and it was], *Wired* Online was the funk-grungiest," Hall writes. "Here, being next to the accounting department meant the never ending dub and hubdub of house music and club tunes—*Wired* rave headquarters." Spirits remained high, even when tension started to surface on the *content versus community* question. There was always somebody around, always some exciting work to do, and during the rare off hours, all of that *dub and hubdubbing* to keep a body distracted. Somewhere in there the group even acquired a name that almost everybody liked. @*Wired* was a contender for a while, but "we could see that @something-or-other was going to be so generic that we thought of something else," Steuer remembers (@Wired's death knell came when *The New York Times* started using "@times"). It was Louis who came up with *HotWired*.

Plenty of other things still needed making up after the site was christened. High on the list were the details of its revenue model. The site's earliest revenues were going to come from advertising—that much had been settled in the business plan. But nobody had much more than the faintest notion of what a Web advertisement looked like—let alone what it cost. Andrew recalls that Internet service provider GNN (Global Network Navigator) once had a hand in underwriting NCSA's "What's New" page—but that was as much as he and the rest of the HotWired staff had to go on. This made for a fairly free-form business planning process. "Literally," Steuer recalls, "Andrew, Louis, and I just *made up* pricing structure for banner ads. I vividly remember the conversation. How much should it cost? Well, what do we charge for the most expensive page in the magazine? Oh, about nine thousand and something. Ten thousand's a round number. Ten thousand? Okay. For a month? Okay. Like that. How did you pick the number? Well, I actually pulled it out of [let's call it thin air]."

The results of HotWired's early decisions, some merrily ad hoc, many long considered and agonized over, are all over the Web, and probably will be for years. This is not because Jonathan Steuer, Andrew, and Louis necessarily came up with the *right answers*. It is rather because they came up with the *first* ones. And in coming up with the answers that they arrived at, and in implementing them first (and in what turned out to be a closely-watched forum), they created precedents that quickly became industry practice. HotWired's first banners were long horizontal rectangles. They hovered at the top of pages. They linked directly to pages and sites dedicated to their sponsors. They were called, well, *banners*. There is no burning reason why they had to turn out precisely like this. Square banners might have worked. Bottom-of-the-page banners might have too. They could have been called "pennants," or maybe "billboards." The standard Web advertisement might also have become a banner or button floating permanently at the bottom of a user's screen, had de facto HTML supported such a trick at the time (ads on the commercial online service Prodigy were like this). And this could have been called a *button*. Or it could have been called a *floater*. Not all of the advertisements on today's Web are identical to their forerunners on 1994's HotWired (and HotWired did not pioneer impression-based pricing, which later became standard for banner advertisements). But not much has changed. Banners are still called *banners*. And most (though not all) are still horizontal strips that perch at the top of Web pages.

Details like these may seem trivial. But they matter. Any form that touches millions of people, countless times, day after day, becomes part of the infrastructure, part of a society's shared experience and vocabulary. And its merits and demerits aside, it can acquire astonishing staying power. Decades ago, somebody made the semicolon one of the eight most easily-reached characters on a typewriter keyboard. Keyboard standards then battled, and the semicolon won. However good the reasons were for giving the ; its little place of honor, it sure seems like a bad idea today. The spacebar, meanwhile, feels like a big win. Whether the banner is itself a semicolon or a spacebar is debatable. But we'll be stuck with it for a while.

The HotWired staff didn't have much time to ponder spacebars and ;'s when they developed their first banners. They had their hands were plenty full with *selling* the blasted things, as selling the Web to advertisers turned out to be a serious uphill battle. Netscape's validating IPO was still almost a year off. And today's umpteen million Web users were still just a blissed-out *yeah, right* theory. HotWired initially turned to *Wired*'s sales force for introductions and feet on streets. But then in September a well-regarded media buyer named Rick Boyce was recruited from ad agency Hal Riney & Partners to head up HotWired's sales efforts. Only 5 of the site's 14 charter sponsorships had been sold by the time Boyce came aboard. This gave him a big docket to fill in very little time, as HotWired's launch was slated for October. He also couldn't fill it with just *anybody*, as Andrew, for one, was anxious for HotWired to live up to *Wired*'s legacy of bringing both consumer and technology advertisers together.

Among Boyce's biggest selling points were the magic of the moment, and HotWired's own considerable sizzle. Syd Jones, one of the IBM marketers who spearheaded his company's involvement with HotWired, recalls that along with the allure of the *Wired* image and HotWired's expected target markets, the office's rough-edged digital glamour and energy made the decision to buy into HotWired an easy one. "Boyce met us at the *Wired* office," he recalls, "and took us a couple of blocks to the HotWired office. It was this old warehouse with lots of workstations, and it had such an exciting and energized environment. It was so new. There was lots of unfinished space, and CD players all over." Jones and his partner "looked at each other once we were inside, and it was just so clear. Yes, we were absolutely doing this. The people were so fantastic."

One issue that Boyce faced frequently was the near-total lack of Web sites among the advertisers that he was targeting (particularly the consumer product companies). This was something of a stumbling block, as HotWired's conception of an *advertisement* was a banner linked to a Web site. The proposed solution to this was that HotWired would host *mini-sites* on its own servers for sponsors that didn't have sites of their own. This was a fine and logical solution, but it came with its own little stumbling block in that HotWired had absolutely no Web development resources that it could lend its sponsors to develop those sites. The obvious solution to this was for HotWired to turn to the Web development community to build its *mini-sites*.

But this community barely existed in the fall of 1994—although fortunately for all parties it did have one early, innovative, and very local member in Organic Online. This was a tiny company that Jonathan Steuer's former Cyborganic partner Jonathan Nelson had founded just a few months before. Nelson's partners in the enterprise included Brian Behlendorf, who was still working for Steuer as HotWired's chief engineer. Organic's original plan was to sell its services to record companies and book publishers. But "it turned out that those were not the companies that had five-digit budgets to spend on exploratory media," Behlendorf remembers. For a while there it didn't look like *any* companies fell into that category. But Organic doggedly stuck to its guns, which turned Nelson into one of the Web's first practically-full-time salespeople—a distinction that "just sucked" at the time, he recalls. Nelson spent much 1994 haplessly pitching the Web to anybody who would listen. He found that "the typical response was that either their minds were blown by the capabilities of this, or it was, 'hey Marv! this guy's trying to sell me the *Internet*!' " Nelson remembers. The *hey Marv!*'s were dismayingly common, and even the few blown minds generally had trouble finding their checkbooks.

But then Nelson learned about HotWired's *mini-site* problem. And soon he wasn't just pitching Organic and the Web to his would-be clientele, he was pitching HotWired—and by association *Wired*, publishing world's the cool, new, digitaller-than-thou rising star. Within weeks, both HotWired and Organic had signed up Club Med and Volvo as customers, among others. In the end, Boyce estimates that Organic had a hand in roughly three quarters of his charter sponsors' sites. This helped spur Organic to tremendous growth. Less than two years after HotWired's launch, the company had over 50 employees and dozens of clients, including Saturn, Levi's and Colgate-Palmolive.

With Organic's symbiotic help, Boyce was able to sell out the site in time for its launch on October 27, 1994. Its 14 sponsorships sold for $30,000 each, Boyce recalls. Pricing covered placement over a fiscal quarter, and included no notion of impressions or click-throughs (those models evolved later). Boyce and his team also succeeded in their mission to bring mainstream advertisers to the Web. This meant that "on the same day, the first magazine, the first automobile site, the first travel site, the first commercial consumer telephone company sites all went up online, as well as the first advertising model," Jonathan Nelson points out, making for a truly "revolutionary" moment in the Internet's history.

The launch itself was a vivid event for everyone involved. Most of HotWired's now 20-strong staff pulled all- or most-nighters the evening before it. One of Steuer's engineers downed "like thirteen espressos in seven hours" to get through the last big push ("he's virtually immune," Steuer explains). When the big moment came, everyone gathered around Brian Behlendorf's Silicon Graphics system to watch him throw the virtual switch and bring HotWired online. At least a few video cameras were pointed at Behlendorf and his computer to record the event. And at least one of them, the biggie (HotWired's own for-posterity camera) was also plugged into the wall. Behlendorf's computer, coincidentally, was plugged into the wall. Around 10:00, Behlendorf threw the switch. HotWired went live to the world. The cameras gazed, the lights dimmed. Maybe 15 seconds passed, then the office went dark and HotWired crashed. After some fuse fixing and camera shuttering, HotWired came up again, more or less for good.

HotWired debuted with several content areas, most of them opaquely named. "World Beat" was dedicated not to reggaelike music, but to first- and third-person accounts of events and travelings throughout the world. "Renaissance" was HotCode for arts and entertainment. "Kino" meant (loosely) digital art and moving images, while "Piazza" meant discussion spaces and other interactive forums. "Signal," meanwhile, took "the Pulse of the Digital Revolution." Its offerings included "Flux," an influential column featuring the weekly rants and *pssssst*s of one Ned Brainard, an imaginary net.specter who was widely rumored to be a mouthpiece for HotWired's upperlings. Piazza's interactive forums included bulletin board–style discussion groups (called "threads"), chat spaces, and live events (i.e., the auditorium-style discussions described above). Louis characterized HotWired to the reporters covering the launch as *"live, twitching, the real-time nervous system of the planet;"* and as dedicated to producing "new thinking for a new medium—context about the Digital Revolution and new art forms from the Second Renaissance."

October of 1994 was a big month on the Web, as it also saw the debut of the Netscape Navigator (né Mosaic Netscape) and of Time Warner's Pathfinder service. Pathfinder managed to beat HotWired out the door by three days. In this it did not truly steal HotWired's thunder, however, as HotWired was unique at its launch (and indeed for months afterward) in its use of the Web as a *sponsored* publishing medium (Pathfinder did not start featuring advertisements until the spring of 1995). HotWired's commitment to creating original content also set it apart. Pathfinder (like almost all of the other newspaper and magazine affiliates setting up shop on the Web at that time) was built almost entirely from repurposed editorial content from its undigital properties. But the fact that Pathfinder did not follow HotWired's *No Shovelware!* edict did not make it an uninteresting or unserious bet on the medium. While *Wired* (after all) had relatively few wares to shovel, Time Warner generated an enormous trove of assets every week. Walter Isaacson was now proposing to make that trove—the crown jewels in a very traditional company—*free to the world*. This was an aggressive and progressive step to take back in the days before Netscape and others showed that *no charge* on the Internet did not necessarily mean *no business model*. The fact that Time Warner, one of the oldest of the old-line pillars of traditional media, was taking that step was a development that no other major publisher could ignore. In this, Time Warner anointed the Web as a *serious* medium, even as *Wired* anointed it as a *cool* one. More authoritative arbiters of *serious*ness and *cool*ness could hardly be imagined. In this, Pathfinder's and HotWired's nearly simultaneous launches served to validate and aggrandize rather than eclipse one another.

HotWired's launch brought on a lot of excitement and *we did it!*

euphoria down on South Park. But the blissed-out moment did not last long, as the fault lines between the *content* and *community* camps had by then grown deep. Both sides felt that elements of both content and community were essential to a successful HotWired. But there was a fundamental rift between them in that the community camp viewed "media as a jam session," Andrew explains, meaning that "if you build this online community space, you'll get all these wonderful contributions coming in from all these different people. You'll have great art, great music, great writing; so it's a big jam. It's like thinking that if you just build a studio and put the instruments out, you'll get the Beatles. But our standpoint was that more often than not, you'll get an awful garage band. We also believe that fundamentally, media is not a jam session—media is about having and articulating a strong point of view."

Steuer paints a fairly similar picture. "My agenda the whole way, and what you should be using the Net for," he says, is "not just [as] another way to broadcast content out, but to find a way to take a community of people . . . and give them a place to connect with each other in addition to providing them with a place to consume your content." He cites a dispute over a section called "Planet Wired" as characteristic of the differences between him and Andrew and Louis. "Howard," he recalls, "had a bunch of friends in different cities all over the world who were avid *Wired* readers and were doing cool shit on the Web. So the idea was that rather than do HotWired Germany, we would have a section of Planet *Wired* where the German sites [i.e., those of Howard's contacts and others] got put."

This didn't happen, Steuer says, as "the idea of [contributors] who were not under tight editorial control really didn't fly for Louis, I think. I mean, Howard's editorial style was very loose. And I personally think that's a good thing on the Net, which uniquely can allow people to combine a strong sense of their individual context and perspective to a reporting medium. And I think that Louis's vision was much more magazine-like than that. And so the idea that there were all these people who he didn't know, and he hadn't met, and whose copy he wasn't getting to read and chew up and spit out in advance, was . . . wrong [to him]." For Steuer, "the bottom line," he says, "is I want to do bottom-up media, and Louis wants to do top-down media, and that's fine. They're both legitimate models, and they work [in] different ways and they involve different people."

For his part, Louis says that he "would disagree that they're [both] legitimate views," because "the thing that is special about media, is that it's *not* your point of view. It's someone else's point of view. That it's not the experience that you create. It's experiences created for you. . . . It's an abdication of responsibility to think that your community is going to make your media. You make the media. That attracts the community. The community discusses it, then you make more media. It's the experience you can't create yourself. It's a complete fiction out there that the Web is making everybody a publisher. Jonathan believes it. Howard believes it. Justin believes it. Dave Winer [an industry pundit and former HotWired columnist] believes it. He said, 'a billion publishers,' and I think that's ahistorical bullshit. It's just not real. Typewriters have made everybody a publisher, or desktop publishing made everybody a publisher, or whatever. It's not true. People don't want to sit down and create their own entertainment. They can. Anyone in America, in the world, can come home from work at the end of the day and sit down and write a novel. They don't. They don't for good reason. They don't because . . . they don't have the smarts to do it, or the inclination, or they prefer instead to let somebody else carry them out of their normal day-to-day life and give them what they can't provide for themselves. That's the function of media. That's a very philosophical, fundamental difference that we have. And no one has persuaded me that there is any other way of looking at media than that. If it's not that, it's not media" (Louis also adds that "it was the reality of getting shit from Howard's contributors—unbelievable rubbish—which convinced us" that Rheingold's Planet Wired idea "was not only apriori dumb, but actually unworkable.").

Sometime in the fall, there was what Louis characterizes as "a fairly unsubtle intervention" to realign the site with his and *Wired*'s perspective ("certainly we ruffled their feathers," he acknowledges). Nobody was fired. But the ruffling of the feathers had its intended effect. Rheingold was the first to leave. Out of town for some time on a book tour, he resigned by E-mail. Steuer left shortly thereafter. By April, 11 more had followed, according to (and including) Justin Hall. Some departures were wholly amiable. Brian Behlendorf, for instance, left for the happy purpose of helping Organic Online's other cofounders keep up with the surging demand for its services. Others left on less cheery terms.

Steuer went on to play an instrumental role in launching CNET's Web site (see Chapter 8). He also continued developing his on- and off-line community notions with Cyborganic, which he had always maintained as an informal organization and Web presence in his off-hours. Cyborganic gradually developed a robust online space with a chat room, member Web pages, and much more. Its weekly Thursday-night dinners ("TND" to regulars) meanwhile became a fixture in the San Francisco Web community's social calendar. Drawing anywhere from dozens to hundreds per week, these came to attract a good deal of media attention. *Rolling Stone* even ran a seven (*seven!*) page article on Cyborganic and TND about ten months after Steuer's departure from HotWired. By the summer of 1996, Cyborganic had grown to employ six full-timers. A few months later it opened its first physical space in San Francisco's SoMa district.

As Steuer chased his online and off-line community dreams, Rheingold started building out an organization modeled on the philosophy he had articulated in *The Virtual Community* and elsewhere. Called "Electric Minds," his company was financed by Softbank, among others (see Chapter 6), and debuted on the Web in November of 1996. Like HotWired, it uses articles from well-regarded writers, as well as other content (including Mark Pesce's "VRML University"; see Chapter 4) as catalysts to discussions. But unlike HotWired, Electric Minds puts the greater emphasis on the *jam session* aspect of its media ("Welcome! Feed your mind and change the world: Join our Conversations" was its front page's opening greeting).

As Steuer and Rheingold pursued their own visions of content/community balance, HotWired did the same. And as 1995 progressed, its staff put the turbulence of its first months behind it and focused on building the site and its business. The Web's first true commercial publisher learned a number of important lessons early on. One related to its innovative membership system, which has since been widely (although in many cases partially) emulated. In its earlymost history, HotWired required all of its visitors to fill out a questionnaire about themselves. Steering clear of the deeply personal stuff, this asked mainly about backgrounds and interests. Responses were fed into a member database. Like I/PRO's I/Code product (see Chapter 5), the membership system was meant to customize the content and (eventually) the advertising that visitors saw based upon their backgrounds. It was also meant to heighten its members' sense of affiliation with HotWired, in that it allowed them to choose user names that they could build into unique identities throughout the site's many forums, giving them "pseudonymity, not anonymity" in their dealings with one another, as Brian Behlendorf puts it.

But member registration went over poorly. Behlendorf estimates that up to 80 percent of HotWired's would-be visitors turned away upon encountering the questionnaire, so the registration requirement was soon dropped. HotWired memberships were thereafter offered as value-added options for site visitors. Membership's privileges included preferred access to certain interactive forums, as well as a free subscription to *HotFlash*, HotWired's weekly E-mailed newsletter. *HotFlash* served to remind members that the site was still there, and to drive traffic to particular pages. Newsletters like it soon became commonplace on the Web.

HotWired's content evolved under the banner of "way new journalism," a term that *Newsday* (later *Time* magazine) journalist Joshua Quittner coined in the debut editorial that he guest-wrote for HotWired. Self-consciously invoking Tom Wolfe's seminal essay "The Birth of New Journalism," Quitter proclaimed that a *way new* era had come to reporting. The *way new* school would be defined by its incorporation of new devices like interactivity, hypertext, instantaneous publishing, media elements like audio and video, and more. HotWired's own definition of way new journalism became one of content tied to context. "Media is about point of view," Andrew explains. "Every piece of media you read has an opinion, and to say that it doesn't is just kidding yourself." Way new journalism embraces this fact, "but also embraces the context within which that point of view lies."

Andrew cites HotWired's response to an alarmist *Time* magazine cover story on *CyberPorn* as an example. Titled "JournoPorn," this response "involved a number of things that would give you, the reader, our perspective, i.e., this is a bogus story, [it is] riddled with errors, and on and on and on. But it also gave you the context within which we made those decisions." For instance, the JournoPorn piece included a hyper-link to the *Time* story, so that readers could see firsthand what HotWired's writer was attacking. It also had a link to a discussion space on the WELL in which the *Time* article's writer defended his work. In this it let readers examine the evidence behind HotWired's opinion and draw their own conclusions, which "*is* way new journalism," Andrew explains. "You can read it on many different levels. You can read it just as an opinion piece from us. You can go deeper into many of the different threads we talked about. You can go read the contrary view and decide to disagree with us. That's what it's about."

It is also about *conciseness*, something which the HotWired staff had not realized at first, as "we started out thinking that this medium was a magazine," Louis recalls, "and that it has a table of contents, and it has features, et cetera, so it has some mass going out of the box." Consistent with this view, the early HotWired commonly posted 3000–5000-word articles. But it soon became clear that the Web is in fact "a bad place to read," Louis says. Cathode ray tubes lack the resolution and portability of printed media, making most people unwilling to use them to read magazine-length articles. In response to this, HotWired's content evolved into concise pieces with quick payoffs, which rarely ran more than a thousand words. The site meanwhile shifted further away from analytic *journalism* to focus on "delivering the granule of experience," Louis explains, a granule that "can be as small as a single page."

Louis's (and many others') thinking on this subject was heavily influenced by the rise of Suck. Now a HotWired property, Suck was the creation of Carl Steadman and Joey Anuff, who first turned up in HotWired's production department in the spring of 1995. Steadman came to HotWired from a job at *The Minneapolis Star-Tribune*, Anuff from work in multimedia (his specialty had been hand-drawn animations). The two did a good deal of talking and thinking about the Web over the summer, and agreed that the medium was becoming plagued with smug "navel-gazing"; that it was "self-serious and self-referential in really the worst sense of the term," Steadman recalls. Even *way new* HotWired had "a very corporate feel" in their view. "It felt like a lot of people working on this product which was crafted to meet a demographic," Anuff says. On top of this, "voices on the Web weren't really there. Which was shocking, because everyone talked about how the Web was this medium in which anyone could participate, and a whole variety of voices would suddenly be there."

"And it's crucial to appreciate the magnitude of the egos involved," Steadman adds. "I mean, even though people had no clue as to what they were doing then, and they still don't now, that wasn't the personality people were projecting back then." Steadman and Anuff prepared to retaliate, and in late August, Suck's first page appeared at the can't-forget-it address *www.suck.com*. In contrast to its lurid putative parent, Suck adopted a spare and spartan form. A single, narrow column of words tumbled down the left side of its daily pages. This was broken only by simple Pepperidge Farm packaging-like illustrations. At a time when many Web sites were starting to choke on mazes of hyper-links and gratuitous graphics, Suck was a relief to the eyes.

But pure as it was, few came to Suck to oggle its layout. Instead they come for its *voice*. Cynical, deeply informed, and for months dramatically anonymous (is it really Marc Andreessen? Stewart Alsop? Sonny Bono?), Suck became the Web's goad and conscience. Each day, prima donnas were taken to task. Stupid Web sites were scorned. Suck's unknown masters quickly became famous for pulling no punches. But the site was funny as well was cynical. And it was never (quite) so bitter as to make readers worry that the guys behind it were heading for a clock tower with an M-16. Suck got all of a hundred hits on its first day on the Web. But within a week it was receiving a thousand hits a day, and within a few months, over a quarter of a million. By the spring of 1996, Suck was drawing over 10 thousand daily visitors, and even *USA Today* was keeping up with it in its own hapless way (see Chapter 3).

Suck's widely imitated example taught the industry a number of lessons. Web users, it turns out, like content with *closure*. They also like *daily* content, content germane to habitual use. Suck was precisely this, in that it was that "just one thing," Louis says, "that you could reliably connect to every day, and you know you got your hit of Suck. The next time you went, you could get another hit of Suck, and it would be as good as the last one you got." In short, it was *that granule of experience*; and it was one whose editorial solitude was integral to it, and could be sustained only on the Web. Suck as a printed broadsheet could never survive economically. Suck as a syndicated newspaper column would be surrounded by comic strips and Art Buchwald, and would just not be the same.

Andrew cites Suck as one of HotWired's own major influences toward the end of 1995, because in its earliest days, HotWired tended to view itself as "this small, little outpost," he recalls, "and the enemy was the Time Warners, the Viacoms, the News Corps; these big, monolithic companies." But in the still-little world of the Web, HotWired was a giant as well. And so, "when people talked about the big Web sites with their thousands of pages, it was Pathfinder, it was us. We were sort of on that list. And Suck came along, and was very effective. It really proved that you don't have to be this big thing, and it really gave us a quick sense of, 'Oh shit! We're one of them big things too! Let's rethink this.' "

HotWired was indeed *one of them big things* when Suck launched, and in more than just the scope of its content. By the late summer of 1995, its head count had almost tripled to 70 people. This growth had been fueled in part by Boyce's team, which was regularly selling out HotWired's capacity. It had also been paid for by Louis's willingness to continue betting the company (or at least a good deal of its capital) on the Web. HotWired's operations lost more than $2 million in 1995. By at least one reckoning, they seemed to be on their way to sextupling that in 1996. But this didn't concern Louis, who says frankly that "we don't plan to make any money today. It would be illogical for us to make any money today. We plan to make money when this becomes the dominant medium," and when that day comes, "We will be at the table." Getting to that table is not a cheap proposition. It involves anteing up, quarter after quarter, while the medium's secrets are gradually revealed by experiments like Suck. And so Louis anted furiously to hang onto HotWired's seat, turning occasionally to a Web-smitten investor community for more chips.

During that time, HotWired—*No Shovelware!*—continued listening to its traffic patterns, to its audience feedback, to find the medium's yet unwritten rules. Writings got shorter. Pages started dancing with Java code. New channels switched on, others switched off. Adrenaline, a sort of HotWired sports page dedicated to pursuits like off-road biking and Ultimate Frisbee, glowed briefly until early 1996. Cocktail, a *granule* on the order of Suck, rose up almost spontaneously to become one of HotWired's most popular features. Described as "an uninhibited celebration of cocktail culture," it now publishes the recipe of a featured drink every week. Another feature, Dream Jobs, became a sort of *granule* help-wanted page that listed only one lone job every day. This would of course be a *Dream Job!* somewhere in the trenches of the Digital Revolution™—and probably out of reach to most of the thousands who glimpsed the page. Still, supplicants were encouraged to E-mail their credentials to the employer du jour—or to simply click through to the Levi's Dockers site, Dream Jobs' perennial sponsor.

An especially promising feature switched on in October of 1995. This was *Rough Guide*, a Web version of the popular, street-savvy travel guide. The series' U.S. edition was posted first, and filled up over 1200 Web pages. It was followed by Canadian and Mexican guides in the summer of 1996, then by European and Australian guides in the fall. The *Rough Guide* site is an experiment with a publishing form that could benefit significantly from the Web's native features, as, more than most published documents, travel guides are meant to reflect an external world. In printed form, they are rather like snapshots in that they reflect point-in-time realities, even as the places, prices, and schedules they report on evolve constantly. But a travel guide on the Web can be more like a live video feed, one that changes continually with the reality it reflects. Still images are of course more portable than *live video feeds*, and it's hard to shove a Web site into a backpack. But it's also easy to print up a few relevant pages from a computer before charging off to the airport. A Web-based guide can also benefit tremendously from the Web's participative nature, as a guide's readers inevitably have more feet on the street, ears to the ground, and mouths at the plate than its writers. The Web can allow publishers to enlist those feet, ears, and mouths in a very dynamic way by inviting reader commentary and integrating it with their editorial content.

HotWired's *Rough Guide* seeks to do all of these things. Its producer, Marci Nelligan, estimates that 50 to 60 editorial changes and updates are made to the U.S. guide's contents alone every week. Reader views are also invited and integrated. But as of this writing, HotWired's *Rough Guide* is still a very rough draft. It lacks media-rich content, interactive maps, regularly updated events listings, and a reservations facility. And unfortunately, its *content* has drawn very little *community* in that reader participation is still minimal. This doesn't mean that the guides are shovelware, but rather than that they have plenty of growing room, and are more than ready to do some growing.

As experiments like Suck and *Rough Guide* unfolded in 1996, HotWired's editors and management worked to integrate their lessons into the site's content model. In January of that year, they decided to move all of HotWired's channels to a "daily format," meaning that at least a feature or two in each would change every day. This was in part a response to the Suck lesson. It was also a reaction to patterns in HotWired's traffic, which indicated that more and more *regulars* were coming into the site daily, particularly from work. This indicated that for at least some people, the Web was becoming a daily habit, much like a newspaper. This was a pattern that HotWired wanted to both encourage and benefit from.

Some time after the move to daily content, management decided to decentralize HotWired. The plan was to make it less of a Web site, and more of a "network or studio . . . producing a series of media products," explains executive producer Chip Bayers. Consistent with the *network* theme, *channels* like Netizen and Signal would now be called *programs.* Each program was meant to grow into a distinct and highly focused entity capable of building brand equity of its own, independent of HotWired. Some of the programs were appropriately reflagged with more accessible names. Piazza, home to interactive forums like chat rooms, became "talk.com." Renaissance, the chronicler of pop culture, was rechristened "Pop." This move was partly a reaction to the rise of a number of successful sites on the Web that were built around highly focused themes. It seemed that people were happy going to Movielink for movie listings, ESPNET SportsZone for sports scores, and CNN for general news, instead of a single source (e.g., a local paper) for everything, as they would off-line. It seemed that HotWired could best capitalize on this trend by having its programs represent their content and themes more boldly than they could as toned-down subsidiaries lurking a level below HotWired's front door.

Creating stand-alone brands would also make it easier to leverage names and content in other media in addition to the Web, which became a priority for the company. Netizen, for instance, soon became a department in *Wired* magazine, and it was announced in the spring of 1996 that it would become a television program on the new MSNBC network. It seemed that if the other programs became unique brands with truly independent identities they would be more compelling products to pitch and promote in other media.

As HotWired continued exploring its medium and its rules, literally thousands of other publications were starting to do the same. Some, like HotWired, were native inhabitants of the Web. These included sites with literary orientations, like Word, Feed, and Salon 1999; professionally-oriented sites like CNET (see Chapter 8); and guerrilla efforts like Suck and Justin Hall's pages. Printed periodicals also came onto the Web by the thousands. Many of these simply sprayed all or parts of their printed editions onto the Web with few Net-native distractions to liven them up.

Newspapers seemed to be particularly averse to the old *Wired—No Shovelware!—*edict. This leads Andrew to view most newspaper sites as "wonderful archives; there's nothing more than that to it." And he is right, in that they *are* wonderful archives. They are accessible, globally available, and in most cases, free. Shovelsome as their wares may be, the Web brings publishers enough native power that even the least imaginative harnessing of it provides real end-user value. Aware of this, and in some cases keen to shore up their classified businesses in the face of inevitable competition from online publishers (e.g., Yahoo!; see Chapter 6) newspaper publishers embraced the Web more than perhaps any other group. By the spring of 1996 there were well over a thousand newspapers publishing on the Web, up from a handful at the time of HotWired's launch.

And by that time, HotWired had itself matured tremendously—or had at least grown a lot. By early summer of 1996, the *live, twitching, real-time nervous system of the planet* had close to 150 full-time employees—roughly double its head count from the previous summer (and more than the head count next door at *Wired*). This staff was still housed in HotWired's first post-Grotto home, a vast and barely subdivided room in which neither cubicles nor Chinese walls rose to muffle the staff's banter or the frequent thrummings of the company stereo. Lighting came from uniform rows of stalky black Halogen mushrooms that glowed beneath the ceiling fans which lazily controlled the climate. Snaking amongst the halogen stalks and the tapping toes of the HotWired proletariat were the hot-pink streaks of the offices Ethernet cabling—a nowhere-but-SoMa touch. Also setting the office apart from those of the sober financial district just a few blocks away was the absence of *company pens*. Pre-digital implements, these were said to be left out of the budget for ideological reasons (rebelling against this dogmatic excess, the Suck staff stocked ample supplies of Suck pens, as well as eponymous lollipops and condoms). The company stereo was also inimitably HotWired. Usually on and often loud, its use was governed by strict house rules. "You can turn it down, but only temporarily," an employee explained. "Even then, it's very much frowned on," because "when you turn it down, you change *everybody's* environment, not just your own."

Three hot meals were served daily in the adjoining *Wired* offices. These weren't free, but they weren't expensive, ranging in price from two dollars for breakfast to three dollars for dinner. Employee meal cards were adorned with slogans that rotated periodically. *I do not actively pursue meat*, declared one. And they didn't, as *Wired* meals were almost invariably vegetarian ("a real beef of mine," complained one carnivore, hopefully intending no pun). Everybody got KP duty about once every three months. Nobody seemed to remember seeing Louis or Andrew scrubbing up, but most of the other senior managers seemed to do regular time. The office's other homelike touches included its dogs (Maria and Mrs. Peel) and the snoring bodies occasionally spied in its bead-curtained *Chill Room*.

In the late spring of 1996, HotWired began gearing up for bigger and better things. Work began on far posher office space just a few blocks away. Spacious, multileveled, and skylit, the new home would include room for production studios, sleeping areas, a big spread of video games, and other distractions. Even more exciting, HotWired and *Wired* magazine announced that they would soon go public under a new umbrella organization called "Wired" Ventures. Things went great with the office, at least.

The rumblings began on the IPO front as soon as the business press ran the numbers on Wired Ventures' proposed valuation. This was $450 million—a lofty 18 times the previous year's revenues in a market that valued most magazine publishers at 1 to 2 times revenues. The hoped-for premium was partly attributable to the fact that Wired Ventures had been growing its revenues at some 300 percent per year—a headier clip than, say, Time Warner. Much of Wired Ventures' gloss came from HotWired, however, and HotWired's value was extraordinary—well over $250 million if *Wired* was imagined to be worth an extravagant 8 times revenues. This was at a time when HotWired's prior 12 months' revenues were around $2 million.

This led to some well-founded skepticism about whether the market would grant Wired Ventures the price it was seeking. All speculation became moot by the middle of the summer, however, when a dismal market for technology stocks helped force the Nasdaq composite down almost 15 percent in a single month. Citing these market conditions, Wired Ventures announced in the middle of July that the deal was off. In October it was ready to try again, although for a humbler $272-million valuation.

A couple of things went wrong this time. The first, Louis says, was the market again. It didn't go into free-fall, as it had over the summer. But it seemed to be looking for a different kind of investment story than it had been earlier in the year. Louis recalls that when Wired Ventures wrote its first business plan geared toward an IPO in early 1996, the recent success of IPOs like Pixar's, and (later) Yahoo!'s seemed to indicate that the market was open to digital media-related companies whose profitability prospects lay in the intermediate future (Wired Ventures was then unlikely to turn profitable for at least two years, perhaps more). But by the fall, "the end-of-summer market meltdown had brought investors to look for a mid-97 profitability story," Louis explains.

Wired Ventures' impending IPO had meanwhile started to attract negative publicity (as had the first). While on the road discussing the IPO with investors, Louis learned that people back at *Wired* were getting gloomy about this. So he wrote up an E-mail for internal distribution that was meant to raise sagging spirits—and to *stay internal*. Unfortunately, somebody took it upon himself to post Louis's E-mail to the WELL—i.e., to the world. The IPO was soon called off. Meanwhile, Louis recalls, *The Wall Street Journal* asked the Securities and Exchange Commission (SEC) what the E-mail meant with respect to its regulations governing IPOs, which brought the SEC to begin an investigation of Louis's "supposed attempt to subvert *Wired*'s 'quiet period' " (in other words, a concern was raised that Louis had orchestrated the leakage in hopes that his optimistic E-mail would heighten investor demand for the IPO, which would have violated SEC regulations). The SEC soon "concluded that no breach had been attempted or occurred," but the whole episode with the *Journal* "add[ed] insult to injury," Louis says.

As this unhappy drama unfolded, the decentralized HotWired *network* continued to churn out new programs. It entered the crowded search engine market with an offering called HotBot in May of 1996. A joint venture with a local company called Inktomi, HotBot claimed to have indexed more of the Internet's content than any of its rivals. In the summer, two programs debuted (Packet and Webmonkey) that shared some of the tricks of HotWired's trade with Web developers. In November, a daily news service switched on. Marketed as Wired News, this was a very ambitious effort that employed dozens of writers and production people. Posting over a dozen articles a day in areas including business, culture, technology, and politics, it looked like a front page for the Internet community.

In this, many viewed it as a competitor to CNET and ZDnet (see Chapter 8). But Andrew points out that Wired News's mandate is broader than those other services', and its coverage of their main areas of focus (e.g., breaking technology news for industry professionals, product reviews for serious, up-to-the-minute users of technology) is corollarily less extensive. For this reason, "We don't consider ourselves to be a direct competitor to the technology trade sites, such as CNET and ZDnet," he says. "We actually think our service is very complementary to theirs. If anything, we think our competitors are general news providers—people like CNN and *The New York Times*." Wired News of course had a home on the Web. But it also brought the *Wired* brand into a number of new distribution channels, including the

Marimba system, PointCast (see Chapters 3 and 8), and even the Reuters wire service (through Reuters, Wired News content could reach hundreds of newspapers world wide).

In all of this—HotBot, Wired News, and other new channels—HotWired was becoming an increasingly diffuse entity in an increasingly competitive, crowded, and complex business environment. This made its mandate harder to discern from the outside, and likewise made it more difficult to determine if the company had remained, or was becoming, a *success*. For many Web content companies, the accepted metric for comparing success across sites had become traffic. This is at least a very quantifiable proxy for general popularity. Traffic also turns pages, turned pages deliver banners, and banners generate revenue, the lifeblood of any enterprise. In the first fiscal quarter of 1996, HotWired served over seven million pages to its visitors. This was a lot of pages, and represented an exponential increase in traffic since launch. But CNET, a relative upstart, was serving almost as many pages every week by then, and Yahoo! was serving almost as many every day. HotWired's traffic subsequently boomed, *septupling* over the next six months. By the end of 1996, the site's monthly page view traffic had seen an awesome twenty-fold jump since the start of the year. Although much of this growth was attributable to traffic at the HotBot search engine (search sites tend to turn a lot of pages, relative to content sites—and also tend to sustain lower advertising rates), traffic at HotWired's content pages had also surged. But traffic had meanwhile boomed at other leading sites, to a degree that made it clear that if HotWired was to be *number one* on the Web by some meaningful metric or quality, traffic was not going to be it—or at least not for the foreseeable future.

This in itself has not concerned Andrew, who says "the whole idea of market share is not one that we are personally subscribing to," because "the goal of this organization is to create brands," not to simply churn pages. Brands are entities, attitudes, and content spheres like Suck, Netizen, and Dream Jobs, and parent company Wired Ventures is developing multiple "avenues to shoot those brands out" to the public. These include the Web, television (e.g., MSNBC's *Netizen* program), periodicals (for now just *Wired*), and books (the HardWired division published its first six titles in the fall of 1996). In this multiple-avenues model, a brand like Netizen might draw relatively little Web traffic compared to, say, CNET, yet still be an enormously valuable property by becoming the basis of a successful TV program or perhaps a magazine. The brand's presence in any one medium could then feed and build its presence on other media. *Suck TV* for instance (you never know . . .), could inspire viewers to check out the Suck Web site, which could itself send its visitors back to the TV show or to the newsstand to pick up *Suck Monthly*.

Cross-media brand building is an intriguing strategy, and is certainly becoming common on the Web, in that players from all media have brought their brands to the Web and some have done quite well. Web-native brands are meanwhile beginning to make their first successful forays into other media. CNET, for instance, produces several successful television shows, and Yahoo! has already established modest beachheads in broadcast and print (see Chapter 6). But outside of the Web, cross-media brands are relatively rare. There certainly are plenty of gigantic cross-media *companies*, but their magazines tend to be just magazines, their cable channels just cable channels. Significantly, there are also almost no instances of magazine publishers becoming successful TV producers (*National Geographic* being one very rare exception to this).

In this, Wired Ventures' cross-media branding strategy is for now a relatively unproven one. The diffusion that it encourages in HotWired's content meanwhile has risks. HotWired itself is a large organization—one of the largest on the Web—with a lot of resources and some extraordinary talent. But its programs compete head-to-head with several organizations in several different markets. Some of these are just as big as HotWired, yet are far more focused. HotBot, for instance, plays in the same market as four publicly-traded companies, each with more cash in its till than all of Wired Ventures as of this writing. And as Andrew notes, Wired News hopes to take on old and very well-established media giants such as *The New York Times* and cable news powerhouse CNN.

HotWired's *brands* are meanwhile still young and relatively immature, which will not make it easy for them to leap into other media. Most are also still known more for their affiliation with HotWired than for their own stand-alone notoriety. The typical visitor to Netizen's Web site, for instance, would almost certainly think of it as a "section of HotWired" rather than a truly separate entity. This perception could change as the HotWired brand is de-emphasized and made into more and more of an umbrella "network" label, allowing the "true" brands beneath it to stand out. But this could easily serve to dilute the HotWired name. There is meanwhile a limit to the exposure brands like Netizen can get within *Wired* magazine without diluting the *Wired* brand. Netizen has long been a monthly *Wired* department. But readers don't read Netizen, they read *Wired*. Most may not even notice the Netizen logo on the front page of the occasional *Wired* article, and even those who do probably view an Alvin Toffler interview in *Wired* as *an Alvin Toffler interview*, not as *this month's Netizen*.

As a labeled focal point for a wide range content that seeks to build up one brand (the company's best), not several, Wired News could become a remedy for some of this diffusion. In November of 1996, HotWired took a step toward using the service for that purpose when it shut down Pop (formally "Renaissance"—a channel chronicling television, contemporary music, and other pop culture) and effectively folded it into the "culture desk" of Wired News (inevitably making Hot-Watchers wonder if Netizen might soon be consolidated with the politics desk).

Also, in presenting its diversity of brands, the HotWired network is putting forth a potentially complementary mix of content and services, in that each HotWired program "is meant to hit a certain niche, and there is a lot of overlapping within those niches," Andrew points out. Traffic at any one program therefore can (and certainly does) serve to build traffic at other programs. A Web developer who is a Webmonkey loyalist, for instance, might end up linking over to HotBot once inside the HotWired Network to do an Internet search, then on to Flux to check out "Ned Brainard's" latest industry gossip. HotWired invites this sort of interprogram meandering with a user interface that keeps links to all of its programs accessible at all times, with cross-promotional banners, and other encouragements. In this, HotWired can play the traditional editorial function of *aggregator* for its visitors, just as it plays the *talent scout* role by providing content that meets consistently high standards. Since the Web is growing more bewilderingly vast every day, filtering functions like these might be valued more and more.

But the relevance of at least one of them, that of aggregator (which HotWired arguably does more completely than any of the Web's other content providers) is for now unclear on the Web, as the Web lets consumers of content act as their own aggregators to an unprecedented degree. Off-line, most of us traditionally turn to a single source (usually a local newspaper) for all kinds of news, community information, listings, and advertisements. This habit could indicate that we value editorial aggregation—or it might just indicate that the physical channel makes it excessively costly or inconvenient for us to acquire our funny pages from one source, our local news from another, and our William Safire musings from a third.

But on the Web, it's easy to get national news from *The New York Times*, international news from CNN, sports scores from ESP-NET SportsZone, help-wanted listings from Career Mosaic, and cocktail recipes from the *live, twitching, real-time nervous system of the planet*. Since the everyone's-an-aggregator model is a new one, it is not yet clear how much self-aggregation people will really want to do, nor how much they will value traditional editorial aggregation on the Web. But the early signs are that the Web's users enjoy acting as their own aggregators. Search services like Yahoo!, Lycos, and InfoSeek are essentially tools for the self-aggregator, and they draw a staggering amount of traffic—far more than any editorial content service. They also draw a great deal of revenue—roughly 70 percent of all advertising revenues on the Web in 1996, according to publishing analyst Sue Decker of Donaldson, Lufkin & Jenrette. This statistic indicates that self-aggregation may not only be more valuable than editorial aggregation, it might be a far better business than content itself. This fact could well obviate the value that HotWired can appropriate from having health advice, cocktail recipes, travel guides, political commentary, industry gossip, Web site creation tips, technology industry news, a search engine, and more under a single, smartly-presented, well-organized roof.

The value that can be appropriated by content in general will be further obviated (for HotWired and for everybody) by the ongoing refusal of the Web's users to pay for it. This refusal has been quite adamant, and most publishers that have experimented with subscription fees (e.g., *The New York Times* in late 1996) have not gotten very far with them. The most obvious problem with subscription models is that it is hard to charge for something when many close substitutes for it are available for free and are only a mouse click away. And since armies of content providers seem to *have their reasons* for putting free content on the Web (e.g., it is an extension of brands in other media, or it helps to market a product, or the capital markets seem to be willing to fund it, or there are big hopes for advertising dollars, or it's just plain *fun*), almost all kinds of content have and will continue to have freebie substitutes somewhere on the Web. This does not mean that it will be impossible for publishers to differentiate their content enough to charge for it—Web-based publishers of professionally-relevant research and analysis are among those who are already ringing up millions in subscription fees (see Chapter 1). But as the Web's openness causes the supply of accessible content to explode, the laws of supply and demand will inevitably bring the price of content down, probably very close to the marginal cost of creating and distributing copies of it—which is to say, zero (industry sage Esther Dyson is among those who have made arguments like this).

None of this means that HotWired is doomed, nor even endangered. It has some of the highest editorial and production standards on the Web, and has long been "paid" well for this in that it has sustained the Web's highest advertising rates ($150 per thousand banners on most of its programs, compared to the $15–75 rate that is prevalent elsewhere). It also has outstanding literary talent, a highly-regarded brand name, and an intangible but important credential in being the first to pioneer and implement so much that is now integral to the Web's landscape. And perhaps most importantly, it has Louis's and Andrew's unflagging determination to keep anteing up, to *stay at the table*. If they can capitalize their company and retain control of it in the process, they will certainly continue to pay whatever it takes to continue playing. Louis first made this clear when he started betting hard on the Web long before it was fashionable, when he had very little to play with and everything to lose. He continued to make it clear throughout 1995 and 1996, when he put even more expensive people behind HotWired than he put behind *Wired*, despite the fact that *Wired* was generating roughly 12 times the revenues as HotWired.

The value of being *at the table* at the end of all this will depend on how big a deal the table actually is, and how many people are sitting there. The early indications are that the table, at least, will matter quite a bit. The Web's ferocious rate of adoption, the levels of accountability it offers advertisers (see Chapter 5), the advantages of ubiquity, immediacy, and cost that it offers publishers, its intermediate-term promise as a commerce channel, and much, much more indicate that the Web is fast becoming *a* if not *the* dominant medium. It is less clear if being a Web *player* will have the same economic value as being, say, a Hollywood studio mogul in the 1980s. If there are in fact *a billion publishers* out there, being one of them will mean a lot less than if there are six.

The reality will of course lie somewhere between these extremes. The Web's liberating openness will always allow room for countless thousands, even millions, of "Web publishers," depending on how that term is defined. But early feel-good imaginings of Disney and Viacom meeting Justin Hall and Suck on level playing fields notwithstanding, a number of factors are already driving consolidation among the Web's top-tier publishers of editorial content. As Joshua Quittner (who coined the term "way new journalism") explains it, "we just didn't realize how damned expensive it would be to create good content." Web production costs money, however cheap Web distribution is. Competitive pressures have also caused production values at Web sites to rise dramatically since 1994, to the delight of those who visit them and the (financial) dismay of those who produce them. As new technologies (e.g., Java) become de rigueur at the better Web sites, more and more skilled artists & engineers are also entering the production equation. And even distribution is not entirely free, as fast Web servers aren't cheap, and keeping a million-plus page-per-day site up and running is a black art that only a few sites have really figured out.

All of this means that it is indeed damned expensive to maintain a topflight Web site—and it will only get damned expensiver in the future. Faster Internet connections will make pricey video content de rigueur for at least some sites. New-new technologies will call for more and more artists & engineers. The marketing budgets that content providers will need to rise above the noise will meanwhile balloon, as they have in almost all mature media.

All of this should one day provide many opportunities for those who have continually anted up, have learned the black arts, have hired the artists & engineers, and are therefore still among the fewish *at the table* as a result. For instance, Louis expects that on the consolidated Web of the future, "if you're small, you'll have a real tough time," because "one of the discoveries of HotWired is that you need critical mass. It's not a casual thing, to create media in this space. It's maybe not like a television network. But it has so many diverse components, and they need to be of such quality, that you can't do it by just putting together twelve people who may be good engineers and writers." The Web's openness alone, then, is not enough to let penniless artists and writers blossom into media moguls. But it can "enabl[e] people to start," Louis says. "It's like lots of garage bands. They don't become stars without connecting to somebody that can add muscle to their existence." He sees HotWired as being that muscle for the Web's garage bands. "You might have a good idea," Louis says, "and you may have done it a little while, but you probably need some coaching. You might be able to do it better if you had some more technology. Come to the studio; we'll help you do it. There are all sorts of possible deals we can do with you. We can buy you, we can license you—let's talk. I think those kinds of relationships are definitely going to come."

They may also come naturally, as HotWired itself was a garage (or at least Grotto) band scarcely two years ago. The garage has since grown large and posh. It has added some floors and some skylights. But its bet-the-company-then-sleep-in-the-*Chill-Room* ethos are still alive and well. It is still too early to say precisely how rosy or gloomy HotWired's future will be. Louis and Andrew still need to capitalize their company as of this writing. They are also taking on an awfully long, disparate, and formidable list of competitors. But they have a number of important advantages to draw on. These, along with their commitment to the medium and their longstanding openness to listen to the Web, learn its rules, and adjust their model accordingly, have put them in a strong position to become one of the publishers *at the table*, and to thereby give HotWired a future on the Web commensurate with its pioneering and agenda-setting past.

CHAPTER 8

HALSEY MINOR
CNET

Merging Media

For one glittering evening in April of 1996, a certain heads-down, hardworking sliver of San Jose, California, had trappings of Hollywood's brash elegance. Not all the trappings, to be sure, but trappings nonetheless. The occasion was the First Annual CNET Awards for Internet Excellence, which were held in conjunction with the Internet World '96 conference and trade show. Like most nonmovieland awards nights, this one drew an industry, not planetary, in-crowd. The awards on offer (best Web browser! best Web server! best Internet development tool!) were also a bit less glamorous than Best Picture, Actor, and Actress. Still, the CNET Awards had something that their peers in most other industries lacked, in the old-line mass media element evident that night in the klieg lighting and the heavy whirring cameras. *TV!* However seduced by the New Medium, most in the industry could still be made a little slack-jawed by the old. And it turned out that the CNET Awards night would be distilled into rollicking old-media content even as it celebrated the new.

This was unsurprising, as CNET (or "C|Net," as it is written in its logo and throughout its site) was all about bringing online and broadcast content together, and using each to build the other. Thus far, it seemed to be pulling this off. Just a year after its broadcast debut, the company was already preparing to launch its second, third, and fourth TV shows, even as it was maintaining two of the Web's most popular sites. Consistent with this, the awards night was not only videocasted and RealAudio-casted live to the Internet, but it was also slated to be *telecasted*, piped into over 67 million homes. True, only about one million of them would actually tune in to the segment. And true, the networks carrying it would have names like "Sci Fi Channel" and "USA Network" rather than "ABC." But a certain magic still came from having the cameras rolling and certified television commentators mastering the ceremonies.

And for a moment it all felt more like New Hollywood than Mountain View. There were attractive young sociable people being attractive, young, and social. There were magazine coverpersons acting removed and drawing pointed fingers. There were fortune-tellers, open bars, live music, and of course, *teevee*. But there were also some more familiar faces from the Valley. There were *propeller-heads*, or socially reluctant engineers. There were *ponytails*, or techno artists, many down from San Francisco's multimedia gulch area. And of course there were *suits*, or the business types who grease the wheels and feed the machine with capital. The neo-Hollywood admixture was drawn from all and none of these groups. It was just this new *community of Web professionals*, it seemed, or at least that community as seen in the flash of the klieg lighting.

In the eye of this happy storm was a guy in a tuxedo; make that *the* guy in a tuxedo (this was still the Valley, after all); Halsey Minor, CNET's founder and CEO. Halsey (yes, it's a family name) was busily churning out the quips and comments and forgetting no names, even as he warily minded the evening's orchestration. Things went off without a hitch (with the exception of Marc Andreessen's nonattendance at a ceremony that culminated with his receiving a Person of the Year award, but nobody could have controlled that). And when the cameras stopped whirring and the crowds dispersed, it seemed that Halsey's Awards had made a credible bid to become a respected industry forum—not a bad flourish to make just a few weeks before CNET's initial public offering.

Outgoing, athletic, and anything but a nerd, Halsey Minor gives the lie to the popular press's knee-jerk fetish for the word "geek" in all discussions of the Internet. As mentioned, his is an *on* company; it's online and it's on-the-air. It's the Valley gone Hollywood, it's *teevee* gone Web. The content at its flagship Web site and on its television shows focuses on computers and technology. It targets a fast-growing and attractive demographic that finds such matters interesting. Halsey's think-big goals for his company include growing its broadcast properties into a 24-hour cable channel and building its Web traffic beyond even Netscape's.

He bases his ambitions on the vastness of today's audience for computer media. This audience has already driven the circulations of the three leading computer magazines (*PC Magazine*, *PC World*, and *PC Computing*) to exceed those of the three leading business magazines (*BusinessWeek*, *Forbes*, and *Fortune*). But much as publishers love them, technology buffs have largely been ignored by television producers. There is plenty of programming for the *BusinessWeek* crowd (e.g., CNBC, CNN*fn*, and innumerable network TV shows), but computing subjects are for the most part explored only in glossy pages. This situation indicates that there could be room for a technology channel, or at least for a lot of technology-related programming, as Halsey is betting.

If anything, online audiences are even hungrier for CNET's kind of content, because diverse as the Internet's users are, they all share the one inevitable fact that they own or have access to computers. Most of them are therefore presumably at least passingly interested in computers. By devoting its online efforts to the massive intersection of the world's *on the Web* population and its *interested in computing* crowd, CNET can therefore play to what is almost by definition the Web's largest audience. Asked about that audience's economic potential, Halsey points to the technology magazines, which capture over 80 percent of the computer industry's almost $3-billion annual advertising budget. The lion's share of that lion's share is seized by giant publishers like Ziff-Davis, International Data Group, and CMP Publications, each of which have several major (and in IDG's case, hundreds of minor) periodicals in their stables. Ziff-Davis (which is wholly owned by Japanese computer distributor Softbank; see Chapter 6) rings up over $300 million in annual advertising revenues from *PC Magazine* alone, which by itself is a couple dozen times more than CNET's 1996 revenues.

These are big competitors to take on. And Halsey is indeed taking them on in that he competes with them more or less directly for both advertising dollars and audience. But their size does not seem to concern him. Indeed, in his brasher moments he confidently predicts that they "are going to get slaughtered," in part because their cumbersome and expensive physical form qualifies them as *the mainframes of the nineties*. No, Halsey has no plans to introduce *CNET Weekly*, nor any other ink-on-paper publication in the near or un-near future. In this he is absenting his company from the online/in-print intersection that all of his print competitors, as well as literally thousands of newspapers and even some Net-native brands like Yahoo! are playing in.

But this does not mean that CNET sees no interplay between media. The company was indeed founded to play in another intriguing intersection: that between television and the online world. This intersection may not seem to be very meaningful while video over the Web is still a grainy, plodding novelty. But the success of cable-branded Web sites like CNN's, ESPN's, and Discovery's has long hinted that the TV/Internet intersection in fact counts for something. And as consumer Internet connections grow faster and increasingly capable of delivering rewarding video content, it will become ever more important.

Or at least Halsey is betting on that—and he is not alone at the table. Microsoft joined him there along with its partner NBC when they jointly funded the creation of the MSNBC cable/Web network. CNN*fn* has likewise been sharing creative and other talent between its on-the-air and online properties for some time, as have some of the other many cable and broadcast brands that are staking out positions on the Web. But while he is not alone in the online/on-the-air corner, Halsey is probably its most tenured occupant, as he has been building CNET as an online/broadcast property since 1992—long before Microsoft and those other newcomers entered the game. CNET is also arguably that corner's purest play, is keeping more eggs in the online/broadcast basket than anybody else. This fact makes the company far more interesting and potentially important than its stand on print, however dramatically Schwarzkopf- or Custer-like that might prove to be.

CNET itself closely reflects its maker's character, as startups so often do. It is a fast-moving place where hard work is expected. It is also a very young place, with at least one key vice president who had his first legal drink shortly before Clinton entered the White House. Youth and just-get-it-done informality give the office a certain *cool hangout* feeling. Cavernous and filled with on-air props, its main room hints of Halsey rallying his first employees with a shout of, "Hey kids, with a bit of work we can turn that old barn down the road into a theater!" Only it's the nineties, and this sure isn't *The Little Rascals*. The barn was a health club, the theater is a TV studio—one cobbled together from onetime hoops courts, squash courts, and even an old railway car (the building once housed the headquarters of a train-themed restaurant chain). Between the TV gear, the mixing studios, CNET Radio's control room, and all of the workstations and Web servers, the place's every nook seems to bleep, hum, or blink. Tucked in amongst all of this are video games, a red British phone booth (go figure), and a Fooz Ball table where Halsey and his lieutenants like to settle their scores.

But CNET's weekending feel has its limits, because if the San Francisco Web scene's black-clad and body-pierced crowd gravitates to HotWired, its heads-down and tasseled-loafered set works at CNET. In this, Fooz Ball tables aside, CNET at its heart is all *suit* and no *ponytail*. It is also, fittingly, quartered on the fringe of San Francisco's button-down financial district not South Park's avant-garde hubbub. But HotWired and CNET do have their weird little similarities. One strange fact is that Jonathan Steuer was instrumental to getting both of them set up on the Web. A-if-not-*the* charter member of the HotWired launch team (see Chapter 7), Steuer's *outtahere* stomp took him more or less directly to CNET, where the company subsequently "got the whole Web site up in six months, and couldn't have done it without Jonathan," Halsey recalls.

Odder still, CNET and HotWired have remarkably similar people at their helms, at least on paper. Halsey and Andrew Anker were born within months of each other, and both grew up on the East Coast. They both went to prep school, then went on to liberal arts educations despite childhood fascinations with computers. Like Andrew, Halsey started his career after college as a Wall Street analyst in 1987, the year of the Crash. Also like Andrew, he left the Street to eventually move West and launch a content-based Web company that he now runs. But unlike the New Yorkerly Mr. Anker, Halsey is not a born-and-bred big-city dweller. He rather was born, grew up, and went to college in the same fairly small, very southern town. This was Charlottesville, home of the University of Virginia.

Halsey lived in comfortable circumstances down in Charlottesville. His father is a successful agricultural real estate broker, his mother a trainer and trader of horses ("or so she says," Halsey chuckles without really clarifying). Never one for parental handouts, Halsey established his first profitable business while still a young teen. His company painted fences, of all things, and came to employ many of the local youths. But despite this early Tom Sawyerly moguldom, Halsey insists that he was a "closet nerd" while growing up. By this he means that he had an early and ongoing interest in computers (and probably relatively few other *nerd* symptoms, one guesses). This started at age 10, when he unilaterally ordered a Heathkit system from a catalog (no, his parents didn't cave in and buy it). Halsey later puzzled and played with many other makes and brands of early-times computers before settling (like Andrew Anker, surprise) on an Apple system.

College was across town at the University of Virginia. There Halsey affiliated with an athletic (and tasseled-loafered) set, and played lots of squash. But though preppy and Wall Street-bound, he passed on the gentlemanly safety of an economics curriculum and instead majored in anthropology because "it would let me study anything I wanted to, because anthropology overlays everything," Halsey explains. His anthropology mainly overlaid art and art history. It also touched on lots of languages—pre–Wall Street tongues like Latin and Arabic. As a senior, Halsey pushed the *overlay everything* concept to its logical limit by writing an honors thesis whose sole footnote referenced the sum of his life experiences (it seems he got away with it).

Although he was no industrial engineering or accounting class regular, Halsey did sharpen his business skills in college by starting a small company called Rental Network. His Network was a few unconnected terminals scattered throughout Charlottesville that spat out information about rentable apartments on request. Stomping around from terminal to terminal in rain & snow & sleet & hail to update their little databases by disk, Halsey not surprisingly found himself "thinking about netlike issues" early on, he recalls. "I was like, 'Wouldn't it be great if they were all just sitting off the network? And wouldn't it be great, rather than having people walk over to the local university bookstore to get access to the information, [if] they could get it in their dorm rooms?' " *Hmmm.*

Halsey had notions of taking Rental Network nationwide. But a friend's father convinced him that he needed the "strong business skills" that investment banking could give him. So after graduating in 1987, he moved to New York and became an analyst at Merrill Lynch. Halsey didn't think much of investment banking ("I did well at it, but I hated it," he shrugs), but he hung in there because he had a project that he wanted to sell Merrill on at the end of his two-year hitch. His plan was to build an infrastructure for distributing information and training resources over the company's internal network using hyperlinks, animation, and graphics. This was an *intranet*, of course, although it predated the word by some years. It was also "the Web done really, really hard," because it came before today's open protocols and authoring environments.

Merrill funded Halsey's proposal, so he set up a teensy company (which he ambitiously named Global Publishing Corporation) and started building his system. The project was a success, and Halsey soon sold Merrill on a more extensive one. This time the objective was "to customize news feeds as they came into the company," Halsey explains, and distribute different news to different people based on their interests and their jobs. His partner in this project was Jeff Bezos, yet another onetime investment banker who has since gone on to Internet glory (Bezos founded and runs Amazon.com, an enormously successful Web-based bookseller; see Chapter 1). Halsey and Bezos signed a lucrative three-year contract with Merrill, and things got off to a promising start. But then one day, Bezos remembers, "we were just sitting in Halsey's office when Merrill Lynch called and said 'we've changed our minds.' " The project was then just a few weeks old. Nobody was concerned about its feasibility or quality. But Merrill was having an awful year and the project's funding just kind of vanished.

Halsey kicked around for a while after that until his then-girl-friend-now-wife Deborah Lee found him some consulting work with an in-flight magazine publisher called EastWest Network. The job paid his bills. But with customers like Eastern Airlines, Pan Am, and Trump Shuttle, EastWest was itself "in a nose dive," Halsey recalls. Indeed, "It was *Aeroflot*," he clarifies, perhaps slipping into some half-forgotten office slang. Halsey's best friends at the company got laid off. But he lingered on for the better part of a year, "working for this guy who was *wacko*," he shudders.

Eventually he had the nugget of another business idea. It was a sort of TV, computer, online thing. And it kind of had something to do with . . . satellites. Yeah—*satellites*. Satellites beaming educational programs into . . . *corporations*. Basically, it needed some work. But before Halsey could quit and write his business plan, he was approached by a friend who worked at a headhunting firm called Russ Reynolds Associates. His friend was calling about a job, of course. But this one wasn't out in the big wide world. It was rather with Russ Reynolds. Like literally; the man. Reynolds was then in his early sixties, and had become his firm's emeritus "ambassador" to the world. At the time he was looking for someone to help him with his emeritus ambassadoring, Halsey remembers, someone who could "basically carry his bags, set up the meetings, fly around the world," and, above all things, *play squash*.

Halsey figured he could do a fair job of all of those things, so he grabbed his racquet and went for an interview. Reynolds won ("for the last time," Halsey points out), and Halsey was offered the job. He decided to sign up for a two-year stint after Reynolds promised that he would be allowed plenty of time to develop his satellite/computer/ TV-thing notion while they were working together. And so Halsey, the onetime entrepreneur, turned investment banker, turned *intranet* consultant, turned in-flight magazine consultant, became a sort of racquet-bearing manservant and immediately started planning his next big move.

In the summer of 1992, Halsey fell ill and stayed home from squash for a few days. Watching a bit of TV, he at one point "noticed that there were three or four channels that were *blank*" on his cable dial (it turns out that they weren't, really, but the inspiration still worked). At about that time, the 486 PC was taking off in the home. Online services were really catching on too. Halsey thought about all this, considered his *blank channels,* and concluded that computers were becoming enough of a consumer phenomenon to warrant "a real cable channel, like MTV," particularly if that channel was supported by some kind of online environment. Since then, he says, his core business model "has never, ever deviated." He left his job to go forth and implement that model in December of 1992. He was convinced that his timing was immaculate, because he had "stepped out in the age of 500 channels" (he indeed remembers cable tycoon John Malone foretelling the dawn of that age in the press during his very last days with Reynolds). *Five hundred channels!* Most of them *blank!* Surely there would be room for an *MTV-like* computer channel on the massive new dial.

It turned out that Halsey's timing was excellent, but not due to anything happening in the cable industry. Because even as he was leaving Reynolds, Malone's brave words goading him onward, Marc Andreessen and Eric Bina were rolling up sleeves, stockpiling Skittles, and preparing to hack out the first Mosaic browser.

Halsey hammered on his business plan and coined some clever slogans (*It's Not Just a Television Network; It's Networked Television!*). He also spent a lot of time checking out the commercial online services like CompuServe, since the pre-Web Internet—the antithesis of a consumer environment—was wholly unsuitable for his *MTV-like* service. Among the early-round investors that he lined up at that time was Shelby Bonnie, an analyst at Julian Roberts' celebrated hedge fund, Tiger Management (who invested on his own, not Tiger's behalf). Bonnie had graduated from the University of Virginia a year ahead of Halsey, although they hadn't known each other there. He had pretty much been on Wall Street ever since, with the exception of a two-year hiatus when he picked up an M.B.A. at Harvard.

Bonnie enjoyed his work at Tiger. But somehow finance just wasn't doing it for him anymore. He had been a spare-hours computer hobbyist for years by then. He had also long harbored an interest in entrepreneurship that Wall Street just wasn't going to satisfy. All of this led him to think about more than just investing when Halsey first brought him his business plan. The business plan itself was exciting. But it was Halsey himself—his manic energy and his Big Ideas—that really blew Bonnie away. The fact that Halsey was hiring was also pretty exciting. Bonnie's first day at CNET was in July of 1993.

By then the company had plenty of *suits* (Halsey had already taken on a Stanford Business School graduate named Bettina Shapiro [now Cisneros] to help write the business plan). So everyone figured that the time was right to start calling on Hollywood. Soon enough Halsey rang the offices of Kevin Wendle. Wendle was then running a production company that he had named (and he worked hard on this) Kevin Wendle Productions. Although only 34, Wendle was already a 20-year veteran of The Industry. He had started his career in the news organization of New York's Channel 5 at age 14. At 17 he was senior producer of the midday news for Channel 11, and at 20 he was producing the flagship six o'clock local news for WABC (Channel 7). Wendle subsequently won an Emmy award and moved to Los Angeles, where, as a wizened and weary 26-year-old, he was one of the six people on the Fox Network's founding team. His development credits at Fox eventually included such shows as "Married . . . with Children," "In Living Color," "The Simpsons," "Beverly Hills 90210," and "America's Most Wanted." By the time Halsey contacted him, Wendle's eponymous company had grown into a successful production house with dozens of full-time employees.

Halsey knew substantially none of this when he called. Wendle had just been highly recommended by somebody-or-other, so he basically rang him up and dove right into his pitch. He told Wendle about how he was preparing to launch a cable network. About how he had this brand-new notion of initially *nesting* its content within another network, and then later breaking it out to become a network in its own right. About this partner of his whose name was—well, it was at least as weird as *Halsey*. Halsey spoke fast, Halsey spoke at length, and

Halsey spoke with conviction. At some point there was a momentary break in the action, and Wendle dove right in.

"So," he started. "This network of yours . . ."

"Yeah?"

"It's gonna be about . . . fish?"

Halsey explained that the network would be called C-Net, not *Sea*-net, and that the "C" stood for *computer*. And everything started making sense to Wendle, particularly the bit about "online" this and that. Wendle started telling Halsey about his own background. When he got to the part about the Fox Network, he heard Halsey cover the mouthpiece (ineptly, it turns out) and hiss *He cofounded* Fox! to somebody.

Wendle smiled. *Nerd.*

Soon enough Halsey was asking Wendle if he would consider consulting for CNET. Wendle figured, "okay, well, the first thing that I'll advise him is save your money and forget about starting a cable network for people interested in computers." But he decided to hold his fire until he had a chance to meet the guy.

Wendle and Halsey finally sat down about a month later. Wendle wasn't expecting much. But he soon found himself "blown away" by Halsey's understanding of the cable industry, particularly by his *nesting* scheme, which in Wendle's experience was a novel idea. Halsey's plan was to start out producing just one or two shows that would be hosted, or *nested* on another network. CNET would then use these to build its brand equity with viewers and its credibility within the industry. It would then gradually expand its programming hours so that the eventual leap to a 24-hour network would be incremental, rather than quantum. *Cool.* Wendle signed on as CNET's consultant in early 1994, and soon after as a full-time CNET staffer.

Around the time that Wendle came aboard, Bonnie raised a couple of million dollars (mainly from "friends and family" of the CNET staff) and the company relocated to San Francisco to be near the technology heartland. Work started on CNET's first pilot episodes shortly after that, and four segments were soon ready. They were "CNET Central" and "The New Edge," both of which eventually made it to the air, a technology industry personalities piece called "The Insiders," and a survey of multimedia and CD-ROM technology called "Double-Click." "CNET Central" looked particularly good; its pilot was hosted by MTV's Adam Curry, who had by then largely left the klieg lighting to start a Web site development company called On Ramp (with Dimension X's Karl Jacob; see Chapter 3). "Double-Click" looked particularly bad; it soon earned the office nickname of "Doesn't Click" (it never did).

Some time in there, Adam Curry showed Halsey Mosaic and this new *Web thing*. The timing was excellent, as Halsey was by then getting very frustrated with the commercial online services. The trouble was that all of them were insisting on exclusive rights to any CNET content that they might host. This was problematic because Halsey wanted to reach everyone online, not just the subscribers to one particular service. Now suddenly it seemed that the Web had the potential to change all of this, because once the commercial services fitted their proprietary online environments with gateways to it, CNET could be accessible to everybody simply by being there. This notion was itself a bit problematic, since none of the commercial services had yet shown the slightest interest in giving their customers Web access. But Halsey was sure that this would change once the Web caught on, as he expected it to. And so, with four (well, three) good pilots under their belts and a promising new medium welling up beneath their feet, everything looked rosy for the CNET team as they roared into what Kevin Wendle now remembers as "the worst year of my life."

By February, CNET's overriding objective was to get a Deal, whether it was with a major cable company embracing its *nesting* scheme, a financier (preferably neither friend nor family this time) funding its expansion, or, better yet, both. But the days when good online-related business plans would draw take-a-number queues of panting investors were still distant. And by the summer's end, it seemed that CNET's senior team had approached almost every major cable player without so much as a nibble. It was beginning to seem that neither cash nor *nest* would be forthcoming—although countless tantalizing near-misses soon brought everybody's life to turn upon static like the tone in a powerful person's secretary's voice (*She sounded* HAPPY! *Happy to* HEAR FROM US! *That must mean her boss has read our business plan, bought in on the nesting scheme, talked it over with the board . . .*)

The summer of 1994 was the company's worst. Senior management went without salaries. Everyone else stomached 50 percent pay cuts. Shelby Bonnie started writing personal checks to cover payroll, and it seemed that the end was near. Matthew Barzan, now CNET's vice president of software services, recalls how sorry the little company newsletter started sounding. It was "like, 'Chris is looking into steam cleaning the garage. Matthew is looking into possible ways to put down strips on the front steps, most likely tape.' And this was dead serious," Barzan insists. "This was not tongue-in-cheek. 'We think we'll get a copier next week. Bid was a little high.' " With little to engage managerial attention other than chasing Deals (and with this now consisting mainly of navel gazing), the company directed its frantic focus to the mundane. "We would have Halsey, Shelby, Kevin—full managerial forces" meet with any salesperson who dared darken the doorstep, Barzan recalls. "It was like, 'Look, we're gonna be a really high-profile company, and we just need a break on this first steam cleaning. And we're only going to get one initially, but who knows? This could turn into a monthly steam cleaning. . . .' We sold that to every single person. We tried to get used furniture, absolutely anything. We must have been so annoying to deal with, because we were always looking for a deal. *Hey, we'll put you on TV!* was our big pitch."

The first ray of hope shot through late in the summer of 1994, when a call came through from Vulcan Ventures, the investment arm of Microsoft cofounder Paul Allen. Allen was known for his big bets on media and technology companies like TicketMaster, Egghead Software, and DreamWorks, the new movie studio. He had heard of CNET through contacts at Fox. Allen ended up coming down to CNET's offices personally after his Vulcan proxylings did some initial sniffing around, which seemed like a promising gesture. In their meeting, Halsey "pitched his heart out for two hours without stopping," Wendle recalls, while "Paul sat there completely silent." Yet Allen seemed impressed and everyone was optimistic. But then a day went by without a phone call. Then another. Doubts spread, anxieties flared. Then finally Vulcan called to say that Allen was interested in investing. He soon bought 21 percent of CNET's equity for some $5 million (a stake that he later expanded by converting some loans).

With its first Deal closed, CNET had a much easier time clinching the second. This was with the USA Network, which agreed to host "CNET Central" (CNET's first TV show) on its eponymous network and on its Sci Fi Channel affiliate in exchange for warrants on some of CNET's equity and some stock. Halsey was delighted to land with USA. It had an extraordinary 67-million household reach for one thing, and its own branding was also not so brash that it would swamp CNET's attempt to develop an identity within it. This would have been a real issue on other strong cable networks like MTV, say, where it would have been difficult to be *CNET* to viewers, as opposed to *MTV's computer show*.

As his two Deals were being inked at the end of 1994, Halsey in a sense decided that there would not be a third one. The commercial on-line networks were then growing at a lightning rate, and the Web was still tiny (Netscape had posted the first beta copy of its Navigator only weeks before). But the commercial services were all still demanding monogamy of CNET, and Halsey had no interest in locking his online doors to all but a single service's subscribers. In light of this, he decided to make a firm strategic commitment to the Web as his online medium.

CNET had all of 12 employees on hand to build its Web site and develop its TV programming when its Deals closed. So with cash in the till and a distribution channel finally open, the company went on a hiring binge. Soon Jonathan Steuer and several other recent HotWired alums were hacking on the Web site. Wendle's team meanwhile staffed up and got busy with "CNET Central." In the end, the company took scarcely six months to launch in both media. "CNET Central" debuted first, in April of 1995. Kevin Wendle describes the show as "the 'Entertainment Tonight' of the digital world." Emceed by two bantersome hosts, it has a light and accessible tone, and surveys a wide range of technology-related issues.

CNET online launched two months later and almost immediately grew into one of the Web's most heavily trafficked sites. By the time of its first anniversary it had more than 40 full-time writers and editors on staff, and was expected to triple this number before its second. The site presents a comprehensive mix of trade news, product reviews, and industry features. Its news pages are especially popular. Built around subjects like Intranets, the Net, and Newsmakers, they have become part of the daily habit of thousands of industry professionals. All of CNET's pages bear a distinctive red, yellow, and green color scheme, and tend to follow a punchy, get-to-the-point editorial arc. Like HotWired, CNET online is supported by a weekly E-mailed newsletter (*The Digital Dispatch*) that is almost surely the Internet's highest-circulation periodical. The *Dispatch* had more than 500 thousand subscribers by the end of its first year, and was expected to cross the one million mark by the end of its second in 1997.

Competing with periodicals like *PC Week* and *PC Magazine* for readership and ad dollars, one of CNET online's goals is "to make paper seem antiquated," Halsey declares. To this end, the site takes full advantage of the Web's immediacy, publishing its content in several daily "editions" that release every few hours. This frequency gives its content a timeliness that no printed publication (certainly not a weekly magazine) can match. CNET's editors can publish the beginnings of a story almost literally the moment it breaks, then fill it in with details and quotes as they become available. While he certainly doesn't call himself a *way new journalist,* Halsey also likes to see his editors make use of the richness that hyper-links, Java, and other online devices can add to a story. He often cites CNET's "Interactive PC Score Board," as a case of "multimedia deliver[ing] what print cannot." A Java-enabled "feature," this queries prospective computer buyers about desired price ranges and feature sets, and pulls system and manufacturer recommendations from a database. The closest analogs that a magazine can offer to content like this is an eye-numbing grid of computer names, sample feature sets, and prices.

CNET's early editorial and (increasingly) commercial successes do not of course mean that its printed rivals are doomed. After all, the Web is a *bad place to read*, as *Wired*'s Louis Rossetto has pointed out, meaning that certain writing (particularly longer pieces) is simply better suited to print than computer screens. And besides, all of CNET's printed competitors have diversified their bets with extensive Web sites of their own. Some are quite ambitious, and a few have even been around since before CNET. The most formidable is probably Ziff-Davis's ZDnet and the magazine sites that link to it (although Halsey sniffs that he hates to be compared to ZD because he finds its online efforts to be "boring as hell").

ZD, whose printed properties include the industry's highest circulation periodical, *PC Magazine*, is able to leverage all of its printed content online, and also enjoys enviably strong and long-standing relations with the computer industry's advertisers. ZD CEO Eric Hippeau says that he expects the Web to help build rather than undermine his core business, because those "who can leverage both mediums and really learn how to make them work together . . . will then be able to transfer readers and customers from one to the other," ultimately creating a bigger audience. While its print readership is still probably much greater than its online following, the Web is already no drop-in-the-bucket distraction to ZD. Hippeau estimates that the company's total online efforts employed roughly one-sixth as many editors as all of its printed properties combined by the middle of 1996, giving ZD an online staff larger than CNET's total head count.

But despite the competition it faces, CNET's Web traffic has grown explosively and continually since its launch. The company measures this traffic (like most Web content companies) in *page views*. A page view is counted whenever a page has been wholly downloaded (and therefore presumably viewed) by a site's visitor. Halsey recalls that CNET logged some 115 thousand page views on the day its site switched on. Traffic then grew tenfold the following year, and Halsey hoped to see another exponential jump, to over 10 million daily page views, in time for CNET's second online anniversary in June of 1997.

Such an increase could have huge economic ramifications for the company, as its revenue potential is closely tied to its traffic. This is because CNET places only a single advertisement on each page that it serves, which means that it can't sell any more banners than it has page views. For this reason, the site's page views are referred to as *inventory* internally. And like any business, CNET can't sell any more *inventory* than it generates. Halsey estimates that on average his sales force sells around 85 percent the site's inventory, although there have been times when the site has been sold out.

The notion of a sold-out Web site suggests an interesting counterpoint to the common contention that "nobody pays for" Web content. When page views translate directly into advertising revenues (as they do very cleanly at a sold-out site, where every new page view literally allows another banner to be sold) people absolutely do "pay for" what they see simply by turning pages. For instance, a habitual CNET user who checks in daily with its news pages might easily turn 10 pages or more per visit. Since CNET sells the banners that it serves with its news pages for $100 per thousand, or 10 cents each, such a visitor's traffic could notionally put one dollar into the company till every day.

Such visitors are clearly valuable enough to merit generous acquisition budgets. To this end, CNET is not only one of the Web's biggest sellers of banner advertising, but it is one of its biggest buyers as well. Some might argue that its bargain banner binge buys have only deepened the red ink perennially found thus far on the company's income statements. But CNET is a young company, and most of its early losses have been associated with building its name and getting its content development staff up to a point of critical mass. Once the baseline costs associated with all of this have stabilized, the economics of distribution over the Web should give CNET tremendous operating leverage, which could make it extraordinarily profitable. This is because if the company can continue to all-but-sell-out its page views, it would acquire practically linear revenue exposure to traffic growth (because more traffic means more inventory, which means more revenue when inventory is selling out). But it would meanwhile have almost no cost exposure to traffic growth, because while big leaps in traffic do call for more data lines and Web servers, and while these are not free, their costs are almost negligible compared to the revenue that their page view capacities can generate.

These economics are very attractive compared to those faced by magazines, which incur significant physical production and distribution costs on behalf of every marginal reader that they reach. Halsey compares his operational advantage over traditional publishers to that of software companies over computer hardware companies, and points out that Microsoft has sustained market capitalizations rivaling IBM's with less than a tenth of its revenues. It is this that leads him to characterize his printed rivals as *the mainframes of the nineties*.

But linear increases in traffic will not bring linear increases in revenues if CNET's sales force is unable to keep up with expanding inventory, as page views that have to be served to visitors without paid-for banners attached on them are worth about as much as empty theater seats when the curtain goes up. For this reason, CNET invests heavily in its sales force. This team started selling banners in October of 1995, four months after CNET's online launch (banners were bundled with TV ads sold on "CNET Central" before that). Less than a year later, CNET had become the leading ad revenue generator among the Web's content sites (only Netscape and two search engines were then outselling it).

CNET differentiates itself to its sponsors with a family of proprietary tools and value-added services that are designed to make their ad campaigns more effective. The tools are developed by CNET's own advanced technology group in New Jersey. Comprised largely of engineers lured from nearby Bell Labs, this division had dozens of full-time employees by late 1996. Its tools let sponsors target their ads based on visitors' backgrounds (a service similar to that offered by DoubleClick, the ad placement agency discussed in Chapter 5). They also let advertisers track the performance of their ads in real time, making it easy for them to pull advertisements that don't work, or to retarget them to the demographic groups that seem to respond to them best.

Supporting these tools are CNET's "Crusaders," who help customers interpret and react to the data that the site's tools generate (among other things). All of this has helped CNET keep its click-through rates in the lofty range of 5–6 percent, Halsey says, which compares very favorably to the 2 percent average that Ariel Poler and I/PRO have noted throughout the Web as a whole (see Chapter 5). Some CNET sponsors do even better than that. John-Scott Dickson of Insight Enterprises (a $340-million direct marketer of computers, software, and services) says that he often gets 10 to 20 percent click-through responses to the ads that he places on CNET. He attributes this partly to CNET's willingness "to let us try new concepts." For instance, one time CNET's sales team helped him place RealAudio buttons on a third of the banners in a particular campaign. The RealAudio-enabled banners (which said *Well, happy http to you, cowpoke!* when clicked) yielded an astonishing 22 percent click-through rate. Dickson, who has conducted a number of experiments like this at CNET, now characterizes the company as "extremely flexible and responsive. We can call [them] on Friday afternoon with an idea and they'll have it on the server in hours," he says. This kind of service helps CNET stay nearly sold out, and its salespeople perpetually hungry for more *inventory.*

There would of course be no inventory without topflight content to draw page-turning eyeballs, which keeps CNET editor-in-chief Christopher Barr busy. Barr came to CNET from Ziff-Davis (specifically, from *PC Magazine*) and has since been joined by several other print émigrés, including *InfoWorld*'s former executive news editor Jai Singh and *Byte* magazine's former editor-in-chief Rafe Needelman. Barr cites the feedback loop that the Web builds between editors and their audiences as one of the medium's great strengths. Log files, he points out (see Chapter 5), can let an editor track the traffic drawn by each article on a site, revealing readers' interest patterns. CNET's log files let Barr know "exactly how popular a story is, [such that if] we put out a bunch of stories that are incredibly popular, we know that, and we can do more of the same. Or if something's a dud we can ignore it, essentially. And we know the next day." The reader surveys that his print-world counterparts have to turn to for similar insights are cumbersome, expensive, slow, and comically blunt instruments by comparison.

The ability to directly audit the interests and reactions of huge audiences is a unique one afforded by the Web. The fact that an audit can be done unobtrusively means that measurements of an audience's behavior will not be colored by any self-conscious ex post facto attempts to re-create or explain behavior. Such attempts can distort the results of a media audit or survey beyond the point of validity. And distortions are all too likely when people are asked to recall the details of casual activities (e.g., flipping through a magazine), or when they feel like they are on stage under an auditor's scrutiny. Distortions like these expose traditional media audits to the Hawthorne effect noted by psychologists and others, in which the very act of observation influences the outcome of the process being observed. But when an online audience's choices are logged exhaustively and anonymously, the impacts of sample bias, the Hawthorne effect, and other such distortions melt away; every reader's choice can then be treated as a vote. Editors who heed the daily elections tallied in their log files can tune their content to reader interests in ways that have not been possible before.

Log files can also make it possible for editors to calculate the financial returns on even tiny pieces of content. Magazines can't do this, because printed articles are embedded components of larger products, and do not by themselves generate revenues. But an article that drives salable page views on a commercial Web site makes measurable contributions to its site's inventory, and when inventory is sold out, allowing every marginal page view to enable a marginal sale, these contributions translate directly into revenues. Articles can also directly impact revenues when inventory is not sold out, as specific writers or subject matters that draw their own distinct audiences might sell out their page views to sponsors trying to reach their audiences. Something very much like this in fact happens regularly at directories like Yahoo!, where banner space on search pages tied to commercially relevant subjects like computing is frequently oversubscribed, even when the site as a whole is only 30 to 40 percent sold out. When this happens, every marginal computer-related search makes it possible for another banner to be sold, even as millions of other page views go unsold every day.

All of this can enable online editors like Barr to literally measure the financial performance of stories. For instance, if a freelancer is paid 75 cents a word to write a 400-word piece, the piece obviously costs $300. If its page views subsequently generate 10 cents each in marginal revenues, the piece might be thought of as profitable if it generates more than three thousand page views, or as a money loser if it generates fewer. Barr does not assess stories in this manner ("I'm not quite that cold," he says). And as CNET's traffic continues to build, he expects that most of its content will comfortably cross the profitability threshold anyway. He has already posted one story that generated more than 90 thousand page views, and believes that even 150 thousand page view outcomes "might seem modest or small" in the near future.

But editors with lower budgets, less traffic, and perhaps colder blood than he could come to track the financial returns on their content very carefully. A "consignment" model for content could even arise, whereby sites provide baseline traffic and a sales infrastructure, and writers and other creatives place their material in exchange for percentage shares of their page view revenues. This arrangement could let creatives retain real financial equity in their work, while letting publishers remove content creation expenses from their fixed cost structures. This might not be the right answer for all artists and publishers, but it is an intriguing economic model that the Web can enable. Far more exotic models may even arise as the Web's extraordinary auditability makes the microeconomics of media attention and marketing easier to measure and understand.

CNET's proprietary software tools are already giving the company real competitive power by helping it peer into those microeconomics. Better-placed ads result in higher click-through performance, and therefore higher ad rates and more satisfied customers. Barr's careful reading of his log files meanwhile results in more and more popularly relevant content being generated and displayed at the site. But CNET's TV studios are meanwhile, ironically, pouring just as much effort and money into creating the broadest, bluntest, and arguably least targeted form of media around. This might seem like a paradox. But CNET's online and on-air operations are actually both integral pieces of a highly coherent media strategy.

As noted, CNET debuted on the air (or *in the ground*, more precisely, as most viewers get its signal via cable) with "CNET Central" in April of 1995. "CNET Central" "throw[s] to online all the time," Halsey says, meaning that it makes regular references to features on CNET's Web sites. As a result, "you can see the blips" in traffic whenever it airs, Halsey says. The show's early success allowed CNET to add three other full-length shows to its lineup in the summer and fall of 1996. These included a half-hour show about new technologies called "The New Edge" (which, like "CNET Central," was one of the first pilot episodes that the company made early in its history) and an hour-long program about the Internet called "The Web." Both of these debuted on the Sci Fi Channel in July of 1996. The third, a half-hour–long Internet-related program called "tv.com," debuted on syndicated stations in September of 1996. Like "CNET Central," all of these newer shows *throw to online* aggressively.

Taken together, they also represent a big step toward CNET's goal of becoming a 24-hour network. Kevin Wendle estimates that only 10 to 14 hours of original content per week are necessary to sustain a 24-hour signal at first. And with its first four shows, CNET was already producing two and a half hours. Halsey is "absolutely" confident that CNET will make the leap to having its own channel, almost certainly before the end of the decade. And this could have terrific implications for CNET's online properties, as Halsey is convinced that over the long term, cable networks will be better positioned than any other content providers to compete on the Web. He believes they are particularly well-positioned relative to magazine publishers, which is why he shuns print so categorically.

One huge advantage that cable companies have when they come to the Web pertains to promotion. Illustrating this, Halsey cites the ESPN network's site ESPNET SportsZone. He estimates that ESPN television draws roughly 20 million viewers per week, and "there isn't a magazine out there in the sports area that promotes to as many people." Its huge audience lets ESPN *throw to online* much more powerfully than any magazine. It can do this with little snippets of dedicated air time, or just by having its announcers make occasional references to the Web site. TV's richness meanwhile heightens the impact of ESPN's promotions. "ESPN Sports can do an ad where they show Boris Becker diving for a ball, or two football players crunching heads, or a baseball player snagging a ball before it goes over the fence, with rousing music in the background," Halsey points out. "*ESPN Sports. Check it Out. . . . You can't do that in a magazine.*"

Even with only a tiny handful of TV shows, CNET was already reaping tremendous promotional leverage from its broadcast properties. It was producing programming at a break-even rate by its second year in production, which effectively gave it hundreds of costless hours of TV exposure per year. By contrast, Halsey estimates that Yahoo! spent $8 million on its first TV advertising campaign—which bought it only a tiny fraction of CNET's total on-air hours.

Great as its promotional leverage is, cable has a potentially greater and more strategic advantage on the Web in the area of *content synergy*. For now this matters little, as most consumers still access the Internet through modems that are too slow to serve up cable content (i.e., video) in a rewarding manner. But this will change. And Halsey predicts that when it does, video will become integral to Web content. If he is right, cable properties will be far better positioned to compete on the Web than periodicals publishers. To appreciate this, consider *The New York Times* and CNN. Both have very popular news sites today. But CNN of course maintains a global video news–gathering operation to feed its non-Web media outlets, while *The New York Times* does not. This means that if video truly infiltrates the Web, it will be "much easier for CNN to basically take that operation and put its video online, and even do some incremental stuff with it [than it will be] for *The New York Times* to build out an entire operation and not have a cable network to amortize it against," Halsey points out.

From this, Halsey concludes that as a cable property, "your relative advantage scales proportionately with bandwidth." And bandwidth, or network and network access speeds, will continue to *scale*, or grow, just as surely as it has almost every year since the Internet's inception. Halsey cites a prototype piece that CNET developed for a high-bandwidth Internet access company (@Home) to illustrate what this could mean. The prototype consisted mainly of video footage. To produce it, one of CNET Central's cohosts "basically spent an extra five minutes in front of the camera one day." Because the infrastructure to create the piece was already paid for, the job was done "for almost no extra money," Halsey points out. And this is good news if you already have video operations. But "if you aren't in the TV business, you don't have cameras and lights sitting out there. You have to go out and basically acquire all that stuff. And that's really expensive."

The synergies that Halsey sees between cable and the Web could make CNET formidably competitive. But others will benefit from them too. One even more self-consciously cross-media experiment that is even better known than CNET is the MSNBC network, a $500-million joint venture between Microsoft and NBC that launched in July of 1996. MSNBC's cable channel debuted with 14 hours of original daily programming. The network's Web site was likewise ambitious. MSNBC's strategic orientation clearly resembles CNET's. And while most of its content falls into the general news category dominated by CNN, the new network did launch a daily one-hour program focusing on the Internet and technology. Called "The Site," this show, like *PC Magazine*, like *PC Week*, like *MacUser*, like *PC Computing*, was a Ziff-Davis production. Like CNET, it also launched with an eponymous Web site. But "The Site" did not launch with CNET's distribution (MSNBC debuted with 22.5 million households, compared to

USA's 60+ million). And it invoked a fairly flimsy Web site (thesite.com) that seemed awfully tangential to its parent's core business. For these and other reasons, Halsey did not deign to view "The Site" as really being in CNET's league.

Halsey meanwhile continued to build out CNET's exposure to the cable/Web intersection in ways that went beyond even the CNET brand. One of these avenues was CNET's partnership with E!, the entertainment network. CNET and E! now jointly own a third company that maintains E!'s branded presence on the Web. The site, called *E! Online*, launched in the summer of 1996. Like the cable network, E!'s Web site focuses on providing entertainment news, gossip, and celebrity information, and also serves up background on innumerable movies and TV shows.

E! President Lee Masters recalls first meeting with the CNET folks back when they were initially pitching their *nesting* concept. He didn't see much synergy between his network and a computer show at the time. But he liked the CNET guys. He recalls being "really impressed with their intelligence," and was immediately interested in partnering with them once a more appropriate opportunity for that emerged. For his part, Halsey was drawn to working with E! because he was convinced that entertainment news would be a huge content area on the Web. He understood that the leading requested search categories at the big Internet directories were entertainment and technology (or at least they were among the family-oriented subject matters that Halsey was willing to consider devoting a Web site to). Working with E! therefore seemed to be a perfect way to diversify CNET's content exposure.

The E! partnership also became a good way to leverage CNET's investments in technology and infrastructure. Because now if the Advanced Technology Group develops a membership registration system, say, they can "pick it up and drop it over," to the E! site as well as to CNET's other sites, Halsey points out, and "there is huge operational leverage" in this. Halsey intends to apply this leverage across more content areas in the future. As he does, his cost advantage relative to companies that must make all of their investments on behalf of single branded sites will grow. It will grow all the more as rising production values, heightening bandwidth, and complex new content technology (e.g., Java) cause the baseline investments that world-class Web sites face to balloon (see Chapter 7).

All of this talk of cable/Web *content synergies* and ever-heightening bandwidth begs the question of whether Web access will get so speedy that Internet connections will be able to take the place of the TV cable, allowing the Web to *subsume television*. Over the very long haul (more likely decades than years) the answer is probably *yes*. But even when the Internet can deliver full-screen video to a mass market, Halsey does not expect TV to *go poof*, because "the linear format has its advantages. Television has its advantages. There's a certain ubiquity about TV that's not going to be replaced overnight by the Internet."

E!'s Lee Masters echoes this notion, and says he expects that rather than subsuming television, the Web will come to cater to the "really small, narrow niches serving every type of magazine interest" that were originally "seen as the future of cable." For instance, Masters points out that while stamp collectors sustain many periodicals, they are not on the verge of getting their own 24-hour *philatelists* cable channel. But, he speculates, stamp collectors might perhaps be a big enough audience to sustain an hour's worth of production-quality video every day, or every few days. If they are, a high-bandwidth Web site could distribute that content, even if it could never elbow its way onto the cable system's constricted shelf.

Once on the Web, focused video content could, like highly targeted audiocasts (see Chapter 2) then benefit enormously from the medium's unique ability to aggregate audiences across time and geography. This could make all kinds of new video content viable, because economic attendance thresholds are naturally far easier to clear when audiences can be drawn globally, rather than from single broadcast networks or (certainly) metropolitan areas. Timeshifting makes it easier still to draw a large crowd, as it enables an audience's members to "show up" over periods of days, weeks, or even years, rather than just at the moment of broadcast (see also Chapter 2). And unlike the broadcast spectrum, the Internet does not force content providers to compete for room on a finite shelf. This means that if the Internet does grow into a global video storage and delivery system, the "shelf space" available to video producers—like that now available to writers and, increasingly, musicians—will effectively become infinite.

An explosion of new content should absolutely result from this. Lower-end video production costs have been tumbling for years, while broadcast and cable shelf sizes have remained fairly static. The simplest laws of supply and demand indicate that *cheaper* content should have resulted in more content. But when content lacks an avenue to its audience, it will not be made, however cheap it is to produce. This has meant that as production costs have dropped, many niche audiences (e.g., stamp collectors) that might have become interesting from a production cost standpoint have remained uninteresting to producers because of distribution bottlenecks (CNET's own early difficulties in getting distribution for its TV shows demonstrated this fact).

Internet video delivery could change this by making it easier to both reach and aggregate audiences. Lee Masters' hour-a-day stamp collecting "channel," as well as countless other niche video concepts, could then become viable businesses. Advertisers might then flock to these niches, as narrowly-targeted content tends to create coherent audiences, which are much easier to sell to than diverse ones (see Chapter 5). Content that has been able to muscle its way onto the broadcast shelf could also benefit greatly from an online video distribution. "CNET Central," for instance, could become as accessible in London and Jakarta as it is in Mountain View. Hundreds of old CNET video broadcasts could likewise be made available archivally throughout the world, much as hundreds of CNET Radio programs are already accessible via RealAudio.

This distribution model is still far from reality. It is not at all certain that people will want to watch videos on their computer screens, for one thing. Most of us are accustomed to interacting and *driving* when we have 150 buttons beneath our fingers, not kicking back, observing, and being driven. Video entertainment of the beer-'n'-popcorn variety would also inevitably lose much of its luster if it had to be watched from office chairs rather than comfy couches. So just as Internet audio might need to pump through our home stereos before it becomes popularly relevant, Internet video might have to find its way into the living room. This move would require some juggling in the infrastructure. But the infrastructure is already being juggled. Video gaming giant Sega recently started adding Web access to its set-top boxes (and thereby to the TV sets they connect to). Startups like WebTV are meanwhile promoting dedicated TV set-top boxes for Internet access. And PC manufacturers like Gateway are already marketing PCs that receive television signals.

But a trickier issue than shuttling Internet connections between devices and around living rooms is the network infrastructure. Progressive Networks can already get okay audio through a mass-market 28.8 kbps modem (and sub-okay audio through a lower-end 14.4 modem; see Chapter 2). But consumer-grade video demands far more bandwidth than RealAudio. Video piped through a 28.8 modem is *ugly* compared to anything that we would tolerate on our TV sets, and as such is still more of a curiosity than a dawning mass medium. For the Internet to become truly relevant to video, consumer bandwidth will therefore have to expand significantly.

Several competing experiments are now underway which could allow this to happen. A particularly closely-watched one is the @Home network, which is headquartered in tidy Mountain View, California. @Home is a joint venture of cable giant TCI and Kleiner Perkins, the venture capital fund that backed both Netscape and Marimba. Its board members include Netscape CEO Jim Barksdale. @Home is building a national network that is meant to bring high-speed Internet access to consumers, businesses, and content providers. Consumers will connect to it via modems attached to their cable TV jacks. @Home is riding the cable network because coaxial cable can offer several thousand times the bandwidth of copper phone lines. The company plans to use a small slice of this total capacity (6 out of 750 megahertz [MHz]) to deliver 10 *mega*bit connections to its users. This is roughly 300 times the bandwidth delivered by 28.8 *kilo*bit modems.

Each multi-megabit node in the @Home network will be shared by up to a few dozen subscribers, according to @Home product line manager Jeff Huber. This means that individual subscribers will not have their 10 Mb connections all to themselves. But Internet traffic is "bursty" by nature. In other words, users requesting Web pages and downloading files typically draw in sporadic bursts of traffic, which are followed by long periods of no traffic as Web pages or files are read or contemplated. This, coupled with the fact that only a fraction of a node's subscribers will tend to log on at any one time, should leave wide swaths of bandwidth available for each bursty request. If the @Home network delivers as planned, it should have no problem distributing short-subject videos to its subscribers in a highly interactive manner (although the network will bog down if too many subscribers try to use it to access movie-length videos).

@Home is now backed by three gigantic cable companies that together reach over 40 percent of the households in the United States (TCI, Cox Communications, and Comcast). Building out its national infrastructure will be no trivial feat. Expensive enhancements will have to be made in every local cable system that offers its services. The network will also need to reach content providers as well as consumers (a 10 Mb end-user connection won't mean much if the server on the other end is on a low bandwidth line). So far, @Home has "the top 100 or so Internet sites" on its bandwagon, Huber says, developing content that shows off its high speed. @Home's backers have also committed a great deal of capital to its cause, and have lined up a technical team that includes some legendary players, such as Milo Medin, NASA's former networking wunderkind. Huber expects that @Home will be available to millions of American households by 1998. Other cable companies including Time Warner and Jones are also working on their own high bandwidth projects.

Telephone companies are meanwhile getting into the high bandwidth game themselves with a technology known loosely as XDSL (DSL stands for "digital subscriber line," and "X" denotes the fact that there are several DSL variations, including ADSL, VDSL, HDSL, and SDSL). XDSL seeks to deliver data rates of up to several dozen megabits per second over traditional copper phone lines. Like cable modem networks, XDSL systems will require significant upgrades to the existing infrastructure in order to work.

It is still far too early to pick a winner between XDSL and cable-based solutions. Halsey even questions whether a clear-cut winner will ever emerge. But this is fine with him, as he believes that ongoing competition will inspire everybody to "spend money like a banshee" just to stay in the game. And this will cause consumer bandwidth to "ramp faster than everybody thinks"—which is good news if the *content synergy* between cable and the Internet sits at the heart of your business strategy. Halsey meanwhile hopes to start benefiting from these synergies even before the banshee spending begins in earnest because of the increasing popularity of something known as off-line browsing.

Off-line browsing was pioneered in the Web's earliest days by products like FreeLoader and Web Whacker, which let their users download and store entire Web sites on their computers. As FreeLoader's name hints, these tools were partly intended to reduce their owners' network connection charges, because once a site was downloaded a user could disconnect from the Internet and browse through it for days without racking up hourly Internet access fees. Most Internet access providers now offer flat monthly pricing plans. But FreeLoader and its ilk remain popular, as Web pages stored on a local hard drive can be summoned much more quickly than they can be from across the Internet. In this, off-line browsing tools offer a fairly convincing imitation of fast Web access.

A company called PointCast took off-line browsing to a new and innovative level when it debuted its PointCast Network, which so inspired the Marimba team (see Chapter 3) in early 1996. PointCast is like a cross between a screen saver and a newsy cable TV station. When a computer running PointCast hasn't been used for a few minutes, its screen fills with stock quotes, news headlines, sports scores, and other dynamic content. PointCast can run on a computer whether it is on- or off-line. When online, the information that the system displays is constantly refreshed with live data from PointCast's servers. When it is off-line, the system recycles information from its most recent connection.

Halsey believes that "this whole off-line browsing thing is going to completely revolutionize the content distribution equation." He points out that the switch utilization in the American telephone network is significantly less than 1 percent late at night. And since many dozens of megabytes can slip through a 28.8 kbps modem during those low-usage wee hours, he figures that "there's no reason why we can't download and have a complete multimedia CNET experience" waiting on computers throughout the world every morning. The phone companies, he figures, would love this new way of utilizing their underutilized assets. He points to Microsoft's "Active Themes" technology as a more likely survivor in this market than PointCast (see Chapter 1). Unveiled in late 1996, Active Themes was to integrate constantly-changing content from sites like CNET's directly into the Windows desktop environment.

Related to the off-line browsing distribution model (in that involves the downloading of large files—and demands commensurate infrastructure on CNET's part) is CNET's software services business, which links out from its download.com site. This business started out as a little adjunct to cnet.com. But soon Halsey came to view it as "the most important thing we've got." The download.com site and its sisters (shareware.com, java.com, activex.com, buydirect.com, freeware.com) point users to software housed in hundreds of different locations throughout the Internet. This includes "freeware" (code for which there is never any charge), "shareware" (code that users are typically invited to "try out" for free, but are in theory meant to pay for at some point), and even some wholly *not-free*ware. Freeware authors have many different motivations. Some are students and researchers intent on serving the public, others are hackers out to make names for themselves, and still others are corporations whose freeware supports the sale of *not-free*ware. Shareware writers more typically hope to eke profits from their efforts, and distribute over the Net in order to avoid the clogged and expensive retail channel.

Scores of Internet sites have hosted shareware and freeware files for public access for years. Many of these rose up from academic institutions, and are maintained by their masters as labors of love. CNET's software services seek to make the contents of all (or at least most) of these archives accessible from a single efficient and user-friendly point. Scarcely a year after CNET's online launch, this service's database listed over a quarter of a million pieces of software (the precise number changes daily) in more than 100 archives. CNET does not typically host that software itself. Instead, users find the software they're looking for through CNET's database, and are then linked seamlessly to its hosting archive, wherever it may be, to enable a download. Users gain from this in that they find what they are looking for quickly, without having to tangle with tricky file transfer protocol commands or path names. CNET gains in that its users gaze at CNET screens and their sponsors' banners throughout their searches and downloads.

CNET's software service was turning over a million pages per day within six months of acquiring its first independent Web address (this was shareware.com; the other addresses, including download.com, came later). And interestingly, it seems that this independent address did a lot to build its traffic. CNET sales vice president Paul Klein recalls that usage "almost tripled" immediately after the shareware.com name was switched on in November of 1995. Before that, most users had linked to the service via the cnet.com home page. It may seem odd that eliminating a few moments of navigation at the start of a 10- to 20-minute download process would so increase demand. And it is odd. But the traffic impact was very real. Stranger still, the new shareware.com traffic did not seem to cannibalize cnet.com's traffic at all.

CNET concluded from this that "the more you spin out, the more people will come," recalls its software services vice president, Matthew Barzan. Heeding this lesson (which they believed they had learned earlier than most), Halsey and his lieutenants decided to acquire every *domain name* that could conceivably host a current or planned service. This was not easy, as domain names are allocated by the InterNIC (Internet network information center), a fairly hands-off body that makes assignments on a first-come, first-served basis. Most attractive names were first-served long ago, including virtually every one that interested CNET. It fell to Matthew Barzan to do something about this.

Barzan was one of CNET's first employees. He was recruited to the company directly from New England's *pink collar* workforce (by his definition, those ranks of sailing, golf, and tennis instructors on hiatus between preppy educations and one-of-these-days "real lives"). Barzan's teeth-cutting *name space* assignment was the shareware.com name that later proved so inspiring. A fairly easy job, this involved little more than slipping $6000 to a NYNEX cable splicer in New Jersey. Emboldened, Barzan bartered & begged & bought until he had download.com, freeware.com, and (what the hell) activex.com. Somewhere in there he also got rights to news.com, which now points to CNET's news stories (this switched on in September of 1996), and search.com, which is now home to a CNET search service (similar to shareware.com, search.com aggregates the resources of hundreds of search services like Yahoo!; it was turning hundreds of thousands of pages daily within weeks of its launch).

When tracking down the owner of a useful domain name, Barzan quickly learned that "The best news is when you get someone who's clearly faked their business address: It says, 'Suite 4B,' or something, which is obviously an apartment. So you know they'll probably be psyched to turn [the name] over. It cost them nothing, they probably don't have a site up at it, and they're just going to get rewarded for registering for it in October of '93." Barzan found a lot of Suite 4Bs out there, and CNET's stable of domain names quickly grew.

Seasoned, confident, and with several successes under his belt, Barzan eventually felt ready to take on java.com, his biggest prey. His initial research revealed that the name was (surprise) already spoken for—and its proprietor wasn't working out of any *Suite 4B*. This was none other than bean-grinding hegemon Mr. Coffee. *Mr. C.* was using java.com to route E-mail traffic, which was distressing, as Barzan knew that a few thousand bucks wouldn't be enough to inspire any substantial company to change God-knew-how-many employee E-mail addresses. It was time to get creative. At this point, the usual tactic would be to barter with banners. But since Mr. Coffee had no Web site, Barzan knew its management probably wouldn't get too excited about banners on cnet.com.

Barzan thought things over and realized that the Mr. Coffee people "only got java because it's sort of a pun on coffee. And they're *really* coffee." So he tracked down the owner of coffee.com, bartered & bought & begged for it, then called Mr. Coffee and offered them *$10,000 and coffee.* But his contact "didn't really see the value in that." Worse, he let Barzan know that CNET had competition. Sun Microsystems, the multibillion-dollar originator of the Java language, was bidding too—and Sun had opened at $20,000. Barzan hung up with a sinking feeling that *ten thousand and coffee* wasn't going to cut it. Desperate, he began a frantic search for *mr*coffee.com, which he tracked down to some guy in Los Angeles ("I have *no* idea what he was doing with it"). He begged & bartered (and ultimately coughed up $1000) then went back to Mr. Coffee and offered to match the cash and throw in mrcoffee.com. He further sweetened the deal by having a $20,000 check cut and ready to go (he figured this would give him a leg up on Sun, as no company that big could ever write a check for something as goofy as a *domain name* as fast as Halsey). And then "all of sudden," Barzan recalls, his Mr. Coffee contact's "eyes were huuuu-uge." *Twenty thousand and mrcoffee* carried the day.

CNET was a little poorer for the transaction. But if the share-ware.com precedent is anything to go on, Barzan's bargain could one day look every bit as sweet as the fabled $24 purchase of Manhattan (CNET's later *unsuccessful* $50,000 bid for the less Net-relevant tele-vision.com address indicates that inflation is already rampant in the Web's name market). CNET meanwhile has coffee.com on its books, and Barzan vows he is going to "call Juan Valdez and those guys and try to get them bidding on it" as soon as he gets a spare moment.

But for now, his hands are plenty full with CNET's software ser-vices, which he runs. One short-term concern that this business faces is that the zero-revenue mini "industry" it is built upon is now under duress. As mentioned, most of the larger archives that CNET points to are maintained by universities. Many of these have been around for years, but exploding Internet traffic has caused demand for their ser-vices to explode. Now suddenly, Barzan says, "The deans are looking at this thing and saying '*Yikes*.' " This may mean that eventually "we can't get around creating CNET FTP and being a massive FTP site our-selves" (FTP, or File Transfer Protocol, is the protocol by which large files like software programs are transferred over the Internet).

Halsey will no doubt support CNET FTP's creation should it come to that, as he knows how big the software industry is, he sees most of it migrating to the Internet, and he believes that his popular software services could help him play a critical role in the new online market. A big step in that direction is a new business called "buydirect.com," (launched in December of 1996) which is designed to facilitate retail software sales. Halsey does not plan to become a Net-based software retailer himself. Instead he intends to act as a middlesite, or broker. Buydirect.com follows the original shareware.com model in that it acts as a central point from which (it is hoped) hundreds and perhaps thousands of companies will offer their products. It will provide its vendors with transaction-clearing services and customer flow, and will charge a 20 percent finder's fee for the transactions it expedites. Buydirect.com will no doubt face some serious competition, as Halsey is by no means alone in thinking about selling and distributing software over the Internet. But he is alone in that he already turns millions of pages per week at services that point people to other people's software. And this is quite a starting point.

Halsey hopes to build his software distribution business even further through his relationships with the big Internet service providers (ISPs). Many of these are now in the habit of giving their subscribers customized browsers in hopes of strengthening their branding. Branding has become very important to ISPs, as they play in competitive and commoditylike markets. A customized browser can bolster an ISP's brand name by pointing its subscribers directly to its home page (instead of Netscape's or Microsoft's) whenever they log onto the Internet. Some also feature ISP logos in their windows, and even some ISP-defined buttons in their toolbars (e.g., some ISPs designate the search services that users are referred to upon hitting the SEARCH button).

But Netscape and Microsoft constantly update their browsers, which means that "If you're Bell Atlantic," Halsey says, "and you give your people a browser . . . and they download a [new] Netscape browser, now it points to Netscape. It doesn't go to Bell Atlantic any more. It doesn't have any of your buttons on it." Halsey figures he can solve this problem through download.com, or some new derivative of it. If people start getting their browsers from him instead of Netscape and Microsoft, he figures, he can diligently figure out what ISP they're using, then "make sure that the Bell Atlantic people get the Bell Atlantic browser, the Bell Atlantic buttons, and the Bell Atlantic logo" when they come to him for upgrades. Many ISPs would no doubt see the value in this, and would encourage their subscribers to use CNET for their software updates. This would not necessarily leave CNET in a position to "assign" browsers to its visitors. But it would give it a great deal of influence over their choices, because positioning within a screen or a click stream can have an astonishing impact on a user's actions (recall how shareware.com's traffic tripled just on the strength of its acquiring an eponymous domain name). In this, becoming the download site of choice for browsers, plug-ins and other Net-critical software could be akin to assigning the shelf space of the world's grocery stores. By dint of occupying a similar, but less dramatically important position, Netscape was able to wring $5 million each from five Internet-search companies in the spring of 1996 (see Chapter 6).

All of this provides Halsey with ample reason to pay attention to the ISPs. And fortunately, this is all that he needs to think about these days: ISP relationships. That, plus cnet.com and the cable properties, with perhaps a bit of time set aside for the E! relationship (as well as *E! Online*). But pretty much that, plus download.com, shareware.com, and the other related sites, are all that Halsey really needs to focus on (with the exception of CNET Radio and the new television shows that Wendle's group is cooking up. Those require just a bit of oversight too). Investor relations, the other financing issues that Bonnie sometimes presents him with, as well as matters relating to the sales force and the advanced technology group (both of which report directly to Halsey) really need some consideration too. But those things, in addition to the above-listed matters, plus keeping Barzan busy with additional domain name assignments, pretty much fills up Halsey's working day.

Okay, so Halsey is busy. But he is happy with his busyness. After all, he's been waiting for this one since he first became an entrepreneur at age 14. Back then "I used to be pissed off that I missed the whole PC revolution, because I thought I'd be good—I thought I would be a good entrepreneur," he recalls. And "it was such an exciting time. The early eighties, when everyone was starting companies like Adobe, Lotus, Microsoft. It seemed like such an incredible time, and I was about ten years too young." That was not an easy thing for an eighth grader to take. But now the Web has come along, and Halsey feels incredibly fortunate to be on hand "at the right age, and at the right time, and with [an] idea." He feels sorry for the young Halsey-come-latelies of today. Because this is it. "The Internet does everything. It does television, it does radio, it does print, it does it when you want it, it does it in a way that's personalized for you, it literally gives you everything." This doesn't seem to leave much, because "how do you improve on it? Other than sensory implants . . ."

Halsey can imagine CNET growing into a $5-billion company some day. And he would naturally like to be the one who takes it there, although he insists that there are other things that he (occasionally) wishes he was doing. He points out that before he got so excited about the Web, his goal had been to make enough money by age 35 to retire and get a Ph.D. in anthropology. He actually misses studying Arabic. And he regrets that what he does now is in some respects not as "mind expansive" as the matters that took up his hours when he was a student. He enjoys business. But in the end, "business is business. It's creative, but it's not, like, *really* creative. And if you get really creative, investors get worried, as they should."

But Halsey should find himself with ample time to *get really creative* someday. Because just as he's no longer 10 years too young, he's also not 10 years too old. He was just 31 when CNET went public, which should leave him plenty of years to look forward to both with and without his company. And after all, the Internet is a wild beast. Halsey could just stumble across a way to make his revenues soar to $5 billion in the next four years. If so, he might just keep to his schedule.

EPILOGUE
Another 1,000 Days

X Mosaic, the crash-prone piece of undergraduate software that touched all of this off, released in early 1993. A few months later, beta versions of Mosaic that ran on the PC and Macintosh released, and some months after that, in the fall of 1993, stable-ish post-beta PC and Mac versions. As noted in Chapter 1, it was these releases that made the Web, and through it the vast and open Internet, popularly accessible and relevant. In this they set off the wildfire expansion of the network that, by some reckonings, had reached more than 50 million people by late 1996.

This does not mean that Mosaic alone should receive credit for everything chronicled in these pages. Mosaic was rather just one piece of a vast edifice that had been long in the making. It was certainly not the most expensive piece. Nor was it the most complex, nor perhaps even the most important one. But it was the last missing piece. And with its release and proliferation, billions of dollars' worth of infrastructure that had been laid over decades began to come together. This included millions of personal computers, the global telephony network, the protocols specified by Tim Berners-Lee and many others, the cable network, the wireless network, and more. Bits and parts of these ingredients had been interconnected for years. But it was only when the lesser networks that they had formed took on a universal and increasingly ubiquitous interface that they began to interoperate, that they began to access one another's resources and to offer their own resources to one another.

In the thousand days that followed, literally thousands of companies were established to facilitate and (they hoped) profit from the Web's expansion. The successful ones created billions of dollars in value for their investors and founders. Billions more were meanwhile being invested by venture capitalists, large Net-savvy (and Net-naive) corporations, as well as individual investors. All of this investment and value creation helped the Web sustain its astonishing rate of growth, and meanwhile helped its content advance in sophistication at almost as dramatic a rate.

Web content began in 1993 at an extremely humble and most unsophisticated starting point. The Web was then still an intriguing obscurity that lacked media elements much richer than CAPITAL-IZED WORDS and had no refined visual interface. By the start of 1994, it had its visual interface and was playing host to thousands of colorful images set against stark white backgrounds and faintly formatted text. By the beginning of 1995, the visual interface had become more stable, had sped up significantly, and could do a much better job of formatting and presentation. By the start of 1996, Web pages were *bleep*ing, singing, displaying static 3-D images, and hosting full-blown computer programs that could themselves drive animations, run calculations, and do just about anything else. And by early 1997, everything had been further enlivened by hundreds of Netscape plug-ins and ActiveX controls, by persistent Java, by *un*-static 3-D images, by dramatically improved audio and video elements, by several intriguing experiments in Internet telephony, and by much more. Throughout this period the number of Web sites expanded by a factor of thousands, and the number of Web users by at least as much.

This is an astonishing arc of growth and improvement for such a short period of time. But dramatic as it all was, it was but a foreshadowing of what is yet to come. The investments that fueled the Web's development are accelerating, not tapering off. And many of the tens of thousands who have gone to work full-time in the medium have just gotten their bearings, are only really starting to apply their full focus and creativity to building it. Another thousand days will of course pass, and another 10 thousand days after that. And then the inevitable time will come when the Web's dawning years will seem as remote as the pioneering days of film seem today. Today's best and most lavishly-funded Web sites will then look as naive and primitive as the earliest silent movies.

The snickering of cynics who argue that the Web *will never amount to anything* because of this or that present-day inadequacy should be considered in light of all this. Perhaps the most commonly made argument is that the Web is *too slow*. This is a very defensible argument, as anybody who regularly connects to the Internet from home will attest. But there is no reason to expect that Web access speeds will improve any less rapidly than they have been. And so far, they have been improving at a dramatic rate. As noted in Chapter 1, the first release of the Netscape Navigator could download and display Web pages up to 10 times faster than Mosaic. Subsequent versions of the Navigator (and of Microsoft's Internet Explorer) have of course run even faster than this. The speed of the average consumer-class modem has meanwhile improved too; threefold in the thousand days following Mosaic's release. These two effects together accelerated consumer Web access by an order of magnitude in the three years following Mosaic's release. And access speeds will continue to improve—perhaps by a factor of hundreds, if certain cable modem and XDSL experiments pan out.

Another argument against the Web is that *there is too much garbage up there*. This is also entirely true—but look at how well television has done. The navigability of Web content also makes it uniquely easy for people to avoid the garbage they don't want to see, and go directly to the garbage (or the ungarbage) that interests them. And as the Web's shelf piles higher and wider and deeper with more and more content, and as people become more adept at being their own aggregators, and at employing searching and screening tools like Yahoo!, the avoidable tedium of the Web's uninteresting garbage will become less and less of a distraction.

Other related arguments about the Web's content quality (e.g., much of it is still static; a lot of it seems like thinly-veiled advertising; production values are often amateurishly low) and infrastructure (e.g., audio and video fidelity is limited; 3-D scenes and computer programs distributed over the Internet run jerkily and slowly) should be made cautiously, and should be considered in light of the dramatic changes that occurred during the Web's first thousand days as a consumer medium, as well as the fact that many more thousands of equally eventful days will inevitably pass.

They should also be considered in light of the common questions—many of them very well-founded—that were asked about the Web's com-

mercial viability early in its history. For instance, when Netscape and
HotWired were inking their business plans in the spring of 1994, many
questioned whether the Web would ever attract an economically interesting audience. At the time it had perhaps a million users, perhaps considerably fewer. Two years later its user base had reached tens of
millions and was growing fast. Also, in the fall of 1994 when HotWired
started peddling its first advertisements, many questioned whether the
Web would ever attract anything more than a curious trickle of advertisers. Two years later, a single Web enterprise—Yahoo!—had over 300
paying sponsors. Also, as Netscape's IPO approached in the summer of
1995, many looked at the company's previous quarter's revenues of just
over $10 million and questioned how a young startup that *gave away* its
products could ever make any money. Less than 13 months after the
IPO, Netscape wrapped up its first $100-million quarter.

The passage of the consumer Web's second thousand days will
bring as many surprises and improvements as the first. It will also lay
to rest many more questions about the Web's commercial viability and
its popular relevance. And it will see the Web continue its explosive
growth. Fueling this growth will be the increasing draw of the network
as it becomes more powerful and ubiquitous, and a corollary increase
in the costs associated with not affiliating with it. Also significant will
be a tremendous expansion in the content categories that the Web can
meaningfully service as the Internet's delivery infrastructure becomes
more robust. For instance, the spread of broadband Internet access
will make video and certain types of audio content far more accessible
and rewarding. The spread of 24-hour Web connections (these are
now commonplace in offices, and systems like @Home's are bringing
them to the consumer market) will make services like phone directories and movie listings far more interesting than they can be when accessing them requires users to boot up their computers and open an
Internet connection. The spread of wireless Web access will meanwhile
make maps, traffic reports, and other mobile content available when
and where people need it, increasing its relevance.

When the next thousand days are over sometime near the end of
the millennium, at least a few of the companies chronicled in these
pages will be large, healthy, and independent. Some may be integrated
pieces of other companies, and some may have disappeared entirely.
But the markets and technologies that they helped pioneer will be extant and thriving. And even then, the Web, its content, its markets, and
its reach will still be in their earliest and most humble dawning days.

INDEX